July 1954

Jack L. Alb

P9-CQY-953

A. CAMPBELL.

Anno Ætat. 65.

Biographies and Sermons
of
Pioneer Preachers

Arranged and Edited by

B. C. Goodpasture and W. T. Moore

B. C. Goodpasture

Nashville, Tennessee

1954

Contents.

(v)

PREFACE

It is now almost a century since this volume was first published under the title, THE LIVING PULPIT OF THE CHRISTIAN CHURCH. The editor and all the contributors to it have long since gone to their reward. It is not, therefore, "The Living Pulpit".

Further the expression, "Christian Church", is not now used in the same sense as in the title of the book. Some whose names appear in the book, if living now, would not likely be, or desire to be, recognized as being members of the "Christian Church". The present publisher has thought it wise to change the title to BIOGRAPHIES AND SERMONS OF PIONEER PREACHERS. This is more accurate.

The work is an exact reproduction of the Biographies and Sermons. A new Preface has been written and the original Introduction has been supplanted with a short sketch of Alexander Campbell and his famous Sermon on the Law.

The publisher deems this collection of Biographies and Sermons worthy a permanent place in "Restoration" Literature. This does not mean, however, that he endorses every sentiment and form of expression they contain. He does not.

B. C. Goodpasture

ALEXANDER CAMPBELL

Alexander, son of Thomas and Jane Corneigle Campbell, was born near
Ballymena in the county of Antrim, Ireland, September 12, 1788. His mother was of
French Huguenot ancestry and his father came from West Scotland.

Early in life he attended an academy conducted by his uncles Archibald and
Enos Campbell. Later he spent some time in the University of Glasgow. His parents
being staunch Seceder Presbyterians, he was brought up in the strictest tenets of
their faith. In August, 1809, he came to America. At the time of his arrival his
father, who had preceded him to this country by two years, was deeply concerned
about restoring the pattern of New Testament unity, teaching, and worship. The son
shared his fathers interest in this worthy effort. They adopted the motto, "Where
the Scriptures speak, we speak; where the Scriptures are silent, we are silent," in
their search for "the ancient order of things." Following this principle in his
study of the Bible, Alexander Campbell was soon convinced that he had not been
baptized; consequently, on June 12, 1812, he, along with a few others, was
immersed by Matthias Luce in Buffalo Creek, near Bethany, W. Va.

It was in the spring of 1810 that young Campbell preached his first sermon.
Six years later he delivered his epoch-making sermon on the Law. His ability
was such that he was soon in demand as a preacher. July 4, 1823, he began the
publication of the CHRISTIAN BAPTIST. This paper was succeeded by the
MILLENNIAL HARBINGER in 1830. The HARBINGER was discontinued at the end of 1870.
Through these papers Mr. Campbell succeeded in getting the truth before the
people. It was never his purpose to found a new religious body. It was ever
his purpose to restore the church of the New Testament in faith, in practice,
and in worship.

In 1841 Mr. Campbell became president of Bethany College, Bethany, W. Va.
He held this position until his death on March 4, 1866. Through his classes in
the college he exercised a profound and far-reaching influence. Several of the

contributors to this volume came under the tutelage of the "Sage of Bethany."

Alexander Campbell was a many-sided man. In addition to his work as preacher, lecturer, editor and college president, he held a number of important debates. These exercised a far-reaching influence on the minds of thousands. The first of these debates was held in Mt. Pleasant, Ohio, June 19, 20, 1820, with John Walker, a Presbyterian, on the general subject of baptism. The second, with William Maccalla, also a Presbyterian, was held in Washington, Ky., October 15-22, 1823. The next debate was held in Cincinnati, Ohio, April 13-21, 1829, with Robert Owen, a skeptic of New Lanark, Scotland. It was the first of the "big-three" debates. About eight years later there followed the debate with Bishop Purcell on Catholicism, in Cincinnati, Ohio, from January 13-21, 1837. The last of his public debates was with N. L. Rice, a Presbyterian, in Lexington, Ky., from November 15 - December 1, 1843. In this, the last and longest of his debates, the subject, action, and design of baptism; the operation of the Holy Spirit; and Creeds, were discussed.

Mr. Campbell was married to Miss Margaret Brown, March 12, 1811. To this union eight children were born; seven daughters, Jane, Eliza, Maria Louisa, Lavinia, Amanda Corneigle, Clarinda, and Margaretta; and one son, John Brown, who died the day he was born. The first wife died on October 22, 1827. Mr. Campbell was married to Miss Selina Huntington Bakewell on July 31, 1828. To this marriage six children were born; three sons, Alexander, Wickliffe (who was drowned while his father was in Europe), and William; and three daughters, Margaret Brown, Virginia, and Decima. The second Mrs. Campbell died on June 28, 1897.

B. C. G.

THE SUBSTANCE OF A SERMON.

Delivered before the Redstone Baptist Association, met on Cross Creek, Brook County, Va., on the 1st of September, 1816.

BY ALEXANDER CAMPBELL,

One of the Pastors of the Church of Brush Run, Washington County, Pa.

"The law was given by Moses, but grace and truth came by Jesus Christ."—John 1:17.

"The law and the prophets were until John, since that time the kingdom of God is preached, and every man presseth into it."—Luke 16:16.

PREFACE.

To those who have requested the publication of the following discourse, an apology is necessary. Though the substance of the discourse, as delivered, is contained in the following pages, yet, it is not verbatim the same. Indeed, this could not be the case, as the preacher makes but a very sparing use of notes, and on this occasion, had but a few. In speaking extempore, or in a great measure so, and to a people who may have but one hearing of a discussion such as the following, many expressions that would be superfluous in a written discourse, are in a certain sense necessary. When words are merely pronounced, repetitions are often needful to impress the subject on the mind of the most attentive hearer: but when written, the reader may pause, read again, and thus arrive at the meaning.

Some additions, illustrative of the ideas that were presented in speaking, have been made; but as few as could be supposed necessary. Indeed, the chief difficulty in enforcing the doctrine contained in the following sheets, either in one spoken or written sermon, consists in the most judicious selection of the copious facts and documents contained in the divine word on this subject.

We have to regret that so much appears necessary to be said, in an argumentative way, to the professed Christians of this age, on such a topic. But this is easily accounted for on certain principles. For, in truth, the present popular exhibition of Christianity is a compound of Judaism, heathen philosophy, and Christianity; which, like the materials in Nebuchadnezzar's image, does not well cement together.

The only correct and safe course, in this perilous age, is to take nothing upon trust, but to examine for ourselves, and "to bring all things to the test." "But if any man will be ignorant, let him be ignorant."

As to the style adopted in this discourse, it is such as we supposed would be adapted to the capacity of those who are chiefly benefited by such discussions. "For their sakes we endeavor to use great plainness of speech."

As the doctrines of the gospel are commonly hid from the wise and prudent, and revealed only to babes, the weak and foolish; for their sakes, the vail of what is falsely called eloquence should be laid aside, and the testimony of God plainly presented to view.

The great question with every man's conscience is, or should be, "What is truth?" Not, have any of the scribes or rulers of the people believed it? Every man's *eternal all*, as well as his present comfort, depends upon what answer he is able to give to the question Pilate of old [John xviii, 38] proposed to Christ, without waiting for a reply. Such a question can only be satisfactorily answered by an impartial appeal to the oracles of truth—the alone standard of Divine truth. To these we appeal. Whatever in this discourse is contrary to them, let it be expunged; what corresponds with them, may the God of truth bless to those to whom he has given an ear to discern and a heart to receive it

ROMANS VIII, 3.

"For what the law could not do, in that it was weak through the flesh, God, sending His own Son in the likeness of sinful flesh, and for sin, condemned sin in the flesh."

Words are signs of ideas or thoughts. Unless words are understood, ideas or sentiments can neither be communicated nor received. Words that in themselves are quite intelligible may become difficult to understand in different connections and circumstances. One of the most important words in our text is of easy signification, and yet, in consequence of its diverse usages and epithets, it is sometimes difficult precisely to ascertain what ideas should be attached to it.

It is the term *law*. But by a close investigation of the context, and a general knowledge of the Scriptures, every difficulty of this kind may be easily surmounted.

In order to elucidate and enforce the doctrine contained in this verse, we shall scrupulously observe the following

METHOD.

1. We shall endeavor to ascertain what ideas we are to attach to the phrase *"the law,"* in this and similar portions of the Sacred Scriptures.

2. Point out those things which *the law* could not accomplish.

3. Demonstrate the reason why *the law* failed to accomplish those objects.

4. Illustrate how God has remedied those relative defects of *the law*.

5. In the last place, deduce such conclusions from these premises, as must obviously and necessarily present themselves to every unbiased and reflecting mind.

I.

In discussing the doctrine contained in our text, we are then, in the first place, to endeavor to ascertain what ideas we are to attach to the terms *"the law,"* in this and similar portions of the Sacred Scriptures.

The term *"law,"* denotes in common usage, "a rule of action." It was used by the Jews, until the time of our Saviour, to distinguish the whole revelation made to the Patriarchs and Prophets from the traditions and commandments of the Rabbis or Doctors of the law. Thus the Jews called the Psalms of David, *law.*—John xii, 34. Referring to the 110th Psalm, they say, "We have heard out of the law that Christ abideth forever."

And again, our Saviour calls the Psalms of David *law,* John x, 34. Referring to Psalm lxxxii, 6, he says, "Is it not written in your law, I said ye are gods." Thus when we hear David extolling God's law, we are to understand him as referring to all divine revelation extant in his time.

But when the Old Testament Scriptures were finished and divided according to their contents for the use of synagogues, the Jews styled them the law, the prophets and the psalms.

Luke xxiv, 44, Christ says, "All things written in the law of Moses, in the prophets, and in the psalms concerning me, must be fulfilled."

The addition of the definite article in this instance as well as all others, alters the signification or at least determines it. During the life of Moses, the words *"the law,"* without some explicative addition, were never used. Joshua, Moses' successor, denominates the writings of Moses, "the book of the law;" but never uses the phrase by itself. Nor, indeed, have we any authentic account of this phrase being used without some restrictive definition, until the reign of Abijah, 2d Chron. xiv, 4, at which time it is used to denote the whole legal dispensation by Moses. In this way it is used about thirty times in the Old Testament, and as often with such epithets as show that the whole law of Moses is intended.

When the doctrines of the reign of Heaven began to be preached, and to be contrasted in the New Testament with the Mosaic economy, the phrase *"the law"* became very common, and when used without any distinguishing epithet or restrictive definition, invariably denoted the whole legal or Mosaic dispensation. In this acceptation it occurs about 150 times in the New Testament.

To make myself more intelligible, I would observe that when the terms *"the law"* have such distinguishing properties or restrictive definitions as "the royal law," "the law of faith," "the law of liberty," "the law of Christ," "the law of the spirit of life," &c., it is most obvious the whole Mosaic law or dispensation is not intended. But when we find the phrase "the law," without any such limitations or epithets as "the law was given by Moses," "the law and the prophets were until John," "if ye be led by the Spirit, ye are not under the law," "ye are not under the law, but under grace," &c., we must perceive the whole law of Moses, or legal dispensation, is intended.

I say the *whole* law, or dispensation by Moses; for in modern times the law of Moses is divided and classified under three heads, denominated, the moral, ceremonial, and judicial law. This division of the law being unknown in the apostolic age, and, of course, never used by the Apostles, can serve no valuable purpose in obtaining a correct knowledge of the doctrine delivered by the Apostles respecting the law. You might as well inquire of the Apostles, or consult their writings to know who the Supralapsarians or Sublapsarians are, as to inquire of them what is the moral, ceremonial or judicial law.

But, like many distinctions handed down to us from mystical Babylon, they bear the mark on their forehead that certifies to us, their origin is not Divine. If this distinction were harmless, if it did not perplex, bias and confound, rather than assist the judgment in determining the sense of the apostolic writing, we should let it pass unnoticed; but justice to the truth requires us to make a remark or two on this division of the law.

The phrase *the moral law,* includes that part of the law of Moses "written and engraved on two tables of stone," called the ten commandments. Now the word *moral,* according to the most approved Lexicographers, is defined "relating to the practice of men toward each other, as it may be virtuous or criminal, good or bad." The French, from whom we have the term *moral* immediately, and the Romans from whom we orginally received it, used it agreeably to the above definition. Of course, then, a *moral* law is a law which regulates the conduct of men toward each other.

But will the ten commandments answer this definition? No. For Doctors of Divinity tell us, the first table of the Decalogue respects our duty to God; the second our duty to man.

Why then call the ten commandments *"the moral law,"* seeing but six of them are moral, that is, relating to our conduct towards men? In modern times we sometimes distinguish between religion and morality; but while we affirm that religion is one thing, and morality another; and then affirm that the ten commandments are the *moral law*—do we not, in so saying, contradict ourselves? Assuredly the legs of the lame are not equal!

A second objection to denominating the ten precepts "the moral law," presents itself to the reflecting mind, from the consideration that all morality is not contained in them. When it is said that the ten commandments are "the moral law," does not this definite phrase imply that all morality is contained in them; or, what is the same in effect, that all immorality is prohibited in them?

But, is this the fact? Are the immoralities called drunkenness, fornication, polygamy, divorces on trifling accounts, retaliation, &c., prohibited in the ten precepts? This question must be answered in the negative.

If it had been asked, is all immorality prohibited in this saying, "thou shalt love thy neighbor as thyself?" we would readily answer yes; but it is the so-called moral law we are speaking of. We affirm, then, that the above immoralities are not prohibited in the Decalogue, according to the most obvious construction of the words. We are aware that large volumes have been written to show how much is comprehended in the ten precepts. But, methinks, the voluminous works of some learned men on this subject too much resemble the writings of Peter D'Alva, who wrote forty-eight huge folio volumes to explain the mysteries of the conception of the Messiah in the womb of the Virgin Mary! And what shall we think of the genius who discovered that singing hymns and spiritual songs was prohibited, and the office of the Ruling Elder pointed out in the second commandment? That dancing and stage plays were prohibited in the seventh; and supporting the clergy enjoined in the eighth!

According to this latitude of interpretation, a genius may arise and show us that law and gospel are contained in the first commandment, and of course all the others are superfluous.

But this way of enlarging on the Decalogue defeats the division of the law of Moses, which these Doctors have made.

For instance, they tell us that witchcraft is prohibited in the first commandment—incest and sodomy in the seventh.

Now they afterwards place these vices, with the laws respecting them, in their judicial law; if, then, their moral law includes their judicial law, they make a distinction without a difference.

There remains another objection to this division of the law. It sets itself in opposition to the skill of the Apostle, and ultimately deters us from speaking of the ten precepts as he did.

Paul, according to the wisdom given unto him, denominated the ten precepts the "ministration of condemnation and of death;" 2d Cor. iii, 7-14. This we call the moral law. Whether *he* or we are to be esteemed the most able ministers of Christ it remains for you, my friends, to say.

Paul having called the ten precepts the ministration of death, next affirms that it was to be done away—and that it was done away. Now the calling the ten precepts "the moral law," is not only a violation of the use of words; is not only inconsistent in itself and contradictory to truth; but greatly obscures the doctrine taught by the Apostles in the 3d chapter, 2d Cor., and in similar passages, so as to render it almost, if not altogether, unintelligible to us. To use the same language of the moral law as he used in respect to the minstration of condemnation and death, is shocking to many devout ears. When we say the moral law is done away, the religious world is alarmed; but when we declare the ministration of condemnation is done away they hear us patiently, not knowing what we mean. To give new names to ancient things, and speak of them according to their ancient names, is perplexing indeed. Suppose, for example, I would call the English law which governed these States when colonies, the constitution of the United States, and then affirm that the constitution of the United States is done away, or abolished, who would believe me? But if the people were informed that what I called the constitution of these States was the obsolete British law, they would assent to my statement. Who would not discover that the giving of a wrong name was the sole cause of such a misunderstanding?

Hence it is that modern teachers by their innovations concerning law, have perplexed the student of the Bible, and cause many a fruitless controversy, as unnecessary as that relating to the mark set on Cain. It does not militate with this statement to grant that some of the precepts of the Decalogue have been re-promulgated by Jesus Christ, any more than the re-promulgation of some of the British laws does not prevent us from affirming that the laws under which the colonies existed are done away to the citizens of the United States. But of this more afterwards.

To what has been said it may be added, that the modern division of the law tends very much to perplex any person who wishes to understand the Epistles to the Romans, Galatians and Hebrews; insomuch that while the hearer keeps this distinction in mind, he is continually at a loss to know whether the moral, ceremonial, or judicial law is intended.

Before dismissing this part of the subject we would

observe that there are two principles, commandments or laws that are never included in our observations respecting the law of Moses, nor are they ever in Holy Writ called the law of Moses: These are, "Thou shalt love the Lord thy God with all thy heart, soul, mind and strength; and thy neighbor as thyself." These our Great Prophet teaches us, are the basis of the law of Moses, and of the Prophets: "On these two commandments hang all the law and the prophets." Indeed the Sinai law and all the Jewish law is but a modification of them. These are of universal and immutable obligation.

Angels and men, good and bad, are forever under them. God as our Creator, cannot require less; nor can we, as creatures and fellow-creatures, propose or expect less, as the standard of duty and perfection. These are coeval with angels and men. They are engraven with more or less clearness on every human heart. These are the ground work or basis of the law, written in the heart of heathens, which constitute their conscience, or knowledge of right or wrong.

By these their thoughts mutually accuse or else excuse one another.

By these they shall be judged, or at least, all who have never seen or heard a written law or revelation. But for these principles there had never been either law or gospel.

Let it then be remembered, that in the Scriptures these precepts are considered the basis of all law and prophecy; consequently when we speak of the law of Moses we do not include these commandments, but that whole modification of them sometimes called the legal dispensation.

It must also be observed that the Apostles sometimes speak of the law, when it is obvious that a certain part only is intended. But this so far from clashing with the preceeding observations fully corroborates them. For if the Apostle refers to any particular part of the law, under the general terms, the law, and speaks of the whole dispensation in the same terms without any additional definition, then, doubtless, the phrase the law, denotes the whole legal dispensation, and not any particular law or new distinction to which we may affix the words, the law.

II, 1. We shall not attempt to point out those things which the law could not accomplish.

In the first place, it could not give righteousness and life. Righteousness and eternal life are inseparably connected.

Where the former is not, the latter cannot be enjoyed. Whatever means put us in possession of one puts us in possession of the other.

But this the law could not do. "For if there had been a law given which could have given life, verily, righteousness should have been by the law" (Gal. iii, 21). "If righteousness come by the law, then Christ is dead in vain." These testimonies of the Apostle, with the whole scope of divine truth, teach us that no man is justified by the law, that righteousness and eternal life can not be received through it.

Here we must regret that our translators by an injudicious supplement should have made the Apostle apparently contradict himself. I allude to the supplement in the 10th verse of Rom., 7th chap. From the 7th verse of this chapter, the Apostle narrated his experience as a Jew under the law, and then his experience as a Christian under the gospel, freed from the law. The scope of the 10th verse and its context is to show what the Apostle once thought of the law, and how his mistakes were corrected. If any supplement be necessary in this verse, we apprehend it should be similar to what follows: "And the commandment (which I thought would give me) life, I found (to lead) to death." This doubtless corresponds with the scope of the context, and does not, like the present supplement, clash with Gal. iii, 21.

Indeed the law, so far from being "ordained to give life," was merely *"added* to the promise of life till the seed should come to whom the promise was made." "Moreover the law entered that the offense might abound"—"For by the law was the knowledge of sin." For these reasons we conclude that justification, righteousness and eternal life cannot by any means be obtained by the law.

2. In the second place, the law could not exhibit the malignity or demerit of sin.

It taught those that were under it that certain actions were sinful. To these sinful actions it gave descriptive names—one is called theft, a second murder, a third adultery. It showed that these actions were offensive to God, hurtful to men, and deserved death. But how extensive their malignity and vast their demerit the law could not exhibit.

This remained for later times and other means to develop.

3. In the third place, the law could not be a suitable rule of life to mankind in this imperfect state. It could not be to all mankind, as it was given to and designed only for a part. It was given to the Jewish nation, and to none else.

As the inscription on a letter, identifies to whom it belongs; as the preamble to a proclamation, distinguishes who is addressed; so the preface to the law, points out and determines to whom it was given.

It points out a people brought out of the land of Egypt and released from the house of bondage, as the subjects of it. To extend it farther than its own preface, is to violate the rules of criticism and propriety.

How unjust and improper would it be, to convey the contents of a letter to a person to whom it was not directed—how inconsistent to enjoin the items of a proclamation made by the President of these United States, on the subjects of the French government. As inconsistent would it be to extend the law of Moses beyond the limits of the Jewish nation.

Do we not know with Paul, that what things soever the law saith, it saith to them that are under the law? But even to the Jews it was not the most suitable rule of life. 'Tis universally agreed, that example, as a rule of life, is more influential than precept. Now the whole Mosaic law wanted a model or example of living perfection. The most exemplary characters under the law, had their notable imperfections.

And as long as polygamy, divorces, slavery, revenge, etc., were winked at under that law, so long must the lives of its best subjects be stained with glaring imperfections. But when we illustrate how God has remedied the defects of the law, the ideas presented in this particular shall be more fully confirmed.

III. But we hasten to the third thing proposed in our method, which is to demonstrate the reason why the law could not accomplish these objects.

The Apostle in our text briefly informs us, that it was owing to human weakness that the law failed to accomplish these things—"In that it was weak through the flesh." The defects of the law are of a relative kind. It is not in itself weak or sinful—some part of it was holy, just and good—other parts of it were elementary, shadowy, representations of good things to come. But that part of it written and engraven on tables of stone, which was holy, just and good, failed in that it was too high, sublime and spiritual to regulate so weak a mortal as fallen man. And even when its oblations and sacrifices were presented, there was something too vast and sublime, for such weak means, such carnal commandments—such beggarly elements— such perishable and insignificant blood, to effect. So that as the Apostle saith, the law made nothing perfect, it merely introduced a better hope. If the law had been faultless, no place should have been found for the gospel. We may then fairly conclude that the spirituality, holiness, justice and goodness of one part of the law, rendered it too high; and the carnal, weak and beggarly elements of another part, rendered it too low; and both together became weak through the flesh. Viewing the law in this light, we can suitably apply the words of the Spirit uttered by Ezk. xx: 25, in relation to its incompetence—"I gave them," says he, "statutes which were not good, and judgments whereby they should not live."

We have now arrived at the fourth head of our discourse, in which we propose to illustrate the means by which God has remedied the relative defects of the law.

All those defects the Eternal Father remedies, by sending His own Son in the likeness of sinful flesh, and for sin, condemns sin in the flesh. "That the whole righteousness which the law required, might be fulfilled in us, who walk not after the flesh but after the Spirit."

The primary deficiency of the law which we noticed, was, that it could not give righteousness and eternal life.

Now, the Son of God, the Only Begotten of the Father, in the likeness of sinful flesh, makes an end of sin, makes reconciliation for iniquity, finishes transgression, brings in an everlasting righteousness, and completes eternal redemption for sinners.

He magnifies the law and makes it honorable. All this he achieves by his obedience unto death. He finished the work which the Father gave him to do; so that in him all believers, all the spiritual seed of Abraham, find righteousness and eternal life; not by legal works or observances, in whole or in part, but through the abundance of grace, and the gift of righteousness, which is by him;—"For the gift of God is eternal life through Jesus Christ our Lord." This righteousness, and its concomitant eternal life, are revealed from faith to faith—the information or report of it comes in the divine word to our ears, and receiving the report of it, or believing the divine testimony concerning it, brings us into the enjoyment of its blessings. Hence it is that Christ is the end of the law for righteousness to every one that believeth. Nor is he on this account the minister of sin—for thus the righteousness, the perfect righteousness of the law, is fulfilled in us who walked not after the flesh, but after the Spirit. Do we then make void the law or destroy the righteousness of it by faith? God forbid: we establish the law.

A second thing which we observed the law could not do, was to give a full exhibition of the demerit of sin. It is acknowledged that the demerit of sin was partially developed in the law, and before the law. Sin was condemned in the deluge, in the confusion of human speech, in turning to ashes the cities of the plain, in the thousands that fell in the wilderness. But these and a thousand similar monuments beside, fall vastly short of giving a full exhibition of sin in its malignant nature and destructive consequences. But a full discovery of its nature and demerits is given us in the person of Jesus Christ. God condemned sin in Him— God spared not His own Son, but delivered Him up. It pleased the Lord to bruise Him, to pour out His soul an offering for sin. When we view the Son of the Eternal suspended on the accursed tree—when we see

Him in the garden, and hear His petitions—when we hear Him exclaim, "My God, my God, why hast Thou forsaken Me?"—in a word, when we see Him expiring in blood and laid in the tomb, we have a monument of the demerit of sin which no law could give, which no temporal calamity could exhibit.

We sometimes in the vanity of our minds, talk lightly of the demerit of sin, and irreverently of the atonement. In this age of novelty, it is said "that the sufferings of Christ were so great as to atone for the sins of worlds on worlds," or at least for the sins of the damned as well as the saved—that "one drop of His blood is sufficient to atone for the sins of the whole world." That is, in other words, the sufferings of Christ so transcended the demerit of the sins of His people as to be sufficient to save all that shall eternally perish. These assertions are as unreasonable as unscriptural. In our zeal to exalt the merits of the atonement—I say, in the warmth of our passions, and in the fullness of our hearts—let us be cautious lest we impeach the Divine wisdom and prudence. Doubtless, if the merits of His sufferings transcend the demerit of His people's sins, then some of His sufferings were in vain, and some of His merit unrewarded. To avoid this conclusion, some have affirmed that all shall be saved and none perish, contrary to the express word of God. Indeed, the transition from these inconsistent views of the atonement, to what is called Universalism, is short and easy. But I would humbly propose a few inquiries on this subject. Why do the evangelists inform us that Christ died so soon after His suspension on the cross? Why so much marvel expressed that He was so soon dead?—so much sooner than the malefactors that were crucified with Him? It might be presumed His last words solve these difficulties—"It is finished, and He gave up the ghost."

From these and similar premises, it would seem that His life and sufferings were prolonged just so long as was necessary to complete the redemption of His people. We are accustomed on all subjects that admit of it, to distinguish between quantity and quality. In the common concerns of human intercourse sometimes the quality of a thing is acceptable when the quantity is not; at other times the quantity is acceptable when the quality is not. If a thousand slaves were to be redeemed and emancipated by means of gold, the person in whose custody they were could not demand any more precious metal than gold—when one piece of gold was presented to him he might object to the quantity as deficient, though the quality is unobjectionable. In respect of the means of our redemption, it must be allowed that the sufferings of Christ were they. These sufferings, then, were the sufferings of a divine person—such doubtless was their quality. And a life and sufferings of any other quality could avail nothing in effecting redemption for transgressors. If but one of Adam's race should be saved, a life and sufferings of such a quality would have been indispensably requisite to accomplish such a deliverance. Again, if more were to have been saved than what will eventually be saved, the quantity and not the quality of His sufferings would have been augmented. The only sentiment respecting the atonement that will bear the test of Scripture, truth or sober reason, is, that the life and sufferings of Christ in quality, and in length or quantity, were such as sufficed to make reconciliation for all the sins of His chosen race; or for all them in every age or nation that shall believe in Him. There was nothing deficient, nothing superfluous; else he shall never see of the travail of His soul and be satisfied; which would be the reverse of His Father's promise, and His own expectation. When the life and sufferings of Christ are viewed in this light the demerit of sin appears in its true colors—all inconsistencies vanish, and all the testimonies of sacred truth, of Patriarchs, Prophets and Apostles harmoniously correspond. But if we suppose that the sufferings of Christ transcended the demerit of the sins of "His people," then we have no full exhibition of the demerit of sin. Nor are "His people" under any more obligation of love or gratitude to Him than they who eternally perish.

That which remains on this head is to show how the failure of the law in not being a suitable rule of life has been remedied.

We noticed that example is a more powerful teacher than precept. Now Jesus Christ has afforded us an example of human perfection never witnessed before. He gave a living form to every moral and religious precept which they never before possessed. In this respect He was the distinguished Prophet to whom Moses and all the inferior prophets referred. In entering on this prophetic office He taught with a peculiarity unexampled by all His predecessors—"He spake as never man spake."

The highest commendation He gave of Moses was that he wrote of Him, and that he was a faithful servant in Christ's house. From the beginning of his ministry to the end of his life, he claimed the honor of being the only person that could instruct men in the knowledge of God or of His will. He claimed the honor of being the author and finisher of the only perfect form of religion; the Eternal Father attested all his claims and honored all His pretensions. Respecting the ancient rules of life, the law and the prophets, He taught his disciples they had lived their day—he taught them they were given only for a limited time. "The law and the prophets prophesied until ᵀohn"—then they gave place to a greater Prophet, and a more glorious law. Malachi, the last of the ancient prophets, informed Israel that they should strictly observe Moses' law, until a person should come in the spirit and power of Elias. Jesus taught us that John the Baptist was he, and that the law and prophets terminated at his entrance upon his ministry; for since that time the kingdom of God is preached, and all men press into it. To attest His character, and to convince the church of His being the great Prophet to whom all Christians should exclusively hearken as their teacher; to weaken the attachments of His disciples to Moses and the prophets, it pleased God to send down Moses and Elias from heaven; the one the law-giver, and the other the law-restorer, to resign their prophetic honors at the feet of the Messiah, in presence of select witnesses. "Jesus took with him Peter, James and John into a high mountain, and was transfigured before them, and His face did shine as the sun, and His raiment was white as snow, and behold there appeared Moses and Elias talking with him." Peter, enraptured with these heavenly visitants, proposes erecting three tabernacles—one for Christ, one for Moses, and one for Elias. But while he was thus proposing to associate Christ, the great Prophet, with Moses and Elias, inferior prophets, a bright cloud overshadowed them, and a voice came out of the cloud, an indirect reply to Peter's motion—"This is my beloved Son in whom I am well pleased, *hear ye him*." Thus when these ancient and venerable prophets were recalled to heaven, Christ alone was left as the great Teacher, to whom, by a commandment from the excellent glory, the throne of the Eternal, we are obliged to hearken. That this transaction was significant of the doctrine above stated must be manifest, when we take into view all circumstances.

Might it not be asked, "Why did not Abel, Abraham, or Enoch appear on this occasion?" The reason is plain—the disciples of Christ had no hurtful respect for *them*.—Moses and Elias, the reputed oracles of the Jewish nation, were the two, and the only two, in respect of whom this solemn and significant revocation was needful. The plain language of the whole occurrence was this—Moses and Elias were excellent men—they were now glorified in heaven—they had lived their day—the limited time they were to flourish as teachers of the will of Heaven was now come to an end. The morning star had risen—nay, was almost set, and the Sun of Righteousness was arising with salutiferous rays. Let us then walk in the noon-daylight—let us hearken to Jesus as the Prophet and Legislator, Priest and King. He shall reign over all the ransomed race. We find all things whatsoever the law could not do are accomplished in him, and by him—that in him all Christians might be perfect and complete—"for the law was given by Moses, but grace and truth came by Jesus Christ." It now remains, in the last place, to deduce such conclusions from the above premises, as must obviously and necessarily present themselves to every candid and reflecting mind.

1st. From what has been said, it follows that there is an essential difference between law and gospel—the Old Testament and the New.*

---

* There are not a few professors of Christianity who suppose themselves under equal obligations to obey Moses or any other Prophet, as Christ and his Apostles. They cannot understand why any part of the divine relation should not be obligatory on a Christian to observe; nor can they see any reason why the New Testament should be preferred to the Old; or why they should not be regulated equally by each. They say, "Is it not all the word of God and are not all mankind addressed in it?" True, all the holy Prophets spake as they were moved by the Holy Spirit, and men

No two words are more distinct in their signification then *law* and *gospel*. They are contra-distinguished under various names in the New Testament. The law is denominated "the letter," "the ministration of condemnation;" "the ministration of death;" "the Old Testament or Covenant, and Moses." The gospel is denominated "the Spirit," "the ministration of the Spirit," "the ministration of righteousness," "the New Testament, or Covenant," "the law of liberty and Christ." In respect of existence or duration, the former is denominated "that which is done away"— the latter, "that which remaineth"—the former was faulty, the latter faultless—the former demanded, this bestows righteousness—that gendered bondage, this liberty—that begat bond-slaves, this freemen—the former spake on this wise, "This *do* and thou shalt

---

were the objects of their address. It is, however, equally evident that God at sundry times and in diverse manners spake to men, according to a variety of circumstances, which diversified their condition, capacity, and opportunities. Thus he addressed individuals, and classes of individuals, in a way peculiar to themselves. Witness his addresses to Noah, Abraham, Daniel, Jonah, Paul and Peter. Witness his addresses to the Patriarchs, the Jews and the Christians. Again, men are addressed as magistrates, fathers, masters, husbands, teachers, with their correlates. Now to apply to one individual what is said to all individuals and classes of individuals, would, methinks, appear egregious folly. And would it not be absurd to say, that every man is obliged to practice every duty and religious precept enjoined in the Bible. Might we not as reasonably say, that every man must be at once a Patriarch, a Jew, and a Christain; a magistrate, a subject, a father, a child, a master, a servant, etc., etc. And, certainly, it is as inconsistent to say, that Christians should equally regard and obey the Old and New Testament. All Scripture given by divine inspiration, is profitable for various purposes in the perfection of saints, when rightly divided, and not handled deceitfully. But where the above considerations are disregarded, the word of God

live"—this says, "Say not what *ye* shall do; the word is nigh thee, [that gives life,] the word of faith which we preach: if thou believe in thine heart the gospel, thou shalt be saved." The former waxed old, is abolished, and vanished away—the latter remains, lives, and is everlasting.

2d. In the second place, we learn from what has been said, that "there is no condemnation to them which are in Christ Jesus." The premises from which the Apostles drew this conclusion are the same with those stated to you in this course. "Sin," says the Apostle, "shall not have dominion over you; for ye are not under the law, but under grace." In the 6th and 7th chapters to the Romans, the Apostle taught them that "they were not under the law"—that "they were freed from it"—"dead to it"—"delivered from

---

must inevitably be perverted. Hence it is that many preachers deceive themselves and their hearers by selecting and applying to themselves and their hearers such portions of sacred truth as belong not to them nor their hearers. Even the Apostles could not apply the words of Christ to themselves or their hearers until they were able to answer a previous question—"Lord, sayest thou this unto *us* or unto *all?*" Nor could the eunuch understand the Prophet until he knew whether he spoke of himself or of some other man. Yet many preachers and hearers trouble not themselves about such inquiries. If their text is in the Bible, it is no matter where; and if their hearers be men and women, it is no matter whether Jews or Christians, believers or unbelievers. Often have I seen a preacher and his hearers undergo three or four metamorphoses in an hour. First he is a moral philosopher, inculcating heathen morality; next a Jewish Rabbi, expounding the law; then a teacher of some Christian precept; and lastly, an ambassador of Christ, negotiating between God and man. The congregation undergo the correlate revolutions; first, they are heathens; next, Jews; anon Christians; and lastly, treating with the ambassadors for salvation, on what is called the terms of the gospel. Thus, Proteus-like, they are all things in an hour.

it." In the 8th chapter, 1st verse, he draws the above conclusion. What a pity that modern teachers should have *added* to and *clogged* the words of inspiration by such unauthorized sentences as the following: "Ye are not under the law" *as a covenant of works, but as a rule of life!* Who ever read one word of the "covenant of works" in the Bible, or of the Jewish law being a rule of life to the disciples of Christ? Of these you hear no more from the Bible than of the "Solemn League" or "St. Giles' Day." Yet how conspicuous are these and kindred phrases in the theological discussions of these three last hundred years! But leaving such phrases to those who are better skilled in the use of them, and have more leisure to expound them, we shall briefly notice the reason commonly assigned for proposing the law as a rule of life to Christians. "If Christians are taught," say they, "that they are delivered from the law, under it in no sense—that they are dead to it—will not they be led to live rather a licentious life, live as they list; and will not the non-professing world, hearing that *they* are not under the law of Moses, become more wicked, more immoral and profane?" Such is the chief of all the objections made against the doctrine inculcated respecting the abolition of the Jewish law in respect of Christians, and also as this doctrine respects the Gentile or Heathen world. We shrink not from a fair and full investigation of this subject. Truth being the only allowed object of all our inquiries, and the sole object of every Christian's inquiry, we should patiently hear all objections—coolly and dispassionately hear, examine, and weigh all arguments *pro* and *con.*

That the first part of this objection is very natural, has been very often made, and strongly urged against the doctrine we advocate, we cheerfully acknowledge. As this objection was made against the Apostle's doctrine concerning the law, it affords a strong probability, at least, that our views on this subject correspond with his. We shall then hear how he stated and refuted it. Romans vi, 15. "What then? Shall we sin because we are not under the law, but under grace?" Here he admits the objection, and in his answer incontestably shows that Christians are not under the law in any sense. If they were in any sense, now was the time to say, "We are not under the law in some sense, or under a certain part of it; but in one sense we are under it as a rule of life." We say the Apostle was here called upon, and in a certain sense bound, to say something like what our modern teachers say, if it had been warrantable. But he admits the doctrine and states the objection, leaving the doctrine unequivocally established. He guards the doctrine against a licentious tendency thus—"God forbid!" "How shall we that are dead to sin live any longer therein?" and in the subsequent verses shows the utter impossibility of any servant of God, or true Christian, so abusing the doctrine we have stated. Now whether the ancient way of guarding the New Testament, or gospel, against the charges of Antinomianism or a licentious tendency, or the modern way is best, methinks is easily decided amongst true disciples. Not so easy, however, amongst learned Rabbis and Doctors of the law.

But, query—Is the law of Moses a rule of life to Christians? An advocate of the popular doctrine replies, "Not all of it." Query again—What part of it? "The ten commandments." Are these a rule of life to Christians? "Yes." Should not, then, Christians sanctify the seventh day? "No." Why so? "Because Christ has not enjoined it." Oh! then, the law or ten commandments is not a rule of life to Christians any further than it is enjoined by Christ; so that reading the precepts in Moses' words, or hearing him utter them, does not oblige us to observe them; it is only what Christ says we must observe. So that an advocate for the popular doctrine, when closely pressed, cannot maintain his ground. Let no man say we have proposed and answered the above queries as we please. If any other answers can be given by the advocates themselves than we have given, let them do it. But it is highly problematical whether telling Christians that they are under the law will repress a licentious spirit. True Christians do not need it, as we have seen: "how shall they that are dead to sin live any longer therein?" And dare we tell professing Christians, as such, that the law, as a rule of life, is a condemning law? If not, then what tendency will the mere affirmation that they are under a law as a rule of life which cannot condemn them have to deter them from living as they list. Upon the whole, the *old way* of guarding against immorality and licentiousness amongst Christians will, we apprehend, be found the most consistent and efficacious. And he that has tried the old way and the new, will doubtless say as was said of old, "No man also having drunk old wine, straightway desireth new: for he saith the old is better." And, indeed, every attempt to guard the New Testament, or the gospel, by extrinsic means, against an immoral or licentious tendency, bears too strong a resemblance to the policy of a certain preacher in Norway or Lapland, who told his hearers that "hell was a place of infinite and incessant cold." When asked by an acquaintance from the South of Europe why he perverted the Scriptures, he replied, "if he told his hearers in that cold climate that hell was a place of excessive heat, he verily thought they would take no pains to avoid going there."

But as to the licentious tendency this doctrine we inculcate is supposed to have upon the non-professing or unbelieving world, it appears rather imaginary than real. It must, however, in the first instance be ascertained whether the Gentiles, not professing Christianity, were ever supposed or addressed by the Apostle sent to the Gentiles, as being under the law of Moses. We have under the second head of our discourse particularly demonstrated that the Gentiles were never under the law, either before or after their conversion. To what has been said on this subject we would add a sentence or two. It was prophesied of the Gentiles that they should be without law till Christ came. Isa. xlii. 4, "And the isles shall *wait* for *his* law." The chief glory which exalted the Jews above the Gentiles, which the Jews boasted of to the Gentiles, was that to *them "pertained* the adoption, the covenants, and *the giving of the law."* They exclusively claimed the law as their own. And why will not we let them have it, seeing Hom whose law the Gentiles waited for is come, and has given us a more glorious law. Whatever was excellent in their law our Legislator has re-promulgated. But shall we say that we are under the law as a rule of our Christian life, because some of its sublimest moral and religious precepts have been re-promulgated by Him who would not suffer one tittle of it to pass till he fulfilled it? As well might we affirm that the British law which governed these States, when colonies, is the rule of our political life, because some of the most excellent laws of that code have been re-enacted by our legislators. Paul, the Apostle to the Gentiles, plainly acknowledged in his addresses to them, that they were without law, aliens from the commonwealth of Israel having no hope, &c. And of them he said that "when the Gentiles, who have not the law, do by nature the things contained in the law, these having *not the law,* are a law unto themselves." But, in so saying, does *he* or do *we* excuse their sins or lead them to suppose that they are thereby less obnoxious to the wrath to come? By no means. For we testify that even natural conscience accuses them of sin or wrong in their thoughts, words and actions according to its knowledge. And consequently "as many as have sinned without law, shall also perish without law." In so testifying, do we cherish a licentious spirit? By no means. For there stand a thousand monuments in this present world, independent of Jewish law, on which are inscribed these words, "For the wrath of God is revealed from heaven against all ungodliness and unrighteousness of men." But one thing demands our observation, that the Apostle sent by Heaven to preach to the Gentiles, in accusing them of sins of the deepest dye, and of the most malignant nature, dishonorable to God and destructive to themselves, never accuses them of any sin which the light of nature itself would not point out, or natural conscience testify to be wrong. Hence it is that in the long black catalogue of sins preferred against the Gentiles, is never to be found the crime of Sabbath-breaking, or transgressing any of the peculiarities of Judaism. And now what is the difference between an ancient Greek and a modern American or European who disbelieves the gospel? Under what law is the latter, under which the former was not? Was the former a sinner and chargeable in the sight of God, as well as the latter? Yes. Would not natural conscience according to its means of knowing right and wrong, or the work of the law written in the heart, condemn the unbelieving Romans as well as the unbelieving Americans? Most assuredly. And what is the difference? Not that the latter is under any law that the former was not under, but the means of discerning right and wrong in the latter are far superior to the former, and consequently their overthrow or ruin will be more severe. In point of law or obligation there is no difference between the unbelieving American and the rudest barbarian; though the former is polished with science, morals, &c., like the ancient Greeks and Romans, and the latter remains an uncultivated savage. They will be judged and condemned by the same law which condemned the Roman who died 1900 years ago. And the condemnation of the latter shall be more tolerable than the former, not by a milder law, but because his knowledge of right and wrong was much inferior to the former; and having heard the gospel of salvation and disbelieved it, he adds to his natural corruption and accumulated guilt the sin of making God a liar, and preferring darkness to light, because he believed not the testimony of God. This is the sole difference in respect of condemnation between the Indian and the most accomplished citizen. From these few remarks it will appear, we trust, obvious to every person who has an ear to distinguish truth from falsehood, that there is no condemnation to them which are in Christ Jesus—that they are under no law that can condemn them—that *he* who was made under the law is become the end of the law for righteousness to them—that being dead to sin, they should live no longer therein—that there is no necessity, but a glaring impropriety in teaching the law as a rule of life to Christians—that all arguments in favor of it are founded on human opinion and a mistaken view of the tendency of the gospel and Christian dispensation —that all objections against the doctrine we have stated as licentious in its tendency are totally groundless. "For the grace of God that bringeth salvation teacheth us that denying ungodliness and worldly lusts, we should live soberly, righteously and godly in this present world. Looking for that blessed hope, the glorious appearing of the great God, even our Saviour Jesus Christ; who gave himself for us that he might redeem us from all iniquity, and purify unto himself a peculiar people, *zealous of good works.*"

3d. In the third place, we conclude from the above premises, that there is no necessity for preaching the law in order to prepare men for receiving the gospel.

This conclusion perfectly corresponds with the commission given by our Lord to the Apostles, and with their practice under that commission. "Go," saith he, "into all the world, and preach the gospel unto every creature." "Teach the disciples to observe all things whatsoever I command you." Thus they were authorized to preach the gospel, not the law, to every creature. Thus they were constituted ministers of the New Testament, not of the Old. Now the sacred history, called the Acts of the Apostles, affords us the most satisfactory information on the method the Apostles preached under this commission; which, with the epistolary part of the New Testament, affords us the only successful, warrantable, and acceptable method of preaching and teaching. In the Acts of the Apostles, we see the Apostles and first preachers paid the most scrupulous regard to the instructions they received from the great Prophet. They go forth into all nations proclaiming the gospel to every creature; but not one word of law-preaching in the whole of it. We have the substance of eight or ten sermons delivered by Paul and Peter to Jews and Gentiles, in the Acts of Apostles, and not one precedent of preaching the law to prepare their hearers, whether Jews or Gentiles, for the reception of the gospel.

This conclusion corresponds, in the next place, with the nature of the kingdom of heaven or Christian church, and with the means by which it is to be built and preserved in the world. The Christian dispensation is called "the ministration of the Spirit," and accordingly everything in the salvation of the church is accomplished by the immediate energy of the Spirit. Jesus Christ taught his disciples that the testimony concerning himself was that only which the Spirit would use in converting such of the human family as should be saved. He was not to speak of himself, but what he knew of Christ. Now he was to convince the world of sin, of righteousness, and of judgment; not by applying the law of Moses, but the facts concerning Christ to the consciences of the people. The spirit accompanying the words which the Apostles preached, would convince the world of sin; not by the ten precepts, but because they believed not on him—of righteousness, because *he* went to the Father—and of judgment, because the prince of this world was judged by him. So that Christ and not law was the Alpha and Omega of their sermons; and this the Spirit made effectual to the salvation of thousands. Three thousand were convinced of sin, of righteousness, and of judgment, in this precise way of hearing of Christ, on the day of Pentecost; and we read of many afterwards. Indeed, we repeat it again, in the whole history of primitive preaching, we have not one example of preaching the law as preparatory to the preaching or reception of the gospel.

This conclusion corresponds, in the third place, with the fitness of things.* That man must be con-

---

*Indeed we have yet to learn what advantage can accrue from preaching the so called "moral law," to prepare sinners for the gospel. In the nature and fitness of things it cannot prepare or dispose the mind to a belief of the gospel. The Apostles teach us that "the law worketh wrath." This is inevitably its effect on every mind which does not believe the gospel. It irritates and excites the natural enmity of the mind against God. A clear exhibition of the divine character in the law, apart from the gospel, tends more to alienate than to reconcile the mind to God. When

vinced of sin by some means, prior to a welcome reception of saving truth, is generally acknowledged. Now, as the gospel dispensation is the most perfect revelation of salvation, it must be supposed that it possesses the best means of accomplishing everything connected with the salvation of its subjects. It must, of course, possess the best means of convincing of sin.

---

a preacher of the law has labored to show his hearers the immaculate holiness, the inflexible justice, the inviolate truth and consuming jealousy of Jehovah, manifested in the fiery law, supposing the gospel kept out of view, he has rather incapacitated and disqualified their minds from crediting the gospel or testimony of the condescension, love, mercy and grace of the Eternal Father to mankind. How opposite is the divine wisdom to the wisdom of many modern scribes and teachers of the law! They preach first the law to natural fallen man, then the gospel. But He who seeth not as man seeth, preached first the gospel to fallen man, and afterwards added the law, because of transgressions, till the seed should come. Eternal life was promised through the seed, and the law added till the seed come.

Nothing can be more inconsistent than the conduct of the law preachers. When they have echoed the thunders of Mount Sinai in the ears of their hearers almost to drive them to despair, and to produce what they call "legal repentance," then they begin to pull down the work of their hands by demonstrating the inefficacy, unprofitableness and danger of legal repentance. Might they not as well at once imitate the Apostles and primitive preachers—preach the gospel, which, when received, produces repentance not to be repented of? Might they not preach Christ crucified, in whom is manifested the wrath and judgment of God against sin; and his condescending love, mercy and grace to the sinner? Might they not, knowing the terror of the Lord, persuade men by the persuasives of the doctrine of reconcilation; rather than to increase their enmity, awaken their suspicions and work wrath in their minds, by an unlawful use of the law? But in order to this, their minds must be revolutionized; they must take up a cross which they at present refuse; and what is difficult indeed, they must unlearn what they have themselves taught others.

This truth, however, does not depend on mere supposition. The fact that the Holy Spirit makes an exclusive use of it in convincing of sin, is a striking demonstration of its superior excellence for that purpose. But independent of these considerations, it must be confessed that the gospel or testimony concerning Christ affords the fullest proof of divine justice and indignation against sin—it presents the clearest view of the demerit of sin, and of all divine perfections terrible to sinners—it exhibits the most alarming picture of human guilt and wretchedness that ever was given, and on these accounts is of all means the most suitable to convince of sin. It was already observed that the eternal Father condemned sin in the person of his Son, more fully than it ever was, or could be condemned in any other way. Suppose, for illustration, a king put to death his only son, in the most painful and ignominious way, for a crime against the government: would not this fact be the best means of convincing his subjects of the evil of crime, and of the king's detestation of it? Would not this fact be better than a thousand lectures upon the excellency of the law and the sanctions of it? But every similitude of this kind falls infinitely short of affording a resemblance of the eternal Father not sparing his Sole Delight when sin was but imputed to him. Having seen that this conclusion corresponds with the commission given by the Redeemer to his Apostles—with their practice under that commission—with the nature of his kingdom, and with the fitness of things, one would suppose that no objection could be preferred against it. But what doctrine of divine truth is it, against which objections, numerous indeed, and strongly urged, and by men who profess to be zealous for the truth, have not been made? Is it the doctrine of sovereign, free, and abundant grace? No. Is it the doctrine of the natural sinfulness and corruption of all men? No, no. Against these, many objections, yea, very many, are urged. We must not suppose, then, that this doctrine we now maintain shall be free from objections. We shall, then, attend to some of those objections which have been made, or which we anticipate may be made against this conclusion.

It may, perhaps, be objected that there are some expressions in the apostolic epistles which imply that the law was necessary to convince of sin, as pre-requisite to a welcome reception of the gospel; such as "by the law *is* the knowledge of sin"—"for without the law sin *was* dead." There is no authority from the original for varying the supplements in these two clauses. If it corresponds with the context or with the analogy of faith, to supply *was* in the last clause, it doubtless corresponds as well in the first clause. But we lay no stress on the one or the other; for before Christ came all knowledge of sin *was* by the law; and "the law entered that the offense might abound." For the law was added to the promise of life, because of transgression, till the seed should come to whom the promise was made. Now we would suppose that when the *seed* is come, and the time expired for which the law was added, it is superfluous to annex it to the gospel, for the same reason it was annexed to the promise made to Abraham. And although it should be allowed that Christians derive knowledge of sin from the law, it does not follow that it is the best means of communicating this knowledge—that Christians are dependent on it for this purpose—nor that it should be preached to unbelievers to prepare them for receiving the gospel.

The seventh chapter to the Romans contains the fullest illustration of the once excellence and utility of the law that is to be found in all the New Testament;

and as this chapter will doubtless be the stronghold of our opponents, we shall make a remark or two on the contents of it.

In the first place, then, let it be remembered that in the fourteenth verse of the preceding chapter, the Apostle boldly affirms that Christians are not under the law. To the conclusion of the sixth chapter he refutes an objection made to his assertion in the fourteenth verse. In the first six verses of the seventh chapter he repeats his assertion, and uses an apt similitude to illustrate it. Having, then, demonstrated that Christians are not under the law, in the seventh verse of the the seventh chapter he states an objection which had been made, or he anticipated would be made, against his doctrine—"If Christians are not under the law, if they are dead to it, if they are delivered from it, is it not a sinful thing?" "Is the law sin, then?" This objection against the nature of the law, the Apostle removes in the next six verses by showing the utility of the law in himself as a Jew under that law; and concludes that the law is holy, just and good. To the end of the chapter the Apostle gives an account of his experience as a Christian freed from the law, and thus manifests the excellency of his new mind or nature by its correspondence to the holiness of the law; so that he most effectually removes the objection made against the law as being sin, and at the same time establishes the fact that Christians *are delivered from it.* Such evidently is the scope of the latter part of the sixth and all of the seventh chapter. We cannot dismiss this chapter without observing, first, that the law or that part of the law which the Apostle here speaks of, is what modern teachers call "the moral law." If so, then Christians are not under it; for the law which the Apostle affirms Christians are delivered from in the sixth verse, in the seventh verse he shows is not sin;

and the law which he shows is not sin, he demonstrates to be holy, just and good. So that here, as well as in the third chapter of his second Epistle to the Corinthians, Christians are expressly said to be delivered from the so-called moral law; and that it is abolished or done away in respect of them. We must remark again that before any thing said in this chapter respecting the utility or excellence of the law can be urged as a precedent for what we condemn—namely, preaching the law as preparatory to the gospel, or a law work as preparatory to genuine conversion, it must be shown that the Apostle gave this account of his experience under the law as preparatory to his conversion. Otherwise no objection can be made from anything in this chapter to the conclusion before stated. But this cannot be; for the account we have of his conversion flatly contradicts such a supposition. Previous to his conversion he was a very devout man in his own way—"touching the righteousness which was in the law he was blameless." See the account he gives of himself, Phil. iii, 4, 5, compared with Rom. vii, 7-12; Acts xxii, 1; xxiii, 1; from which we learn that he was taught according to the most perfect manner of the law, and was a Pharisee of the strictest kind: had clear ideas of sin and righteousness; and, externally considered, was blameless and lived in all good conscience until the day of his conversion. But it was not the law, it was not a new discovery of its spirituality, but a discovery of Christ exalted, that convinced him of sin, of righteousness and of judgment; and instantaneously converted him. So that nothing in his previous life or attainments, nothing of his experience as a Jew, nothing of his knowledge of sin or of righteousness by the law previous to his conversion, can be urged in support of preaching the law or a law work to unbelievers, to prepare their mind for a welcome reception of the truth.

When we shall have mentioned a favorite text of the law preachers, and considered it, we shall have done with objections of this sort. It is Galatians iii, 24. We shall cite from the 23d verse: "Before faith [Christ] came we were kept under the law, shut up unto the faith which should afterwards be revealed. Wherefore the law was our schoolmaster *to bring us* to Christ, that we might be justified by faith. But after that faith [Christ] is come, we are no longer under a schoolmaster." Methinks it looks rather like an insult to the understanding of any person skilled in the use of words, to offer a refutation of the use that is frequently made of the 24th verse. But let the censure rest upon them who render it needful. Every smatterer in Greek knows that the 24th verse might read thus: "The law was our schoolmaster until Christ" came; and this reading unquestionably corresponds with the context. Now is it not most obvious that instead of countenancing law-preaching, this text and context condemn it? The scope of it is to show that whatever use the law served as a schoolmaster previous to Christ, it no longer serves that use. And now that Christ is come we are no longer under it. We see, then, that this conclusion not only corresponds with the commission to the Apostles, with the nature of Christ's Kingdom, with the apostolic preaching, and with the fitness of things: but that no valid objection can be presented against it, from anything in the apostolic epistles.

Some, notwithstanding the Scriptural plainness of this doctrine, may urge their own experience as contrary to it. It would, however, be as safe for Christians to make divine truth a test of their experience, and not their experience a test of divine truth. Some individuals have been awakened by the appearance of the aurora borealis, by an earthquake, by a thunder-storm, by a dream, by sickness, etc. How inconsistent for one of these to affirm from his own experience, that others must be awakened in the same way! How in-compatible with truth for others to preach such occur-rences as preliminary to saving conversion!

But the difference between ancient and modern con-versions is so striking as to merit an observation or two. Now that the law is commonly preached to pre-pare men for Christ, it must be expected that modern conversions will be very systematic, and lingering in all. While preachers will not condescend to proclaim the glad tidings until they have driven their hearers al-most to despair by the thunders of Mt. Sinai—while they keep them in anxious suspense for a time, whether the wounds of conviction are deep enough; whether their sense of guilt is sufficiently acute; whether their desires are sufficiently keen; whether their fears are sufficiently strong; in short, whether the law has had its full effect upon them: I say, when this is the case, conversion work must go on slow; and so it is not rare to find some in a way of being converted for years; and, indeed, it is generally a work of many months. It would be well, however, if, after all, it were com-monly genuine. Compare these conversions with those of which we read in the Acts of the Apostles, and what a contrast! There we read of many converted in a day, who yesterday were as ignorant of law and gospel as the modern Hindoos or Burmans. To account for this we have only to consider and compare the dif-ferent sorts of preaching and means by which those were and these are effected.

But some may yet inquire, Are unbelievers under no law or obligation by which conviction may be commu-nicated to their minds? Or they may ask in other words, How does the testimony of Christ take hold of them? And why do they welcome the gospel? We have already shown that there is a law written on every human heart, which is the foundation of both law and prophets, under which both angels and men exist, whose obligation is universal and eternal. It is inscribed more or less distinctly on every heathen's heart. It is sometimes called the law of nature, but more correctly called by the Apostle, *conscience*. This natural conscience, or sense of right and wrong, which all men possess in different degrees, according to a variety of circumstances, but all in some degree, is that in them which God addresses. This natural conscience is fitted to hear the voice of God, as exactly as the ear is fitted to hear sounds. This renders the savage inexcusable. For the invisible things of God, even his eternal power and godhead, are manifested to his conscience in the natural world. Now God addresses conscience in those whom he brings to himself in a variety of ways. Sometimes even where his word is come, he speaks by awful events to the consciences of men. In this way he awakens inquiries that lead to the saving truth. Witness the jailor and his house, of whom we read in the Acts of the Apostles. God spake to his conscience by an earthquake, and put an inquiry in his mouth that was answered to his salvation and that of his house. That which fits the savage to hear God's voice in the natural world, fits him or the man of civilization to hear his voice in the gospel, when it is sent to them in power.

Are we to preach this law of nature, then, some will inquire, or are we to show men that they possess this natural conscience, previous to a proclamation of the glad tidings? I would answer this question by proposing another. Am I to tell a man he has an ear, and explain to him the use of it, before I condescend to speak to him? One answer suits both inquiries. We should consider the circumstances of any people before we address them. Do we address Jews? Let us address them as the Apostles did. Persuade them out of their own law that Jesus is the Messiah. Do we address professed Christians? Let us imitate the apostolic addresses in the epistles. Do we preach to barbarians? Let us address them as Paul preached to the Lycaonians—speak to their consciences. Do we preach to polished infidels or idolaters? Let us speak to them as Paul spake to the Athenians—speak to their consciences.

4th. A fourth conclusion which is deducible from the above premises, is that all arguments and motives, drawn from the law or Old Testament, to urge the disciples of Christ to baptize their infants; to pay tithes to their teachers; to observe holy days or religious fasts, as preparatory to the observance of the Lord's supper; to sanctify the seventh day; to enter into national covenants; to establish any form of religion by civil law;--and all reasons and motives borrowed from the Jewish law to excite the disciples of Christ to a compliance with or an initiation of Jewish customs, are inconclusive, repugnant to Christianity, and fall ineffectual to the ground; not being enjoined or countenanced by the authority of Jesus Christ.

5th. In the last place we are taught from all that has been said to venerate in the highest degree the Lord Jesus Christ; to receive Him as the Great Prophet, of whom Moses in the law, and all the prophets did write. To receive him as the Lord our righteousness, and to pay the most punctilious regard to all his precepts and ordinances. "If we continue in his word, then are we his disciples indeed, and we shall know the truth and the truth shall make us free—if the Son shall make us free, we shall be free indeed."

It is remarkable how strong our attachments are to Moses as a teacher: though Moses taught us to look for a greater prophet than he, and to hearken *to him!* It is strange that three surprising incidents in the history of Moses would not arrest our attention and direct us to Christ. With all his moral excellence, unfeigned piety and legislative dignity, he fell short of Canaan. So all who cleave to him will come short of the heavenly rest! His mortal remains, and his only, the Almighty buried in secret; and yet we will not suffer his ashes to rest in peace! He came down from heaven to give place to the Messiah, to lay down his commission at his feet; and we will not accept it! Strange infatuation!

If Moses was faithful in Christ's house as a servant, shall not Christ be faithful as a son over his own house? Let us as his disciples believe all he teaches, and practice all he enjoins in religion and morality; let us walk in all his commandments and ordinances; and inquire individually, What lack I yet? If we are then deficient, let us say with the Jews who disowned him, "We are Moses' disciples, but as for this fellow, we know not whence he is." But let all remember that if he that despises Moses' law died without mercy, of how much sorer punishment, suppose ye, shall he be thought worthy, who despised Christ as a teacher! His commandments are not grievous to his disciples —his yoke is easy, and his burden is light.

Let every one that nameth the name of Christ depart from all iniquity. Let us walk worthy of Him. Let us take heed lest by our conduct we should represent Christ as the minister of sin. Let us not walk after the flesh but the Spirit; and then we shall show that the righteousness of the law is fulfilled in us. Then shall no occasion be given to the adversary to speak reproachfully. And if any should still urge the stale charge of Antinomianism, or affirm that we live in sin that grace might abound, did evil that good might come, or made void the law through faith, let us put to silence the ignorance of foolish men, by adorning the doctrine we profess with a blameless conduct. Let us not merely rebut such insinuations with a "God forbid!" but evince, how shall we that are dead to sin, live any longer therein.

May he that hath the key of David, who openeth and no man shutteth, and shutteth and none can open, open your hearts to receive the truth in the love of it, and incline you to walk in the light of it, and then ye shall know that the ways thereof are pleasantness, and all the paths thereof are peace! *Amen.*

THE LIVING PULPIT OF THE CHRISTIAN CHURCH.

DAVID STAATS BURNET.

[WHILE preparing for this volume a short notice of the life of this distinguished brother, we received the sad intelligence of his death. His discourse was already partially in type, and the engraving nearly ready. Under these circumstances, it was thought best to retain him in the book, although the original intention was to have no one appear in it but living preachers.

The lesson which this sad event teaches is one of solemn warning. While preparing a book, in which none but the living were to occupy a place, one of those selected is suddenly numbered among the dead. Truly, in the midst of life we are in death.

In consultation with the publishers, it was decided to give a more general notice of the deceased than was at first intended. It was believed this would be just and proper, and highly appreciated. In accordance with this decision, we have collected what material we could, in the short time allowed, from which to write a biographical sketch, and present the following as the result of our labors.]

DAVID STAATS BURNET was the eldest child of ISAAC G. and Mrs. K. W. BURNET, and was born in Dayton, Ohio, July 6, 1808. His ancestors, on both sides, were Scotch, and of very respectable character. His maternal grandfather was Capt. GEORGE GORDON, a native of Philadelphia. His paternal grandfather was Dr. WILLIAM BURNET, of Newark, N. J., a member of

3 (33)

the Congress of 1775. He claimed lineal descent from GILBERT BURNET, Bishop of Salisbury, so conspicuous during the great English Revolution, under William, Prince of Orange.

When he was eight years of age his parents removed to Cincinnati, his father having formed a law partnership with the late NICHOLAS LONGWORTH. Subsequently the father served twelve years as mayor, employing the son as clerk, when at the age of thirteen. While in this employment, under the watchful care of his father, young David acquired those habits of industry and faithfulness which characterized him through life, and which laid the foundation of his future career.

He was educated in the Presbyterian faith, and was sprinkled, in accordance with the custom of that sect, about the time he entered his father's office as clerk. But his mind had already begun to investigate; and owing to the interest which he subsequently took in the cause of Sunday schools—having at the age of sixteen become associated with a Presbyterian official in conducting a very successful one—he was led to a close examination of the Word of God. This examination convinced him that some of his religious positions were wrong, and could not be reconciled with the Divine teaching. After prayerful consideration, he determined to change his religious connections, as his views had undergone a radical change, especially on the subject of human creeds and the ordinance of baptism. Accordingly, on the 26th of December, 1824, he was immersed by the Rev. JOHN BOYD, and received into the Enon Baptist Church.

It is worthy of remark that, at this time, he was unacquainted with the teaching of ALEXANDER CAMPBELL and those associated with him in pleading for a return to primitive Christianity; and yet, he rejected the authority of human creeds, and declined to accept any test of faith but the Word of God, basing his application for baptism on Rom. x: 6–10, not knowing that any one else had done so before. On this account, it was with some hesitation that he was received by the Baptists, his views being, in many respects, at variance with their established usage.

Immediately after his baptism he commenced preaching in the name of the Lord, notwithstanding, at that early age, he was offered admission to the West Point Military Academy by his uncle, the late Judge JACOB BURNET.

His life at this time becomes an interesting study, and the moral sublimity of his character challenges our unaffected admiration. Surrounded by a large circle of influential relatives and friends, who, if religious at all, had little or no sympathy with his views of Christianity; with wealth and worldly honors offered him without stint, he turned his back upon them all, and, like the great Lawgiver of Israel, chose rather to suffer affliction with the people of God, than to enjoy the pleasures of sin for a season; esteeming the reproach of Christ greater riches than all the treasures and honors of the world. It is only now and then that a young man, under such circumstances, deliberately selects the profession of an humble preacher of the Gospel. And when one does have the moral courage, by the help of God, to do it, his name should be held in everlasting remembrance among those who "contend for the faith once delivered to the saints."

Although little more than sixteen when he began to preach, such were his piety and earnestness, and such his devotion to study, that he made very rapid growth in his profession; so rapid, indeed, that at the age of twenty he was called to the pastoral care of a church in Dayton, O., and was held in great esteem as an earnest, faithful, and eloquent preacher of the Gospel.

In the autumn or winter of 1827, the youthful preacher united with Elder WILLIAM MONTAGUE, of Kentucky, in the organization of the Sycamore-street Baptist Church of Cincinnati. This church numbered about eighty members at the time of its organization, and adopted a platform of principles much more liberal and progressive than those usually adopted by the Baptist churches at that time. But the principles of the Reformation, as advocated by ALEXANDER CAMPBELL, WALTER SCOTT, and others, now became very generally known, and their influence upon the Baptist churches throughout the West was very great, in some places completely absorbing whole districts, and enlisting a very earnest interest in favor of the plea for a return to Primitive Christianity. The Sycamore-street Church was not free from this influence, and it was not long until a division took place, the two portions forming different congregations, and finally growing into the present Ninth-street Baptist Church, and the Christian Church, corner of Eighth and Walnut streets. Brother BURNET adhered to the latter-named organization, and from that time until the day of his death was thoroughly identified with the movement, and a zealous defender of the principles and practices, as advocated by the Disciples of Christ.

And here again we find him yielding to his honest convictions in opposition to every worldly interest. It is difficult to conceive of a more self-sacrificing act than that which breaks away from wealth, position, fame, friends, relatives, and last, though not least, religious associations, and unites present hopes and an eternal destiny with a movement which promises nothing in this life but ignominy and shame, and, in the popular estimation, nothing in the life to come but everlasting ruin. Only honest and earnest convictions could induce any sane man to enter upon such an unpromising adventure. And yet this is just what the subject of this sketch did. The people with whom he associated himself religiously were, at that time, held in very low esteem by the different religious parties into which the Protestant world was divided. Nor could it be expected otherwise. The plea which they made struck at the very foundation of all the existing religious sects; hence it is reasonable enough to suppose the sects would bitterly denounce a movement which had for its object their complete destruction. This very attitude of the Reformation arrayed all the hosts of sectarianism against it. The contest was a fearful one, and the odds against the little Spartan band who plead for a return to apostolic Christianity were truly appalling. But truth is mighty and will prevail; and our brother lived long enough to see his brethren, who were so heartily despised at first, rise to be one of the most powerful and influential religious people in all the land. And to reach this success, no one labored more steadily and earnestly than he himself, sacrificing ease and comfort, traveling at times from one end of the country to the other, working by day and by night, preaching the Gospel, organizin; churches, writing for the papers, editing books, teaching school, in fact, doing any thing that was necessary toward pushing on the cause which lay so near his heart.

On the thirtieth day of March, 1830, he was married to Miss MARY G. GANO, youngest daughter of Major-general JOHN S. GANO. She had been immersed in 1827 by Rev. JEREMIAH VARDEMAN; and it is due to her to say here that she always faithfully co-operated with her husband in all his efforts to spread the Gospel of the grace of God. In 1833, he entered actively upon the work of an evangelist. He made an extensive and successful preaching tour through the Eastern States, passing through Virginia, then further north to the seaboard cities. The result of his labors in the cities visited was highly satisfactory. Great good was accomplished in stirring up the Disciples to a more active zeal, while a very general interest was created in favor of the Primitive Gospel. Many of the churches that now exist in those localities are the results of good seed sown during this tour.

On returning home he commenced his career as editor and publisher. From 1834 to 1840, he published the "Christian Preacher," a monthly magazine, containing choice discourses and essays on the great themes connected with man's redemption. This exerted a good influence, and had considerable circulation. In 1846, he published "The Christian Family Magazine;" then the "Christian Age," for several years. At another time he published simultaneously "The Reformer," "The Monthly Age," and "The Sunday-school Journal." He also edited the "Sunday-school Library," of fifty-six volumes, and an edition of the "Christian Baptist," in one volume. In all these publications he showed considerable ability, though his powers as a writer were not equal to his speaking talent. His home was in the pulpit, and he was never so able in any other department of labor.

As an educator he had considerable experience; and although he may not have excelled in this profession, his career was highly creditable to him. For two years he was President of Bacon College, Georgetown, Ky., and afterward Principal and Proprietor of Hygeia Female Atheneum, situated on the heights, seven miles back of Cincinnati. In both of these places he gave evidence of good executive talent and respectable ability as a teacher; but it was not the work he most desired; consequently, in 1844, he resumed the pastoral charge of the church on Sycamore street, Cincinnati, and subsequently at the corner of Eighth and Walnut streets, serving in all sixteen years.

His ministry in Cincinnati was attended with a steady and permanent success. He never produced any very marked impression on the city, but kept the church in a growing condition, receiving always the confidence of his brethren, and the respect and esteem of all who knew him. While occupying this position, he devoted himself closely to study, taking a very general course of reading, especially in some of the departments of ancient and modern history. Here also he became acquainted with pastoral work, a department of labor not very well understood at that time by preachers of the Christian Church. Owing to the small number of preachers, it was impossible to supply many of the churches with regular pastors. The preachers had to do chiefly evangelical work, and, consequently, had little or no experience in developing the resources of a single church. Brother Burnet saw that pastoral labor must be done in the churches, and especially the city churches, before they could ever reach that spiritual growth which would enable them to exert a proper influence on the world. Holding these views, he labored not only for an increase of the ministry, but for such a ministry as would be able to build up the *churches* as well as convert the world. He did not measure power by *many*, but by *much*. Numbers in a church are well enough, but strength is not always in numbers. Discipline, long and patient discipline, is necessary to develop *real power*, and this can not be had without a thorough organization, and some one to take the oversight, who feels the responsibility of watching for the souls of the people. He did not argue that the pastoral office is a distinct office from the eldership, but that it is a part of the work of the eldership. But as the elders selected by the churches are generally not competent, or else will not perform this work, such men should be provided as conscientiously feel it to be their duty to "feed the flock of God." This course would alone give such prosperity to the churches as would make them the "pillar and support of the truth."

In 1857 he was called to the pastoral care of the church on Seventeenth street, in the city of New York. At the conclusion of one year's labor he resigned, and spent the following year along the seaboard from New York to Texas. The next year was spent in Missouri and Kansas, where his labors were greatly blessed, several hundred additions being made to the churches. It was during this tour that he conducted one of the most remarkable meetings of his life, at Paris, Missouri. For several weeks the interest was so great that all the merchants in the place, by common consent, closed their business houses every day at ten o'clock, to enable them to attend church. It is said by those who heard him, that his power in the pulpit during this meeting was truly marvelous.

When he returned from this tour, he again took charge of the church corner of Eighth and Walnut streets, Cincinnati, but in the fall of 1860, at the earnest solicitation of many brethren, he was induced to resign and take the corresponding secretaryship of the American Christian Missionary Society. This placed him again actively in the general field, and gave him additional opportunities for extending his travels and his already large acquaintance among the brethren. But our civil war beginning in 1861, and the resources of the Society being largely cut off, he gave up the secretaryship, removed to Balti-

more, Maryland, and became pastor of the church in that
city. There he remained until his death, which took
place on the 8th of July, 1867, being just fifty-nine years
and two days old.

His last hours were in accordance with his whole life,
full of faith and hope. His sickness, in its aggravated
form, was of short duration. He had not been well for
some time, but no one considered him seriously ill. He
had just resigned his pastoral charge at Baltimore, and
was about to remove to Louisville, Kentucky, where he
had been called to the pastorate of the church on the corner of Walnut and Fourth streets. He preached his
farewell sermon to the church which he had so faithfully
served, on Lord's day, June the 30th, and the labors of
that day apparently developed the germs of the disease
of which he died. On the day following, he sought in
quietness to relieve himself of his distress, but without
success. On Tuesday morning, although quite feeble,
and severely suffering, he insisted on meeting an engage-
ment to administer the ordinance of baptism to two persons who had made the confession the previous Lord's
day. In the performance of this act he had to be supported to and from the church. On Wednesday he was
too ill to rise, and was at once placed under rigorous
medical treatment; but the most skillful and unremit-
ting attention was unavailing. The work of death from
this time proceeded, and on Monday morning, at eleven
and a half o'clock, was accomplished

It is a pleasant reflection to his friends to know that
during his entire illness his intellect was unclouded and
his faith undimmed. The evening before he died, he
said to those at his bedside: "Brethren, my faith is
strong in God; I die in the faith of the Gospel, and
have no fears." Next morning, just before death, he

said: "My path is clear before me, and I have nothing against any one." Many of his last moments were spent in repeating the Psalms, especially the twenty-third, alternately in Hebrew and English.

On the Wednesday following his death, a large concourse of the brethren and friends assembled at the Christian Church in Baltimore, to pay their last respects to the honored dead. An appropriate discourse was preached by Brother A. N. GILBERT, of Syracuse, N. Y. His remains, in charge of his brother JACOB BURNET, Esq., and two brethren appointed by the Baltimore church, were then taken to Cincinnati, where, on Friday afternoon, his funeral took place, from the church corner of Eighth and Walnut streets. An eloquent funeral discourse was delivered by ISAAC ERRETT, of Cleveland, Ohio, a valued friend of the deceased, and, for many years, a co-laborer in the Gospel, after which the remains were followed by a large number of relatives and personal friends to Spring Grove Cemetery, where they were interred in the family burying-ground.

Thus ended the earthly career of a noble hero of the Cross. His life had been glorious, and his death was triumphant. He rests from his labors, and his works do follow him. In deep sorrow, though not as those who have no hope, we adopt the sentiment of the poet:

> "Fallen—on Zion's battle-field,
>   A soldier of renown,
> Armed in the panoply of God,
>   In conflict cloven down!
> His helmet on, his armor bright,
>   His cheek unblanched with fear—
> While round his head there gleamed a light,
>   His dying hour to cheer.

> "Fallen—while cheering with his voice
>   The sacramental host,
> With banners floating in the air—
>   Death found him at his post.
> In life's high prime the warfare closed,
>   But not ingloriously ;
> He fell beyond the outer wall,
>   And shouted, Victory !
>
> "Fallen—a holy man of God,
>   An Israelite indeed,
> A standard-bearer of the cross,
>   Mighty in word and deed—
> A master-spirit of the age,
>   A bright and burning light,
> Whose beams across the firmament
>   Scattered the clouds of night.
>
> "Fallen—as sets the sun at eve,
>   To rise in splendor, where
> His kindred luminaries shine,
>   Their heaven of bliss to share.
> Beyond the stormy battle-field
>   He reigns in triumph now,
> Sweeping a harp of wondrous song,
>   With glory on his brow !"

Brother Burnet was in stature somewhat below the medium height; but his presence was so commanding as to impress upon the observer that he was no ordinary man. He had a healthy physical organization, susceptible of great endurance, and a large well-balanced brain; and this accounts for the immense amount of physical and intellectual labor he was able to accomplish, his whole life being characterized by great activity and energy.

His manners were somewhat formal and stiff, arising, doubtless, from a too sensitive nature, which instinctively shrank from familiar contact with any but the most intimate friends. He was always, however, deferential and courteous to even the humblest individual, but his natural reserve sometimes subjected him to the charge of exclusiveness. Nevertheless, he was one of the most social and agreeable of men, but his sociability was not of that free, outspoken kind which disarms criticism and makes every one feel perfectly at home. It was none the less genuine, however, on this account.

As a scholar, he had respectable attainments, having made considerable progress in the study of the languages, especially Hebrew and Greek. He was also very fond of the sciences, and was quite familiar with natural history.

As a speaker, he was more of an elocutionist than a rhetorician. His declamation was easy and graceful, his voice rich and melodious, and his power to control an audience, when fully aroused, unsurpassed by any preacher in the ranks of the Disciples. But, like all great orators, he was not always equal to himself. It required a suitable occasion to bring him out in his full strength. It is said by those familiar with his preaching, that he never was so powerful as when conducting a successful protracted meeting. At such a time he seemed to be inspired, and spoke as if his lips had been touched with a Divine eloquence. His ability as a writer, however, was not so great. His style was too diffuse, and was not always free from rhetorical blemishes, especially in the use of metaphors.

He had fine executive talent, and always made his successes permanent. He never lost any ground. If he did not always go forward, he never went backward. He did not stop in the *formative* state of a work, but carried it forward to *organization*. In fact, he was distinguished as an *organizer;* and the present system of societies among

the Disciples owes its origin to his efforts more than to
those of any other man.   In a letter to the editor of this
work, dated Baltimore, February 28, 1867, he says: "I
consider the inauguration of our Society system, which I
vowed to urge upon the brethren, if God raised me from
my protracted illness of 1845, as one of the most important acts of my career."   He was President of the Bible
and Missionary Societies while they co-existed, and was,
at the time of his death, President of the General Missionary Society, having been elected to fill the vacancy
occasioned by the death of the venerable and lamented
ALEXANDER CAMPBELL.

He was also a growing man.   He never ceased to
devote himself to constant and laborious study.   He
felt it to be his religious duty to make every sermon he
preached better than any he had ever before preached.
Hence he did not belong to that class of preachers, who,
after preaching a few stereotyped discourses, have nothing
more to say.   His mind was fertile in resources, and his
industry equal to the severest demands of his profession.
As he grew in years, he grew also in power, so that his
last years were the years of his greatest usefulness.   His
success in Baltimore, though made at an advanced age, was
by far the most decided of his whole life.   The church
there was in a very low condition when he took charge of
it, and owing to the civil war which was then raging, he
found many difficulties in the way of any permanent progress.   Nevertheless, he continued to work on, trusting in
God that good results would come by and by.   These results did come; for, during the last year of his ministry,
the most gratifying success attended his preaching of the
Gospel.   Large numbers were added to the church, while
the older members were built up in their most holy faith.
Never was the cause more firmly established in the city

of Baltimore, and never were the prospects more flattering than on the last days of his ministry there.

While it is a source of great regret that he was cut off
in the midst of so much usefulness, it affords no little
satisfaction to reflect that a life, so full of self-denial and
labor, closed at last in the midst of such triumphant
success.

THE GOOD CONFESSION.

BY D. S. BURNET.

"Jesus Christ witnessed a good confession."—1 TIM. vi: 13.

THE Good Confession, more than any other peculiarity, distinguishes the people who choose to be
called Christians or Disciples of Christ. What the text
calls the good confession is exacted of every candidate
for baptism, and upon it, rather than any other consideration apart from his hearty faith in it, the party is admitted to that holy institution. Confident of the corect-
ness of the practice, beloved, I ask your attention to some
suggestions in regard to its import, its scripturality, its
uses, and its abuses.

The reasons of the course now proposed are simply
these: Surrounded by a multitude of religious denominations, within the last forty-five years a community has
grown from zero to a half million, without a denominational aspect, and stands to-day unmarked by a human
formula. It is founded upon the good confession that
JESUS IS THE CHRIST, THE SON OF THE LIVING GOD.

The world has a right to know whether this is a scriptural method of constituting the Church, and what are its
practical workings in society. What the world demands,
we as a people fully concede. As far as this address can

(47)

answer the demand, it is my purpose to show that the
Primitive Church had no other doctrinal foundation;
that the convert had no other claim upon baptism; and
that the recent recovery from the apostolic ages of this
formula has justified the terms, "Reformation of the
Nineteenth Century."

What is the Good Confession? The text is part of a
valuable passage, which in the authorized version reads,
"Thou hast professed a good profession, before many
witnesses. I give thee in charge in the sight of God who
quickeneth all things, and before Jesus Christ, who before Pontius Pilate witnessed a good confession," etc.
The Greek words represented by "a good profession"
in the 12th, and "a good confession" in the 13th verses,
are the same—την Καλην ὁμολογίαν—and therefore should
be rendered by the same words in both cases. It should
be *confession* in both verses, for the verb ὁμολογέω, of the
context, means to confess. It is defined, "to speak one
language; to say together; to hold the same language;
to agree with another; confess; to be connected with one;
to come to terms of surrender." Out of twenty-two
occurrences in the New Testament, it is never translated
"profess" but twice; and one of those cases is in the text.
We will, therefore, translate the passage thus: "Thou
hast confessed *the* good confession before many witnesses.
I charge thee in the sight of God, who makes all things
alive, and Jesus Christ, who, in the time of Pontius Pilate, witnessed *the* good confession, keep this commandment." In the prosecution of our inquiries, it will be
necessary to recur to this translation. It will be noticed
that the article in the Greek requires the amended version to read "*the* good confession." There is the width
of the seas between *a* and *the* in this connection. Doubt-

less Timothy often confessed *a* good confession, but allusion is made here to one particular and peculiar confession, which the apostle designates, *par excellence*, *the* Good Confession—a formula pronounced once, and but once, in his lifetime, as a religious act.

Both Jesus and Timothy made this confession. In what, then, did it consist? In reply, it is affirmed:

I. That the good confession is the historical and logical aspect of the Gospel.

The Apostle John sums up his memoirs of Christ in these remarkable words: "These are written that ye might believe that Jesus is the Christ, the Son of God."* It would be safe to suppose that Matthew, Mark, and Luke wrote their several works for the same purpose. It is inevitable, then, that the only recognized account of Jesus, embracing half the New Testament, is a historical and logical defense of the Messiahship and Lordship, the mission and the Divinity, of Jesus of Nazareth; in other words, that those books elaborate and defend the proposition which has been called the Good Confession. As they contain the matter-of-fact grounds on which Christ must be obeyed, they have for ages been called the Four Gospels.

In the record of that most touching interview between Jesus and the sisters of Lazarus, which has been the legacy of the children of sorrow for near two thousand years, Martha but represents the expectations of the pious Israelites, when she declares, "I believe thou art the Christ, the Son of God, *which should come into the world.*" The coming one was to be, they thought, both Messiah and Son. They supposed the new kingdom would be inaugurated by the resurrection of many of the prophets, the

---

*John xx: 31.

4

reappearance of Moses and Elijah, and that the Messiah, who had often appeared to the nation as its deliverer, would reign in unexampled splendor.*

But the instrument of salvation, called the Gospel, was committed to the apostles to be preached and administered to people of all nations. The *Acts of Apostles* is the only inspired record of their preaching. It fully sustains the proposition that the words of this Confession are the staple of the Gosple. These heaven-qualified and commissioned preachers either ignored all other issues or used them in subservience to the elaboration and enforcement of this Confession. To a careful reader, nothing will be more apparent than that the whole purpose of the apostolic ministry was to argue and enforce the claims of Jesus upon the faith, reverence, and heartfelt obedience of all classes of persons, as the heaven-provided Savior of a lost race. They drove this one point to the conviction and submission of all but the incorrigible. They had nothing to do with doctrines. They preached a person, Jesus, made of a woman, as human as his mother, and having been declared to be the Son of God with power, as divine as his Father. Every discourse tended to this conviction, whether addressed to saint or sinner. The reign of grace opened among men by the triumphant carrying of this point under the formula "Let all the house of Israel know assuredly that God hath made Jesus whom ye crucified, both Lord and Christ;" and it was "when they heard this, they were pierced to the heart;" and that day three thousands of them surrendered to the conquering Crucified, by being baptized in his name.† By a

---

*See Kinnoel, Lightfoot, Schoetgen, Bloomfield, Townsend, etc.
†Acts ii: 36, 37.

similar argument the same inspired apostle opened the door of faith to the Gentile world.* Philip, in Samaria, "preached Christ unto them."†

It is but necessary now to examine the method of preaching adopted by the remaining great actor of this book of primitive church history, Paul the apostle. Here we are happily relieved from all darkness or doubt in regard to the didactic course of this most renowned champion of the Cross. "Paul, as his manner was, went in unto them, and three Sabbath-days reasoned with them out of the Scriptures, explaining and alleging that the Christ must needs have suffered and risen from the dead, and that this Jesus whom I preach unto you is the Christ."‡ Enough has been said to demonstrate our point, that there was no gospel, and it may be added, there *is* no gospel, which is not founded on this primitive formula.§

The moral rather than the logical side of the Gospel, the love of God to the world, the sympathy of angels, and the persuasion of the Holy Spirit, not to mention objectionable forms of expression, have been unwisely permitted to usurp pulpit and popular attention, while the apostolic method of presentation, including the moral and logical, has been ignored.

II. The Good Confession, that Jesus is the Christ, the Son of God, is the creed and foundation of the Primitive Church.

The Jews never had an uninspired creed. The Bible was their only divine book. Israelites and Samaritans

---

*Acts x: 34, 43. †Acts viii: 5. ‡Acts xvii: 2, 3.
§ The celebrated metaphysician and Christian, John Locke, wrote a volume to prove this first proposition of this discourse. It is long since out of print.

had the same Pentateuch. Pharisees and Sadducees worshiped in the same Synagogue. God never contemplated
any substitute for his Word. It alone is to enlighten,
govern, and save. The legacy of the apostle to the
Ephesian elders was this sacred treasure: "I commend
you to God and to the Word of his grace, which is able
to build you up and to give you an inheritance among
them which are sanctified."* Thus Jesus adopts the Good
Confession as the rock of his kingdom.†

The church was not yet in existence, but it was to be
erected upon this foundation when built. "Thus saith
Jehovah God, Behold I lay in Zion for a foundation a
stone, a tried stone, a precious corner, a sure foundation;
he that believeth shall not make haste."‡ This was the
basis of faith. In Corinth Paul laid the same foundation: "I have laid the foundation." "Other foundation
can no man lay than that is laid, which is Jesus Christ;"§
that is, Jesus Christ doctrinal—Jesus Christ in this formula, with its accompanying proofs, illustrations, and
enforcements. Until some one shall arise—no one has
yet done so—and show that God ever authorized a religious society, Jewish or Christian, to be founded upon
an uninspired document, it will be taken for granted that
Jesus meant what he said in these utterances, and that
the Good Confession, as defined in the conversation between Jesus and his disciples, is the doctrinal foundation
of the Church, as it is of the individual faith of each of
its members. It may be objected that the whole New
Testament is considered the rock of the Church. Truly,

---

*Acts xx: 32.

†Matt. xvi: 16–18. By the laws of language, the rock is the confession which Peter had just made. So wrote Chrysostom.

‡Isaiah xxviii: 16.   §1 Cor. iii: 10, 11.

it is the Divine directory of the Church. The Ten Commandments were the constitution of the Jews, or the old covenant, the bulwark of the unity of God against Polytheism. The Good Confession sustains the same relation to the Christian Church. It is the new covenant and the development of divine society in God—the Father, Son, and Spirit. The Confession was laid as a foundation in Zion by the Father (Isaiah xxviii: 16), and Jesus built the Church upon it throughout the Roman empire before the New Testament was written and compiled.

There is a religion of the New Testament as well defined as the religion of the Athanasian or Augsburg Confessions, or the miscalled Apostles' Creed, and perfectly distinct from either of them. The New Testament comprises the "church standards" of Christianity. In taking the Bible we accept all truth—in taking the Bible *alone*, we reject all error.

III. The Good Confession is Divine.

There is a sense in which all the Bible is Divine—it is inspired. But it is not intended in this statement to say that the Good Confession is inspired. The words of all the sacred writers are inspired, by whomsoever spoken— saint, sinner, angel, or demon; that is, God had them written. But it is claimed for this Confession that God made it, that it is the foundation which *he* laid in Zion. He gave these words to no prophet, angel, or apostle to announce. He charged the atmosphere with them himself. "Blessed art thou, Simon, son of Jonah, for flesh and blood hath not revealed it unto thee, but my Father which is in heaven."*

Though there is some disputation as to the time when

---

* Matt. xvi: 17.

the Father made this revelation to Peter, the record seems to point to the baptism of Jesus in the Jordan as the occasion. God made the revelation, and when others were appalled by the disproportion between the common appearance and lofty claims of Jesus, Peter remembered and rightly interpreted it. For this his Master gave him the blessing. Heaven grant that it may be a revelation and a blessing to us all! John the Baptist's testimony sustains this view. "I knew him not; but that he should be made manifest to Israel, therefore I am come baptizing in water."* By saying, further, that God had told him that upon whom he should see the Spirit descending and remaining, "the same is he that baptizeth in the Holy Spirit," he fully identifies the revelation with the events of the baptism. Those events themselves teach us the same lesson. The heavens opened while the yet uninaugurated Son and his harbinger were but coming out of the waters of the sacred river—the heavens opened in the face of the shining sun! Was the miracle in the circumambient space, or in the eyes and ears of the beholders? Stephen, by an exaltation of vision, saw Jesus at the right hand of God, as a man by the aid of a telescope sees volcanoes in the moon. To the spectators the heavens opened, and to connect those heavens with Jesus by a visible link, the dove-like Spirit, the power and the heart of God came down in beautiful gyrations, bearing the olive-branch of glory—the Messiahship. For what is Messiah in Hebrew, and Christ, its equivalent, in Greek, but anointed? Jesus was christed by the Spirit's descending and remaining on him. This was in fulfillment of prophecy. "The Spirit of the Lord God is upon

---

* John i: 31. *In,* in the Greek, in verses 31 and 33.

me, because the Lord hath anointed me to preach good tidings unto the meek."*

The first three Evangelists coincide in the statement that, following the Spirit-anointing or christing, "There came a voice, saying, This is my beloved Son, in whom I am well pleased."† This established the Sonship of the Confession. The two, the anointing of the Spirit and the avouching of the Father, embrace its two elements, making it divine, in the sense of done and said of God in person. Again, the evangelical prophet is justified by the evangelical annals: "Behold my servant whom I will uphold, mine elect in whom my soul delights, I have put my Spirit upon him."‡ This accuracy of delineation transforms the prophecy into history. We have the Father's words interpreted—Behold the anointed—he is my Son—my delight.

God, who has many oracles—the Spirit, angels, and men—seldom speaks in person. He spake, and it was done. He gave us a world. He spoke in Eden, and organized a family with language and religion. After a silence of twenty-five centuries, he stayed his cloud-chariot over Horeb. The heavens lighted their fires, and uttered their thunders. The terrified mountains trembled like aspen leaves. He uttered his voice, the earth melted. He spoke "the ten words," and organized a sacred nation. Fifteen centuries more passed and the heavens open again, now over the sacred river, lying deep in the bosom of mother earth. The voice and Spirit of the Father are poured in the dove form of mercy, and the

---

* Isaiah lxi: 1.   Compare Luke iv: 16–21; Acts x: 38.
† Compare Matt. iii: 17; Mark i: 11, and Luke iii: 22.
‡ Isaiah xlii: 1.

utterances of affection—My Son—my delight. This Confession, thus completed, is in the highest sense divine.

It is difficult to exaggerate the importance of this third proposition. If the Good Confession is the marrow and fatness of the Gospel, if it is the rock chosen on which to found the Church, no one could object to its being called divine. But the word divine receives a new power in this connection, where the act of the Spirit and the word of the Father are proved to constitute the Confession itself. The Church of Christ is pre-eminently a divine institution, and is degraded by the thought of an uninspired basis. The convert is not called upon to emasculate his reason and humble his manhood by bowing to a humanism in the vestibule of the temple of truth. His "faith and hope rest in God." This preaching is "in demonstration of the spirit and power, that your faith should not stand in the wisdom of men, but in the power of God."*

There is something peculiar in the employment of ὁμολογία as the name of the confession, and the verb ὁμολογεω to express confess. There are several other Greek words which signify confess and confession, but they do not have the superadded idea of repeating after another, or "holding the same language." In the Greek, then, those who confess, repeat what was first said by the Father concerning his Son Jesus Christ. This appears more obvious from the consideration that the noun ὁμολογία is compounded of ὁμος, one and the same, and λέγω to speak, declare, recount. The confession by a penitent is a repeating after the Father, Son, and Holy Spirit, as did Peter, who got the blessing. Although this Confes-

---

* 1 Cor. ii: 4, 5.

sion is never quoted as an authority for sponsors, yet it is the nearest approach to the idea of sponsors which the Bible contains. The Spirit visibly rests upon Jesus, and the aspirant for baptism cries, "Jesus is the Christ." The Father says, "Behold my Son;" the candidate responds, "I believe Jesus is the Son of God." The Hebrew יָדָה, rendered confess, means, first, to pronounce, to utter, and, after, confess; in its very common use, "give thanks, praise, celebrate, glorify, i. e., name aloud, with the accusative of the object." *

In one of his controversies with the Jews, in the array of evidences of his mission, Jesus said, "Though I bear record of myself, my record is true;" † and the Baptist said, "He that hath received his testimony hath set to his seal that God is true." ‡ God avouched Jesus, and requires that we should solemnly declare his testimony correct; that we should indorse the Father's testimony of the Son.

In John v, Jesus appeals to his countrymen to believe the testimony of the Baptist and his own daily miracles, triumphantly adding to these evidences, "The Father himself who sent me hath borne witness of me. Did you never hear his voice, or see his form? or have you forgotten his declaration?" This translation of Dr. Campbell, the President of Marischal College, Edinburgh, has been objected to as not being true to history. Nevertheless, the weight of evidence seems to sustain it, and harmonizing admirably with the object of this discourse, it casts a flood of light on the transaction at the Jordan,

---

* Fuerst's Lexicon.

† John viii: 14. In v. 31, "Jesus said, If I testify of myself my testimony is not true;" i. e., in a court of justice, I alone am not a legal witness in my own case. ‡ John iii: 33.

when the visible anointing of the Spirit, and the audible testimony of the Father designated him of whom Moses in the Law and the prophets did write. The Spirit descended in a bodily shape like a dove upon him.* The invisible God, who dwells in light inaccessible, has often assumed a form, and once became flesh, and tabernacled in clay for years. We beheld his glory as the glory of the only-begotten of the Father, full of grace and truth, like the fire of God in the unconsumed green and flowering shrub on Horeb.

The Greek for confession, in ancient military language, was the word which designated the terms of surrender. There is great propriety in thus styling the words by which a sinner publicly concedes the victory to the Prince of Peace

IV. The Good Confession is the most liberal confession of faith on record.

This may be inferred from its simplicity. There is nothing intricate in it. It involves the great fact of the Bible, the central truth of the whole revelation. Jesus is the Alpha and Omega of all sacred literature. It is truly a confession of faith, and not of opinions. In this respect it is unlike any symbol of any denomination. *It* relates words from the lips of Jehovah—*they*, words of uninspired men regarding real or fancied principles supposed to be, or implied, in the statements of the Bible. Man recoils from man clad in undue authority. It is a lesson taught by Jehovah: "Cursed be the man that trusteth in man," (himself or another,) "and maketh flesh his arm." † The time will never come when the body of Christ will be based upon any one sectarian symbol or creed, and be

---

* Luke iii: 22.   † Jer. xvii: 5.

clad in its parti-colored garment. A prayer for union in
that direction is a vain hope. The intercessory of Jesus
is for those who should believe on him through the word
of the apostles, that they all might be one.* The religious world gives its homage to the Word of God. It is
to be regretted that their leaders of the people will not
permit them to renounce their creeds and unite on it.

This formula is disentangled thus from the innumerable vexed questions of religious strife. Perhaps each one
of us has a preference among the religious philosophies
which have been christened after their authors, Augus-
tine, Calvin, Arminius, etc.; but all intelligent persons
separate them from Christianity. Holding or withhold-
ing assent to any of them does not necessarily make
either a good or a bad man. But to confess true faith in
Christ materially improves the character and advances
the prospects of sinful men. As the confessor naturally
takes the name of the confessed, the convert is, and he
is called, a Christian. Illiberality has been charged upon
the assumption of our leader's name, as though it were
ostentatious and invidious to be named after our Master.
If one may be called a Platonist or a Calvinist, may you
not be named a Christian? Does not James intimate
that the name of Christ was called upon all disciples?†
When will the time come for all followers of Jesus to be
called Christians? Would there be any thing invidious
in that? But one will say, "We are all called Christians;
it is invidious in you to appropriate the name to yourselves." We deny no one the right to confess and follow
Christ, and to wear his name. We simply refuse to wear
any additional name, or to hold any thing as matter of

---

* John xvii: 20, 21. † James ii: 7. See Greek. Compare Acts xi: 26.

faith, not found in the New Testament. This can not
be illiberal! The highest Christian liberality consists in
standing up for Jesus and his Word, and inviting all
others to do the same. We deny the right of any one to
assume the name of an uninspired leader, as Luther, or
Wesley, or Campbell, great and good as those men were.
Therefore, none of our hymn-books or periodicals are
thus designated. We are equally opposed to calling a
church after any system of ecclesiastical polity, as Episcopal, Presbyterian, Congregational, etc. These are not
descriptive. Our Church claims all these terms, but puts
them upon none of its books, papers, or houses of worship, or willingly wears an uninspired style. There is no
denominationalism in Christianity.

V. Christ made the Good Confession before the Jewish
high-priest and Sanhedrim, during the administration of
Pontius Pilate, and died for the making of it.

The authorized version of our text reads, " Jesus *before*
Pontius Pilate." I have rendered the words επὶ Ποντίου
Πιλάτου, in the time of Pontius Pilate, in the sense of,
during the administration of, etc. Επι signifies the time
in which something happens. On the subject of date, it
is thus used both in the classics and in Scripture.* Attention is called to this criticism, because Jesus made his
confession, truly, in the time of Pilate, but in the presence of the high priest. The incident is most important
and touching. In the trial before the Sanhedrim, the
complaint against Jesus came near being dismissed for
want of evidence. A comparison of Matthew, Mark, and

---

*See the Greek of Luke iii: 2. During high priesthood (singular) of
Annas and Caiaphas, Mark ii: 26, common version rendered correctly
επι 'Αβιά θαρ, in the days of Abiathar. See also Mark xv: 1, Luke iv:
25, John iv: 27, where επι means during.

Luke shows that many witnesses were presented by the prosecutors, but their testimony was irrelevant. At last, two agreed to say that Jesus had threatened to destroy the temple of God. As he had indeed said, if *they* should destroy the temple, meaning and pointing to his body, he would rear it up in three days, they had but to garble the statement to rouse the national hatred. But they failed again, as the testimony of the two did not circumstantially agree. When they were baffled at every point, the presiding Hierarch, coming to the aid of the prosecutors, cried out, "I adjure you by the Living God," (I put you upon your oath,) "tell us whether thou be the Christ the Son of God. Jesus said unto him, Thou hast said."* It is here we find the ground of his condemnation. He died for the Good Confession! The high priest rent his clothes, an action emblematical of fear and sorrow, sometimes of indignation, and also employed when giving the accused up to the rigors of the law. The consul Paulus rent his garment through indignation, and Julius Cæsar did the same to appease the infuriated multitude. The fact is twice related of Augustus. Caiaphas tore his pontifical robe in irrepressible rage, making more impressive his surrender of the darling Lamb of God to the punishment of blasphemy, for he instantly put to vote the question of his execution on the charge of that crime. The Jews of the present day justify their ancestors and themselves in rejecting the greatest of men, as some rabbis call him, on the ground of the blasphemy involved in his claim of Divine Sonship.

In every attitude assumed by Jesus in the evangelical history, he excites our admiration and love; but that he

---

* Matt. xxvi: 63.

himself should furnish the ground of his immolation, when his foes had failed, transcends all our conceptions of the morally sublime, and bankrupts love itself in its adoration.

"Come, then, expressive silence, muse his praise."

VI. The Confession by which Jesus died is appointed for our life.

The deep-felt conviction of all races and all ages coincides with the Bible statement that man is a sinner. "The whole head is sick and the whole heart faint. From the sole of the foot even unto the crown of the head, there is no soundness in it; but wounds, and bruises, and putrefying sores."* The prophet is confirmed by the apostle. "I find then a law, that, when I would do good, evil is present with me."† The heathen poet experienced the same internal struggle:

> Aliudque cupido,
> Meus aliud suadet. Vides meliora proboque;
> Deteriora sequor.

Confession of Christ is a condition of salvation from sin. Confess me before men, and I will own you before the burning throne, is the promise of Christ. There is no recognition before God and angels without it.‡ The relation of the Confession to the cure of sin will be noticed hereafter; it is enough now to show that the Confession which brought death to Jesus brings life to us. The apostle says: "With the heart man believeth unto righteousness, and with the mouth confession is made unto salvation." §

---

*Isaiah i: 5.   † Rom. vii: 21.
‡ Matt. x: 32, 33. Luke xii: 8, 9.   § Rom. x: 10.

What mercy! Jesus died by our sin, and for it, and we live by his righteousness. He died for acknowledging himself to be our Messiah and God's Son—the God-Man Savior. We live by believing and confessing the words which condemned him. He died confessing, that we might live confessing! It is a brazen serpent cures the serpent's bite!

VII. The import and value of this formula entitles it to the designation Good or Beautiful Confession.

Can a man believe that Jesus is the Christ, and not have the spirit of obedience? Can he be a rebel against him? When about to ascend to heaven, Jesus observed to his disciples: "All authority in heaven and on earth is conferred upon me."* This was simply stating that he was the Messiah of the old covenant—the Christ of the new. Antiquity, weary of exhausting all the stores of its rhetoric for designations of David's son, fell upon the expedient of calling him the מָשִׁיחַ, Messiah, anointed, in Daniel,† and ever after so styled him. When the Jews adopted the Greek language, they employed Χριστος, Anglicised Christ, because it was of the same import. As all authority, sacerdotal and regal, was conferred by anointing with oil, to call "him that was to come" the anointed, was to say precisely what Jesus affirmed—all authority, celestial and terrestrial, is conferred upon me. The Jews on Pentecost were pierced to the heart, when they understood from the fisherman apostle that God had made the person whom they had consigned to ignominy and death both Lord and Christ, and nothing could be more natural than their agonizing shriek, Brethren, what shall we do? Then, verbally, Christ is anointed, but evangeli-

---

* Matt. xxviii: 18. † Daniel ix: 25, 26.

cally, he receives all authority and power. Faith in the Christhood admits the regal authority of Jesus, and is the very germ of obedience.

But it is more. The anointed is Priest—High Priest. Paul beautifully unfolds the idea in the Hebrews. Christhood is sacrifice and offering; blood at the altar and blood at the mercy-seat. It is death for sin, the innocent for the sins of the guilty, and ceaseless intercession in heaven for the erring. No man intelligently believes this without feeling that he is a sinner needing a Savior. To confess the Christhood of Jesus is to avow one's self a sinner, and to come to God bearing this precious Lamb that taketh away the sin of the world in his heart. He sings with Watts:

> "My faith would lay her hand
> On that dear head of thine,
> While like a penitent I stand,
> And thus confess my sin."

Can one say Jesus is the Son of God without admitting the divinity of his mission? Can any make the Confession of the Sonship without acknowledging the Fatherhood? Can any one recognize a Father and a Son in God without acknowledging God in both? Is the Father divine? So is the Son, else there were not the community of nature imparted by those two relations; for Jesus is not *a* Son of God by creation, but *the* Son of God by birth—the only-begotten of the Father.

The Confession presents Jesus objectively in all his official and personal relations to the universe—the Lord of all, God manifest in the flesh, and the Savior of sinners. Blessed be his holy name! Subjectively, the confessor stands before God a sinner, meeting Jehovah at the altar

of sacrifice and the mercy-seat upon the blood of Jesus.
Here God exclaims,

"My Son, in whom I delight!"

The confessor responds, "He is the chiefest among ten
thousands, and the one altogether lovely!" The Cross
of Christ is the pacification of the universe. Blessed are
all they who put their trust in him!

The words τὴν καλὴν of the text, translated "the good,"
as applied to the Confession, may be rendered "the beautiful." It is defined beautiful, applied to visible things
and persons; to man's inward nature, morally beautiful,
noble; serving a good end, good, fair. The noble, the
beautiful Confession! So honorable to God, so invalu-
able and creditable to man! During a ministry of over
forty years, it has been the delight of your speaker to
take this good, noble, and beautiful Confession of thousands. No pearl so priceless or diamond so bright to
the eye of faith as the pure distillation of sorrow on the
cheek of penitence! and no music so tender as the sweet
response of the heart, "I do believe, and I wish to serve
Jesus!"

The reception of thousands upon the simple confession of faith and obedience has caused some nervousness
among those who require a recital of inward struggles,
and delineations of the various shades of darkness and
light, doubt and confidence, which may have marked the
progress of the soul to final submission. Who has produced one precedent or precept for the admission of
persons to baptism upon any other basis than the Confession? Echo asks, Who? and asks in vain! It must,
however, be admitted that, like every other good thing,
the noble Confession is liable to abuse by both adminis-

5

trator and subject. The preacher is warned against care-
lessness in building upon this foundation wood, hay, or
stubble.* His work shall pass the ordeal of fire. Let
him look well, then, to the materials of his spiritual edifice. As a wise man, he will ascertain whether the candidate understands the Confession. He has Philip for his
authority.† An age too tender to have such understanding should be held back till more mature. He should
be persuaded of the sincerity of the offer, and of the felt
force of a correct understanding. No man whose habits
render his failure a certainty, is in that state fit for the
kingdom of God. The necessity of restraint, however, is
the exception, not the rule. The great difficulty is to get
persons willing to serve Christ. It is believed that the
practice recommended in this discourse is more uniformly
successful, when carefully and intelligently guarded, than
any other in making numerous and stable converts. Disasters, indeed, have occurred by the inconsiderate zeal of
some impulsive men, more desirous of multiplying trophies than of securing a lasting victory.

The want of sufficient pastoral labor has systematic-
ally invited apostasy. Traveling preachers should be dis-
suaded from leaving bodies of new recruits in new places
without regular drill, done by themselves or those whom
they provide.

The position of the Confession in the Gospel economy
heightens its *beauty*. It immediately precedes baptism in
the name of Christ, for the remission of sins through his
precious blood and the gift of the Holy Spirit.‡ Before
heaven and earth the candidate states his faith in the Jesus

---

* 1 Cor. iii: 8–15. † Acts viii: 30.
‡ Acts, ii: 28; xxii: 16; viii: 37, 38.

of the New Testament, and his desire to serve him ; that he is thus dead to the world in heart, as he is dead before the law; that he desires to consummate this death in an actual leaving of the world. As we bury the dead, we bury him. "As many of you as are baptized into Jesus Christ are baptized into his death; therefore we are buried with him by baptism into death, that like as Christ was raised up from the dead by the glory of the Father, even so we should walk in newness of life."* The confessor is immersed both into the death of Christ, and into *his own* death to the world. He enacts, in a living tableaux, an allegorical death, burial, and resurrection. In the light of this and similar passages, nothing can claim to be baptism that does not fulfill its conditions of burial and rising.

In this discourse, Acts viii: 37, I believe that Jesus is the Christ, the Son of God, has not been quoted, because, on the authority of the Bagster Greek Testament, Tischendorf, Alford, etc., it is rejected. Yet the Bible Union Revision, Bengal, Benson, and many others having retained it, it is best to consider its authenticity an open question. If it is genuine, its testimony is decisive. If it is rejected, it is scarcely less. If it is an interpolation, it is a historic proof of the universality of the practice of taking the good Confession from the convert. That the exclusion of verse 37 leaves the eunuch's question— "What doth hinder me to be baptized?"—unanswered, must forever stand a presumptive argument in favor of the authenticity of that verse. The Bible is never silent on direct questions of that class.

· VIII. All men will be compelled to confess Christ at the close of this dispensation.

---

* Rom. vi: 3, 4.

As a different Greek word is employed in these words, "Every tongue shall confess that Jesus is Lord to the glory of God the Father," * this acknowledgment of all in heaven, earth, and hades will not be making the Good, the Noble Confession. Though indeed it shall be the result of conviction, and shall be a voluntary accord from all who have loved the world too much to love Christ, it will be too late for that class. The nobleness of confessing Christ as the sinner's friend is not to be confounded with the acknowledgment of him as judge when dragged before his tribunal. Indeed, many in that day shall call upon overhanging rocks and towering mountains to hide them in their opened graves, that they be not dragged like culprits from their cells, before the face of God and the Lamb, now become the Lion of judgment. To look upon him whom they have pierced, and gaze upon the brow once lacerated with thorns, but now encircled by the diadem of universal dominion, were a terrible retribution, even if there were no lake of fire nor shoreless abyss below. Is it better, friendly alien, to receive an irrevocable sentence on the knees and confess the power of justice after a life's resistance, or to compound your difficulties in accepting the offered grace of the inevitable conqueror, by an expressive confession of his well-established claims, and a union of your interests and efforts with his rising cause? "Kiss the Son lest he be angry, and ye perish from the way when his wrath is kindled but a little. Blessed are all they who put their trust in him!" *Amen.*

---

* Phil. ii: 11.

My truly
H. T. Anderson

HENRY T. ANDERSON.

THIS distinguished scholar and preacher needs no lengthy introduction to American readers. His Translation of the New Testament has made his name quite familiar in this country, and he is not altogether unknown in many portions of Europe.

HENRY T. ANDERSON was born in Caroline County, Virginia, on the 27th of January, 1812. His parents, who were also natives of Virginia, were Baptists, though quite liberal in their views. Hence, Brother ANDERSON's early religious training was nearly in harmony with the position he now occupies. The Bible was the text-book, and its teachings had a very powerful influence upon his youthful mind.

At the age of twenty-one he made the confession, and was immersed by his elder brother, who had left the Baptists and united with the Disciples. By giving diligent attention to the study of the Scriptures, he made such rapid progress in the Divine life that he began to preach in May, 1833, not more than ten months after his baptism.

His method of studying the Scriptures was such as left nothing unnoticed. The Bible was read and re-read again and again. Every sentence was studied, both in the original and English, with the most prayerful interest. Scripture was used to illustrate and explain Scripture, until every subject in the Word of God was examined in the light of Divine Truth. This method of investigation made his preaching didactic rather than hortatory, practical rather than ornamental. Hence, in the popular style, he is not an orator. Nevertheless, his discourses are always highly entertaining, because they are full of instruction, and delivered in an earnest, impressive style.

He remained in Virginia, preaching at various places in Caroline, Hanover, and some other counties, until the year 1837, when he removed to Kentucky, and for several years taught school and preached in the southern portion of the State. In November, 1847, he took charge of the Walnut-street Church in Louisville, and continued there six years. After this he was engaged for about eight years in teaching classical schools, and preaching the Gospel in various parts of the State. In December, 1861, he began to translate the New Testament, a work upon which his reputation chiefly rests. For many years he had made the New Testament original a constant study. He had been blessed in early life with a fine classical education; and such was his devotion to the Greek, that, when he began to make his translation, it was equally as familiar to him as the English. Of the translation itself we need not speak, except to say that it has been pronounced by competent judges the best in the English language. Whether this be true or not, it certainly has superior merits, and will doubtless take a high position among standard works of its kind. He is now engaged in giving an exact translation of the text of Tischendorf. His present home is in Harrodsburg, Ky., where he has preached for the Church for several years.

His prominent characteristics are originality of thought, simplicity of manner, and great faith in the providence of God. He is emphatically a *thinker*, and every thing that he says gives unmistakable evidence that he is not satisfied to simply appropriate the labor of others. He seeks the foundation of things, and though his views may not always be correct, they are always highly suggestive.

His whole nature is childlike. The most perfect simplicity marks every thing he does. His purposes are as transparent as light itself. No one could be freer from affectation. But that which distinguishes him above every thing else is his wonderful faith in God. We do not think we have ever known a man who gives himself more unreservedly into the hands of his Heavenly Father. In this world's goods he has been poor all his life, but he has certainly been rich in faith. The circumstances under which he began his translation afford a fine illustration of this peculiarity. Having a large family to support, with a salary not exceeding six hundred dollars, and no other means that he could command, there was little prospect that he could do any thing beyond supplying the necessities of the hour. But he had faith in God, and entered upon the work with full confidence that the "Lord would provide." In speaking of this subject, in 1863, he says: "The Lord raised me up friends. Some from a distance sent me a few dollars. Two worthy sisters paid one hundred and twenty dollars each last year. Those near me have, some of them, remembered my wants, and generously supplied me with food and clothing. Though the war swept away what little I had, God has never forsaken me. I have a Father in heaven, a Redeemer at his right hand. My prayers have been heard. Friends are near me, and I live, a monument of the truth that God will not forsake those who put their trust in him."

JESUS OF NAZARETH IS THE THEANTHROPOS.

BY H. T. ANDERSON.

"And thou shalt call his name JESUS: for he shall save his people from their sins."—MATT. 1: 21.

WHAT think you of the Christ? whose son is he? The Jews answered: The son of David. Jesus replied: How, then, does David in spirit call him Lord, saying, Jehovah said to my Lord, Sit thou at my right hand, till I put thy enemies under thy feet? The Scripture makes it evident that the Christ is the son of David. The answer to the question, that he is David's son, was and is correct. But this first question led to the second, to which the Jews gave no answer. The son of David, according to Scripture, should sit at the right hand of Jehovah till his enemies were put beneath his feet.

We are to suppose that the Jews either would answer this second question, and could not, or that they could, and would not. The Scriptures furnished the answer. The writer, Matthew, says: "No one was able to answer him a word." This inability of theirs did not proceed from ignorance; for the Scripture had said that David's son should be the Son of God: "I will be to him a father, and he shall be to me a son." The Christ, as Son of God, would have a right to sit at the right hand of Jehovah. It is probable that the Jews understood this, and their inability to answer the question arose, not from ignorance, but from a consciousness that an answer would have entangled them in a snare from which they would not have been able to escape.

Jesus is the son of David, and Son of God. As such he is son of two kings—one, the king of earth; the other, king of the heavens. The Scripture had made many promises to David and to David's son. His throne and his kingdom were to be of endless duration. To the Jews there was something fearful in the answer to this second question. Jesus had been called the son of David, and while they were willing to acknowledge that the Christ was the son of David, they were not willing to answer a question which they saw would lead to an acknowledgement that Jesus the Nazarene was that person, who should possess endless as well as universal dominion.

The words "Sit thou at my right hand, till I put thy enemies under thy feet," involve the overthrow of all who are not friends of Jesus. Hence an answer to the question, "What think you of the Christ?" involves the eternal destiny of every man. If the question be answered as Scripture requires, and become, when answered, the guide of life, then it is well for him that answers it. But if an answer be given which Scripture does not justify, and the answer become the guide of life, then the answerer becomes the enemy who shall be put beneath the feet of the Christ.

It not unfrequently happens that men surround themselves with necessity which leads them to perdition. Jesus, on another occasion, put a question to the Jews which they could not answer: "The immersion of John, whence was it? from heaven or from men? But they reasoned among themselves, and said, If we reply, From heaven, he will say to us, Why, then, did you not believe him? But if we reply, From men, we fear the multitude; for all regard John as a prophet. And they answered and said to Jesus, We know not."

How easy for men to involve themselves in such a necessity. We set up our gods in our own hearts; we determine to worship them; we see that an answer to certain questions will involve us in inconsistency; we can not endure to contradict our own theories, and for fear of the reproach that others may cast against us, we determine to follow our delusions, and perish in them. Each man that holds an error ties a millstone about his neck, that will drown him in the depths of the sea. Men's opinions are the millstones that they fondly tie about their necks; and these opinions are the cause of their ruin. The traditions of the Jews, their fondness for their rites, their love of the favor of men proved their destruction.

There are many Christs. As many as are the opinions of men, so many Christs are there. But there is but one Christ—the Christ of history. He it is of whom Moses in the law and the prophets did write. He it is who is written of by the holy apostles. He, and he alone, is the Christ. Jesus the Nazarene, the son of the virgin, is the Christ, the Son of the living God. Whatever has been written of him must be received as true. Our reason, our intellectual nature, our spirit, our mind, whatever is within us, require of us to accept as true the testimonies which have been preserved to us from the days of the apostles. I desire life. Jesus gives eternal life. I die. Jesus will destroy death. I am a sinner. Jesus died for

our sins. I wish to be just before God. Jesus rose again
for our justification. There is not a wish in my whole
nature which is not fully satisfied in Jesus of Nazareth.
To the testimonies, then, concerning Him. What say
they?

Let us ignore all creeds and formulas of faith as made
and published by men. Rise we, at once, to the pure
fountain of eternal truth. "Behold, a virgin shall be
with child, and shall bear a son, and they shall call his
name Immanuel, which, when translated, is, God with us."
This is Matthew's THESIS. His testimony sustains his
thesis. Note well his words. Immanuel is God with us.
That being conceived by the virgin of the Holy Spirit, is
God with us. Here let skepticism lay her hand on her
mouth, and dare not utter one word of dissent. Was deceit found in Jesus's mouth? Did Herod find in him any
thing worthy of death? Did the Jews find any witness
that could testify to aught that he did amiss? For what
crime did he suffer death? Was it a crime to acknowledge
himself the Son of God? For this he suffered, not for
aught that he had done amiss. Then there was in him
no sin. Judas, who betrayed him, testified to his innocence. He was in life pure and spotless. Surely, then,
he is God with us. Though in flesh, he was not of flesh.
Though in form as man, he was not of man. Hence his
sinlessness. Being sinless, he is God with us.

Let this be our first proof of the true Godhead of
Jesus. The manner and the matter of his speech shall
be our second proof. "You have heard that it was said
to the ancients, You shall not kill; and whoever shall
kill, shall be liable to the sentence of the judges. But I
say to you, Whoever is angry with his brother, shall be
liable to the sentence of the judges."

The words, "I say to you," so often repeated in this discourse, exhibit a consciousness of authority to make law which no other human being ever possessed. Indeed, the multitudes felt this peculiarity of manner, for they were astonished at his teaching; for he taught as having authority, and not as the scribes.

Hear him again: "I am the light of the world; he that follows me shall not walk in darkness, but shall have the light of life." And again: "For the Father judges no one, but has given all judicial authority to the Son; that all may honor the Son, as they honor the Father." Language such as this needs no comment. It is the utterance of one who knows what he says, conscious of what he is.

When he had risen from the dead, he gave to his apostles the last commission in these words: "Go, therefore, make disciples of all the nations, immersing them into the name of the Father, and of the Son, and of the Holy Spirit." This commission is based on a fact stated in the preceding words: "All authority in heaven and on earth is given to me." Note well the words "All authority." We can conceive of authority legislative, authority judicial, authority executive, no more. In his person is centered all this. What, then, is the argument to be drawn from this? Evidently that he is God; for none other than God can make law for all in heaven and on earth; none other than one possessed of all knowledge and wisdom can judge all; and none other than God can execute the laws after judgment has been given. Look through the vast array of beings intellectual in heaven and on earth. For all these law must be made. To their condition the laws must be adapted. In judging them, mercy and justice must combine. Their varied condi-

tions, the unnumbered circumstances that govern their
actions, must all be considered. Who is sufficient for
this but one who has all knowledge, and all wisdom, and
all justice?"

"The Father judges no one." Well may we rejoice
in this saying. One will judge who has been in the flesh,
tempted in all points as we are; consequently, knowing,
from his own experience, what it is to be in the flesh,
what it is to be tried, and, therefore, knowing how to
judge of the actions of men.

Between man and the Infinite One called the Father
there was a gulf of infinite breadth and depth. Look
abroad to the heavens; behold their immeasurable vast-
ness! How could man approach, come near to, such a
being? We feel overwhelmed by the unsearchable greatness of God. But turn, now, and look at Jesus. He
is Immanuel, God with us. In him God comes near us;
God ceases to be at an immeasurable distance. The incomprehensible grandeur and unsearchable greatness of
God, now clad in flesh, are not such as to overawe our
souls, and make us shrink within ourselves, terrified,
alarmed, and awe-struck. No; through Jesus we draw
nearer to God, for he has come very near to us. That
measureless gulf has been filled with the presence of Immanuel, God with us. He is our lawgiver and our
judge. In him dwells all the fullness of the Godhead
bodily. Yet he is the MAN Christ Jesus. Dear to every
Christian is the truth that such a one has all judicial authority committed to him.

The Apostle Paul tells us that Jesus is the heir of all
things. If he is the heir of all things, then he has the
knowledge of all things, and the wisdom with which to
govern all things. What man would give to a son an

estate, knowing that he had not understanding sufficient to enable him to manage it with prudence? The wisdom of the heir of all things should be such as to enable him to control all things. Who, then, but God can know all things, manage all things, and control all things, so as to cause them to work together for good for those who love him? Messiah is God over all things, forever blessed. We are also told that he is head over all things to the Church.

There is good reason why he is the heir of all things. He created all things. Let us hear an apostle: "For by him were all things created, things in heaven and things in earth, visible and invisible, whether thrones, or lordships, or principalities, or authorities; all things have been created by him, and for him: and he is before all things, and by him all things consist." Note well this language. He is before all things, and by him all things consist. Evident, then, is it that he who was before all things, and by whom all things consist, is not a creation. And, further, he who created all things has a right to all things, and is, consequently, the heir of all things.

But there is another argument connected with this. The apostle adds: "For it pleased *the Father* that all his fullness should dwell in him." If, then, all the fullness of the Father dwells in him, how can he be not equal to the Father? He did not think it an act of robbery to be equal with God. The Jews understood that the Son of God was equal with God. The Apostle John tells us that the Jews sought the more to kill him because he had not only broken the Sabbath, but also said that God was his own Father, making himself equal with God.

It is argued, however, that he himself says, "My Father is greater than I." Yes, and it is true, too, that he was made a little lower than the angels. There is a vast difference between the *nature* of a being and the *position* of a being. As a Son, he was less than the Father. But when did he become a Son? When he was born of the virgin. As a man on earth, he was less than the Father. As such, made subject to death, he was a little lower than the angels. The relation of son to a father supposes the one greater than the other; but let the relation be no longer considered, and the one is equal with the other. Whatever the father is, the son is. Is David the father of the Christ? Then the Christ is flesh. Flesh is equal to flesh. Flesh can not be less than flesh. So the Christ, being the Son of God, is equal to God. God can not be less than God. In other words, the divine nature can not be less than the divine nature. The το Θειον is the το Θειον. Θεοτης is Θεοτης. It can not be less. The Christ is Theanthropos, God-Man. As God, he is fully so; as man, he is fully so. In the Christ dwells all the fullness of the Godhead, Θεοτης, bodily. It is evident that the less can not contain the greater. But the Christ has all the fullness of the Θεοτης in himself. Hence, apodictically, equal to God.

The apostle of the Gentiles, in his letter to the Romans, says of the Christ, that he was made or born of the posterity of David, according to the flesh, but declared to be the Son of God with power, according to his holy spiritual nature, by his resurrection from the dead. The learned may differ somewhat in their understanding of this passage. But one thing is evident and beyond dispute, that there is a contrast—his sonship according to the flesh, and his sonship according to the opposite nature. As the son of David, he was flesh, and consequently weak; as Son of God, he was possessed of a holy spiritual nature, and consequently had ϑυναμις, power. To this state of weakness he refers when he says, "My Father is greater than I."

I will not here press into service that passage found in 1 Tim. iii: 16, because I am satisfied that the reading in the common Greek text can not be supported. Instead of reading, "God was manifested in flesh," I shall read, according to Tischendorf, "He who was manifested in flesh, was justified in spirit, seen by angels," etc. It is a question, then, well to be considered, Who is he that was manifested in flesh? When this question is duly considered, we shall arrive at a conclusion as safe as though we should retain the common reading. It is evident that some one was manifested in flesh. He who was manifested in flesh was more than flesh.

The apostle John will give us an answer to the question, Who was this? "And the WORD became flesh, and tabernacled among us, (and we beheld his glory, the glory as of the only-begotten of the Father,) full of grace and of truth." The WORD, Logos, Wisdom, was made flesh, and hence manifested in flesh. It is worthy of remark that Jesus, on two occasions, uses the term Wisdom when speaking of himself. "For this reason also the Wisdom of God said," (Luke xi: 49.) "For this reason, behold, I send you prophets," etc., (Matt. xxiii: 34.) "Yet Wisdom is justified by her children," (Matt. xi: 19.) In these places the term Wisdom seems to stand for the Messiah. Of the first quoted, there can be no doubt, for in the parallel place in Matthew we find him using the pronoun I. That which is by him called Wisdom is by John called The Logos, the WORD. Let us approach the first of John, and weigh the contents of his first verse.

"In the beginning was the WORD, and the WORD was with God, and the WORD was God."

This beginning can be no other than that mentioned by Moses; "In the beginning God created the heavens and the earth;" for the apostle goes further, and says, "He was in the beginning with God. All things were made by him, and without him not one thing was made that exists." Let the reader compare Prov. viii, in which Wisdom is represented as being with God in the beginning.

Let it be well noted that creation is attributed to the Logos or WORD: "By him all things were made." "He was in the beginning with God." "The Word was God." I will not permit myself to attempt to explain what human language can not explain. I call attention to the facts stated. That being, who is here called the Logos, was with God, and active in creation. Jesus, in his prayer recorded by this apostle, says: "Glorify me with thyself with the glory which I had with thee before the world was." He did exist, then, before the world existed. He began the creation. He was before all things. He is not, then, as the Nicene Creed says, "God of God," but he was God. In the simplest, broadest, only sense, he is God; for to him is creation attributed. No one can create but God.

Here we might make an end of our argument; but as the testimony is not exhausted, let the argument be continued. The Apostle Paul applies the following words, quoted from Psalm 102, to the Messiah: "And thou, Lord, in the beginning didst lay the foundation of the earth, and the heavens are the works of thy hands. They shall perish, but thou remainest: and they all shall grow old as a garment; and as a mantle thou shalt fold them up, and they shall be changed; but thou art the same, and thy years shall not fail."

In Micah, v: 2, we find the birth of Jesus foretold: "But thou, Bethlehem Ephratah, though thou be small among the thousands of Judah, out of thee shall he come forth to me that is to be ruler in Israel; whose goings forth have been from of old, from everlasting."

Jesus was born in Bethlehem. Yet his goings forth had been from old, from everlasting. Does this language require comment? Can it be made more full, more comprehensive, by aught that we can say? Let it stand as found in the holy Scripture, fully testifying to the eternal duration of that being who was once in flesh. We have made it evident from Scripture that Jesus is the Theanthropos—the God-Man. We have given answer to this question, What think you of the Christ? Be it known that this is our answer, that this is what we have to say of the Christ. Ignoring all creeds and confessions of faith as made by men, we come to the oracles of the living God, and decide this question on which hangs the destiny of the human race. Jesus the Nazarene is Immanuel, God with us; in the true sense, God; and in the true sense, Man.

He must have been such as we have found him described in Scripture, otherwise he could not be a Savior. He came to save man from sin, and he must meet and overpower all the adversaries of man. Satan is the prince of the hosts of darkness, the author of all evil, the murderer of the family of Adam. Jesus must meet him and subdue him. Jesus is the head over all the hosts of light, directing them by his wisdom in his great conflict with the powers of darkness. It requires infinite wisdom so to control these powers of light as to finally gain the victory

6

over the enemies of God and of man. Behold, then, one who wears our nature, sitting at the right hand of the throne of the Majesty on high, clothed with all authority in heaven and on earth, and this for the purpose of bringing honor and glory to the sons of God. As man, he sympathizes with us in all our sufferings, feels our sorrows, intercedes for us; as God, he will put under his feet every enemy that stands opposed to our honor, our glory, our life, and our incorruptibility. What, then, shall we say of him in conclusion?

We will say that which God has said: "Let all the angels of God worship him." He whom all the angels of God worship, is worthy of the worship of all the sons of men. "And I saw, and heard the voice of many angels round about the throne, and the living creatures and the elders; and the number of them was myriads of myriads, and thousands of thousands. And they said, with a loud voice: Worthy is the Lamb that was slain, to receive power, and riches, and wisdom, and strength, and honor, and glory, and blessing. And every creature that is in heaven, and on earth, and under the earth, and such as are in the sea, even all that are in them, I heard saying: To him that sits on the throne, and to the Lamb be blessing, and honor, and glory, and strength, from age to age."

What argument shall we draw from universal worship? All the angels of God, and all created beings unite in giving to Jesus the Nazarene the homage of their hearts. In the midst of this universal homage, can there be found a mortal, a being who calls himself a man, that refuses that honor and glory and blessing which are due to the Lamb? If there is one, then all the angels of God will unite in saying, Let such a one be put among the enemies of Jesus beneath his feet.

"Behold, he comes with clouds, and every eye shall see him, and those also who pierced him." He comes again, even as he ascended into heaven. He was despised and rejected by men; he was a man of sorrows, and acquainted with grief. Yet he comes to be glorified on earth. A kingdom is in reservation for him, that all peoples, nations, and languages may serve him. He comes as the Son of Man, to visit the sons of men, to give reward to all that have faithfully served him. To those who look for him he will appear the second time, without a sin-offering, for salvation. But to those who have corrupted his holy religion, who have disregarded his saints, who have despised his little ones, he will appear in flaming fire for destruction. He will come in the glory of his Father and of the holy angels, and he will reward every one as his work shall be.

Blessed Redeemer, come quickly. Thy saints are weary, they mourn thy absence, they long for thy coming. Again we say, Blessed Redeemer, come quickly.

Yours in the good hope
Thomas Munnell

THOMAS MUNNELL.

THIS earnest, energetic, and successful preacher of the Gospel is a native of Ohio County, West Virginia, and was born February 8, 1823. He remained at home with his parents until he entered Bethany College, where he graduated, in 1850, as one of the "Honor men" of his class. While at college he was distinguished for high intellectual and moral qualities, and, during the last session he remained there, began to exercise his gifts in preaching the Gospel. After graduating, he entered at once actively on the work of preaching and teaching. Seven years of his life were spent in this double employment, the greater portion of the time, filling the chair of Ancient Languages and Literature in the Western Reserve Eclectic Institute, located at Hiram, Portage County, Ohio. While holding this position he gave abundant evidence of fine executive talent, as well as that energy and persistence for which he has always been distinguished. It was largely through his instrumentality that the institution in which he labored was placed on the road to success; and whatever prosperity has attended its subsequent career is owing, in a great measure, to his efforts to give it a consistent and permanent organization while he was one of its professors. Since leaving Hiram he has been offered several times the Presidency of the Institute, but has never felt it his duty to accept.

In addition to his experience as a teacher at Hiram, he has, at different times, been Principal of flourishing academies at Williamsburg, N. Y., Mt. Sterling, Ky., and New Castle, Ky. At all these points he gave evidence that he possessed superior qualifications to impart knowledge to the youthful mind, and a proper moral direction to the youthful heart.

In 1857, he entered upon the duties of pastor of the Christian Church corner of Eighth and Walnut streets, Cincinnati, Ohio. His labors in this church were constant and arduous. Visiting from house to house, and especially among the poor of the congregation, was an every-day duty. The strong were made stronger, the wavering confirmed, the indifferent

(85)

warned, the prodigals persuaded to return to their Father's house, while a general interest was created in the Sunday-school, prayer-meeting, and all the other agencies of the Church. Such labors, as they deserved to be, were greatly blessed. The spiritual strength of the Church was largely increased, Christian sympathies and activities developed, while the Lord added many converts from the world to the cause of Christ.

In 1860, he removed to Mt. Sterling, Ky., where he divided his labors between the Church and an Academy until the war compelled him to discontinue the latter. He was with the brethren there during their severest trials, and did much, by his prudent counsels, prayerful labors, and constant watchfulness, to save the Church from division, and the cause from utter ruin.

For the last four years his time has been chiefly occupied as Corresponding Secretary of the Kentucky Missionary Society, and his success in this department of labor has proved him to be the "right man in the right place." His present home is Mt. Sterling, Ky.

Brother Munnell is five feet nine inches and a half high, weighs about one hundred and forty pounds, has a tough, bony frame, high, projecting forehead, dark-brown hair and beard, with a sharp, black eye, that always looks you straight in the face. His whole organization is indicative of a character distinguished for great mental and physical activity; such a character as is capable of a large amount of good, honest work.

His preaching is chiefly practical, and always instructive and entertaining, though not remarkable for logical arrangement, rhetorical finish, or oratorical display. He is a much better writer than speaker. He is very fond of discussion, and, with the pen, is a formidable opponent, as any knight of the quill may learn by attempting to cross his plans. Notwithstanding this, he is kind in the social circle, and has, in a remarkable degree, the power of attracting all classes of society to him.

ATONEMENT.

BY THOMAS MUNNELL.

"But God commendeth his love toward us, in that while we were yet sinners, Christ died for us."—Rom. v : 8.

IN approaching the philosophy of reconciliation to God, involving the profoundest principles of moral government, no humble minister will feel very confident of his ability to equal the lofty theme. It is said that Handel, when composing his oratorio of "Creation," always went to the piano with the prayer "that he might praise God worthily;" and the anxious inquiry of every proclaimer of the love of Jesus is,

"How shall I my Savior set forth?
How shall I his beauties declare?
Oh! how shall I speak of his worth,
Or what his chief dignities are?"

If there be such a science as moral philosophy, its length and breadth, and depth and height, are all involved in the Cross of Jesus Christ. Believing that its principles are as fixed and indestructible as those of natural philosophy or chemistry, I propose to show, from evidences wholly undeniable, that the Cross was not an arbitrary, but a necessary, antecedent to the pardon of our sins. It must

(87)

be remembered, however, that no analogies, drawn from governments as developed among men, should be required, in all respects, to illustrate the doctrine of Atonement. Notwithstanding this, the purpose is to make our way through the thickest of the difficulties inherent in this deepest of all theological subjects, and to show that, contrary to all skeptical deductions from inadequate premises, it is consonant with all other truths well recognized in the governments of men; and as the necessities that impelled the death of Christ were of a governmental character, we must, first of all, look into the very foundation of government itself, as developed in the several sections that follow.

I. Most men will admit, without argument, that, when God made man, *it was necessary to place his moral as well as his physical nature under law;* that, just as a child is unequal to all his future relations, is unable to project that course of life that will be best for him in old age, to have pursued in youth, and, therefore, needs the wisdom and guiding counsels of parents, so man, being also of himself unequal to all his future interests, and in this life unable to project a course that would prove, a million years to come, to have been the best, surely needs the law of wisdom from the heavenly Father to guide him as a frail child through a perilous future wholly unknown to him. This principle, by following out one of the plainest analogies suggested in common life, plainly says that man needs, and must have, *a law* to keep him from evil.

It must not be forgotten that a written moral law was necessitated by the physical, mental, and moral constitutions given us by our Creator—was anticipated by these. The fact that our bodies may be injured by gluttony demands a law forbidding gluttony, to shield us from the punishment inherent in that sin. Would it not be unkind in the Lord to form our bodies so that they inevitably would be injured by debauchery, and yet utter no word of warning against it? Again: our moral constitutions are so constructed that falsehood, dishonesty, and all impurity of heart are damaging to the soul; and as the simple child of nature does not know of these results except by a terrible experience, it was both wise and merciful in the Almighty to issue a law, saying, "Thou shalt," and "Thou shalt not." The presence of the Bible in the world does not *create* the penalty of sin; it only *foretells the natural results* of sin, and shows the way of escape. Strong drink would ruin the body just the same as if there was no law in the Bible against it. The penalty is inherent in the sin itself, and not in any arbitrary appointment of God, and unless we go back of our creation and inquire, *"Why hast thou made me thus?"* why hast thou made my body and soul liable to be affected pleasantly or unpleasantly by good or bad actions? it is useless to complain of the laws of revelation, which were not first, but came in after we were made, and that with a view of meeting our constitutional necessities as already established. The vital practical truth is, that "All have sinned and come short of the glory of God;" then "The wages of sin is death." We have received a law which is "holy, just, and good," the violation of which brings on results more terrible than we are willing to admit.

II. It is readily admitted that the transgression of natural and civil law *is justly followed by punishment;* nor do the most skeptical as to punishment, as taught in the Bible, ever complain of injustice in this. While it is fully admitted that "the wages of sin is death," both in our natural and civil relations, the human heart is slow to believe the same thing true of the moral law. Man does not wish to believe a bad account of his future, and this may be the reason why the Savior occupied three times as much space in describing the condition of Dives as in describing that of Lazarus. Also in Deuteronomy 28th, nearly four times as many verses are required to tell of the curses as of the blessings. It is pleasanter to believe in heaven than in hell.

That the transgressor of moral law should feel the consequence as expressed in the compunction of conscience in this life is not often denied, but that the results of conduct here should extend to worlds unseen is a conviction by no means well settled in the minds of many. Whatever may be the nature, intensity, and duration of future punishment, one thing must be admitted : that the value and the necessity of the death of our Savior are to be strictly measured thereby. If he died to save us from an hour's pain, we should feel somewhat obliged to him. If his death should deliver us from a life-long threatened torture of mind and body, we should be very grateful, but could scarcely for that be bound to him through eternal cycles, to serve him and love him with every thought and emotion of our whole being. But if he saved me "from so great a death," from the "worm that never dies," from the fire unquenchable, from the "left hand," and from hell, then will I sing

"Love so amazing, so divine,
Demands my soul, my life, my all."

If my sin had incurred the intensest sorrows of the mind, the fracture of every bone, the crushing of every muscle, and the rupture of every blood-vessel, and if this

were to be endured for threescore years and ten before
my rest should come, even then the death of our Sacrifice
would not have been absolutely "necessary," for time
would bring me through. But the history of Dives and
Lazarus turns heaven and hell both inside out, and reveals the fearful truth that no emigrant ever came out of
hell to heaven. The gulf is fixed; the damned can never
be redeemed, and, blessed be God! the redeemed can
never now be damned. "He that is holy will now be
holy still, and he that is righteous shall be righteous still;"
but it is equally and fearfully true that "He that is unjust shall be unjust still, and he that is filthy shall be
filthy still." The result of sin, then, is not temporary,
but eternal, and our obligation to Jesus, therefore, is unlimited, and can only be discharged through endless years.

The very beginning of all true conceptions of the doctrine of atonement is found in a true conception of sin
and its consequences. To underestimate the "exceeding
sinfulness of sin" is to underestimate the atonement or
reconciliation to God. To suppose, also, that the consequences of sin are but trifling, destroys all faith in the
necessity of the death of Christ. Hence all parties who,
either wholly or partially, deny the doctrine here being
treated, will be found with conceptions more or less indifferent as to the nature and condemnation of sin. If
sin be a trifle, its effects can not be serious, sin itself can
not be "exceedingly sinful." The Savior, consequently,
did but little for us in delivering us from it; our gratitude
to him is, therefore, weak, and all our notions of the worth
of the "unspeakable gift" are brought low. As no patient can feel very grateful to a physician for relief administered if he thought himself in no great danger, so our
cheap convictions of sin and its fearful work upon the

soul destroy our gratitude and love and faith in Jesus. Our sins seem small, rather innocent, and very pardonable. Being so small as to escape our eyes blinded in their favor, we conclude they escape the eye of God. But Paul has said: "Though I am conscious of no fault in myself, yet am I not hereby justified, for he that judgeth me is the Lord." Our not perceiving our little sins does not prove their absence from us; for David prays, "Cleanse thou me from secret faults"—the smallest, most hidden, and most insidious faults—for the animalcule will in time become leviathan, and the insect sins of this life will rise like mountains before us in the next.

Once more before leaving this point—for here the real difficulty lies. Men would readily accept Christ if they were convinced of the wickedness and deep damnation of sin. They are fond of believing that sin has no eternal consequences; that its wounds will all heal up by the recuperative force of the soul itself, without the aid of a Savior; that it will amount to some inconvenience truly, but even that for no great length of time. "These shall go into everlasting punishment" is not a very palatable saying, but is an exceedingly "faithful saying, and worthy of all acceptation," or else Jesus Christ had no great errand into this world. He came to save us from *something*, or there is no Savior. His greatness as a Redeemer is measured by the greatness of the danger from which he redeemed us, and when we believe that he saved us from "everlasting punishment," we feel that he has wrought out "eternal redemption for us."

Who can prove that the soul will repent and get rid of sin beyond the grave? Dives was still an unbeliever in the power of God's word after death, and thought the spirit or ghost of Lazarus would have much more influence with his five brethren than would Moses and the prophets. Besides, if a man will in this life break over all the barriers placed in his way to hell, is it not reasonable to suppose that after death, when public opinion, self-respect, and Gospel influences can no longer operate, his speed in sin will be accelerated rather than retarded? Sin, then, will remain in the soul, in the will, for evermore; and if sin be the prime cause of pain, the pain itself must be eternal. The flesh will feel the thorn as long as the thorn is in the flesh, and the only redemption from the pain is redemption from the thorn, and the only redemption from death spiritual will be found in salvation from sin, the sting of death. Now, Jesus undertakes to deliver man from sin by his atoning blood, that death may have no sting, and that we may be saved from its eternal consequences. To show on what principles he proposes to accomplish this great salvation shall be our purpose in the pages following, that we, each one, may see

What Jesus Christ " has done for me
    Before I drew my breath,
What pain, what labor to secure
    My soul from endless death."

III. An impression has been spread wide in the public mind implying that God the Father has always been hard to persuade to pardon the sinner, and that it is only after long and hard pleading on the part of our Advocate that he consents to our release. Poets have worked it into their rhymes, and pulpit orators have made it the pabulum of pathos, but the Bible teaches precisely the opposite. "God so loved the world;" "We love him because he first loved us;" " In this the love of God was manifested;" and many other passages, demonstrate his willing-

ness to forgive as soon as it could be done on principles
that would not involve the destruction of moral government.   If a civil ruler pardon one who truly deserves
punishment, he is as unjust as if he were to punish an
innocent person, for justice consists in treating each one
just as he deserves.   When man had sinned, the problem
was to ascertain how he might be pardoned, and yet not
impugn the justice of God.   If man receives his dues,
mercy is "clear gone forever," but if he be pardoned,
how can it be reconciled with justice, which demands his
punishment?   This was a problem which no human governor had ever been able to solve.

In the days of the Roman consuls, it is said that a certain commander, named Brutus, had his army drawn up
in form of battle just before the enemy, who confronted
the whole length of his lines.   Brutus commanded his
men not to accept a challenge from the foe to single combat to decide the issues of the day; and knowing how
hard it was for his soldiers to be mocked for cowardice,
he denounced the penalty of death upon any one who
should violate this order.   Soon a strong man came forward into the middle space between the two armies, and
bantered the stoutest Roman that ever handled a sword
or hurled a spear.   And after indulging the usual brag-
gadocio and insult for their seeming cowardice for a long
time, the martial spirit of one of the sons of Brutus was
so stung and aroused by his abusive language that he
rushed into the midst, accepting the challenge, fought a
terrible duel, slew the enemy, stripped him of his armor,
won the day for his countrymen, and returned amid the
shouts of all his comrades in arms.   But a certain sadness soon settled over the countenances of all.   *A military
order had been disobeyed.*   The act could not be ignored

with safety. Army discipline, army effectiveness, and consequently national safety, would all be imperiled by passing over this disobedience of martial law. A father's heart cried out for mercy; military necessity demanded justice. Had Brutus spared his son, he could not have punished the son of any other man, and this would have disorganized and demoralized his whole army, and given up the whole nation a prey to the enemy. He resolved that the nation should see that he who spared not his own son would spare no one else, and that strict obedience in the army was indispensable to the safety of all. Here was a governmental difficulty involving a contest between justice and mercy, in which justice took the lead, because no arrangement could be made securing the exercise of both. The question with Brutus was, how he could be just, and still show mercy to his son, which is the same principle involved in the salvation of sinners. How can God be just, and yet the justifier of the unpunished offender? If justice be exacted, every sinner will feel the bottom of perdition; if mercy prevail at the expense of justice and the law, it would ruin the universe, for all intelligences would see the weakness and unrighteousness of the supreme government, and other angels might be found unwilling to "keep their first estate." God must preserve his rule, must magnify his law, and make it honorable before all angels and all men.

I will not say that any illustration, drawn from the governments of men, can fully represent the point just now before us; but I will suppose a case, which I think will explain some of the principles involved in the doctrine of atonement through Jesus Christ. Suppose ten thousand subjects of the English Crown should rise in sedition and rebellion against the lawful authority; that

they have been tried, convicted, and sentenced to banishment to St. Helena for ten years. The government
would gladly pardon them, were it safe to do so. But
the law must be respected; sin must be punished before
all, that others also may fear; and while mercy pleads in
the heart of the executive, justice demands the penalty of
violated law. Now, it is plainly impossible for English
law, or any other *law*, to show mercy, for "law workith
wrath." When Darius had signed a decree that threw
Daniel into the lions' den, and yet desired to save him
from the penalty of that law, he "labored till the going
down of the sun" to harmonize the working of justice
and mercy—to save his favored Daniel, and yet preserve
his law—but failing in this, the law must take its course,
and the penalty be felt in all its force. So, in the absence
of what Mr. Jenkins calls an "expedient," the ten thousand must bear their own reward. But, lo! an expedient
is suggested, a substitute, one that will suffer in their
stead. Who must he be? One of the guilty party?
They must each one suffer for their own sins, and have
no merit to spare for others. Will the banishment of a
common subject of the government, although an innocent
one, meet the emergency! Such would not be "found
worthy," for his punishment would call no attention sufficient to satisfy an account with the whole empire. But
if a son from the throne, the Prince, will come forward,
not only innocent as a lamb of any political offense, but
governmentally worthy to be a substitute, and will, through
love for these offenders, offer to endure the ten years' exile in their stead, the government may, without the least
fear of losing its proper tone and authority with the people, accept the noble substitute, and remit the penalty of
the transgressors. The Prince, remember, is not in jus-

tice bound to do this, but in compassion for his future subjects he kindly makes the offer. The government is not
bound to accept him as a substitute, and to release them;
but being from the first anxious to deliver them, and now
seeing a way in which it may be done, in pity for the
convicts, and in the grandest admiration of their noble
Prince, the system of mercy is agreed to, and carried into
effect.

The Prince returns from his exile amid the acclamations
of the whole nation, who are ready to crown him Lord of
all. In due time he is coronated king of the realm. He
has not only won the admiration of all the people, but
the love, unbounded love, of the ten thousand who, if
not dead to every noble impulse, will be the most loyal
subjects of his empire; because, no sooner had the new
king ascended his throne, than he announced himself as
their ransom, having fully paid, in his own person, the
debt they owed; and now, upon certain terms honorable
both to him and them, he is ready to proclaim their pardon. But if any portion of them, ungrateful for all he
has done for them, will now refuse to have him "reign
over them," what will be their political status in the eyes
of all the world? Can they be forgiven? Was the exile of the Prince alone sufficient to reinstate them without
an humble recognition of the proffered mercy, and a grateful acceptance of it? Are not their cordial services due
to their benefactor? Their original offense was grievous
enough, but if that is to be emphasized by this basest
of all ingratitude, it would double the aggregate of their
guilt. If they refuse this arrangement for pardon, will
any one else try to save them? Will there "remain any
more sacrifice" for their political offenses? Or will it not
be rather a "fearful looking for" the execution of the

7

penalty of sin now exceedingly aggravated by this meanest exhibition of heartless ingratitude?

The parallel intended is easy, and does not require me to name at length the points already made luminous enough by the figure just used. Jesus is our Prince. He volunteered his humiliation to redeem our souls from hell. He returned from the grave to the throne, and issued his proclamation of pardon to all for whom he died: "He that believeth and is baptized shall be saved." He died *for* us, instead of us, in place of us, "bore our sins in his own body on the tree," "took our infirmities, and bare our sicknesses," "by his stripes we are healed," so that whoever now "believeth on him shall not perish, but have everlasting life." The Divine government will not now suffer loss when allowing the sinner mercifully to pass unpunished, for when Jesus had become *legally* responsible for the sins of the world, even he was not allowed to escape the penalty. Even though in the days of his flesh he, in Gethsemane, "offered up prayers and supplications with strong crying and tears," the "cup could not pass from him." Surely, "he that spared not his own son," who was but legally responsible for sin, will spare no other one who is both legally and morally amenable to a broken law. Sin must be punished, whether the substitute or the original offender be responsible for it. If the sinner accept the substitute, he may be forgiven, and in that case both mercy and justice are satisfied. The demands of the law were met, in the Prince, in a way that secures the stability of government, which is now enabled to exercise the desired mercy with safety. If the sinner accept not the sacrifice made for him, he becomes responsible for all his sins in his own person; for no prince could pardon a subject who would not even recognize the mercy sought to be conferred upon him. Atonement, then, is simply reconciliation to God, effected as soon as pardon is conferred upon the sinner; and this is done by every merciful governor as soon as it can be done with safety to the government, the actual realization of pardon being dependent both upon the control of the governmental difficulty and also upon the acceptance of the terms of freedom by the offender.

Ten years' banishment may be sufficient punishment for certain crimes committed against the State; and this has induced some to conclude that moral evil may also be worn out by time and by personal suffering, without the death of Christ. But it must be patent to every fair thinker, that after the civil punishments have been exhausted, the moral obliquity of the criminal may be the same as before. The civil law never takes away the stain of moral guilt, but leaves the offender to settle that account with his God and Judge; for no lacerations of the body, nor sorrows of the mind, nor infliction of civil penalties can ever atone for sin.

> "Could my tears forever flow,
> Could my zeal no languor know,
> This for sin could not atone,
> Thou must save, and Thou alone."

Could our own sufferings, either in this world or in limbo, or in purgatory, or in hell, as some believe and teach, dispose of our sins, then would heaven at last be won, not by the Savior, but by our own powers of endurance; then is Jesus Christ no Savior in any sense, for whoever suffers for all his sins is not saved from sin by Jesus, or by any one else. If you owe a relentless creditor a thousand pounds, and instead of granting your prayer,

as an insolvent debtor, for forgiveness of the debt, he
compel you "to be sold, your wife, and your children,
and all that you have, and payment to be made," could
it be said that you were saved from the debt? No more
can Jesus be called our Savior if we must suffer out our
own demerits. Then is the world without mercy, Christ
a mere pretender, and sinners left to count unnumbered
years in pain. The duration of this must be measured by
the continuance of sin in the soul. As long as disease is in
the body we must be sick, and as long as sin unrepented
of and unforgiven remains in the soul, be that a million
years, the sting of death will still be felt. Forgiveness
and cleansing from all unrighteousness are promised in
this life to all who obey the Gospel. Now, if there be
any assurance of mercy beyond the grave, in what chapter and verse may it be found? Jesus said to the Jews:
"Ye shall die in your sins, and where I am ye can not
come;" from which it is plainly inferable that if a man
die in sin, his condition is fixed forever. And this harmonizes with Abraham's language to Dives: "Between
us and you there is a great gulf *fixed*;" they can not pass
from you to us. Besides these fearful intimations of the
"wrath to come," it is said, in the last chapter of Revelation, after the judgment is past, "the righteous saved,
the wicked damned, and God's eternal government approved," "He that is filthy let him be filthy still, he that
is unjust let him be unjust still," stereotyped in sin forever. Some one has thrown Solomon's faithful saying
into verse:

> "Just as the tree, cut down, that fell
>   Northward or southward, there it lies;
> So man departs to heaven or hell,
>   Fixed in the state in which he dies."

The fabled Gorgon head was said to have power to pet-
rify every one who ventured to look upon its horrid face.
Some artist, trying to represent this idea upon the canvas, drew a thief who had happened to turn his eye upon
the Gorgon just while in the act of stealing, and, lo! with
his hand upon his neighbor's purse, he was horrified into
a solid statue, petrified in his guilt. Death will stereo-
type every sinner, for then the seed-time will be gone, the
summer ended, and the fixedness of the eternal state be
realized. The certainty, then, that some "will go away
into *everlasting* punishment," should alarm the stoutest
heart and pale the bravest sinner as he flies on to the bar
of God. But to avert the unfathomable woe, and turn
the curse away, Jesus "was made a curse for us,"

> "To shame our sins he blushed in blood,
> He closed his eyes to show us God,"

dwelt among the dead that we might be forever with the
living; for by his atoning blood we are reconciled to God,
justice is content, the law is highly magnified, while mercy
and full forgiveness are proffered to all; for "He that
believeth and is baptized shall be saved, but he that believeth not shall be damned."

Lord, help thy poor servants to preach this Gospel with
holy zeal and quenchless love, that sinners may be saved
from the wrath to come, and thy great name be glorified
through Jesus Christ our Lord.

Very Truly Yours

L. L. Pinkerton

LEWIS L. PINKERTON.

LEWIS L. PINKERTON was born in Baltimore County, Maryland, January 28th, 1812. His paternal grandparents were Irish; his maternal, German. In the winter of 1821, when LEWIS was in his tenth year, his father settled in Brooke County, West Va., having previously moved from Maryland to Chester County, Penn., the place of his nativity. Ten years of the son's life were spent among the romantic hills of West Virginia. Those years, as he says himself, were full of "incessant, hard, ill-requited toil;" but they were useful in developing in him the virtue, self-reliance, and fidelity to principle which have ever since characterized him.

He was trained in the Presbyterian faith, but becoming perplexed with the doctrine of "the Decrees" as taught in the "Shorter Catechism," and having carefully studied the Word of God, he was, in 1830, baptized under the personal ministry of Alexander Campbell.

In 1831 he left West Virginia, and, after visiting several localities, settled in Trenton, Butler County, Ohio. Here he engaged in teaching a common school, and in the study and practice of medicine. He was married in 1833, and in 1835 attended a course of lectures in the Medical College of Ohio, at Cincinnati. In 1836 he removed to Carthage, Ohio, then, and for some years later, the place of residence of the lamented WALTER SCOTT. He continued to study and practice medicine till May, 1838, when he gave up his profession, in which he had been quite successful, and began to preach the Gospel.

He at once entered upon his new calling, with energy and success. During the years 1838, 1839, and 1840, he traveled almost constantly, preaching the glad tidings to thousands, and witnessing the baptism of a great number of converts. In 1841 he removed to Lexington, Ky., and took charge of the Church in that city. During the winter of the same year he attended a course of lectures in the Medical Department of Transylvania University, and received the degree of M. D. He resigned his connection with the Church in Lexington in the fall of 1843, and spent the remainder of that year, and the greater part of the next, in preaching and soliciting subscriptions for Bacon College, located at Harrodsburg, Ky. He removed to Midway, Ky., in the spring of 1845, where he taught a successful Female Academy, with only occasional and slight assistance, until the summer of 1851. Meantime he conceived the idea of a Female Orphan School, and communicated his plans to J. WARE PARISH, a noble Christian gentleman, who at once took hold of the enterprise with the warmest zeal. In the winter of 1846–47 a charter was obtained from the Legislature of Kentucky, and the Orphan School located at Midway was put into successful operation.

The establishment of this school may be regarded as one of the most important events in Dr. Pinkerton's career. It was his own conception; and to him, more than to any other man, are the Disciples in Kentucky indebted for this magnificent monument of Christian liberality.

From 1851 to 1860 he was principally engaged in preaching and teaching. The churches at Versailles, Paris, and Midway were those for which he labored most of this time, and at all these points he was eminently successful.

In 1860 he removed to Harrodsburg, having been elected to the chair of Belles-Lettres and Political Science in Kentucky University. When the University was removed to Lexington, he removed also to that city, which is the place of his residence at this time. In February, 1866, he resigned his professorship in the University, and has since been preaching at various points. He delivered a course of lectures at Hiram the present year.

Besides being a successful preacher and teacher, the Doctor is one of the most accomplished writers in the ranks of the Disciples. In 1848 he edited and published the "Christian Mirror." In 1851 he was senior editor of the "Ecclesiastic Reformer." In 1853–54 he edited the Kentucky Department of the "Christian Age;" and, in 1844–45 the "New Era," a weekly newspaper, the organ of the Sons of Temperance in Kentucky.

During his life he has been offered the Presidency of several colleges, but has uniformly declined, because he never considered his scholarship equal to such a position. To use his own style, he is an *educated* man, but not a *scholar*. Nevertheless, his scholarship is quite respectable, such as a man of less modesty would regard sufficient for any of the places to which he has been called.

Both as a writer and speaker, his style is very original. His imagination is chaste, though somewhat tinged with an autumn sadness. His logical powers are above mediocrity, and his thoughts always fresh and vigorous. He is distinguished for great independence of character, and, on this account, his actions are not always well understood. He is thoroughly conscientious, and possesses, in a high degree, a generous, sympathetic, and forgiving nature.

JESUS THE FIRST AND THE LAST.

BY L. L. PINKERTON.

"What think ye of Christ?"—MATT. xxii: 42.

THE *science* of Christianity, Theology, whether orthodox or heterodox, will not, at any time this side
the Millennium, become the possession of any considerable number of those who "profess religion," not even of
those whose lives are shaped and controlled by it. Ninety-
nine of every hundred who are to be saved, if saved at
all, "by the grace of God," shall not fully comprehend
the *methods* of that grace. The very great majority of
men and women are poor, and from all we can now see,
are likely to remain so. They can not have time, therefore, for theological studies, nor can they possess the
mental training which such studies must ever require.
The minister of Christ strangely mistakes, then, who
treats the men, women, and children that meet him in
the house of prayer as though they were students of
theology, before whom he is to discuss "doctrines"—
doctrines which he himself but feebly apprehends, after
years of careful study. He mistakes still more fatally,
if he shall persuade himself that these doctrines are the
matters of *Christian faith*, and that the salvation of sinners or of saints is involved in the understanding of

them. Jesus was, in all respects, pre-eminently *the* Teacher; but he was not a teacher of doctrines; he did not teach "systematic divinity." The poor people to whom Jesus spoke—the Marys and Marthas, the publicans and sinners, the rough men who caught fish in the sea of Galilee, and the plain women who sold the fish in the neighboring villages, the small artificers, the shepherds and the vine-dressers of Galilee—would have made nothing of the debatable doctrines of our modern Christianity. If a clear apprehension, not to say comprehension, of what are called "the doctrines of the Bible," is, indeed, essential to salvation, may we not pertinently and sorrowfully ask, Who, then, *can be* saved? It is strange that this quite radical mistake as to the real objects of Christian faith should have been perpetuated so long, seeing that those most devoted to the maintenance of "orthodox views," as being essential to "vital godliness," can not get forward in the work of the ministry without involving themselves in perpetual and practical contradictions. As thus: Grave and learned ministers, after years of patient and laborious preparation and study, will discuss before their congregations the most recondite principles of the Divine government, the most perplexing problems ever submitted to the contemplation of mankind, and earnestly, and even vehemently, insist that the *conclusions* they may have reached in regard to these difficult themes contain the truth of God; that these conclusions are necessary to "true and saving faith;" and yet these same ministers will receive into the Church men, women, and children—perhaps their own wives, and children, and servants—*not one in fifty of whom has the slightest conception of the doctrines in question!* Alas! one is tempted to exclaim, when will this great folly of

preaching philosophy, instead of preaching Jesus, come
to an end? But few of God's people seem to be aware
that the misapprehension as to the real objects of faith,
from which this strangely inconsistent procedure springs,
lies at the foundation of nearly all the divisions that now
distract and alienate the Protestant families; in fact, that
the Protestant parties, with few exceptions, were born of
the misapprehension. These sad divisions will not be
healed; nay, they must increase in number till this quite
radical misconception is corrected. We are cheered and
comforted by the hope that, even now, the much-needed
correction is in the way of being effected; and our present
discourse is designed to aid, in some small degree, to bring
on the day of Renovation, when, as in the beginning, there
shall be but one flock, as there is but one Shepherd. No
objection ought to be raised against the discussion of any
question that may fairly arise out of the Divine testimonies. Let these questions be discussed, then, by those
who may have taste and talent for such discussions; discussed in books and periodicals, by the fire-side and in
lyceums; but let us not *elevate our reasonings into Divine
oracles*, and make them causes of strifes and divisions
among the people of God—the foundations of warring,
antagonistic sects.

A knowledge of religion, *as a science*, is not more necessary to salvation than is a knowledge of geology, min-
eralogy, botany, physiology, and chemistry, to farming and
gardening. As men manage, by a knowledge of simple
facts, to cause the earth to yield her increase, and as they
live without any knowledge of the processes of digestion
and assimilation, even so may the poor and the uneducated hear, believe, and obey " the glorious Gospel of
the blessed God," and rejoice in "the great salvation,"

without having heard any thing whatever on the subject
of Total Hereditary Depravity, Imputed Righteousness,
Effectual Calling, the mode in which the Holy Spirit operates in conversion, the "doctrine" of the Trinity, or
its opposite, or, indeed, on any other of the vexed questions that have originated and that perpetuate religious
parties. Do we mistake utterly? If not, then is it true
that an overwhelming majority of all who are brought to
God by the preaching of the Gospel, even in the most enlightened communities, know only that they are sinners;
that they ought to be holy in heart and in life; that they
are helpless; that they are disquieted, and fearful, and mis-
erable. They believe that God has pitied and loved them;
that Jesus died for their sins; that God will forgive them
for Christ's sake; that he will comfort and sustain them
through life; and that he will take them to a glorious home
in heaven finally, if they live and die in Jesus. And these,
we may add, remain the chief articles of their creed through
life; these and similar simple truths, apprehended with a
clearness and force, varied by difference in temperament
and culture.

   To pursue the train of thought we are in yet a little
further.   Let any one competent to do so, set himself to
ascertain the amount and kind of "doctrinal" *knowledge*
possessed by any congregation of Christians of average
general intelligence and of average piety. Beginning with
the creation, let him pass leisurely over the four thousand
years of Old Testament history and prophesy. He will
see what the merchants, farmers, mechanics, their wives
and children, the clerks, shop-boys, and the women of
the various handicrafts, know about "Cosmogony," the
Science of the Deluge; what ideas are entertained of the
wonderful and astounding providences of God, as dis-

played in his dealings with the Patriarchs, with the Egyptians, with Israel during their journey to Canaan, with the same people under their judges and their kings, and with the idolatrous nations with which the people of Israel came into conflict. The examiner will, doubtless, find *faith* enough in all that is written, so far as the record has been read and remembered; but he will find, also, that to the vast majority, the things revealed have but a shadowy, misty existence, and that, except in rare instances, *generalization* has not been even so much as thought of; in no instance quite satisfactorily accomplished. Let the same course be pursued with New Testament revelations, the object being to determine with exactness the "views" entertained by the *masses* on the subjects of debate among Protestant Christians. He will find beautiful, all-conquering faith, triumphant hope, and love and joy that pass understanding, but very little "Theology"—none, in fact. Decided partisans will have at hand a few "proof texts," which they will quote at random, and often incorrectly; a few will remember definitions and doctrines which they learned from catechisms in childhood, and of which they understood as much at ten years of age as they now understand at thirty. Ah, well, sinners are saved by grace, through faith, and this faith has for its objects *persons and facts*, not "doctrines," not dogmas, not scientific formulas.

The knowledge absolutely essential to salvation takes its range far within the limits of the whole revelation of God, and yet we believe he has not spoken one word in vain. So we believe he has not made any thing in vain, although the wisest naturalist fails to apprehend the uses of thousands of objects that offer themselves to his contemplation.

In the attempt to unfold, in part, the theme of our present meditation, we shall assume that Jesus understood his own religion—that he knew in what respects the human race was wrong in the sight of God, and the means by which the wrong was to be corrected—that he knew, absolutely and completely, all that men ought to believe and to do in order to justification, regeneration, salvation—that he taught the essential truths of his religion, and illustrated its principles of action *in his own life*. We shall find that, in the apprehension of the Savior, the faith, love, and obedience which his religion requires, *have respect to himself*.

I. Christianity meets us first, and, perhaps, at the last, not as a theory, not as a series of doctrines, not as truth expressed in scientific formulæ; but—and blessed be God that it is so—*as a history*, a biography—the history of a life and of a death, of a burial and of a resurrection, and of an ascension into heaven. To the hearer or reader of that most wonderful, simple, but sublime story, the single question is asked: "What think you of Christ?" Every thing, in the religion of Jesus, turns on the answer that may be given to this far-reaching inquiry. We need not stop to ask nor to answer the quite difficult questions that speculative and ingenious minds may raise concerning the freedom of the will, the decrees of God, the *philosophy* of the Atonement, the mode of the Divine existence, the plenary inspiration of Scriptures. On these, and similar subjects, good and great men have differed in opinion for sixteen hundred years, and are likely to differ for sixteen hundred more. "What think you of Christ?"

II. The question which constitutes our text is, so to speak, a "fair question;" that is, it is one that every intelligent being to whom the story of Jesus is submitted,

ought to *feel bound to answer.*   If the facts and statements
of the four Gospels are taken together, and in their plain,
most obvious import, no analysis or generalization is
required. *The essential truth lies on the surface.* It has
respect to a *person*, and not to a doctrine, we repeat, with
emphasis. Multiplied thousands of the best men and
women on earth this day, if asked, What do you think of
the doctrine of predestination? of the Trinity? of Unitarianism? of election? would hesitate to answer—would
feel themselves wholly unable to answer, but who would,
nevertheless, even die for Jesus's sake, if challenged to
do so. Shall Protestants evermore refuse to learn from
the Word of God, from the history of religious controversy, and from their own observation, the folly—shall we
say it?—of attempting to unite the people of God in the
belief of "speculative divinity?"

That we shall meet with mysteries in the New Testament, is cheerfully conceded. The *central* being in the
whole revelation of God, even *Jesus Christ, our Lord, is
" a great mystery."* And here we must be indulged in a
passing remark on the controversies that for fifteen centuries have been waged between Trinitarians and Unita-
rians. These sad controversies seem to us to consist, for
the most part, of unintelligible jargon, of a childish and
absurd *balancing* of texts of Scripture, and of attempts to
force from stubborn facts and plain declarations more than
they contain, or to lessen their obvious signification. And,
after all, do not the greatest and best men on both sides
of the controversy admit that the relations of Jesus constitute a *necessary* and an effably glorious *mystery?* Why,
then, make attempted explanations of that which is inex-
plicable, the basis of Christian fraternization? Why not
admit the "*great mystery of godliness, God manifest in the*

flesh," and then affirm and teach all that the divine testimonies declare of the nature, relations, office, and work of
the Lord Jesus? We so deal with other mysteries of revelation, why not with this, perhaps, the greatest mystery
of them all?

We would speak with caution and with unaffected dif-
fidence, and yet it does appear to us that neither the Trin-
itarian nor the Unitarian formulæ can be made to include
all the phenomena of the case. The earnest student of
"the record that God has given of his Son," as he reads
and ponders, will say of Jesus, "this is, indeed, 'the son
of man,' my near kinsman, and yet he is 'Immanuel, God
with us;' this is 'the Christ, the Son of God and the Savior of the world.' I can *believe* all this, and stake eternal
issues on it, but I can not *explain* it. It is matter of faith,
not of philosophy. I believe it because it is sustained by
ample testimony, not because I am able to classify and so
bring into *scientific order* all the facts and declarations that
set forth the nature of One who, as the Word, 'was in the
beginning with God, and who was God,' but 'became flesh
and dwelt among us,' and who will, in the end, 'deliver
up the kingdom to God even the Father, and *himself be
subject*, that God may be all in all.'" Dogmatism on
such a subject, what ought to be said of it? Nothing
here and now. Few sadder things have occurred in the
history of the human race, than the divisions and bitter
strifes among Christ's disciples, that have grown out of
futile attempts to explain an unspeakable mystery; and
the controversy may, we think, be fitly and indefinitely
postponed. Within the circle of our own human sympathies, Jesus meets us, and weeps with us, and is "a man
of sorrows," but we immediately perceive that his nature
passes on beyond our nature, and over into the Infinite,

and we not only trust without limit, but adore. "Who by searching can find out God? Who can know the Almighty *to perfeƈtion?*" *

They who, by faith, dwell in Immanuel's land, are like those who would inhabit a *small island* far out in mid-ocean. They have the glorious heavens over them; they live amid beauty, and verdure, and bloom, and fragrance, and fruit; their groves are vocal, and their fields yield a hundred-fold; they have all things richly to enjoy. But they have no line with which to take the soundings of the deep sea that surrounds them, and they can see but a little way out over the heaving waters. Beyond the line that bounds their vision all is mystery. Balmy breezes come to them across the deep, they know not whence, but

---

* "He who dwells in infinity is at once a God who reveals and a God who conceals himself. We can know, but we can know only in part. The knowledge which we can attain is the clearest and yet the obscurest of all our knowledge. A child, a savage, can acquire a certain acquaintance with him, while neither sage nor angel can rise to a full comprehension of him. God may be truly described as the Being of whom we know the most, inasmuch as his works are ever pressing themselves upon our attention, and we behold more of his ways than of the ways of any other; and yet he is the Being of whom we know the least, inasmuch as we know comparatively less of his whole nature than we do of ourselves, or of our fellow-men, or of any objeƈt falling under our senses. They who know the least of him have, in this, the most valuable of all knowledge; they who know the most know but little, after all, of his glorious perfeƈtions. Let us prize what knowledge we have, but feel, meanwhile, that our knowledge is comparative ignorance. They who know little of him may feel as if they knew much; they who know much will always feel that they know but little. The most limited knowledge of him should be felt to be precious, but this mainly as an encouragement to seek knowledge higher and yet higher, without limit and without end. They who in earth or heaven know the most, know that they know but little after all; but they know that they may know more and more of him throughout eternal ages."—*McCosh*, "*Intuitions of the Mind.*"

8

they are full of health and fragrance. Shall they dwell together in peace and love, and enjoy together the varied beauties and bounties of their island home? or shall they quarrel and strive endlessly about what may be the depth of the surrounding sea, and what may be beyond it? It were well could God's people remember always that now we see through a glass darkly, that we know but in part, that we walk by faith. In religion, faith is philosophy; obedience, the perfection of science.

I. We propose now, by citing a few of the declarations made by the Savior concerning himself, to determine what were his own conceptions of his relations to the race he came to save. We say a *few* of these declarations, for *Jesus spoke very often of himself*, a circumstance which seems not to have received the attention its deep significance demands.

1. *Jesus claimed to be the teacher, the leader, and the guide of mankind.*

"Come to *me* all ye that labor and are heavy laden, and I will give you rest. Take *my* yoke upon you, and learn of *me*, for I am meek and lowly of heart, and you shall find rest to your souls." (Matt. xi.) In this declaration, this most affecting invitation, of the beauty and graciousness of which we are not able to speak, Jesus certainly makes *himself* the first and the last. Is it not singular that though the Savior so often speaks of himself, yet nothing he says has the appearance of egotism? "Never *man* spake as he spake." The sentences above quoted are every way most wonderful, if we well consider them. Here is a very poor and very friendless young man, who had been brought up in an obscure village of Galilee, proverbial for the meanness of its general circumstances, declaring that he had not where to lay his head, yet proposing to give rest to the souls of the laboring and heavy laden, if they would come to him and learn of him. Let us try clearly to apprehend the peculiarity of the case. Suppose an uneducated, poor, and friendless young man, from one of our obscure, disreputable, out-of-the-way towns, were to come here to Lexington, Kentucky, in one of these passing weeks, and gathering about him some hundreds of poor men and women, should propose to give them rest to their weary, disquieted souls, what would be thought of him? He would be regarded as an amiable, sorrowful *lunatic*, and some humane person would have him placed in an asylum. But Jesus was not a lunatic. *I defy you to think so.* And if not, then is he *all that he claimed to be*; then is he "the Son of the living God," and we are all of us on our way to his judgment-seat. "If weak thy faith, why choose the harder side?" "What think you of Christ?"

2. Jesus proposed himself *as the object of the faith by which sinners are to be saved.*

"God gave his only-begotten Son, that whoever believes *in him* might not perish, but have everlasting life. Verily I say unto you, he that believeth *on me* hath everlasting life. This is the work of God, that you believe on him, whom he hath sent. The Messiah cometh which is called Christ: Jesus said unto her, *I that speak to thee am he.* Jesus said unto him, Dost thou believe on the Son of God? He it is that talketh with thee." There is something in this constant recurrence of the Great Teacher to himself that demands our closest attention. No one, as before observed, can regard this as egotism. Every reader of the New Testament *feels* that it behooved Jesus thus to press his claims. The world could not be saved by philosophers. It needed that One of infinite perfections should dwell among us and show us the Father—one whom all can trust without limit, in whom they can believe "with all the heart." Though Jesus was, indeed, "meek and lowly of heart," and though he had not where to lay his head, yet, whenever he would win the heart of man to holiness and to God, he spoke of himself as being the object of faith.

3. As Jesus proposes himself as the object of faith, so he constitutes *himself the subject of the confession of faith.* Under circumstances of extreme personal peril, Jesus "witnessed a good confession," and he was *himself* the subject of it. "The high-priest asked him, Art thou the Christ, the Son of the Blessed? And Jesus answered, I am." (Mark xiv.) Wonder not, then, that he requires the same confession from all who would hope in his mercy. "Whosoever, therefore, shall confess *me* before men, him will I confess also before my Father who is in heaven; but whosoever shall deny me before men, him will I also deny before my Father who is in heaven." (Matt. x.) This makes the controversy which Jesus has with the human race not a doctrinal, but a *personal* controversy, so to speak, and it becomes infinitely serious. Men may not be obliged to accept any given interpretations of a chapter in the letter to the Romans, or in the Apocalypse. The primary question is not concerning doctrines, but concerning Jesus. "Who do you say that I the son of man am? Peter answered, Thou art the Christ, the Son of the living God. Blessed art thou, Simon; on this rock I will build my Church, and the gates of hell shall not prevail against it." It is blessed, then, to confess that Jesus is the Christ, the Son of the living God; and on this all-comprehensive truth Jesus *builds his Church.* Thus do we see that in the apprehension of the Redeemer

he is the subject of the confession of Christian faith, and he has given us the form of words in which that confession is to be made. Should any one object that the "form of sound words" in which "the good confession" is appointed to be made, is susceptible of various interpretations, our reply is: So is *any form of words*, and especially any that the wisdom of man may devise. Indeed, from of old, on all the deeper things of God, theologians have found it needful to comment on their own commentaries, and to explain their own explanations. "What think you of Christ?" Is he, indeed, "the Son of the living God?"

4. *Jesus claimed for himself the supreme love of mankind.*

We are not here arguing that men *ought* to believe in Jesus, that they ought to confess and love him, but that he himself so taught. In all things he claims the preeminence. "He that loveth father or mother more than me, is not worthy of me, and he that loveth son or daughter more than me, is not worthy of me." (Matt. x.) "If any man come to me, and (comparatively) hate not his father, and mother, and wife, and children, and brethren, and sisters, yea, and his own life also, he can not be my disciple." (Luke xiv.) This is decisive on this point. Jesus must be first in the heart's affections, or he will not be there at all. And in this appointment of God does not a Divine philosophy shine forth upon us? What so powerfully and constantly controls human life as the love of friends, living or dead? How hopeless would be the prospects of the human race if the duties of life were to be performed only under the guidance of moral philosophy! What philosophy could bind the mother, through days and nights of weariness, to the cradle of her helpless infant? What formula of duty would nerve the arm of

the poor father as he toils ceaselessly, through the heats
of summer and the frosts of winter, that his home may
be one of comfort?   Love is more than dogma, more than
philosophy.   The wayward youth, far from the home of his
innocent childhood, still remembers the tender accents of
a mother's or a sister's voice, and weeps.   They incessantly
call him away from his follies and his crimes, and, from
beyond the grave, they invite him to the Fountain opened
for sin.   These sad, sweet memories of the loved and lost
are often more powerful for good than is the rhetoric or
logic of the pulpit.   The remembered wishes of friends
that have passed the Jordan, how they wrap themselves
about the heart!   And what can be said of the remembered
wishes (shall we say?) of the blessed Jesus?   Shall not the
consideration that he who has done every thing for us,
directs and invites us to a given course of life, be omnipotent?   Yes, *if we love him, we will keep his commandments.*

Alas for us! we find it, perhaps, much easier to love
our party, our church, and its forms and its policies, than
to love the Lord that bought us.   How many of those
in all lands, who have professed to believe in Jesus, can
go out under the starlit sky in the solemn night, and, looking up toward heaven, say with penitent Peter: "Lord
Jesus, thou knowest all things; thou knowest that I love
thee?"

Men can do but little, except as mere partisans, under
the influence of dogmas, whether religious, political, or
moral; but the love of country, the love of mankind, the
love of family, above all, the love of Jesus, what can not
be achieved under its influence?   Even an enemy can be
forgiven, and fed, and clothed for Jesus's sake.   His poor
disciples can be sustained and comforted, because he asks
it of us as if it were for himself.   Men and women, too,

can go cheerfully to the very ends of the earth to seek the lost, and to tell them of God's great love for a sinful race, because Jesus commands it, and we can not *deny him*. Love is greater than faith, for the faith that overcomes the world must work by love. "Love is the fulfilling of the law, and he that dwells in love, dwells in God and God in him, for God is love." When love for Christ shall so possess the hearts of his people as to be ever the regulating influence of their lives, then will the day of millennial glory break, then will Zion rise and shine, then will the Church go forth to the speedy conquest of the world. Meanwhile, he who shall set himself to keep the commandments of God without being *constrained* thereto by the love of Christ, will surely fail. And is not Jesus, the meek and lowly One, is he not "the chief among the ten thousand, and the one altogether lovely?" What think you of Christ? Is he not worthy the adoring love of all hearts?

5. *Jesus claimed Divine honors.*

"For the Father judgeth no man, but hath committed all judgments unto the Son, that all men should honor the Son, *even as they honor the Father*. He that honoreth not the Son, honoreth not the Father who hath sent him." And should any poor sinner be staggered at this? If so, we remand him to "the testimony that God has given of his Son." True, indeed, the humiliation of Jesus was infinite. "He *took not on himself* the nature of angels, but the seed of Abraham; for in all things it behooved him to be made like unto his brethren, that he might be a merciful and faithful high-priest in things pertaining to God, to make reconciliation for the sins of the people." But because of this humiliation, because, "being in the form of God, he thought it not robbery to be equal with God, but made himself of no reputation, and took upon him the form of a servant, and became obedient unto death, even the death of the cross," on this very account "God has highly exalted him, and given him a name that is above every name, that at the name of Jesus *every knee should bow*, of things in heaven, and things in earth, and things under the earth; and that every tongue should confess that Jesus Christ is Lord, to the glory of God the Father." (Phil. ii.) We need not fear to go where God directs, and if he has appointed all the angels to worship his Son, sinners for whom he died may "honor him, even as they honor the Father."

6. *Jesus required that mankind should serve and obey him.*

"If ye keep my commandments, ye shall abide in my love. Ye are my friends, if ye do whatever *I command you*. If ye love me, keep my commandments. He that has my commandments and keepeth them, he it is that loveth me." These citations must suffice. In varied forms of words, Jesus claims to be a leader and commander of the people. The government is on his shoulder, and he declares that all authority in heaven and on earth has been given to him. His apostle declares that "he has become the Author of eternal salvation to all them that *obey him*."

If we have rightly apprehended the import of the teaching of Jesus, then does he make *himself* the object of the faith that brings the sinner to God; he aims constantly to make men his own disciples; he requires men to confess, to honor, to love, and to obey him. This is religion—the religion of the New Testament—and *nothing else is*.

And here we must close this very imperfect survey of these most fundamental and essential instructions. We say *imperfect*, for much less than a tithe of what Jesus said of himself has been cited. Without any marked order, however, we quote a few additional sayings of the great Teacher, some metaphorical, some literal, but all of widest, deepest significance, and all illustrating and confirming our general proposition, namely, that, in the apprehension of Jesus, he was himself the beginning and the end of his religion, objectively considered.

1. "I am come a light into the world, that whosoever believeth on me should not abide in darkness." 2. "I am the good Shepherd, and *give my life for the sheep.*" 3. "No man cometh to the Father *but by me.*" 4. "I am the way, and the truth, and the life." 5. "I am the resurrection and the life." 6. "All that are in their graves shall hear his voice and come forth, they that have done good to the resurrection of life, and they that have done evil to the resurrection of damnation." 7. "The Son of man shall sit on the *throne of his glory*, and before him shall be gathered all nations, and he shall separate them one from another, as a shepherd divideth his sheep from the goats." But we desist. According to these most wonderful declarations, Jesus makes himself King, Priest, Sacrifice for sin, Guide of the world, Judge of all nations. What think ye of Christ?

II. All that Jesus declared of himself, as to his nature, offices, and work, is, in various forms of words, reiterated by his inspired apostles and evangelists in both their preaching and teaching.

1. "Go into all the world and preach *the Gospel* to every creature." Such was, in brief, the great commission under which the apostles went out from the presence of the Lord, "to call men from darkness to light, that they might be translated from the kingdom of Satan into *the*

kingdom of God's dear Son." Let the earnest inquirer after the "truth, *as it is in Jesus,*" carefully read the inspired discourses recorded in the Acts of Apostles. Take, as specimens, the second, tenth, and thirteenth chapters. "Christ, and him crucified," buried, risen, ascended, and seated at the right hand of the Father, constitutes the burden of the apostolic proclamation. They "preached Jesus" to Jew and Gentile, and testified that "*through his name* whosoever believeth on him should receive the remission of sins." The "evolution of doctrines" had not then been begun; the children of God *by faith in Christ Jesus* were one; and "mightily grew the word of the Lord and prevailed." With the evolution of doctrines began the evolution of sects, and they must continue to evolve and to revolve till all shall have returned to the ancient paths, till all shall perceive that the truth concerning the Christ, *practically* accepted, is the sum of all truth essential to Christian life and Christian fraternization. When we shall have closed our examination of the "sermons" of the apostles, the great, primary, all-comprehending inquiry is still with us, "What think ye of Christ?"

2. Our citations from the apostolic letters must be few. Indeed, were all that is there declared of the nature, dignity, offices, and work of Jesus taken away, *a few shreds only would remain,* and these would be meaningless.

1. "*Jesus must reign* till he has put all enemies under his feet." 2. "We have a *high-priest* at the right hand of the throne of the Majesty in the heavens; his priesthood is unchangeable, everlasting. Jesus ever lives to make intercession for us, being the Mediator of the new covenant." 3. "He is made unto us wisdom, and righteousness, and sanctification, and redemption, and by him we draw nigh to God." 4. "We are redeemed by the *precious*

blood of Christ, and he is able to save to the uttermost all that come to God by him." 5. "The Church is the *body of Christ*, and if any man have not the spirit of Christ, he is none of his." 6. "If any man love not the Lord Jesus Christ, let him be anathema." 7. "He has left us an example that we should follow his steps." 8. "Jesus will judge the living and the dead at his appearing and kingdom." Thus by the hour might we repeat the declarations of apostles, in which they have exhausted the capacity of literal and metaphorical language to express the glory, the grandeur, the majesty of Christ. In their *teaching*, assuredly, he is the first, and the midst, and the last. Truly God's thoughts are not our thoughts, nor his ways our ways; for it hath pleased him, through the foolishness of preaching [Jesus], to save them that believe. At the close of our readings of the apostles' letters, the question still returns, if possible, with increased force, "What think you of Christ?"

III. The "ordinances" of the Christian religion—the *Lord's* Day, the *Lord's* Supper, and Baptism—declare the Gospel. They preach Jesus, *and derive all their significance and value from their relations to him.* Let us not suppose that this is accidental.

1. What means the general stillness of the Lord's-day morning, as, in the round of the weeks, it breaks over Christian lands? The engine has ceased to puff, the rattle of machinery is stopped. No teams are being driven afield, but the unyoked cattle rest in the stalls, or repose at will in the green pastures. There is an unusual quiet in most households, for they feel that the day is hallowed. The places of merchandise are closed, and busy trade pauses to breathe. The poor man looks joyfully on the morning of this day, for he, too, may rest, and sing, and

be glad. The bells ring out at length, to tell that the hour of prayer has come; and the rich and the poor together, the father, and mother, and children, and servants pass quietly along the streets or the country highways to their chosen shrines. Touching and beautiful is this, but *why* is it? A voice comes down through the centuries—the voice of inspiration, the voice of angels, the voice of God, —saying, "Now is Christ risen from the dead, and become the first fruits of them that slept." This oracle explains it all. As Jesus died for our sins, so did he rise for our justification. "The first day of the week" hath this inscription: "Sacred, evermore, to the memory of the resurrection of Jesus of Nazareth from among the dead." It celebrates the triumph of the sinner's Friend over death and the grave, and thus preaches one great item of the Gospel of the grace of God. Ah, ye sorrowful ones, who, in garments of woe, and with heavy-laden hearts, go up on this day to the house of the Lord, cling to the faith of Christ's resurrection, for if he rose not, then all faith is vain, we are all in our sins, and our dear ones gone, whom we had hoped to see again, are perished forever. No speculations, no philosophy can help us here. *If Jesus does not come again to this earth, the dead will never rise out of their graves.* But the first day of every week proclaims to all the ages that Jesus *is* the resurrection and the life, as he himself said, and that the dead will one day hear his voice and come forth—that "spring shall yet visit the moldering urn, and the morning of an eternal day break, at last, on the darkness of the tomb." "O Death, where now thy sting? O Grave, where now thy victory? The sting of death is sin, and the strength of sin is the law, but thanks be to God, who giveth us the victory *through our Lord Jesus Christ.*"

2. "On the first day of the week the disciples came to-gether to break bread—to eat the Lord's supper." The appointments are the simplest—a loaf of bread and a cup of wine, but they signify much, even this: "Jesus died for our sins according to the Scriptures." The "Man of Sor-rows" ordained that his disciples should thus show forth his death, *until he shall come.* "The bread—is it not the communion of the body of Christ? The cup—is it not the communion of the blood of Christ?" (1 Cor. x.) "Do this," said the sorrow-laden Jesus, "do this in *remembrance of me.*" Was there in his nature, too, what we find in our own—a desire not to be forgotten? However this may be, he knew how important it is that his disciples should keep in memory the great love wherewith he loved them, that they should often think of Gethsemane, of the agony and bloody sweat, of the crown of thorns, of Calvary and the Cross, and of that cry which was wrung from the break-ing heart of the smitten Shepherd: "My God! my God! why hast thou forsaken me?" By means of the "Sup-per" we go back over the centuries, and look upon the "Lamb of God, as he bore our sins in his own body on the tree," and we say, it is enough—God has, indeed, *loved* the world, since Jesus died to save it. "O Lamb of God, was ever pain, was ever love like thine?"

3. "Go ye, therefore, and teach all nations, *baptizing* them into the name of the Father, and of the Son, and of the Holy Spirit." In obedience to this commandment of Jesus, the apostles *baptized all who yielded to their preaching.* It is, perhaps, worthy of remark that baptism is the only act that can be performed, in which the name of Father, Son, and Holy Spirit may be called *by Divine authority.* It becomes, in view of this fact, a sublime, and even an aw-ful solemnity. But what is its significance? Even this:

the believing penitent is "*baptized into the death of Christ;*" he is "buried *with him* by baptism into death;" he is "baptized *into Christ*, and thus *puts on Christ*." (Rom. vi.) We cite no other Scriptures; it were needless to do so. In this institution, whose very form sets forth a burial and a resurrection, the sinner puts on the Lord Jesus, and, through his name, obtains remission of sins. Thus do the ordinances of the Gospel preach Jesus crucified, buried, and risen, and derive all their significance and efficacy from their relations to him. "*What think you of Christ?*"

Finally: God has placed before a sinful world, for its faith, its love, and its obedience, a *person* wearing human nature, and bearing its infirmities, yet possessing divine and infinite perfections and attributes. Jesus of Nazareth is a historic personage, whose individuality, so to speak, is marked with wonderful clearness. His manner of teaching—the things taught, as well as his beautiful life, are altogether peculiar, single, alone. The New Testament is the miracle of literature. In the person and claims of Jesus our faith is demanded; for his divinely-beautiful character our all-trusting, adoring love is asked. The commandments of Jesus are not doctrines, but plain rules of life, of action, to which submission is required. These three things: faith in Jesus, the love of Jesus, and obedience to Jesus, as Lord of all, constitute the Christian religion, and are possible to the poor and to the unlearned, as well as to the wealthy and the wise. Not so with theology, with scientific Christianity, about which most religious controversies arise, and which constitute the foundations of religious sects, regarded as such merely. Touching the commands of the blessed Redeemer, we may say, it is not easy for the honest-hearted seriously to mistake them. The general import of the whole is, as illustrated by his own beautiful, Divine life, "to do justly, to love mercy, and to walk humbly with God." This is orthopraxy, without which orthodoxy is but an impertinence and a cheat.

Complainings, on all sides, of the want of earnest religious living have become chronic. The general tone of religious life will not be improved till God's people shall come to apprehend with greater clearness, and to feel with far deeper intensity, the claims of their Redeemer on their affections, until they shall love him more than they love wealth, and friends, and life—until the love of Christ shall *constrain* them. Religious partyism has long been the opprobrium of the Church. The Church will never be united in "doctrines" of any kind. She must be one in Christ Jesus, or divide still more, and remain divided till the Lord shall come.

Jesus is with the sinner in his first faint glimmerings of faith; he is before him, the embodiment of infinite sorrow and of infinite love, when alone he heaves the first sigh of penitence; he is in his heart when, before men, he makes confession unto salvation; the penitent clings by faith to the Cross when he is buried with his Lord in baptism; when, as a child of God, he takes his seat at the table of the Lord, Jesus lifts up his bleeding hands before him, and says: "Do this in remembrance of me." When he bows the knee in prayer, he remembers that Jesus ever lives to intercede for him; in hours of calamity, he finds support in the words of Jesus: "Let not your heart be troubled, you believe in God, believe also in me." When his heart sinks in view of death and the grave, he remembers the words of the Savior: "I am the resurrection and the life; he that believeth in me, though he die, yet shall he live again;" and he remembers that Jesus will be his Judge in the last terrible solemnity in the history of the human race. From the lips of Jesus shall fall a sentence that shall raise the redeemed to heights of inconceivable glory, and a sentence that shall banish his enemies, those that deny him, "into everlasting fire prepared for the devil and his angels." From these sentences there can be no appeal for evermore. The Lamb of God will lead his people to fountains of living water in the abodes of immortality, while his redeeming love shall forever constitute the theme of their loftiest anthems.

The sum is this: Instead of abstract, scientific formulas, God has given us every thing in the concrete. He has embodied for us, so to speak, in the person and character of Jesus, his own idea of human life, rendered divine, and has revealed the divine through the human. Instead of "doctrines" he offers to us a mysterious *person*, who draws the hearts of men to him because he is their brother, and who, at the same time commands their devotion, because he is "the only-begotten Son of God." O, ineffable "mystery of godliness, God manifest in the flesh."

Our controversy, then, if we have one, is not with "the Church," nor our chief concern with "*doctrines*" and religious philosophies, but with Him who is "the first and the last, who was dead, but is alive again for evermore, and who has the keys of hell and of death." What think ye of *Christ?* "Blessed are they who do his commandments, that they may have right to the tree of life, and may enter in through the gates into the city." *Amen.*

In the One hope
Jas Challen

JAMES CHALLEN.

FEW preachers among the Disciples are better known than the subject of this sketch. Early in the beginning of the current Reformation, he became identified with its fortunes, and has remained a firm and consistent advocate of its principles till the present time. Although considerably advanced in years, he has not laid aside the armor, but is still preaching, with great acceptance to the Church, at Davenport, Iowa.

JAMES CHALLEN was born in Hackensack, New Jersey, January 7, 1802. His parents were from England, and emigrated to this country soon after the War of Independence. His father was a Methodist, and his mother a Baptist, and this led him to examine the Word of God for himself. The result of this examination was the acceptance of the religious position which he now occupies, and in defense of which he has given the greater part of his life.

He confessed the Savior, and was immersed under the ministry of Dr. JAMES FISHBACK, of Lexington, Kentucky, on the 18th day of January, 1823, and united with the Baptist Church, of which Dr. FISHBACK was pastor. He soon commenced preaching, but, feeling the necessity of a more thorough preparation for the work of the ministry, he entered Transylvania University, with the view to obtain a first-class education. While in the junior class of that institution, he was called to the charge of the Enon Baptist Church, Cincinnati, Ohio, which he accepted, and entered at once upon the duties of his new position. He remained with this church till the Sycamore-street Church was formed. This last was composed principally of members who had been brought in under his personal ministry; consequently were well instructed in the simple truths of Christianity, and fully prepared to "take their stand on the Bible, and the Bible alone."

He was immediately elected pastor of the new church, in which position he was instrumental in establishing firmly the "Ancient Gospel" in the Queen City. In 1834 he removed to Lexington, Kentucky, where he organized the church which exists there at present. He remained at this

9   (129)

point for several years, meeting with encouraging success in the proclamation of the Word.

In 1850 he took charge of the church in Philadelphia, and spent about eight years in that city. In 1860 he removed to Davenport, Iowa, where he has remained ever since.

Brother CHALLEN is of small stature, but has a tough, wiry frame, which is capable of great endurance. He has a high, commanding forehead, small, sharp, penetrating eye, and a mouth that indicates decision and firmness of character. As a speaker, he is pleasing and instructive; sometimes, forcible and eloquent. He has great compass of voice, and always speaks with considerable animation.

His literary attainments are quite respectable, having, for many years past, made the best English authors his constant companions. But he has not pursued this branch of study to the neglect of his ministerial labors—he has found it the best way to prepare himself for his life-work.

He writes rapidly, and with great ease. Besides being a regular contributor to the periodical press of the Disciples, he has written a number of useful works, some of which have had considerable circulation. Of these, we mention " The Gospel and its Elements," " Christian Evidences," " Baptism in Spirit and in Fire," " Frank Elliot," and " Christian Morals." He has also written two volumes of poetry: " The Cave of Machpelah and other Poems," and " Igdrasil, or the Tree of Existence;" and edited " Challen's Juvenile Library," numbering forty-one volumes. For several years he published a monthly, called " The Ladies' Christian Annual," and the " Gem," a neat and well-conducted Sunday-school paper. His writings all breathe a deeply-earnest Christian spirit, and leave little doubt in the mind of the reader concerning the religious position of their author.

RECONCILIATION.

BY JAMES CHALLEN.

"And all things are of God, who hath reconciled us to himself by Jesus Christ, and hath given to us the ministry of reconciliation; to-wit, that God was in Christ, reconciling the world unto himself, not imputing their trespasses unto them; and hath committed unto us the word of reconciliation. Now then we are ambassadors for Christ, as though God did beseech you by us: we pray you in Christ's stead, be ye reconciled to God. For he hath made him to be sin for us, who knew no sin; that we might be made the righteousness of God in him."—2 COR. V: 18–21.

THAT man is alienated from God, and at enmity with him, are truths every-where taught in the Divine oracles; and although many know him not, and are living in ignorance of what he has revealed, yet their whole moral nature and life show aversion to his government, and departure from his ways. The "carnal mind is enmity to God," and "the friendship of the world is enmity *with* him." The Gentiles, before the Gospel was preached to them, are said to be "alienated from the life of God through the ignorance that is in them."

It is not necessary that men shall know God, or be acquainted with his ways, to be alienated from him. As darkness is opposed to light, and error to truth, and sin to righteousness, so the heart and life of man are opposed to his Maker. "The wrath of God is revealed from heaven against all ungodliness and unrighteousness of men" wherever it is found. His nature is eternally opposed to all that is sinful.

The Gentiles were without excuse; "for when they knew God, they worshiped him not as God, neither were thankful; but became vain in their imaginations, and their foolish heart was darkened. Professing themselves to be wise, they became fools, and changed the glory of the incorruptible God into an image made like to corruptible man, and to birds and four-footed beasts, and to creeping things." A fearful picture is drawn by the Apostle of the character and condition of the heathen world in his own day, and it is equally as true now as then. (Rom. i: 20–32.)

The Jews, who were blessed with a verbal revelation, were equally inexcusable as the Gentiles. Indeed, they were involved in deeper guilt. They despised the riches of God's goodness, and forbearance, and long-suffering. They treasured up wrath against the day of wrath and the righteous judgment of God, who will render to every man according to his deeds. The Scriptures have concluded all men under sin. This is the condition of the world, and in this attitude the word of reconciliation is sent us.

The spectacle is an appalling one. If the relation of man to man is one of enmity, that of man to his Maker is of a deeper hue. It is estrangement of heart and life from all that is pure and good; of hostility to the spirit and principles of his moral government over his rational creation. The race of man presents to angels a vast ruin— greater than all the cities of dead empires; a desolation more fearful than the wreck of conquering armies, or the waste of fields and vineyards by the devouring locusts, or by sword and famine.

God sees all this, and remembers whence we have fallen,

and what our sins will lead to unless redeemed by the blood of his Son ; and in his pity and his mercy he has sent us deliverance.

The Ministry of Reconciliation.

The One Great Minister sent of God on this embassy of reconciliation is Jesus Christ, the Son of the living God. He is his special servant in accomplishing this work. He came from heaven with full powers to treat with men on this subject. He represents all the dignity, authority, and glory of the Father who 'sent him ; and all the weakness, poverty and suffering of those he came to reconcile. In his person, we see all that is divine in his Father, and all that is human in his mother. He touches the throne of the Majesty in the heavens, and stoops to the lowest condition of our race upon the earth. His divinity rises as high as the heaven of heavens—over the Bethlehem in which, as a child, he was born, and the Nazareth in which he was subject to his parents. The supernatural shines forth in every stage of his mission, as in the Mount of Transfiguration, and at the tomb of the rich Arimathean. He unites the tears of human sympathy with the voice of omnipotence, and walks with human feet upon the stormy Galilee, while he lays his hand of might upon the turbulent billows, and with divine majesty cries, " Peace, be still." We feel no surprise or astonishment at the "signs and wonders" attesting his mission, as they seem to be the natural accompaniments of it. They appear as his own and proper "works," as fruitage from the tree, or grain from the sower's field, or words and deeds from living men. His mission is "the end of a boundless past, the center of a boundless present, and the beginning of a boundless future."

His life, though human, did not move on the plane of the world's history. He stood apart, and alone, in the grand objects of his mission. He had no popular favor to seek; no worldly plans to accomplish; no honors to gain; no emoluments or earthly ambitions to acquire. He allied not himself with party or sect; with the rich or the poor; with the Sanhedrim or Cæsar. He came not to receive, but to give. He was of the race, and acted for the race. He came as the world's reconciler. The very conception of such a purpose is Divine, and places him incomparably above all who preceded him.

His mission, though to "the lost sheep of the house of Israel," was for the benefit of the world. Not a single nation, but the whole race, were the objects of his ministry. He came, not to elevate Judea from its oppressed condition, nor yet to ally himself with imperial Rome; but to gather, out of the families and tribes of earth, a people for his name; a chosen generation, a royal priesthood; and to found an empire of redeemed, regenerated, and reconciled subjects, which should stand forever.

So far was he from conciliating the favor of the leading parties, the Pharisees, Sadducees, and Herodians forgot their mutual prejudices in opposing him. Pilate and Herod made friends in plotting his destruction. Both the ecclesiastical and political governments were hostile to him; and the only part of the nation that sympathized with him were the poor and the neglected—the outcasts from society—"publicans and sinners." His poverty and pity drew him to the masses, from whom he could receive nothing; and his princely gifts and his humble garb attracted their attention and won their confidence. He was "the Divine man" for which the ages had looked; and suffering and sorrowing hearts responded to his tears and his words of

hope. He knew that a man was greater than his condition; and that learning, wealth, and position were but as
the leaves of the forest, short-lived and temporary, soon
to wither and die, and would give place to the foliage
of returning seasons. His mighty soul heard the deep
moanings of the troubled sea of humanity, and the wail
of ages from the four winds of heaven. He stood in the
very heart of the race, the one perfectly developed man;
the only full-blown flower on the stock of our humanity.
He would draw all men to him, and make them like himself—"holy, harmless, undefiled, and separate from sinners"—that he might elevate them higher than the heavens. Though daily in contact with pollution, he was
never defiled. Though breathing the tainted atmosphere
of a sinful world, he was never infected with its poison.
Though walking in the midst of guilt and shame, of pride
and selfishness, he was proof against it. With the world
grown old in sin and folly, and in arms against him, he
was not only able to meet, but to conquer it. Great as
was the temptation of our first parents, it was nothing,
when compared with what "the Son of Man" endured,
and without sin. He not only realized in person what
men have to encounter in striving for a purer life, but he
showed what latent virtues, and what powers of resistance
the soul of man possesses, and can summon to his aid.
His daily contact with suffering did not harden, but softened his heart. The greatness of our guilt and of our
grief did not fill him with despair, but summoned his
mighty energies to the work of relief. The tears he shed
at the grave of Lazarus, and over Jerusalem, were not the
tears of weakness arising from the inability to relieve and
to conquer, but from the well-spring of sorrow, in view
of the awful ravages of human transgression. "The man

of sorrows"—this inheritor of human grief—is the world's reconciler! How deep thy agony! how lonely thy sorrow! What to thee was the crown of thorns, the scourging and the spitting, the cry of "Crucify! crucify!" the cross, and its shame! These but poorly represented "the man of sorrows." They only gave outward form and expression to the unutterable burden which pressed upon his spirit, in view of the ravages of sin and its appalling consequences.

He saw that sin had made the race "captives;" he came to bring them deliverance. They were condemned criminals; he came to bring them pardon. They were in a state of rebellion; he came to bring them peace. They were dead; he was "the resurrection and the life." They were self-destroyed; he brought good news of salvation. They were alienated from God; he came to reconcile them.

It was the region of the shadow of death into which he entered; the darkness and bewilderment of the race were growing deeper and deeper. To one so sensitive to evil, so averse to wrong-doing, so perfectly in harmony with God and all righteousness, so happy and rich in the memories of the past, so exultant and joyful in the hopes of the future, pity oppressed him beyond the claims of justice, and mercy rejoiced over the demands of violated law. If it had not been for the consciousness of his ability to save, the bloody sweat of Gethsemane would have been the baptism of his life; and the cry, "My God, why hast thou forsaken me," the death-cry of his mission. But "God was in Christ reconciling the world to himself," and he felt sure of success; and "for the joy that was set before him, endured the cross, despising the shame, and has taken his seat at the right hand of the throne of God."

The Ambassadors of Christ.

It was not the design of Christ to leave the world without selecting suitable persons to represent his cause, and carry out his gracious purposes in its reconciliation. He therefore chose twelve men from the humble walks of life, who should be with him during his public ministry, and be fully taught his doctrine. In the early part of his labors, he separated these men from the multitude of disciples, and they were constantly with him in private and in public. They heard his instructions to the people, and his many conversations with the Scribes and Pharisees, and others in Judea. They heard his discourses to the people, and enjoyed the peculiar advantage of his private instruction. They had every opportunity of learning his ways and knowing his will. He kept back nothing from them. They saw his "works" —the signs and wonders which he did. In so many aspects did they view him, that it was impossible for them to be ignorant of his person, his teaching, or his claims. He did nothing in secret. In the synagogue and in the temple, in the open fields, by the seaside, and in the desert, in populous cities and in the villages, and in private houses, they were his daily attendants. They saw his mighty works, and were convinced that God was with him. Diseases in every form departed at his word. The lame, the halt, and the blind were healed, and death, in all its stages, acknowledged his power. The daughter of Jairus, in youth and beauty having just expired, and the son of the widow at Nain, in the strength of his manhood, was being borne to the grave, and at his will they are brought to life; and Lazarus, a disciple, rapidly dissolving in the tomb, awoke and was restored to his weeping sisters. These were the first precursors of the mighty demon-

stration of his own resurrection.   As we see him wading
through the floods of great waters to the mount of sacrifice,
we hear him saying: "I will ransom them from the power
of the grave; I will redeem them from death; O death, I
will be thy plague ; O grave, I will be thy destruction."

Jesus had informed the disciples of the fact that he should
die, and on the third day be raised again.   They did not believe it, and, even after his resurrection, it was with difficulty they could be convinced of its reality.   But by many
infallible proofs he appeared and satisfied even the most
incredulous among them.   They saw him, handled him,
examined his person, conversed with him, and enjoyed such
direct and personal intimacy with him as to assure them of
his identity and triumphs.   They were to be his witnesses:
"Ye also shall bear witness, because ye have been with me
from the beginning."   In choosing an apostle to fill the
place of Judas, who by trangression fell, Peter said to the
disciples: "Wherefore of these men who have companied
with us, all the time that the Lord Jesus went in and out
among us, begininng from the baptism of John, unto that
same day that he was taken from us, must one be ordained
to be a witness with us of his resurrection."   To be a witness with the other apostles of the resurrection of Christ,
it was needful that the person chosen should have known
Jesus intimately from the day of his baptism to the hour
of his ascension.   So much depended upon this great demonstration, that the most certain and unerring testimony,
above all dispute, and free from all doubt, must be afforded.   Jesus, after his death and resurrection, said to
the apostles: "Thus it is written, and thus it behooved
the Christ to suffer, and to rise from the dead the third
day : and that repentance and remission of sins should
be preached in his name among all nations, beginning at

Jerusalem. And ye are *witnesses* of these things." (Luke xxiv: 46–48.) The apostles declare that they were "witnesses of all things that he did, both in the land of the Jews and in Jerusalem; whom they slew and hanged on a tree: him God raised up the third day, and shewed him openly; not to all the people, but unto witnesses chosen before of God, even to us, who did eat and drink with him after he rose from the dead." (Acts x: 39–41.)

In order more fully to qualify the apostles for the work assigned them, he promised, in view of his departure, the Holy Spirit, the Comforter, and the Advocate, to teach them all things, and to bring all things to their remembrance whatsoever he had said to them; and in addition to their testimony, he himself should testify concerning the Savior. He renewed this promise to them before his ascension, and told them that they should be baptized in the Holy Spirit not many days hence; and to tarry in Jerusalem until they should be endued with power from on high.

On the day of Pentecost the twelve, as ambassadors of Christ, opened the seals of their commission, and spoke with the Holy Spirit sent down from heaven. Their minds were wholly immersed in all the splendid powers of the world to come. They were brought fully under the influence of "the spirit of Truth," and being filled with his presence, they began to speak with other tongues, as the Spirit gave them utterance. Three thousand enemies were made friends. The betrayers and murderers of Christ were the first to be reconciled to God by the death of his Son. From thence they went through all Judea and Samaria, preaching the Word; and in connection with Paul, called afterward to be an apostle and ambassador by our ascended Lord, they spread the knowledge of salvation to the ends of the earth.

It was with great propriety that the apostles were called ambassadors. No word could more fully set forth their work, and the authority under which they acted.

An ambassador is a special minister, of the highest rank, sent by one prince or government to another, to manage the affairs of state. They are either ordinary or extraordinary. They represent the authority and dignity of the state that sends them. In the Old Testament such officers are frequently referred to, and their functions are known, and have been respected, in all ages of the world.

The apostles were extraordinary ambassadors. They received their commission in person from their Prince; and their names are mentioned in the instrument that bears it. They brought a special message to the world from him, containing the grounds of reconciliation, and the terms on which they should enjoy it. He left nothing to them, but fully declared in what way he would treat with an alienated and rebellious world. In their words and deeds they satisfactorily displayed, through "signs and wonders," the evidences of their commission. They did nothing in their own name, but in the name of the Prince and Savior of the world, they submitted, in the most grave and solemn manner, the *ultimatum* of their sovereign Lord. They won to his cause multitudes of men and women, and planted churches in the land of the Jews and in the Gentile world. They fully made known the Gospel on every continent then known, and to the islands of the seas; and left on record, for all succeeding ages, the fruit of their labors—the life of their Leader and the conditions of their embassy.

The Gospel they preached did not perish with them. It remained entire, in all its force and in all its elements, for succeeding ages. Others were required by them to " hold fast the form of sound words which they had heard from them, and to keep that good thing intrusted to them by the Holy Spirit that dwells in us." The things they had heard from the apostles were to be "committed to faithful men, who should be able to teach others also." The Church they established on the earth was to last, with all its institutions, until Jesus should come again. The Savior promised that "their work should remain." The terms of reconciliation they proposed to men in his name, are as binding now as they were then. The Gospel, as the incorruptible word, abideth forever.

As the work of ambassadors in secular matters is respected as sacredly after their death as when alive, so the work of the chosen twelve is of perpetual obligation. The crowned Prince has never revoked the message he sent by them, or superseded their embassy. It is still "the word of reconciliation." It is "the word of faith" to the unbelieving, exhibiting all the great facts of the Gospel, its commands and promises. It is "the word of truth" from him who is the true and faithful witness, and who is "the way, the truth, and the life." It is "the Word of Life" to those who are dead in trespasses and in sins, from him who has brought "life and immortality to light." It is "the Gospel of God," because it originated with him, and displays to us his unutterable philanthropy and good-will. It is "the Gospel of grace," as it shows the benignity of God, and the utter helplessness of man. It is "the Gospel of salvation," as it shows the way of escape, and gives us the means of deliverance. It is "the Gospel of peace," because it proposes the terms of reconciliation to a world in rebellion, and shows that every obstacle is now removed in the way of its enjoyment. This word of salvation was given by the Father to his Son, and by him to the apostles, and by them to the world, who beseech men in Christ's stead to be reconciled to God; for he has made him, who knew no sin, a sin-offering for us, that we might be made "the righteousness of God." They urged their plea under the direction of him who had "all authority in heaven and upon earth."

The terms of reconciliation are an immediate surrender, "body, soul, and spirit," to God, according to the Gospel they preached. To believe in Jesus as the Christ, the Son of the living God, with all the heart; to repent and to bring forth fruits worthy of the new life to which they are called; to confess him openly before men as their Lord and Christ; and to be buried with him in baptism, in order to rise in that new kingdom over which he reigns. These terms are enforced by all the arguments drawn from the love of God, and the helplessness of man; from his guilt, and exposedness to the wrath to come; by the long-suffering of God and his unspeakable pity; by the gift of his only-begotten Son, that we might live through him; by his life of sinlessness, of tenderness and love; by his deep humiliation, sufferings, and death; by the Cross and its agony, the grave and its ransom; by the grace which he offers, and the glories which he promises; by the reconciliation which he sends us, and the eternal shame and dishonor which await those who reject it.

The reconciliation will result, finally, not only in uniting together both Jews and Gentiles here on the earth, "by the blood of the Cross," into one body, but all things or persons, whether in earth or in the heavens; "the spirit of the just made perfect" in all ages; the redeemed of God out of every tribe, and tongue, and people under the whole heaven. Angels, who by their purity and holiness have only ministered to us as servants, shall unite with us as friends; and shall, once again and forever, share in our fellowship and partake of our joys; "that in the dispensation of the fullness of the times, he might gather together in one all things in Christ, both which are in heaven and on earth; even in him, in whom we have obtained an inheritance, being predestinated according to the purpose of him who worketh all things after the counsel of his own will."

Most fraternally
L B Wilkes.

LANCEFORD BRAMBLET WILKES.

THE subject of this sketch was born in Maury County, Tennessee, on the 24th of March, 1824. His paternal ancestors were English. His father (EDMUND), grandfather (JOHN), and great-grandfather (MINOR WILKES), were natives of Virginia. His grandfather moved to Middle Tennessee in 1810, and settled in Maury County. His father was the youngest son of a large family, was born in Franklin County, Virginia, in 1797, and was married, in 1819, to C. H. HOUSTON, second daughter of JAMES, the son of CHRISTOPHER C. HOUSTON. The maternal grandfather was of Scotch descent, and a native of Iredel County, North Carolina. The maternal grandmother was the daughter of DANIEL BILLS, of Surrey County, North Carolina, and was of Irish descent. In the spring of 1829, when the son was five years of age, the father left the State of Tennessee, and located in what is now Miller County, Missouri. In that new and growing country, L. B. WILKES spent his boyhood years. As there were few schools, and still fewer churches, within his reach at that time, his educational and church privileges were quite limited till he was twenty years of age. From 1844 to 1848 he spent the time in alternately teaching and attending the best schools accessible to him. During this time he attended an academy at Springfield, Missouri, and made considerable progress in the rudiments of an education.

It was only a short time before entering this academy that he first heard the Disciples preach. Those he heard were illiterate, and, as he thought, heretical in their religious views; and, to use his own language, he "despised them." But while attending the academy, he heard the Gospel preached in its fullness, simplicity, and beauty, by his relative, J. M. WILKES, and J. H. HADEN. Father HADEN, as he was familiarly called, was one of the best and wisest of the preachers of that country. His preaching had a great influence on the mind of the subject of this notice, who, having heard the truth as it is in Jesus, believed, and was immersed in James River, near Springfield, Missouri, on the second Lord's day in August, 1848, by J. M. WILKES.

10   (145)

In the spring of 1849 he entered Bethany College, West Virginia; but in the summer of the following year, at the urgent solicitation of Father HADEN, from whom he received temporary aid, he returned to Missouri, and, in 1852, graduated at the State University, then under the presidency of the distinguished JAMES SHANNON.

In 1853, at the request of the church at Hannibal, Missouri, he became its pastor; and, in February of the next year, he was married to Miss. R. K., youngest daughter of LEWIS BRYAN, of Palmyra, Missouri.

In 1854 he formed a partnership with Dr. W. H. HOPSON, in the management of "Palmyra Female Seminary;" and, in 1856, he was elected President of "Christian College," now presided over by J. K. ROGERS.

In 1860 he was again called to the church at Hannibal, Missouri, where he remained for five years, greatly beloved by the congregation for which he labored, and respected by all who knew him. In November, 1865, he located in Springfield, Illinois, which is his present field of labor.

Both as a preacher and teacher, Brother WILKES has been successful. True, he has never been remarkable for holding "big meetings," and having great success in the evangelical field, though his successes even here have been by no means small; but he has been eminently successful in developing a permanent growth among the Disciples, wherever he has labored. He succeeds better as an instructor of the head, than as a mover of the heart. And yet he is capable of using very powerful persuasive influence, though he seldom resorts to this method, preferring rather to present his subject in the strongest light to the calm judgment, and await the desired result, which, if not so certain, is always more satisfactory when obtained.

His mind is rigidly logical, and yields only to legitimate arguments. He has very strong and decided convictions, and although somewhat reserved in expressing himself on any mooted question, is, nevertheless, always perfectly willing to share the full responsibility of any position he may occupy, and, if necessary, will defend it in the face of all opposition. He is naturally, however, unostentatious, quiet in his general movements, and "seeks after those things which make for peace."

He is about six feet high, has light hair, blue eyes, a sallow complexion, and weighs about one hundred and sixty pounds. He is a close, laborious student, and this fact is clearly marked on his physical organization.

CHRIST'S PRECIOUS INVITATION.

BY L. B. WILKES.

"Come to me, all you that are weary and heavily burdened, and I will give you rest. Take my yoke upon you and learn of me; for I am meek and lowly in heart; and you shall find rest to your souls. For my yoke is easy and my burden is light."—MATT. XI: 28–30.

THIS passage does not say, nor does any one in the Scriptures, that Christ is to come to the sinner, but the sinner is to come to him. Religious teachers are, certainly, some of them, not a little in error on this point. The appliances used, in too many cases, in order to the conversion of sinners, intimate that there is a time to which the sinner is to look and for which he is taught to pray, when God will *incline* to him, when HE will be gracious. The sinner's effort is, of course, influenced by such teaching, to *induce* the LORD to have mercy, instead of *himself* becoming willing to submit, unreservedly and with the whole heart, to terms already plainly propounded, to which he is invited.

This error in practice is founded upon an error in theory. 1. It supposes that God is not, at all times, willing to accept the sinner, though he should come just as he ought. 2. That some work on the sinner's part is necessary to make HIM willing. But, in truth, God is at

(147)

all times willing.   His nature is love, and Jesus's nature is the same, fully the same.   Nor can we conceive what HE would be, if, at any time, he were unwilling to be merciful to a sinner.   One thing we can see clearly—he would not be the God of the Bible.   It would follow hence that we could have no premises from which to infer that any act on the sinner's part would induce willingness on HIS. All such works are, therefore, works of supererogation, based upon the commandments of men, and not upon the will of God.   Notice: I speak of *the* sinner, not *a* sinner, and of God's being willing to pardon the sins of such an one.   If it should be asked: Why, if God is really willing at all times to have mercy upon the sinner, does he not actually and at once have mercy upon all?   I reply: it is because he *can not*, not because he is not *willing*.   True, in a sense, God can not be willing to do what he can not consistently do.   While the sinner is impenitent God can not pardon him; can not *will* to pardon him.   It would be offering a premium for sin to do so.   But still God does will the salvation of every sinner, and he has also willed expressly the conditions upon which he saves.   Now that a given man is not saved, is not proof that God is unwilling to save him, while as yet the man fails of the conditions upon which the salvation is contingent.   But if it could be established that *no* conditions are imposed upon *man*, that God's will to that effect is alone the condition of the sinner's forgiveness, then it would follow, that, if a man is a sinner, it is because God is not willing to make him a saint.   But, for those who believe that the Scriptures express the will of God, *arguments* are not necessary. The plain statements and necessary implications of the sacred volume put the question to rest at once.   (See Ezek. xviii: 23; xxxiii: 11; 1 Tim. ii: 4, etc.)   The passage at the head—"Come unto me," etc., necessarily implies the willingness of Jesus to give rest, life, and salvation. It also informs us that though Jesus is willing, anxious, pleading, bleeding, and dying that the sinner might be saved, yet it is necessary, in order to find *rest*, to *come* and take the yoke divine.

When the faith of the preacher is settled, firmly settled, that God can not be made, nor wished, more ready or willing than he is already, to be merciful to the sinner, then his energies and earnest work will be spent in impressing upon the heart of the poor lost one the awful and calamitous nature of sin. Then will he point him to the Cross of Christ, the best possible expression of the heinous character of that which brought the Savior there. This he will do with earnestness, and with such manifest confidence that, if the sinner will yield in child-like faith and simplicity to the will of God, he shall in nowise be turned away, that he will have good reason to hope the best possible results.

It is implied in the words "Come to me," that Jesus and the sinner are apart. This separation is one suggesting a space, not that may be measured by yards, feet, and inches, but that must be reckoned by degrees of moral quality. Even the parties whom Christ addressed were not supposed to be absent from him by a literal space, but they were morally apart. Among men, we frequently find persons mingling together, whose hearts are not at all in harmony; who are morally wide apart. The mathematical and logical condition of persons and parties being one, of their being together morally—that they love the same thing, then will they love one another—being wanting, they can not be together. So it was of the parties before us. "The righteous Lord loves righteousness, and hates

iniquity; whereas the sinner loves iniquity, and hates righteousness." Hence were they apart. Now, before they can
be together, they must be alike; and ere this is possible,
they must change, one or both. But Jesus already occupies, morally, the position of righteousness, the rallying
point, so far as abstract principle is concerned, for all accountable intelligences in the universe. It follows that
there is no change to take place in him of the kind in
question; and since a physical change is out of the question, therefore no change at all. Hence the *sinner* must
change if he would be saved.

Sin is the cause of the separation. Of this God is not
the author. If he were, I can not see the reason for holding man responsible for it. If man is not responsible
for sin, then there can be no such thing as salvation; and
therefore, no Savior, and Jesus was wrongly named. Nor
shall I suppose that man is the *responsible* author, while
God is the *real* author of sin. That God should be the
real author of sin, but should so shift the responsibility of
it that man—an innocent party—must bear it, is revolting
to my common sense; is little, if any, short of the veri-
est blasphemy. Besides the reason of the case, which I
think I have with me, I have something infinitely better—
the Word of God. Paul says (Rom. v: 12): "Wherefore,
as by one man sin entered into the world," etc. Here it
is declared that sin came by *man*. To say that God is the
author of sin, in any sense, is, I think, far from the truth.
Some are inclined to make God in some way, or to some
extent, responsible for sin, since, say they, HE *permitted* it.
But I do not see that God did, in any proper sense of the
word, *permit* sin. To say that a person permits any given
thing, is to say that he could prevent it. Now, before
any one should conclude that God *permitted* sin, and is to

that extent responsible for it, he should see distinctly
that God could not, in harmony with his nature, with the
principles of his government and the nature of man, have
prevented its existence. That God's physical power is
adequate to the accomplishing of any purpose compatible
with his moral nature, I grant, is true. But that his
omnipotence would or could be exercised to accomplish
that which would be inharmonious with the principles of
his moral government, is not true. Before, then, we
should allow that God could have prevented sin, and
hence that he may have permitted it, we must see that in
so doing he would not have outraged any principles of
his nature or of his dealings with man. Such knowledge
would include a full view of *all* the principles of God's
moral government, which we ought not to presume to
have. But do we know any thing of God from which we
may infer certainly that he could not consistently have
prevented sin? The fact that sin is, to my mind, proves
that God could not have prevented it, and that, therefore,
he did not permit it. Again, if man was so made, or
circumstanced by the Maker, that he *must* do any given
act—*must*, from no matter what cause—I deny that it was
possible in such case that he sinned. The power without
him, not himself, was to all human reason really and re-
sponsibly the actor, while man should be regarded as only
the instrument, the machine. The man did not act; he
was *acted*, rather. The executioner of the criminal is not
held to be guilty of murder, only because he is not supposed to be the one who takes the life of his fellow, except in the sense that the machine thrashes the wheat.
As well may we say that the machine is the responsible
actor, as that man is, where he is *absolutely forced* to act.
I believe it is a dictate of conscience in every case, that,

where a man could not have avoided doing an act, he did not sin when he did it. This is a rule of law in the courts of every civilized nation, and savage too.

Now, if MAN *sinned* in the Garden—and the Bible says he did—and was responsible for it—and the Bible says he was, in that he was punished for it—it follows that *man* was the *real* doer of the deed, and the *responsible* doer, too, and that God, therefore, was not. It follows, also, that it was not *impossible* for man to have avoided the sin. But if man had such power in himself that *he* controlled the event—sin—it follows that it was not another's power that controlled it; that is, it follows that God could not have prevented sin and left man what he made him, and himself the God that he is. So if we allow, as we must, that the creation of man and the manner of his being are but the outcroppings of the Divine nature, we must conclude that the principles of God's government are such that he could not have prevented, and, therefore, did not permit man to sin. This same conclusion may be reached in a much shorter way, thus: God commanded man to not sin. Now, I may assume that God's will, which is the essential feature in his every command, has his entire omnipotence to execute it, so far as his moral government will allow. But his power *did not* prevent sin; therefore, it could not. And since he could not prevent sin, he did not permit it. Again, remembering that sin is the transgression of Law, it follows that God can not be responsible for it, either as causing it or permitting it, unless we suppose it possible for HIM to violate his own law.

That the sinner is the responsible agent for his sin, is argued from the fact that he is recognized as being able to come back, the way being opened, the reasons and motives being furnished, and the invitation being extended. That he is able, under these circumstances, to come, is proved from the fact that *Jesus calls* him, coupled with the fact that the Savior is too good to be so unkind as to tantalize the suffering one with a pressing invitation, to which he knows the sinner to be unable to respond. This tender language from the eloquent lips of the Crucified One is proof enough for me, that the poor, lost ones *can* come back.

May all persons come to the Savior in harmony with this call? I do certainly think that all may come, can come, and ought to come, provided they are the characters, and will comply with the conditions precedent to their coming. But I also think that there are persons or characters who are not included in this call; who, in their present condition, ought not or can not come.

I. The infant is not included for the reason: 1. That it is not capable of understanding the call; of receiving and acting upon it. Now, I reason that Jesus would not invite a human being to perform an act, for the doing of which he is wholly incompetent. That an infant, but a few days old, is entirely incapable of rendering the obedience implied, I shall not attempt to prove. It needs no proof. Therefore, the infant is not included. 2. But this conclusion must be true for another reason: It *need* not to come. Sin being a neglect, disregard, or violation of law, and the infant being entirely incapable of any one of these things, it has, hence, never sinned, and therefore needs no salvation *from sin*. Though it does need a Savior, it is not from *sin*. Salvation contemplates more than simply the remission of sins. It includes the redemption of the body, its resurrection, and preparation for the final and blessed state of the saved. The child, though not a sinner, needs a Savior for these reasons. Moreover, the

Lord declares that unless men shall "turn and become as little children, they shall not enter into the kingdom of heaven." And again: "Of such is the kingdom of heaven." The necessary implication from these sayings is, that the infant child is not a sinner, and needs not to come, and is not, therefore, included in the invitation.

A second class of persons not invited is the righteous. Jesus says: "I come not to call the righteous, but sinners to repentance." The "whole need not a physician, but they that are sick." I have long thought that the poorest excuse of the many offered by sinners for not coming to Christ is, "I am not good enough yet;" whereas it is precisely because they are sinners, great sinners, that they need to come. Such language, too, is presumptuous on their part. It implies that they feel themselves capable of, to some extent at least, fitting *themselves* for acceptably appearing before God for his favor. The more or the better prepared any sinner is for acceptable approach to the blessed Lord, the more plainly does he see and keenly feel that he is all unworthy, all unclean. I would not be understood as intimating that he has *no* preparation to make. Far from it. He has much of that to do, and it must be *thoroughly* done, else every attempt must be a failure. I only mean that he can not, *of himself*, make himself any less a sinner than he is; that he can not deduct from the aggregate amount of sins standing against him. But if, by the phrase, "good enough," he means only preparedness for *coming*, the *act* of *coming*, I make no objections. Let that preparation be well made. What this consists in, and its radical nature, shall be unfolded as we proceed.

A third class of persons not included in this invitation of the Savior is the infidel. "He that comes to God"—

and coming to Jesus Christ is the same thing—"must believe that he is, and that he is a rewarder of them that diligently seek him." (Heb. xi: 6.) "Without faith it is impossible to please God." "What is not of faith is sin." (Rom. xiv: 23.) From the first of these quotations we see that one essential condition of acceptable approach to God is faith. From the second, we see that faith is essential in every case in order to please God. Now, since no one would be invited to come who "must" not; and since no one would be invited to come who would not please God in coming; and since no one can please God without faith, it follows that no one without faith is included in this invitation of the Lord. In the last of these quotations we have a principle of broad and universal application. The apostle, having shown what acts would be sinful, and what would not, finally draws the conclusion that though an act should be of such a nature that it might be done or be left undone without sin, still, in either case, faith must necessarily accompany. I shall not try to prove that the stated principle is applicable in cases of purely a worldly nature. I apply it only to acts of *religious worship*. To all *these* it does certainly apply, if not to *all* human actions. Among those acts which the text does certainly include, is that one, or all those, by which the sinner comes to Jesus Christ, and takes his easy yoke upon him. Now, since the Lord Jesus could not, and therefore has not, invited any one to take a step or perform an act that would be sinful; and since it is shown that any act of worship or obedience to God, performed without faith, would be sinful, it follows that the *infidel* is not included in this invitation. The reasoning will be the same if we should suppose the words, "Come to me," etc., to be a command instead of an invitation. (Rom. x: 14.)

Paul says: "How, then, shall they call on him in whom they have not believed?" The answer evidently is, that it shall not, as it certainly can not in sincerity be done. It seems to me that the way from this orthodox, apostolic faith is not long nor tortuous to the conclusion which we would establish. Whether this text speaks of the simple vocal act of calling upon God, or whether it includes, as it most likely does, all that must be done in order to please God and secure his favor, there is one indispensable condition: *faith must first be had*. Now, I think it easy, leaving the intelligent hearer to exercise but a moment's reflection, to draw the conclusion that the infidel shall not, *can not* come to Jesus Christ. And what he shall not do, it is morally certain the Savior does not invite or command him to do. I leave those who instruct the sinner to call on God, in whom he does not yet believe, for faith, to settle the conflict which their practice involves, with both reason and the express word of God. There is one mode of escape from this awkward dilemma, to which resort is sometimes made. It is said that there are several *kinds* of faith; that while it is true that one kind, mere historic faith, is necessary to calling on God, still the faith which is unto salvation may be called for; that the calling may be, nay, *must be*, BEFORE this saving faith, and in order to it. The first objection that I make to this reply is, that it is not known to be true. The Bible says not one word about *kinds of faith*. It distinguishes between a dead and a living faith; but this is a distinction not of kinds of faith. It refers only to the fact that a faith that does not work is dead, but makes not even an intimation that there are *kinds* of faith. Secondly: But suppose that there *are* kinds of faith, is it known that the Apostle Paul had his eye upon a *mere historic faith*, a kind

of minor importance, which, though needed for calling on
God, is, nevertheless, not the faith which is essential to
salvation? This is not known to be true, *nor is it true*.
The faith of which Paul speaks, is that without which we
can not please God, that is unto salvation. This conclusion will become apparent by a brief reference to the
context: "The word is nigh thee, in thy mouth, and in
thy heart; that is, the word of faith which we preach; that,
if thou shalt profess with thy mouth the Lord Jesus, and
believe in thy heart that God raised him from the dead,
thou shalt be saved. For with the heart man believes
unto righteousness; and with the mouth profession is
made unto salvation." (Rom. x: 8–11.) Thus we see
(even if we must allow that there are *kinds* of that which
is philosophically and Scripturally a unit), that the faith
of which Paul speaks, is that by which we are justified;
that it is a faith of the *heart;* that it is the faith in order
to *salvation.* It is of this faith that the apostle speaks,
when, at the fourteenth verse, he says that a man *can not
call on God without it.* We therefore press the question
again: How can a man call on God *for it?*

A fourth class, not included in this invitation, is the
impenitent sinner. Though a man should have faith, if it
should not work to the breaking of his stony heart; if
it should not bring him in deep poverty of spirit and con-
trition of soul to Jesus, his faith is not of that *degree* necessary to his coming acceptably. This state of things is
not only possible, but it has actually existed. John xii:
42 says: "But yet many even of the rulers believed on
him; but, on account of the Pharisees, they would not
confess him, lest they should be put out of the Synagogue; for they loved the glory of men more than the
glory of God." Here we have persons who did actually

believe on HIM, but they lacked that *degree* of faith
that takes hold of the heart; hence, they would not confess him, as, in that condition, they ought not. In such
a state they could not draw near to the Christ. He would
spurn them from his presence. Such men will appear to
come when they may obtain the thing they want—the
glory of men. I fear that there are many such half-con-
verted souls in the Church. You will know them by
their fruits. They are hard to please. Having itching
ears, they are forever clamoring for teachers who will pan-
der to, and pamper their carnal appetites. They have no
gift for doing any earnest heart-work for God. They are
generally absent from prayer-meeting, and when there, they
have no heart to work. They are nearly always late at
church; and when there they occupy a seat as far from the
speaker as possible, lest his words of burning force should
set fire to their stubbly hearts, or unmask their worthless
and deformed souls. Let the glorious light of the knowledge of the blessed God flash around them, and beam
upon them, that they may be driven from the Church, or
to a speedy and deep repentance. Of all the classes mentioned, this one is most unprepared to come acceptably to
Jesus Christ. Like the Pharisees, which they are, they
are whited sepulchers, fair as to the exterior, but within
are full of rottenness and corruption.

We are now prepared to answer the question—Who may
come to Jesus Christ? This we do in the gracious terms
of the great Teacher: "Come unto me all you that are
weary and are heavily burdened." This language is not
ambiguous. No soul need be at a loss for one moment
in gathering its meaning. It means what it says, and
says plainly what it means. The sinner must *see* and feel
himself a sinner. This implies faith in Christ. For,

where no law is, there can be no sin; and where the law
is not *perceived*, sin can not be discovered. But the law
is seen to be law only when it is seen to emanate from
some rightful source, otherwise it is no more than idle
talk. Hence, if the sinner sees and feels himself to be a
sinner, it is because he has seen not only the law as LAW,
but that he sees the law-giver as LAW-GIVER; that he does
exercise *faith* in the law-giver. But, as already said, this
faith must work, must deepen, until the Gospel's light and
love shine upon the soul, revealing to the sinner's eye all
its enormous pollutions. His mind rests for a moment
upon the revealed beauty, purity, and deep loveliness of
Jesus's character and life, and especially of HIS sufferings
and "death for our sins, according to the Scriptures;"
and he feels to exclaim, "O wretched man that I am!"
Then he looks into his own sinful heart, and it is as
though he looked into the bosom of night itself. Every
pain that Jesus felt, which he now sees was for him, he
feels. Every groan of Gethsemane and of Calvary wrings
from his penitent and burdened heart an echo of grief—
deep heart-grief. Like the porter who has carried long
his burden, and is almost sinking under its weight, so is
he burdened by his sins. He is weary and heavily burdened. Now he may come, because *he* is invited to come.
Now, like the prodigal, he has come to himself, and may
arise and go to God, assured that HE will in nowise turn
him away. O that ministers, that all Christians, indeed,
may more faithfully and effectually point sinners to the
Lamb of God who takes away the sin of the world. Let
them be earnest as those who plead for life; nay, for something that is better than life. But it may be said: The
sinner should not "come" till he is drawn, divinely impelled, to "come." But find a sinner burdened and grief-

stricken, such as I have described, and you find one already drawn, divinely drawn, to God. No matter *how* it was done, the work is certainly and *rightly* done. But the Savior has told us *how* it is done. John vi: 44, 45, Jesus says: "No man can come to me, unless the Father, who sent me, should draw him: and I will raise him up at the last day. It is written in the prophets, And they shall all be taught of God. Every one that hears from the Father, and learns, comes to me." The lesson in this extract is simple and natural. 1. No one *can* come to Jesus whom the Father does not draw to HIM. 2. The sinner first hears, then learns—is thus drawn, and then comes to the Savior, with the assurance that HE will be raised up at the last day. With this agrees Paul, when he says: "So, then, faith comes by hearing, and hearing by the Word of God." The sublime story of the Cross is issued by Jehovah in a proclamation to sinful man. He *hears* and *learns* the glad tidings of the Father. He learns them, as near as may be, in all their unsearchable depths of meaning; in their bearings upon the questions of sin and holiness, of life and godliness. He learns that this Magna Charta of life and endless joy is so well attested by evidence homogeneous that there is simply no room for doubt. He believes, he feels, he trembles, at God's Word—he comes.

While Jesus was on earth, men might literally come to him, though this kind of coming is certainly not the one meant in our subject. But, now that Jesus is not here, where is the sinner to go? for I doubt not but that the lesson is in as full force to-day as when first pronounced. Where shall the sinner go? To *Jesus,* is the answer. With Simon Peter I would say: "Lord, to whom shall we go? Thou hast the words of eternal life." Anciently God dwelt in the Temple. It was his house. There, and not just anywhere, the true worshiper always found him. HE has a house now, also. 2 Cor. vi: 16 says: "For ye are the temple of the living God; as God said: I will dwell in them, and walk among them." This is spoken of the Church. Again, Paul says that the house of God "is the Church of the living God." (1 Tim. iii: 15.) In Eph. ii: 22 it is said of the Church that it is the "dwelling-place of God by the Spirit." In these Scriptures we are taught that the Church is the temple in which God lives.

So far as *place* on earth, for receiving and blessing the sinner, is concerned, I doubt not but that the Church is that place. The O. S. P. Confession of Faith says of the Church: "Out of which there is no ordinary possibility of salvation." So I believe. This Church in which God dwells by his Spirit, is the body of Christ. So teaches Paul (Eph. i: 22,) *et al.* It is from this stand-point— Jesus's capitol for Divine government *on earth*—that all his precepts and commandments, threatenings and promises, are issued. It is to the Church—Christ's body, the temple of God, the resident capitol of the Godhood, on earth—that the sinner must come, in order that he may come to Jesus Christ. All the spiritual blessings of Heaven are yea and amen to that man *who is in Christ Jesus.* This conclusion receives further, and, I think, final confirmation from Hebrews xii: 22, to close of the chapter:

"But ye are come unto Mount Zion, and unto the city of the living God, the heavenly Jerusalem, and to an innumerable company of ángels, to the general assembly and Church of the first-born, which are written in heaven, and to God the Judge of all, and to the spirits of just men made

11

perfect, and to Jesus the mediator of the new covenant, and
to the blood of sprinkling, that speaketh better things
than that of Abel. See that ye refuse him not that speaketh, for if they escaped not who refused him that spake
on earth, much more shall not we escape, if we turn away
from him that speaketh from heaven: whose voice then
shook the earth: but now he hath promised, saying, Yet
once more I shake not the earth only, but also heaven.
And this word, yet once more, signifieth the removing of
those things that are shaken, as of things that are made,
that those things that can not be shaken may remain.
Wherefore we receiving a kingdom which can not be
moved, let us have grace, whereby we may serve God acceptably, with reverence and godly fear. For our God
is a consuming fire."

From this passage, it will be seen that the Christians in
Paul's day were taught to believe that in being saved they
had "come" to Mount Zion, which, I believe, is literally
the Church. The term Church, on earth, may not *exhaust*
the idea in the expression Mount Zion; but I confidently
believe that it is *included therein*, else it is not true, as asserted, that the Hebrew Christians "have come to Mount
Zion." They had then come to the Church. Here they
met the blood of the covenant, the Mediator, the Savior,
the Spirit of adoption, the spirits of just men made perfect, and, finally, God, the judge of all. This coming and
meeting was, of course, not the *literal* or *physical* coming
and meeting of persons and parties, as when one man meets
another on a journey; but the Christians then and now,
in coming to the Church, the heavenly Jerusalem, enter
into spiritual and joyous union and communion with all
the transcendently glorious persons and privileges cata-

logued in all the holy oracles of God, so far as they accrue
to man in the flesh. Of course, when I speak of coming
to the Church, I mean " the Church of the living God."
There is, or seems to be, as great a mania for inventing
new churches as new machinery, and for about the same
reason—to please the dear people. The fashion-mongers
of infidel Paris are not more intent upon pleasing the carnal longings of their mammon-worshipers, than are creed-
mongers and sect-makers to adjust the Church to suit the
tastes of the world.

The *time* for the sinner to come is *now*. When this
life is in danger, man never fails to at once avail himself,
if possible, of every means of escape or recovery. How
strange that any one should be less careful of the true
life—of the life to come.

But I must state the result—rest. Freed from every
galling yoke of bondage imposed by the tyrant sin, the
soul lifts up its head toward the hills whence its help
comes. Now it spreads its wings for an upward flight,
and ever and anon it rises. The sense of rest, of the love
of God shed abroad in our hearts by the Holy Spirit which
is given to us, is the pearl of great price, the very climax
of blessing here below. With but little change, the following lines are in point:

> "One hour of passion, so sacred, is worth
>   Whole ages of heartless and wandering bliss;
> And, O, if there *be* an Elysium on earth,
>   It is this, it is this."

And when life has gone on apace, and death's dark, cold
shadows are settling around, then the soul needs rest, and
feels most blissfully the value of this gift Divine.

It is when the world recedes and disappears, that the soul whispers to itself: "Tell me, my soul, can this be death?"   If so, "O the pain, the bliss of dying."

"There remains a rest for the people of God."   "Let us strive to enter into that rest."

Truly Yours for

O. A. Burgess

OTIS ASA BURGESS.

O TIS ASA BURGESS was born August 26, 1829, in the town of
Thompson, Windham County, Connecticut. Thomas Burgess, one
of his paternal ancestors, joined the Pilgrim Colony in 1637. His maternal ancestors were of the same stock.

He remained in Connecticut till eight years of age, when he removed
to Norwich, Chenango County, New York. The next nine years of his
life were spent in attending school four months in the year, and working
the remaining eight months " amid the rocks and stumps of a sterile farm."
During this time, and when about fourteen, his mother died. This event
made a strong impression on his mind. His religious training had been
after the straightest sect of Calvinism, but his mother's death melted him
down so that he laid aside the "doctrine of the decrees," and began to
earnestly "seek after God." Accordingly he went through the entire
programme of the popular method of "getting religion" at the "mourners'
bench," but did not succeed. Others professed to have "got" it at the
same meeting, but all his prayers and tears were unavailing. He finally
concluded that he was either predestined to be damned, or given over to a
hardness of heart. In this terrible state of mind, he was led to almost hate
God, and utterly reject all revealed religion.

At the age of seventeen he entered "Norwich Academy," a flourishing
institution of its kind, about six miles from home. He remained here only
a few weeks, but made sufficient progress during his stay to teach successfully a common-school during the remaining portion of the year. In the
spring of 1847 he re-entered "Norwich Academy," and in fourteen weeks
finished the entire course, except the classics. In the fall of the same year
he removed to Metamora, Woodford County, Illinois, and taught school
till the summer of 1851. At this point he first heard of the Disciples.
They were vulgarly called "Campbellites," and spoken of in the most
disrespectful terms by all the religious parties in the place. Being already
a scoffer at religion, it did not require much effort for him to join in the
general outcry against the Disciples. He formed the most unfavorable

(165)

opinion of them, and was more than willing to believe that they were false teachers and mere pretenders. Of course, he did not go to hear their preachers, and, consequently, was under this misconception for some time. Finally, in the good providence of God, he was permitted to hear "Old Father Palmer," as he was familiarly called, preach the Primitive Gospel. The discourse was founded on Acts ii: 38, and was a clear and forcible presentation of the Gospel and its conditions. Concerning the effect of this discourse, Brother BURGESS says: "It was new, wonderful. It opened a new world. I could scarcely refrain from joining that day, but did not fully believe what he said. I had heard that the Disciples had a Bible of their own, and, believing this, thought Palmer quoted Acts ii: 38, from his own Bible. I was at least positive the text was not in mine." But it was there just as he had heard it; and when he went home, and saw it in his own Bible, with his own eyes, he could not get away from the truth, but confessed, and was immersed on the 21st of July, 1850. He soon formed a resolution to go to Bethany College, where he could hear, from Mr. Campbell's own lips, the great truths with which he was now partially acquainted. This resolution was carried into effect in the fall of 1851. Arriving at the college with only $4 50, his prospects for long remaining there were indeed gloomy, and would have discouraged any one with a less determined spirit. He secured boarding on trust, and, by constant perseverance and industry, was able to work his way through college— at one time teaching in the "Primary," at another laboring with his own hands at whatever work would best yield a support.

In 1854 he graduated, and returned to Illinois, and took charge of the Church of Christ in Washington, where he remained one year. He was next Professor in Eureka College a year, after which he divided his time between the churches in Metamora and Washington. In 1862 he took charge of the Church of Christ in Indianapolis, Indiana, where he has remained ever since. At this point his labors have been greatly blessed, the membership of the Church having more than doubled since his connection with it as pastor. He has always taken a deep interest in missionary work, and was at one time Corresponding Secretary of the A. C. M. S.

His chief characteristics are energy, persistence, and force. He is never idle, knows no such word as fail, and, in whatever department he may choose to labor, wields a decided and powerful influence. As a speaker, he is logical, pointed, and forcible, but gives little attention to the graces of rhetoric or the charms of elocution. And yet, if the true orator is the man who *carries his point*, Brother BURGESS need not be concerned about the tinseled drapery which is too often the principal staple of modern oratory.

WHAT MUST I DO TO BE SAVED?

BY O. A. BURGESS.

"Sirs, what must I do to be saved?"—ACTS XVI: 30.

IT is the purpose of the present discourse to answer, in the light of the New Testament, the above question. To exaggerate its importance would be impossible; to give it a wrong answer would be fatal to the best interests of humanity, and bring eternal ruin upon the individual soul. The question alike affects personal interests and human destiny, because the race must be lost unless the individual can be saved. The Scriptures are vast as eternity in their generalizations, yet so special that not one infant can draw the breath of life, not one sparrow fall to the ground, but they assure us of the Father's notice. By a simple analysis of the question now before us, it will be found to contain two distinct clauses; one looking to personal activity, expressed by the words "What shall I do;" the other looking to entire passivity, expressed by the words "that I may be saved." These two will be found to contain not simply the principles involved in the salvation of a certain Philippian jailer, but those involved in the salvation of every man from that day to this. If a further analysis of the question be made, it would be eminently proper to emphasize the word *do:* "What must I DO?"

This becomes the more obviously just and necessary, because, amid the Babel ideas of salvation, the words "think,"
"believe," "feel," "enjoy," *et al.*, are almost universally
substituted for the word DO, whereby many are led astray,
and very few trembling sinners are ever truly answered the
momentous question involving their salvation; whereby
also many of the so-called saints are in great doubt and
perplexity a large part of their lives, because the road they
travel being life-long, they are tremblingly awaiting the
end, to know if they are in the right way; whereas, it was
their most gracious privilege to have certainly known at
the beginning; and this they would have done, had they
been answered the question according to Christ, and not
according to men.　　But before the question as to what the
sinner must *do* can be truly answered, the word "saved,"
in the second clause, must be well understood.　What,
then, is salvation, and in what respect, or from what, is any
human being to be saved?

Of course, it will not be necessary to pause here, to note
any cavils that may arise with reference to the special case
in hand; for, if any one should so far forget the candor and
fairness necessary in the discussion of any question, and
particularly one of such grave import, as to affirm that the
jailer desired simply to be saved from punishment, because
the prison-doors were open, or from danger, because there
was an earthquake, such an one need only be reminded
that the sequel shows entirely another state of facts; shows,
indeed, that the jailer had only been aroused by these
things to comprehend his own situation, and, to some good
extent, the character of the men whom he had imprisoned;
and that, therefore, he appealed to them in their character
as ministers of Jesus Christ; and his willing and immediate compliance with the terms of their answer to his

question shows, beyond honorable dispute, how easy of understanding, and how easy of application, was the Gospel for the salvation of that sinner, and, therefore, for any other sinner.

But from what is man to be saved? If this were to be answered in the light of the religion of the present day, wherein the uprising and outflowing of joyful emotions is to be taken as both the condition and proof of religious life, then it could be supposed that to become a Christian, or "get religion," is to be saved from all "the ills that flesh is heir to." It may be well to answer the question first negatively, and ascertain from what man is not to be saved. The following may be safely affirmed: Christ does not propose to save man from the sorrows of this life, for the righteous are often most cast down and afflicted; nor from the poverty of this life, for the wicked wax rich, while the righteous beg bread; nor from temptations, for himself was tempted of the devil; nor from death, for Paul and Nero alike go back to dust; nor from eternal judgment, for every one must appear before the judgment-seat of Christ, to give an account of the deeds done in the body. From these specifications, showing what men are not saved from, it might, almost in great alarm, be asked: Pray, then, from what are they saved? The first direct and unmistakable declaration on this subject may be found in the words of the angel to Mary: "Thou shalt call his name Jesus, for he shall save his people from their sins." This declaration was never changed or modified. If Christ made special cases of salvation while he was on earth, it was only to demonstrate his ability and willingness to perform the great salvation. The great object before him was salvation from sin. Of this the prophets spoke; for this John the Baptist prepared the way, saying, "Behold the Lamb of God that taketh away the sin of the world." Toward this the whole life of Christ tended, and for the consummation of this even his life was offered up. Not an offering burnt upon Jewish altar, not a lamb bled by the hand of Jewish priest, that did not look toward the offering of an acceptable sacrifice for the forgiveness of sin. Whatever details of doctrine may hereafter appear, here, at the very threshold of every religious inquiry, stands the unalterable truth, that without the shedding of blood, there is no remission of sin. If, therefore, the central idea in the offering of Christ was the shedding of his blood for the remission of sin, it follows that the central idea in the salvation of man is salvation from sin.

There are now two features in the question of salvation from sin, which deserve particular attention: these are salvation from the effects of sin already committed, and salvation from the overt act of committing sin. It must be apparent to the careful observer that the blood of Christ applies primarily and principally only to the former, and only incidentally to the latter. Incidentally, because to one already washed from the stain of sins past, there is supposed to be given a strength to resist sin; a strength which comes through a knowledge of Christ, and a trust in his name. And it can only be when this strength is lost through lusts of the flesh, weakness of faith, or general inattention to the means of grace, that such an one washed becomes, in the ordinary sense, a sinner, and has need again of the cleansing power of the blood of Christ. This brings the question, beyond dispute, to apply to the sins of the past; and to this Paul bears testimony, saying: "God hath set forth Christ to be a propitiation through faith in his blood, to declare his righteousness for the remission of the sins that are past, through the forbearance of God." This gives the true initial point from whence all observations are to be made touching the salvation of a sinner, and shows in clear light, and unmistakable terms, that when the solemn question comes— "Sirs, what must I do to be saved?" it is equivalent to the inquiry: What must I do to be saved from, or receive forgiveness of, my past sins. This may seem reducing the question to even too narrow limits. If such a thought arise, it will be very readily removed by a few simple questions, such as, Why do men need salvation at all? The answer: Because of sin. Why is man alienated from the life of God? The answer: On account of sin. Why do you fear the judgment of God? Invariably and always the same answer: Because of sin. If, then, man be freed from sin, what need he fear? Not the ills of this life, for, though he must bear them, Christ will give him strength; not the power of the devil, for, though tempted by him, Christ is mightier than the devil; not the grave, for, though he must slumber in it, Christ has lighted its darkness, and broken its bonds; and surely not the future judgment, for, though he must stand there, Christ is his shield and his eternal defense. In a word, if man be freed from sin, life and death, time and eternity are all his, for he is Christ's, and Christ is God's. "Sirs, what must I do to be saved"—from my past sins?—is a question, therefore, of such vast proportions and infinite import, that in it is more of human weal or woe than by the same number of words can otherwise be uttered by human lips.

With the true scope and intent of the word "saved," as used in the text, now clearly marked out, the real question, "What must I do?" may be considered. It has already been intimated that the force of this question is often lost, just at the time its true use is most needed, by the substitution of other terms for the word *do*. To show that this word is not the accident of occasion, or the creature of the caprice of man, let the Scriptures testify. On one occasion three thousand cried out, saying: "What shall we *do?*" Paul himself, when met by the Savior, inquired what he should *do?* And the blessings of God, in the dispensations of the past as well as the present, are pronounced upon those who *do* his commandments. It having already been shown that the salvation spoken of, is a salvation from sin, it will plainly enough appear that whatever the sinner is called upon to *do*, is to be done in order to that salvation. One of two things will, therefore, follow: there must be something definite in form or doctrine, in the observance of which the sinner may know his sins are forgiven, or the answer may depend upon the ignorance or caprice of him to whom the question is addressed. If the latter be true, revelation may be set aside; for if a preacher, "on the spur of the moment," may give such answer as seemeth good in his own eyes, all revelation on that point would be a work of supererogation, a proposition so manifestly absurd and wicked that it should but be mentioned in order to be rejected; and yet with its manifest absurdity, it is the system at the present time most constantly practiced upon among those attempting to answer the question, "What must I do to be saved?" On the other hand, if there be a definite scriptural answer, those receiving and acting upon a *wrong* answer, their feelings and imaginations to the contrary notwithstanding, will fail to receive the pardon of their sins.

It is now to be affirmed that the Scriptures do contain an explicit answer to the question in the text; that this applied in the days of apostolic teaching equally and alike to all; that whatever elements entered into the answer as given to one sinner, entered into it as given to every sinner; and that, as Christ has not changed his laws, the same answer should be given to an inquiring sinner to-day. If it now be asked, what are the elements which make up a Scriptural answer to the question, "What must I do to be saved?" this is the reply:

1. Faith in the Lord Jesus Christ. 2. Repentance toward God. 3. Immersion into the name of the Father, and Son, and Holy Spirit.

These, it will be shown, enter into each and every individual case; and that whenever the express mention of any one or more of these is omitted, that very omission will be found as proof that those elements have already entered into the occasion, and accomplished their work. It will be observed in passing, too, that there was little or no delay; that, immediately upon hearing the terms of salvation, they were complied with, and the promised pardon realized. It is true, indeed, that God requires fruits worthy of repentance; but it is equally true that he has graciously given the poor sinner the privilege of offering a broken spirit and a contrite heart, as richer than the pains of penance, and a willing obedience as more precious that the fat of rams.

A few words concerning each of the three above propositions separately.

1. *Faith in the Christ.* It is much to be regretted that, at the very first step toward a religious life, the inquirer is met by the disputes of theology and the subtleties of metaphysics, until he almost calls in question either the reality of religion itself, or the sincerity of those who profess it. The great question of faith has not escaped these snares. The tendency of the human mind to search

for hidden causes, trace remote results, and attempt deep diving, when the truth rests in clear and beautiful light just upon the surface, all lend obscurity and darkness, rather than dispel the clouds. Faith, for instance, is held as a sort of creature of anatomy, liable at any time to receive the theological dissecting-knife; and, as a student in medicine is not supposed to understand the human system until he has dissected and separately examined every part of that system, so it is held that man may not have "evangelical faith" until he understands its firstly, secondly, etc. How strongly this contrasts with the simple Scriptures, three or four of which will give the key to the whole subject of faith:

"These are written that you might believe that Jesus is the Christ, the Son of God, and believing, you might have life through his name."—*John.*

"With the heart man believeth unto righteousness."—*Paul.*

"Faith without works is dead, being alone."—*James.*

Here it must be seen that faith is comprehended in few words. It has its object, Christ, and testimony that Christ may be believed in; its subject, man, with motives before him to induce him to believe; and its action or works, else it is dead, being alone; and it thus at once and forever lifts itself above the doubtful issues of intellectual combat, or the *dicta* of grave and reverend seniors, to that sublime height where, amid the pure and serene light of its Divine home, it may make its appeal to the *heart* of man, and offer him the deathless joys of the new and better Paradise of God. And this word *heart* simply signifies all the strength of intellect, all the warmth and depth of the emotions, and all the services of the life. So faith simply says to the inquiring sinner, Lay hold on

Christ with your whole heart, and surrender to him your whole life.

2. *Repentance toward God.* Repentance, like faith, is easy of apprehension when freed from the mysticisms of the schools. Repentance may be stated thus: Repentance is a sorrow for past sins, and such a sorrow as impels the sinner to turn away from those sins, and sin no more. Whatever terms may be used to explain or expand this statement, they will not add to its value, or increase its force. It may be urged, for example, that there should be a godly sorrow for sin; yet what sorrow can be more godly or more heart-felt than that which turns the sinner away from his sins to sin no more? God does not require penance of the sinner. The sooner, therefore, he ceases to sin, the sooner he may cease his sorrow; and as God desires joy to fill the heart, it is evident that repentance should be a speedy work, so that the man may dry his tears and rejoice in God.

But repentance is said to be "toward God." This is eminently proper, because his law has been broken by the sinner, and his character as a law-maker thereby challenged; for whether man will so acknowledge it or not, it is most certainly true that, whenever any law is broken, the immediate effect of that transgression is to call in question the ability or goodness of the law-making power. It is saying to that power, we will take the law into our own hands; we will be a law unto ourselves. Nor will it change the issue to complain that the law is based simply in authority; for there can be no higher test of obedience than by the simple recognition of authority. But whether the sinner be regarded as violating a law of moral qualities, or a law absolute, in either case he must be held as having committed the gravest of offenses against

God, and, therefore, his early and sincere repentance should be "toward God."

3. *Immersion into the name of the Father, Son, and Holy Spirit.* Of this it need only be said, it is the illustrative sequence of the above arguments. It places man in position to know for himself whether he will or will not surrender himself without reserve, and without conditions, to the authority of an absolute law-giver. And this test is put in the form of an immersion, in order that the entire burial of the body may show the entire giving up of body, soul, and spirit to Christ; and, whereas, no other single act can do this, so no other mode, institution, covenant, law, ordinance, commandment, or by whatever other name things or principles may be designated, can, by a single act, bring the penitent sinner into relation with Father, Son, and Holy Spirit. The ordinance, therefore, must not only be immersion, but immersion into these three names.

It only now remains to be shown, that the apostles of the Savior taught every man or woman asking what they must do to be saved, to believe in the Lord Jesus Christ, repent of their sins, and be immersed into the name of Father, Son, and Holy Spirit. Let the case in hand, from which the text is taken, be the first. The jailer at Philippi, but a few hours ago, was nearly or altogether ignorant of the character of Christ and the mission of his apostles; and, under the command of his superiors, united, doubtless, with a will of his own, he had inflicted needless severity of punishment upon Paul and Silas, and thrust them into the stocks. He knew little till that night of the faith of Christ. It was, therefore, but the dictate of common sense, as well as Scripture order, that faith should be the first thing preached to him. As the preaching proceeded, the simple narrative states that "the Word of the Lord" was preached unto the jailer and those in his house. The same hour of the night, the jailer was immersed. Now, it is to be admitted, that in the narrative repentance is not mentioned. To this apparent neglect of inspired men to present an element of the Gospel so important in the work of salvation, there may be two answers: first, the doctrine of repentance is held by all religious people to be of such consequence that an inference in its favor in this case might be presumed, and the concurrent assent of such would be, as is often done, taken by the inquirer as sufficient evidence of its necessity; second, and without this mere *argumentum ad hominum*, it is the true argument, simply to remind the querist or objector that "the Word of the Lord" was preached to the jailer, and that repentance was an integral part of "the Word of the Lord," since the Lord himself had commanded that repentance and remission of sin should be preached in his name among all nations.

Paul and Silas could not, therefore, have been true to their Master on that occasion without preaching the entire Gospel. The history of the jailer now stands thus: That faith was preached to him, is known by positive declaration of Scripture; that repentance was preached to him, is known by inference amounting in effect to demonstration; and that immersion was preached, is also known by declaration of Scripture, for he was immersed the same hour of the night. To determine the immediate effect of all this upon the jailer as touching his question, "Sirs, what must I do to be saved?" the Scriptures declare that he rejoiced, believing in God with all his house; and, if rejoicing is to be taken as an evidence of pardon, as so commonly held, or as properly held, the effect of the

12

knowledge of pardon, then, in either case, it must be conceded that the jailer obtained, the same hour of the night,
just the salvation for which he asked.

Here the whole subject of this discourse might be
rested, in the confident assurance that, as the Scriptures
can not contradict themselves, the answer to a sinner at
Philippi would be equally good in any other latitude or
longitude of the world; and the answer, because eighteen
hundred years old, is more than eighteen hundred times
better than answers of more modern date and more popular fashion, its very antiquity taking it into the purity
of apostolic teaching. But it has been promised to be
shown that the other cases of the New Testament contain
the same elements in answer. Let the attention, then,
next be turned to Acts ii: 37, 38. Here, in effect, is the
same question—What must we do? The answer, properly enough, begins with repentance. Faith is not mentioned. Here, too, the *argumentum ad hominum* might be
resorted to. Every body holds faith necessary to salvation; and, therefore, every body will hold that faith was
in some manner connected with this occasion, though not
mentioned. The solution is, they were pricked in their
hearts, and thus gave, in the estimation of the apostles,
sufficient evidence of faith; and, without wasting words
on learned disquisitions on faith, its parts or philosophy,
the apostles moved right forward, commanding every one
of them to repent and be immersed. In this they were
promised the pardon of their sins, which, obeying, they
received, as evinced by their rejoicing and gladness. In
this, as before, it is found that faith, repentance, and immersion were preached in answer to the question, "What
shall we do to be saved?" and that, without delay, the

terms were accepted, the salvation obtained, and their hearts made glad.

Let Paul's conversion come next. He asked directly of the Lord what he should *do*. The Lord honored him with no other answer than to go into Damascus, and there it should be told him. Then the Lord sent to him Ananias, who made a long sermon very short, by simply commanding him to Arise and be immersed. Paul obeying, straightway received his sight, ate his food, and was told without delay to preach the faith he once labored to destroy. In Paul's case, doubtless, above all others, the tricks of the sophist could be brought to bear, to show that nothing but immersion was preached to him; and thus give a far more plausible plea for salvation by water alone, as the Christians are sometimes slanderously reported as saying, than could be found for others in the plea for salvation by faith alone. But the Christians make no such plea. Paul, like others, had received, on his way to Damascus, abundant evidences on which to build a faith in Christ. He had, in the very blindness with which he was stricken, a clear vision of his sins, of which he at once repented. There remained but one thing to save him from his past sins, and that Ananias immediately announced—Arise and be immersed. It is not to be doubted but Ananias might have discoursed eloquently on faith in all its parts; on repentance in all its emotions; but no such work was needed. The discourse that was needed was given, was obeyed, the salvation obtained, and the great question, "What must I do?" again answered in the same terms, "Believe, repent, and be immersed."

It will now be proper to point out the chief characteristic on account of which these three instances have been made representative. It is this: that at whatever point the preaching was needed, that being determined by the facts in the case, *just at that point the preaching began.* Thus, with the jailer, it began with faith, and ended with immersion; with the three thousand it began with repentance, and ended with immersion; and with Paul, it began and ended with immersion. In one of these, the mention of faith is omitted; in another, the mention of repentance; and in the other, the mention of both faith and repentance. Now, it has particularly been shown that these were not absent in fact because absent in name; and this, too, not because any body doubts their presence, but in order to show the proper argument for their presence, viz., that "the Word of the Lord" was preached; for while, by a common consent, the sectaries admit the presence of faith and repentance, even by remotest inference, they are equally ready to exclude immersion, though it be plainly mentioned. The burden of the argument, therefore, has been to repudiate the mere common consent plea, and show that if "the Word of the Lord" can not be preached without preaching faith and repentance, neither can it be without preaching immersion. And every candid person must admit that we have the argument clearly, since, in the three cases already used, or in those about to be used, the mention of faith and repentance is often omitted, the mention of immersion never.

No matter now which way the attention be turned, these principles remain unchanged. If the Ethiopian be inquired of, he will simply narrate that while reading Isaiah, without so much as knowing whether the prophet spake of himself or some other man, a preacher came along, and, beginning at the same Scripture, preached Christ. Not a word of the details of the sermon is given, but a result reached is plainly stated: they came to a certain water, and the Ethiopian was immersed. If the Samaritans be inquired of, they simply respond that they believed Philip preaching the things concerning the kingdom of God and the name of Jesus Christ, and were immersed, both men and women. The city of Corinth gives the same response, for, many of the Corinthians hearing, believed and were immersed. Sister Lydia's heart is opened, and immersion immediately follows. If Peter and the Gentiles are sought after, that bold apostle is found demanding who dare forbid water for a grand immersion. And if the palaces of the Eternal City, so long echoing to the tread of the mighty Cæsars, be laid under contribution, behold, Paul is there, though in clanking chains, declaring that every Roman that received Christ had been immersed into him. Galatia and Colosse add their testimony, until, like colossal monuments, these truths tower to the very heavens, more splendid than gilded palaces, and more durable than marble and brass.

To make now a brief note of the negative of this whole subject, there will be found but one argument that ever has assumed even the show of plausibility; this is in the question, "What shall I do?" as addressed by a certain young man to the Savior. Various modifications of the same objection are found, as in the thief on the cross. These, however, will all receive the same answer. If, indeed, the answer which the young man received be taken as the standard, it would be quite as well to desist from all efforts to save men; for a part of that answer was, "Sell all thou hast, and give it to the poor." Such a method of salvation failed even in that case, though it was received from the Savior's own lips. There must be something wrong, either in the answer or in its application; the former can

not be true, for the Savior could not fail to suit the occasion; the mistake, therefore, must consist in attempting
to make a general application of a special case, for nowhere
afterward did Christ command that method of salvation
to be preached. The same is true of the thief on the cross,
and all similar cases of special salvation. The answer
to the whole objection is, that while Christ was on earth,
he used his power to forgive sin, as his power to raise the
dead, just as it seemed good in his own eyes; but, being
about to depart from earth, never more in person to minister to the wants of men, he gave to his apostles a short
and simple law, which should be equally applicable to the
beggar and the prince, and in the acceptance of which all
might be saved. This law he commanded them to preach
in all the world, and this law contained the three terms,
Faith, Repentance, and Immersion. If, therefore, any man
or woman will inquire "Sirs, what must I do to be saved?"
let them consider for themselves how far their desire for
salvation has already led them; if so far that they believe
in Christ, let them repent; if so far that they have repented, let them be immersed; and let this be done according to Scripture example, immediately, that they may know
they are pardoned, and be filled with joy and gladness.
Moreover, let the servants of Christ, to whom such a
momentous question may be addressed, consider well the
occasion and surroundings, and, if like the jailer, there be
an ignorance of Christ, let faith first be preached, but immerse, if need be, the same hour of the night; if like the
three thousand, they already believe, preach repentance,
and immerse the same day; but if like Paul, there be but
one thing lacking, preach that one thing, and if the inquirer be as honest as Paul, he will be immersed straightway.

Thus, in any and under all circumstances, when a sinner cries out, "Sirs, what must I do to be saved?" the answer, in clear and explicit terms, is always at hand: "Believe on the Lord Jesus Christ, repent of, and turn away from, your sins, and be immersed into the name of the Father, Son, and Holy Spirit."

Happy is that minister of Christ, who knoweth to give such an answer; and thrice happy that man or woman honest enough and humble enough to receive and act upon it, for they shall receive remission of sins, and rejoice with joy unspeakable and full of glory.

May the day be not far distant, when the jargon of doubtful creeds, and the disputes of zealous sectaries shall be displaced by the Divine symmetry of heaven's own truth, and the earnest pleadings of a united Church; when salvation shall flow as a river, and all the ends of the earth be saved.

Very respectfully,
Geo W Sougan

GEORGE W. LONGAN.

F EW of our readers, outside of Missouri, are familiar with the name of
this excellent brother. His labors have been confined chiefly to his
native State, and even there, seldom, if ever, operating beyond the southern
portion. Although he has contributed some able articles to our periodicals, these have generally appeared without his proper signature, and, consequently, have done little or nothing toward introducing his name to the
people. He is esteemed, however, by those who know him, as one of the
ablest and most useful men among the Disciples in the State where he resides.

GEORGE W. LONGAN was born in the town of Charleston, Missouri,
December 31, 1819. Missouri was then a Territory, and as he has always
resided there, he is quite familiar with the history of that young, but
rapidly-growing State.

His parents removed from Virginia to Kentucky, and thence to Missouri. They were poor, and went to Missouri soon after their marriage,
in order to identify their fortunes with that promising country. The
father was a member of the first Legislature of the State after its admission
into the Union. Reared in a frontier country, where there were no colleges, and few good schools of any grade, the son had little or no opportunities to obtain a first-class education. But, by diligent application to study,
he acquired a fair knowledge of English, and also made considerable progress in Latin; so that he is now a respectable scholar, notwithstanding the
difficulties under which he has had to labor. He is emphatically a *self-
made* man, and has all the vigor, zeal, and independence that usually characterize that class of men.

His parents were Baptists, but, after a careful examination of the Word
of God, he embraced the views of the Disciples, and was baptized by the
well-known evangelist, ALLEN WRIGHT, in 1844. In forming his religious
convictions, he was much indebted to the writings of ALEXANDER CAMP-
BELL, and especially the translation of the New Testament, which he published with prefaces, annotations, etc. Referring to his religious position,

Brother LONGAN says: "When I became a Disciple, I stood alone among my relations; not one of them, so far as known to me, occupying the same ground." His only uncle on his father's side was a pioneer preacher among the Baptists, of great natural ability and large influence.

He commenced preaching about two years after his immersion, but for a number of years was very much circumscribed in his labors, having to toil on a farm or in the school-room to support his family, preaching only Saturdays and Sundays, and that almost entirely at his own expense. In speaking of those discouraging times, he says: "The brethren were very few in the section where I then lived. I remember when brother WILLIAM WILLIAMS, who still lives, was the only advocate of the ancient order of things in the bounds of my acquaintance—perhaps in several counties."

More recently he has devoted himself almost exclusively to the preaching of the Gospel, and although he has never been noted as a successful recruiter, his labors have not been in vain in the Lord. He has done much toward giving permanent success to the cause in Southern Missouri, and is justly regarded as one of the ablest preachers in the State. His present field of labor is Sedalia, Dresden, and Warrensburg.

As a speaker, he addresses the judgment rather than the passions; is more of a logician than a rhetorician or elocutionist; is devoted to the primitive Gospel, and has no faith in innovations or improvements in religion. As a close, logical reasoner, with either the pen or tongue, he has few superiors in the ranks of the Disciples, though his natural modesty, as well as the unfavorable circumstances by which he has been surrounded, have kept him from becoming very generally known.

THE CONDITIONS OF THE GOSPEL REASONABLE.

BY G. W. LONGAN.

"For the Jews ask for a sign from heaven, and the Greeks demand a system of philosophy; but we proclaim a Messiah crucified, to the Jews a stumbling-block, and to the Greeks a folly; but to the called themselves, whether they be Jews or Greeks, Christ, the power of God and the wisdom of God."—1 Cor. 1: 23, 24, (Conybeare's Trans.)

JESUS, the Son of God, is the great central personage of the Divine history. All human characters, however great and good, are subordinate to him, and their names appear in the Sacred Volume only because of the relationship they bear to him in his fleshly lineage, or in order to the better unfolding of his mission of mercy to the world. So the Cross of Christ is the grand central idea in the System of Redemption. Every other conception in the wide range of revealed truth is subordinate to this, and is more or less important, as it is more or less closely related to this grand center of the remedial economy. "Christ," the "Cross of Christ," and "Christ crucified," are to be taken as comprehensive generalizations, including every precious truth which enters into that wondrous system revealed upon the blessed pages of the Book of books. To preach "Christ," or "the Cross of Christ,"

(187)

or "Christ crucified," is, therefore, to preach the Gospel in its broadest amplitude. "Philip began at the same scripture, and preached to him Jesus. And as they went on their way, they came to a certain water, and the eunuch said, See, here is water; what doth hinder me to be baptized?" Here we learn that "to preach Jesus" is to preach the whole Gospel. When Philip preached Jesus, the eunuch learned that it was his duty not only to believe, but even to be baptized. The expressions "Christ" and "Christ crucified," in the text, are clearly to be understood in the same way. They stand for the entire Gospel. Of this, I presume to say, there can be no doubt whatever. Substituting, therefore, for "Christ crucified" its proper equivalent, Gospel of Christ, and omitting, without violence to the meaning of the apostle, what is unnecessary to my present purpose, we have the following somewhat startling proposition distinctly enunciated, viz.: The Gospel of Christ is both the power and wisdom of God. To the latter affirmation in this apostolic deliverance I propose to call your attention in this discourse. I shall accept the apostle's words in the fullness of their meaning. I am troubled with no skeptical misgivings on this question. I believe, with my whole heart, that the Gospel of Jesus Christ is the wisdom of the infinite Jehovah. I shall proceed to give some of the reasons for this faith.

The created universe, in all its visible, tangible, substantive forms, is merely phenomenal. Change is written all over it in legible characters by the finger of the Almighty himself. The mighty forces which are ceaselessly working throughout the domain of matter only obey his behests, and accomplish the counsels of his will. That will is law to the farthest bound of the creation, and in that which is purely material has never been disobeyed. Laws which are but the outgoings of the will of Jehovah, underlie all the sublime and wondrous manifestations beneath us, above us, and around us. It is impossible for a thinking man to escape the conclusion that God works throughout nature by laws as eternal as are the foundations of his own throne. The laws of mind are no less fixed and unchangeable than the laws of matter. The principles which form the basis of God's moral government are as immutable as those by which he determines the manifold phenomena of the physical creation. Whatever is reducible to necessary principles is, therefore, in harmony with the highest wisdom. If, then, the Gospel of Christ, in all its provisions and in all its requirements, is based upon unchanging principles, and springs up necessarily from the very relations which subsist between God and men, for whom it is intended, then is God's wisdom in giving the Gospel vindicated, and our obligation to obey it certainly established. The enlightened Christian does not fear an appeal to reason. He does not deify reason, and fall down and pay it idolatrous homage; he does not depend upon it for the knowledge of God, nor dare to rationalize into myth and fable the teachings of the Divine Word; but grounding the highest and holiest beliefs of his heart upon that Word, and accepting every sentence and every syllable as divine, he does not fear either the logic or the laugh of any daring infidel who may assault the faith that sustains his soul. He believes that as right reason is from God, and is one of his best gifts, so God's Gospel, though confessedly above reason, is, nevertheless, in perfect harmony with its most exalted demonstrations.

If these premises are true, then every thing in the Gospel has its reason. Nothing has been done without an end, and nothing is required without a necessity. When God sent his Son into the world, there was a reason for it; there was an end to be gained that could not be gained in any other way. When Jesus died, there was a necessity for it. It was not merely an arbitrary arrangement, that might as well have been dispensed with as not. God does nothing without a reason; so in the conditions of the Gospel there is a reason for every thing that God requires. There is no condition imposed without a corresponding necessity. God does nothing without a reason himself, and demands nothing without a reason from men. If the Gospel of Jesus Christ is reasonable, then it is adapted to man as he is; to man in his present attitude to God's throne, and law, and government; to man in his relations to time and to eternity. Such an adaptation demonstrated, and the Gospel is shown to be Divine, and its wisdom vindicated as the wisdom of God.

The Gospel scheme is built upon the assumption that men, in their present relations to God, are sinners. There is no attempt in the Bible to develop this conclusion by logical processes or philosophical speculation. The first preachers of the Gospel proceeded in this matter very much as Moses did in opening up to the world the grand drama of the creation. He does not philosophize to establish the existence of Jehovah, but breaks upon us suddenly with the startling announcement, " In the beginning God created the heavens and the earth." So the apostles approach men just as though it were a potent and undeniable fact that all are sinners. They appeal to universal consciousness, and all hearts respond to the appeal, as the eye to light, or the ear to sound.

The Gospel is intended for sinners. It is adapted only to sinners. If, therefore, men are not sinners, they do not need the Gospel. If men are not lost, or in danger of being lost, they do not need a Savior. If men are not guilty, they do not need forgiveness. Come, then, scoffing infidel, laughing at the wisdom of God with heaven-defying presumption, as though it were worse than human folly, come, meet us now at this first step in our investigations, and overturn the very foundation upon which the Gospel rests. Deny, if you will, that you are a sinner. Let there be no faltering here. Meet the issue like an honest man. The day is coming when the secrets of that heart can no longer be buried in the mysterious depths of your own consciousness. Be candid, speak out, and let heaven witness the integrity of your avowal.

There never was a heart thus questioned that answered honestly, but the answer was the same. "There is none righteous, no not one; there is none that understandeth; there is none that seeketh after God; they are all gone out of the way; they are altogether become unprofitable; there is none that doeth good, no not one." Such is the universal proposition that underlies the Gospel of Jesus Christ. If this be not true, the Gospel is a delusion, and Jesus an impostor and cheat. But this true, and we have this the first link in that grand chain of adaptations that demonstrates the Gospel to be divine, and vindicates the wisdom of God in the redemption offered to the world. God is the rightful Lawgiver in the universe which he has made. All men on earth, as well as all angels in heaven, are under law to him. The eternal distinction between right and wrong has been disregarded. Our entire race has trampled upon the Divine will and defied the Divine authority. If these things are not so, then the axiomata of science, the intuitions of the understanding, are a delusion, a dream, and all human knowledge a myth, a fantasm, an airy gambol of the unbridled imagination. The first great want of our race is, therefore, the favor of an offended God, the forgiveness of sins, the salvation of the soul. Deep in the recesses of every heart, that has by law obtained the knowledge of sin, reposes this conviction. You could as easily overturn the very foundations of all thought and all faith as eradicate this conviction, thus obtained, from the soul where reason holds its sway.

Assuming, then, as a great first truth this undeniable fact regarding our relations to the God that made us, the Gospel comes to us tendering a heaven-originated remedy for the danger to which we stand momentarily exposed. It offers pardon of sin, peace with God, and a home in heaven. If this Gospel is divine, then there is balm in Gilead; there is a physician come to us whose skill we may trust with a confidence that knows no fear, and is strongest still when the storm-cloud of danger lowers darkest above us. But if this Gospel is not divine, then is the world a desert waste, and life a burden to be borne with ceaseless sighs and tears.

In the Gospel tender of salvation, every thing is based upon what Christ has done for us. His blood is "the fountain for sin and uncleanness." He, himself, is the "Lamb of God, that taketh away the sin of the world." He is the antitype of every bleeding victim slain as a sin-offering from the very morning of time. It is only through him that God proposes to be merciful to men, and it is only in him that we find peace with God, and the forgiveness of sins. It is no part of my present purpose to enter into the *rationale* of this part of heaven's grand remedy for human guilt. That a philosophy, as profound as the depths of the Infinite Mind, lies at the foundation of the death of Jesus, I believe as devoutly as I believe in God, or in the conscious emotions of my own soul. But the

theme were too broad for my present limits, too grand for
one who feels himself but a child in the deep things of God.
Waiving, then, for the present, all inquiries into this sublimest of all subjects, I pass to consider the conditions
upon which the tender of salvation has been made. I devoutly believe that these conditions are precisely what they
ought to be. I am sure there is an adequate reason for
each step that the sinner is required to take. I am certain nothing is demanded which is not worthy of the Jehovah that makes the demand. To show this to be true is
my present task.

It will be perceived that I assume it as certain, that the
salvation tendered in the Gospel is not an unconditional
salvation. The Gospel itself is not an universal declaration of amnesty to sinners without a proviso or a limita-
tion. The amnesty offered can only be enjoyed by complying with the terms prescribed. Without the death of
Christ, the grace of pardon would not, could not, have
been offered. But with the death of Christ, the wisdom
of God still declares that other questions are involved,
which must not be overlooked in granting the boon of
forgiveness to the world. These other questions concern
the status of the sinner himself. Is his present position
to the law and government of the Almighty such as to
justify his forgiveness? No earthly ruler would feel himself authorized to extend clemency to an offender against
the law, without considering the status of the offender
himself. Does he realize the magnitude of his crime? Is
there reason to believe that, if he shall be pardoned now,
he will not again repeat the offense? How is he at present affected to the law? And what reasons are there to
conclude, if past infractions are overlooked, that he will
obey it faithfully in time to come. And what influence

13

may the exercise of clemency in this case have upon others who may be tempted to similar offenses? Will others, seeing the impunity in this case, and looking for a like impunity themselves, be thereby encouraged to disregard the authority of the state, and trample under foot its most solemnly enacted laws? Wisdom demands that questions like these shall be duly considered, and the earthly ruler, who should act in disregard of the principles here implied, would justly incur the contempt of all right-thinking men.

In dispensing the clemency of the Divine government, nothing is overlooked that Infinite Wisdom perceives to be important. Every consideration, bearing however remotely upon the contemplated action of the Sovereign of the Universe, is given all the weight to which it is entitled. Every contingency is fully provided for, and all apparent antagonisms fully harmonized. In making salvation possible, God has done just enough—nothing more. God has never performed, since the universe began, a single unnecessary act. This his Infinite Wisdom clearly necessitates. As, therefore, God, in providing salvation, has done just enough—no more, no less—so, in granting salvation, he will demand from the sinner, in the way of condition, just so much as, and no more than, the eternal fitness of things requires. God proposes to meet and forgive the sinner at the right point. The only reason he interposes a condition at all, is that Infinite Wisdom declares conditions necessary. The conditions must, therefore, be just so many as this wisdom demands. If the sinner can, by making a single step, put himself into a position where it will be proper for God to meet him and forgive him, then he will be required to make only that step. If more than one step is required, it is because Divine Wisdom perceives that more than one step is necessary. I there-

fore reiterate the position, God in the Gospel proposes
to meet the sinner in precisely the right place.   There is
no reason why there is a single unsaved sinner on earth
to-day, other than this one, viz.: that all sinners do not
stand in such an attitude to God's law and government as
to make their salvation possible according to the perfect
wisdom in which that government is administered.   What
else can be in the way of salvation?   What else can ob-
struct the free course of the love of God.   If it were
simply a question of philanthropy, God would save every
body.   If it were a question of physical power, he would
save every body.   Just at this point the Calvinist and
the Universalist are alike crazy.   The one will have it,
because God is sovereign, and some are lost, that, therefore, from all eternity, God willed and determined them
to endless perdition; while the other, with a well-affected
pathos, persistently declares that God is good, and all,
in the end, must be saved.   There is more involved in
this matter than either of them has ever dreamed.   Infinite Wisdom made man a free agent, and Infinite Wisdom will not ignore that agency in saving him.   God wills
the salvation of men, but not upon principles that might
loosen the foundations of the eternal throne.   God wills
to save the sinner, but the sinner must put himself in a
position where God can bestow the boon in harmony with
unchanging and eternal laws.   One such law violated, and
the universe would never recover from the shock.   The
reign of chaos would come again.

As regards the salvation of men, God has removed out
of the way every obstacle that he could remove.   Of that
which was necessary to be done, every thing which depended on his agency alone, has been done.   Every difficulty on the side of the Almighty has been taken out of

the way. Antagonisms seemingly to man irreconcilable, have been fully harmonized in the Great Sacrifice, and now all that remains is for the sinner himself to move in the matter. Will he put himself in a position where the love of God and the blood of Christ can reach him? This is now the great question on which hangs the eternal weal or woe of the entire race.

What, then, must the sinner do? How many are the steps he is required to make? What are those steps? I answer: He must believe in Jesus Christ; this is the first step. He must heartily repent of all his sins; this is the second step. He must be solemnly baptized upon a confession of his faith in the Son of God; this is the third and last step required in the Divine arrangement. Now, I affirm that the hand-writing of the Almighty is as clearly legible here, as in any one of the tens of thousands of adaptations in the physical universe. I do not now argue the New Testament authority for the successive steps here laid down. For the present, this is assumed. I only assert that the offer of pardon, on these conditions, may be vindicated by an appeal to reason. I declare it as my conviction, that traces of the wisdom of Jehovah may be as clearly discovered here as anywhere in the universe. Let us see.

The sinner can do nothing to change the past. This is clearly impossible. The conditions of the Gospel are not then intended for this purpose. The past, with its hopes and its fears, its joys and its sorrows, is now history. The poor sinner can not undo a single deed, or cancel a single sin. No faith, however genuine, no repentance, however deep and sincere, no act of obedience, however plainly commanded, and however necessary to be performed, can affect a single transaction in the record already made. The things to be done now, can only affect one's present attitude to the law and throne of God. More than this is simply impossible. Omnipotence even (with reverence I speak it) can not change the past. God can forgive sin, but can not change the fact. At whatever point, therefore, God may meet and forgive the sinner, it is clearly an act of grace. It does not matter how many steps the sinner may be required to make, the principle is just the same. It is just as much grace if three steps should be required as if there were but one. This is too clear to require further argument. All that the sinner can do, is to put himself in the proper attitude. The conditions of the Gospel accomplish this much, and nothing more. This is all that is possible to him, and, blessed be God, no more is required. Forgiveness is a merciful boon, an unbought gratuity; and yet all men are not in a proper condition to receive it. The very laws which influence the being of Jehovah himself, forbid the extension of this boon to any who will not stand where it may be consistently bestowed. The point where God proposes to meet the sinner, is, therefore, the point indicated by his wisdom as the proper one. In the face of all the religious and irreligious skepticism of the day, I declare it as my firm conviction, that right reason harmonizes with the Word of the Lord in locating the forgiveness of sins immediately after the third step in the pathway of obedience. I am not ashamed of the Gospel. I maintain that its conditions are wise and just, and shall stand by and defend them as such till the Lord comes.

I lay it down as self-evident, that while the sinner continues to love and practice sin, his forgiveness is simply an impossibility. Every attribute of the Divine nature forbids it. He must lay down the weapons of his warfare against God. He must cease to rebel against the Divine government. He must give up his unholy opposition to the Jehovah, whose right it is to rule. This necessity is as stern and unbending as the laws which influence the being of the Almighty Ruler himself. It springs up necessarily out of the very relations that men sustain to God as Law-giver of the Universe. Deny this necessity, and you destroy the Divine government and overthrow its very foundations. It is impossible, in the very nature of things, for God to forgive an impenitent sinner. Every stone in the universe would cry out against it. It would excite the astonishment of the demons in the infernal regions, and fill all heaven with amazement and alarm. It does not matter about the Divine philanthropy. It amounts to nothing that God is love. It is of no avail that Christ has died. Impenitence is an impassable barrier between the sinner and his God. Infinite love can not surmount such an obstacle as this. Infinite power, directed by Infinite Wisdom, can not remove it when the Gospel fails. Away with all idle cant about the sovereignty of grace! Let us have no dreamy and delusive sentimentalism concerning Infinite Love. The universe contains no remedy for a sinner that will not repent. It is time that this were fully understood. It will be too late when the thunders of the last day shall burst upon the world. Thousands of souls, drugged and crazed with Calvinian nostrums, have gone into eternity waiting for the Lord's good time. Thousands now are living under the delusion that Almighty Love will restore all things in the end. I forewarn you to-day that God proposes no remedy for impenitence. He appeals to you in the Gospel, and if you will not hear that appeal, there is no hope for you. He made you free, and will not violate that freedom, even to save you. Can you not see, sinner, that you must move in this matter, or go down to perdition? God can not come to you where you are. He spreads wide the arms of his love, and entreats you to come to him. Sinner, will you come? The barrier is on your side, and you alone can remove it. God has made you free, and you must use that freedom, or perish forever. So decides the Book of God, and right reason vindicates the decision. The command to repent is not an arbitrary command; it is not a tyrannical edict; it is not an exhibition of authority simply as such, but authority rightful and unquestioned, grounding its exercise, however, upon necessity and the eternal fitness of things. This necessity, this fitness of things, is the reason which underlies the command. The existence of this necessity is the vindication of the Great Lawgiver in making the requirement, and suspending upon our compliance with it the forgiveness of sins and the hope of eternal life. It were as easy to deny any other self-evident truth in the universe as the existence of the necessity here contended for. God makes his appeals direct to the honest intentions of the soul, and the response is instant and universal. The position is, therefore, immovably established. It is as certain as any other proposition in the wide range of human thought, that God requires the sinner to repent, simply because that, in the nature of things, and from the very relations subsisting between the parties, the sinner's forgiveness is impossible without it. So let it be understood and acknowledged till the Lord comes.

But why is the sinner commanded to believe? Infidels sometimes put on a wise face, and stand up and reason against God. Faith, say these wiseacres, is involuntary. A man can not help his beliefs, and therefore it is wrong that he should be held responsible for them. This is a false and dangerous philosophy. A man can help his belief. A man can help believing a falsehood when the truth

is within his reach, provided he will honestly search for the
truth. I do not believe there is an honest infidel on earth
to-day that has patiently and prayerfully sought to know
the truth. A man's beliefs are not wholly involuntary.
Away with such reasoning against God; there is not a word
of truth in it. Again: it has been said that there is no
moral value in faith, and that to justify or condemn on the
ground of believing or disbelieving, is, therefore, clearly
preposterous. I grant, freely grant, that faith is not in
itself righteousness; that it is no moral equivalent for
obedience to a righteous law. But this is not the reason
that God requires men to believe. Such is not the philosophy that underlies this part of the law of forgiveness. The
reason is here: the sinner can not be pardoned in impenitence, and he can not repent without faith. Faith is necessary as a means to an end. Repentance, in this case, is the
end, and you can not reach it otherwise than through faith.
"First fact, then faith, then feeling." The truth must be
heard, understood, believed, pass through the understanding into the heart, and thus become the power of God to
stir the depths of the moral nature. To me, at least, it
is self-evident that God works every-where by established
laws, and upon every thing according to its nature. Matter and mind are subject to different laws, and God does
not ignore this fact in operating upon them. He influences
mind, according to the laws of mind. He works upon
matter in harmony with its nature. The wisdom of God
in the Gospel is seen in this, that every thing is adapted
to man just as he is; to his condition, his relations, his
organization, to every thing that touches at any point the
grand scheme of mercy to the world. If it were God's
plan to change the heart, to renovate the affections by a
direct touch of the Holy Spirit, then it could be done as

well without faith as with it, as well without the Gospel
and where the Gospel has never been, as where it is preached
and understood.   But the plan of the Heavenly Father is
to take man as he is, to influence him and save him, if he
saves him at all, in perfect harmony with all the laws of
his being.   In pursuance of this plan, he addresses his understanding in the Gospel; he appeals to his heart by all
the motives and influences contained in the Gospel.   This
is grounded upon a necessity growing out of the very laws
of thought and feeling.   I repeat, I assume it as true that
God operates throughout the universe upon every thing
he has made, in harmony with the nature he has given to
it.   If this may not be taken as self-evident, then there is
nothing self-evident in the universe, and all human knowledge is simply a stupendous folly.

When Jesus opened the eyes of the blind, unstopped
the ears of the deaf, restored the paralytic, or raised up the
dead, it is as certain that there was a demand for the immediate energies of the omnipotent and all-creating Spirit
as when the universe was made.   Nothing less, according
to the established laws of material things, could meet the
exigencies of the occasion.   But when a soul in ruins is
to be restored, the work is not the same, neither is the way
of God the same.   God does not work alike upon matter
and mind.   The power that he employs in moving the soul
would be folly in the work of raising the dead; while the
energy that brought a Lazarus from the grave would be as
illy suited to stir the heart with a sense of guilt, or destroy
in it the love of sin.   Purblind, indeed, must have been
the venerated fathers of denominational orthodoxy, never
to have caught a glimpse of this grand truth.   Strange that
Doctors of Divinity should stumble where it would seem
that babes might walk without a fear.   The Gospel is the

power of God to save the soul.   But in the Christ-idea—
to borrow a happy expression from one whose work of faith
and labor of love will be rewarded at the resurrection of the
just*—lies the secret of its wondrous might.   Jesus, the
Christ, is not only the center and sum of all Gospel truth,
but the center and sum of all converting and saving power.
The tale of Calvary has stirred more hearts than any other
tale that was ever told.   The Hero of Redemption has
elicited a higher admiration, a holier love, than any other
hero that every lived.   The compassion of the dying Jesus
for sinful men has awakened a loftier gratitude than ever
throbbed in any heart at the mention of any human name.
Blessed be God for the mighty, heaven-born energy con-
centrated in this single, grand idea of a suffering, dying
Christ.   The soul may realize it, but the tongue can never
tell it.   There is more power in this single conception,
taken in its manifold relations, to elevate the race, to en-
noble our humanity, to make men better, and truer, and
purer, than in the speculations of all earthly philosophy,
from Confucius to Cousin.   The Gospel of Jesus is itself
the highest philosophy known on earth or in heaven.   The
angels in glory bend in astonishment and rapture over the
stupendous display of God's wisdom in the redemption
of sinners through the Gospel.   In this whole arrangement
the wisdom of the Infinite One shines out as grandly as
the noonday sun from a cloudless sky.   But the power of
a fact is felt only by those who accept it as a fact.   This
history of all hearts offers no exception to this law.   God
influences mind according to the laws of mind.   Hence the
Gospel is only the power of God to "the called," to "the
saved," to "them that believe."   By one of those unchang-

---

* J. J. Trott, missionary to the Cherokees.

ing laws, therefore, which God will not violate, the influence by which repentance is induced is made to depend upon faith. Faith is the substratum upon which repentance reposes. You can no more have repentance or a change of heart without faith, than you can have a building without a foundation. You can not rear a gorgeous temple in mid-air. You can not have a superstructure without a substructure. God saves man according to the laws of thought and feeling. He does not propose literally to create man over again in the process of renovation. He comes to him as he is. He takes hold of him with the Gospel, and saves him, if he saves him at all, without violence to a single law of his nature. From this fixed point, I reason with the fullest assurance of understanding. Upon this foundation I build without a fear. Sectarian theology unsettles every thing, turns every thing into chaos. It has no logical foundation. It has no reason and no philosophy. God's Gospel is a golden chain of cause and effect. Every link in this chain has been wisely wrought. Nothing is without its reason, nothing without its end. Looking off from this stand-point over the long centuries that have passed away since this grand Christ-idea was first made known to the world, and contemplating what God has wrought by it, who can refrain from exclaiming with the apostle: "O, depth of the bounty, and wisdom, and knowledge of God! how unfathomable are his judgments, and how unsearchable are his paths! Yea, who hath known the mind of the Lord, and who hath been his counselor? or who hath first given to God, that he should deserve a recompense? Unto him be glory forever. Amen."

But what more? When the sinner believes in Jesus, and is deeply penitent for his sins; when his understanding is enlightened and his heart is changed, what then?

Why, then, "He that believeth and is baptized shall be saved." To the law and to the testimony; how readest thou? But why be baptized? Jesus commands; is not that enough? Nay, but is not the commandment wise? And may not its wisdom be vindicated? I answer, yes. My faith is as firm, that there is a Divine reason lying beneath this Divine commandment, as that God is all-wise. Let us reverently attempt to look for it. It may, perhaps, lie deeper than our ken, but it can not be wrong to look.

First, then, I confess that if there were no universe beyond God and the single offending sinner, whose case may be supposed to be under consideration, I can see no reason why baptism should be enjoined. Such a reason might still exist, but, in such a case, would lie deeper than our vision. Were it commanded in such a case, the existence of the reason might be inferred with certainty from the Divine Wisdom, even though our profoundest search failed to discover any trace of it. If, however, God and the single sinner were the whole universe, all that would be necessary to put the sinner within the reach of Divine clemency, seems to be gained, when the sinner believes and repents. His understanding is then right, and his heart is right. His status is known to himself, and fully known to God, and beside these there is supposed to be none else. Human reason, it seems to me, in such a case, fails to discover a necessity for any thing more. But this supposed case is widely different from the real case. The sinner, in point of fact, is only one among millions equally guilty. And besides the guilty millions, there are millions of beings that have kept their first estate, and never sinned. In forgiving a sinner, God must take into account the moral influence of the act throughout all ranks of created beings under law to him   The point at which he proposes to forgive the sinner, must be the one that all right-thinking subjects of the Divine government will recognize at once as the proper one. The angels around the throne must be able to see and vindicate the wisdom and justice of the Almighty Ruler. But God only can read the heart. In all the universe, the penitent sinner's *status*, until developed in an overt act, is known only to himself and to God. But he has sinned openly. With a bold front he has measured arms with Omnipotence. His rebellion has not been confined to his heart. It has not exhausted itself in sympathy. Men on earth, the partners of his crime, have been the witnesses, and angels in heaven have looked on with astonishment at his defiant airs. Now, what does the nature of the case seem to demand? Where does it appear to be proper that God should meet this once bold and defiant, but now humbled and stricken, outlaw? Where should God require him to stand, when he bestows upon him the boon of a merciful forgiveness of all his past sins? I answer: Out before heaven and earth, confessing his guilt, avowing his repentance, and pledging himself to unflinching fidelity in all time to come. His faith and repentance must be embodied in an overt act, that men and angels can see. Surely this is clear beyond cavil. Sinner, in this issue between God and Satan, your rightful Lawgiver demands that you shall define your position. He requires you to choose whom you will serve, and to declare your choice before heaven and earth. Are you for your rightful Sovereign, or do you stand in the ranks of the enemy? God has established an institution, and made it the line of separation between his kingdom and that of the opposing power. This institution is Christian baptism. In this overt act, you externalize your faith and repentance, and make them visible to your fellow-men. In this act you formally and solemnly dedicate yourself to God. In it, you vow eternal allegiance to his throne. In it, all the holy desires and heaven-born resolves of the inner man, take upon them an outward form, and can be seen and read by your associates. Is it strange that God should demand such an expression of your faith in him? such a pledge of eternal fealty in time to come? Nay, it would have been strange, indeed, if God had tendered forgiveness without it. It has its foundation in the eternal fitness of things. Its reason is clear as a sunbeam. It is not the value of the thing done. It is not that it has saving merit in it. It is not that water, as such, has power to cleanse from guilt. Baptism is no charm. It has in it no mystery. Its sole value is this: That as an open, public avowal of your faith and penitence, as a formal and solemn dedication of yourself to God in a heaven-appointed way, it places you in a proper position before heaven and earth to receive the free and gracious forgiveness of your past sins. Sinner, why do you hesitate? Humble, stricken, sin-sick believer, "Arise and be baptized, and wash away your sins, calling on the name of the Lord."

Blessed be God for a reasonable religion! a religion that can be defended alike against the sneers of the bigot, and the scoffs of the infidel. To his name be the glory forever. *Amen.*

Yours Respectfully
Robt. Graham

ROBERT GRAHAM.

THIS distinguished preacher and teacher was born in Liverpool, England, on the 14th of August, 1822. The parents were rigid Episcopalians, and the son was, consequently, brought up in the communion of the Established Church. When only fourteen years of age, during a protracted meeting among the Methodist Protestants of Alleghany City, Penn., he was deeply impressed with the importance of religion, and was led to doubt the correctness of the position he occupied in the Episcopal Church. Although failing to experience the miraculous change, which at that time was a popular evidence of conversion, he was, nevertheless, received on probation, and finally into full membership in the Methodist Protestant Church. He was now conscious of a great change in his views, feelings, and conduct, but he was still unsatisfied with reference to his religious state. There were many passages of Scripture he could not harmonize with the teachings of the Church to which he belonged.

In the fall of 1838 he made the acquaintance of the congregation of Disciples in Alleghany City, Penn., and was thus brought to review the grounds of his religious belief. This examination led to his immersion, on the 17th of February, 1839, by Elder SAMUEL CHURCH, then pastor of the Christian Church in Alleghany City.

At the time he united with the Disciples he was an apprentice for five years, "learning the art and mystery of house-carpentry," in the city of Pittsburgh, and, of course, had very little time to devote to literary pursuits. Nevertheless, he collected quite a library of useful and entertaining books, and devoted all his spare hours to the acquisition of knowledge; and having joined a literary society, made considerable progress in the study of history, Belles-Lettres, Biblical Criticism, Natural Science, etc.

On the 1st of January, 1843, he entered Bethany College, and, in the following year, began to preach for the church at Dutch Fork, seven miles from Bethany, and continued to labor there on Lord's days for three years. By the sale of his library, carpenters' tools, the small salary received for preaching, and occasional help from President CAMPBELL, he was enabled to support himself at college. He subsequently returned all the means Mr. CAMPBELL advanced, with interest on the same from date. While a student at Bethany, he was married to Miss MARIA THORNLEY, of Alleghany City, Penn.

He graduated in July, 1847, dividing the first honors of his class with A. R. BENTON, and delivering the Latin salutatory. In December of the same year he entered upon a collecting tour for Mr. CAMPBELL, and spent nine months in traveling through several of the South-western States. It was during this tour that he co-operated with JOHN T. JOHNSON, in a protracted meeting of great interest, at Fayetteville, Arkansas, which resulted in the establishment of a fine church in that place, to the pastoral care of which he was soon afterward called. He removed to Fayetteville with his family in January, 1849. Here he finally succeeded in establishing Arkansas College, an institution which flourished till the war broke out, in 1861.

In September, 1859, he left Arkansas for Harrodsburg, Kentucky, to take charge of the Chair of Belles-Lettres and History in Kentucky University, to which he had been unanimously elected. He held this position one year, during which time he gave great satisfaction to the friends of the University. He was induced to resign his professorship in 1860, and return to Fayetteville, with the view of becoming the General Agent of the Southern Christian Missionary Society. But the war breaking out, the whole arrangement failed, and, in the fall of 1862, he took charge of the First Church in Cincinnati, Ohio, where he labored with great acceptance till 1864, when he resigned and removed to Santa Rosa, California, and preached for the church, and taught an academy at that place, one year. He then spent one year in San Francisco, and succeeded in establishing a promising church in that city. In January, 1866, he was elected Presiding Officer of the College of Arts, and Professor of the School of English Language and Literature, in Kentucky University. He accepted, and entered upon his work in the following October, which position he now occupies.

ROBERT GRAHAM has a finely-balanced organization—there being perfect harmony between the intellectual and physical natures. He is of low stature, but heavy-set, and weighs about one hundred and eighty pounds. He has a bright, florid complexion, large, light-blue eyes, and an orator's mouth. He is a ready extemporaneous speaker, and, on a great occasion, is capable of exercising wonderful power over an audience. He possesses a strong, active, sympathetic nature, and this gives him great influence in the social circle. Few men have more ability to control the masses, but this is never attempted at a sacrifice of dignity, or any characteristic of a Christian gentleman.

REGENERATION.

BY ROBERT GRAHAM.

"Of his own will begat he us with the word of truth, that we should be a kind of first-fruits of his creatures."—JAMES 1: 18.

IT may be truly said that one-half of all the debates about the Gospel arise from a misconception of the nature of Regeneration. We are glad to think that many persons are regenerated who can not give a consistent and Scriptural view of this subject, even as many are refreshed by the cooling spring who know not the composition of water, and are regaled by the breeze of heaven who can not tell whether the atmosphere is a chemical or a mechanical combination. But this by no means implies that we ought to be satisfied with crude views upon a matter, the importance and interest of which is confessed by all; for while we may not be regenerated by merely understanding the nature of the process, it is equally clear that through this knowledge we may be saved from many pernicious errors, and become the recipients of greatly increased religious enjoyment.

It is generally believed that Regeneration is one of "the things hard to be understood;" and, indeed, this is true, if we thread the labyrinth by the rush-light of modern theology. Following a light so pale and inconstant,

14

"spectres and chimeras dire" will start up on every hand, pit-falls will dimly reveal themselves at every step, and we shall be in constant danger; but once take the bright and sure light of God's Word, follow the guidance of Christ and his inspired apostles, and what was dark is at once illuminated, the difficulties are bridged, and we find ourselves in a hall built as by enchantment, filled indeed with wonders, but wonders revealed, not less to warm our hearts than to quicken our understandings. To speak without a figure, we affirm our conviction that with the New Testament in our hands, and free from the subtleties of scholastic divinity, Regeneration, in its source, instrumentality, and purpose, can be understood as clearly as any other fundamental item of the Christian revelation.

As it has pleased God to reveal all for duty and nothing for mere curiosity, it is our interest and our happiness to obtain well-defined conceptions of the divine process by which we are quickened to a new life, for herein has our Father displayed his kindness to us "who were dead in trespasses and sins." His parental love, shown in the efficient means and final cause of our regeneration may well be to us, as it was to primitive saints and martyrs, the theme of perpetual meditation, gratitude, and praise. What is there so well calculated to elevate our minds as the contemplation of the simplicity and benevolence of the Gospel which reveals God's plan of saving sinners by faith, and causing their lives to abound with the fruits of righteousness to the praise of his glorious grace!

As this discourse is for those mainly who depend not on Greek, but on English, for their knowledge of the living oracles, I shall not speak in a dead language to a living people. Moreover, I may say, once for all, that, in my opinion, it is not absolutely necessary to a clear understanding of this subject that we should draw nice distinctions respecting the Greek words rendered in the common version sometimes begotten and sometimes born. We do not think the apostles, in their use of the words, made any refined physiological discriminations between generation and birth. With them, our new life in Christ begins when we enter his kingdom, and we enter his kingdom by a birth of water and Spirit—a process including the inception, progress, and consummation of a change in both character and state, without which, the Savior says, no one can see the kingdom of God.

We shall then use the words *begotten, regeneration*, and *born again*—as we apprehend the New Testament uses them—to denote a *process*, and not an *act*, without stopping to inquire, in the case of each passage adduced, the particular stage of the process which may be uppermost in the mind of the sacred penman. I feel satisfied, from a careful examination, that the New Testament writers used the Greek words in their literal sense for both begotten and being born; and we are confident that, in their metaphorical sense, they may be similarly used without danger of ambiguity. The reason for this opinion will appear as we proceed.

My method of discussion shall be direct and simple, suited to the humblest capacity, and as best serving the end in view. I shall endeavor to show:

I. THE NATURE OF REGENERATION.
II. ITS ABSOLUTE NECESSITY.
III. ITS BLESSED CONSEQUENCES.

And may he who never withholds his presence and blessing from those who humbly seek him, aid us by his Spirit, that we may understand the truth as it is in Jesus!

I. The Nature of Regeneration.

In elucidating this part of our theme the text suggests a method at once clear and natural:

1. The Source of our regeneration—"Of his own will."
2. The Agent—"He," that is God, "begat us."
3. The Means—"By the Word of Truth."
4. The End—"That we should be a kind of first-fruits of his creatures."

This passage sets before us four items in our Regeneration; as these are fundamental, mistake is dangerous; as it is clearly done, misapprehension is perversity. Indifferent to the beautiful in statement must be the mind that does not see in this verse a perspicuity worthy a divinely-inspired teacher. Is the first item clear? the second is no less evident. Is the third worthy of God's wisdom? the fourth is not less so of his benevolence.

1st. *The source of Regeneration is the will of God.* It is alone of God's free and spontaneous volition, acting without necessity and without constraint, that men are begotten to a new life: it is of "his own good pleasure." Neither is it because of any worthiness in us, as is set forth in Titus iii: 5: "Not by works of righteousness which we have done, but according to his mercy, he saved us, by the washing of regeneration, and renewing of the Holy Spirit." To keep our minds steadily fixed on this essential point, and to introduce—

2d. *The Agent of our Regeneration*, we quote a most expressive passage from John i: 11–13: "He came to his own, and his own received him not. But as many as received him, to them gave he power to become the sons of God, even to them that believe on his name: which were born, not of blood, nor of the will of the flesh, nor of the will of man, but of God." The meaning and application of this passage are plain. Our Lord came to his own people—the Jews—and, with few exceptions, they rejected him : but, to the few that received him, who believed on his name, he gave the privilege of becoming children of God. The apostle, keeping up the figure suggested by the word children, observes that those who received him were born, not of blood, nor of the will of the flesh, nor of the will of man, but of God.

We become children by virtue of birth. By a birth of flesh, we wear the image of Adam ; by a birth of Spirit, we wear the image of Christ. Our flesh is born of flesh; our spirit is born of spirit. So Christ teaches. "That which is born of the flesh, is flesh; and that which is born of the Spirit, is spirit." (John iii: 6.) Being, then, begotten by God, and born into his kingdom of grace, we are his children, and Christ is our elder brother. We are to each other brethren, not in Moses, nor in Plato, but in Christ. This being taught in very many passages of God's Word, and being generally conceded, we may pass on to consider the next item.

3d. *The means employed in our Regeneration.* As this is the point about which there is most disagreement, I will be indulged, I hope, if I labor it at greater length than would otherwise comport with the unity of this discourse.

"He begat us with the word of truth." This settles it that the word of truth is *a* means. Are we prepared to go one step farther, and say it is *the* means? We feel so constrained. There may be ten thousand secondary causes employed to bring men to the knowledge of the word of truth, for we and the powers of heaven and earth may be employed in carrying the Gospel to those sitting in darkness, and in the region and shadow of death, just as the air and its happy denizens bear the seeds and pollen of fruits and flowers to the ends of the earth. While the will of God continues to be the source of our new life, and he himself the efficient cause of it, as long as he is our Father, so long will his word be "the seed of the kingdom;" and not till plants can be produced without seed, and animals without parents, will sinful men be made partakers of the Divine nature—the new life in God— without "the word of truth, the Gospel of our salvation."

But it seems to me that the nature of the case excludes every other instrumentality. Does God beget some children by the word of truth, and others by *different means?* It behooves those who so affirm to show it by express Scripture statement or necessary implication. This, we are confident, never can be done. But the idea that God has a way of regenerating men by his word ordinarily, and by something else extraordinarily, is not less repugnant to the analogy of nature than contradictory to the analogy of faith. Correct views are removed equally from the extravagance of the fanatic, the obscurity of the mystic, and the cold philosophy of the rationalist.

The common view of Regeneration is that it is an act performed by the Spirit of God before faith, and in order to faith; and that by it the heart of the sinner is instantly changed from the love of sin to the love of holiness. There is great variety of statement, from the wildest rant to the most carefully-worded proposition, but in meaning they are all the same. In opposition to this, we maintain that "the seed is the word of God," that this is his chosen instrumentality, and that when that word is received by faith into a good and honest heart, that heart is quickened into new life. That the Spirit of God is always with his word, and that if men are not regenerated the fault is to be found in themselves or the unfavorable circumstances of their condition, and not in the will of God, nor the want of power in his word.

To see what is the teaching of Scripture on a matter so vital and interesting, I quote from Peter's first epistle (i: 22, 23): "Seeing ye have purified your souls in obeying the truth through the Spirit unto unfeigned love of the brethren, see that ye love one another with a pure heart fervently. Being born again, not of corruptible seed, but of incorruptible, by the word of God, which liveth and abideth forever." Can language be plainer than this? We are regenerated, not of corruptible seed; our bodies are generated of that, as we are informed by John, but our spirits are regenerated of this incorruptible seed of the living God. As he only hath life in himself, he communicates it to us through his word of truth. What James calls "the word of truth," Peter calls "the word of God," as the Savior teaches in his sacerdotal prayer, (John xvii: 17): "Sanctify them through thy truth, thy word is truth."

The Savior, John, James, and Peter do, in these passages, teach a simple, but most important truth about Regeneration. We have only to remove from our eyes the films of prejudice and mysticism to see the admirable agreement of all these teachers, and the simplicity of their instruction.

But you are ready to ask me, What is this word of God, which Peter, in this connection, calls the incorruptible seed of the kingdom? Read the concluding verses of this chapter: "And this is the word which by the Gospel is preached unto you." The germ, then, is the word of God in the Gospel of Christ. That word was given in charge to this man and his fellow-apostles, in the great commission to disciple the nations: "Go ye," says Christ, "into all the world, and preach the Gospel to every creature. He that believeth and is baptized shall be saved." Compare, now, with this Paul's language in 1 Cor. iv: 15: "Though ye have ten thousand instructors in Christ, yet have ye not many fathers, for in Christ Jesus I have begotten you through the Gospel." That is, I, Paul, preached the Gospel to you Corinthians, by hearing and believing this Gospel, in which is the incorruptible seed, you have been begotten, and therefore I am, under God, your spiritual father.

That such is the meaning of the apostle is more than conjecture. What did he do when he first preached at Corinth? In the eighteenth chapter of Acts, we have the report of his labors in this celebrated city, and it is singularly explicit: "After these things, Paul departed from Athens, and came to Corinth," the account goes on to say: "And he reasoned in the synagogue every Sabbath, and persuaded the Jews and the Greeks. And when Silas and Timotheus were come from Macedonia, Paul was pressed in the spirit, and testified to the Jews that Jesus was Christ." The result of all this is given thus: "And Crispus, the chief ruler of the synagogue, believed on the Lord with all his house; and many of the Corinthians hearing, believed, and were baptized." Such is the simple and unfigurative account of Paul's evangelical labors in Corinth. He preached the Gospel, testifying that *Jesus is the Christ;* the Corinthians, hearing, believe the testimony, and are immersed. Were not these persons born again? If so, how? It certainly was according to the will of God; and is it not just as certain that it was through the word of truth? That word was, beyond all cavil, the seed of the kingdom—the germ of their new spiritual life.   The fact is, language can not make any thing plainer than does this passage the following propositions:

1. The Corinthians heard Paul prove Jesus to be the Christ.

2. They believed his word.

3. They were baptized.   Consequently they were born of water and of the Spirit.

The reference made by the apostle himself in the beginning of the 15th chapter of his First Epistle to these same Corinthians, confirms us in this view, if farther confirmation is necessary.   He says: "Moreover, brethren, I declare unto you the Gospel which I preached unto you, which also ye have received, and wherein ye stand; by which also ye are saved, if you keep in memory what I preached unto you, unless ye have believed in vain.   For I delivered unto you first of all, that which I also received, how that Christ died for our sins according to the Scriptures: and that he was buried, and that he rose again the third day according to the Scriptures."

Comparing this passage with the one quoted from the 15th verse of the 4th chapter, and both of them with Luke's account in the 8th chapter of Acts, we can not see how any unprejudiced mind can avoid the conclusion that to be born again is to hear, believe, and obey the Gospel; that the Gospel is the good news concerning the death, burial, and resurrection of the Lord Jesus; that these prove him to be the Christ, the Son of God; that this is the great central truth—the germ of spiritual life—which received into a good and honest heart, by faith, becomes the incorruptible seed of which we are begotten of God; and that when we are baptized into Christ according to the Gospel, and come forth out of the water, we are born of water and the Spirit.   I confess that if this be not to be born again, then is the whole thing a myth, and Christ's teaching to Nicodemus incomprehensible.

How natural it is that Paul should say, (Philemon, 10th verse,) that he had begotten Onesimus in his bonds; and we can be at no loss to understand his meaning. Again, John affirms, (1 John v: 1:) "Whosoever believeth that Jesus is the Christ is born (begotten) of God; and every one that loveth him that begat, loveth him also that is begotten of him." How sweetly does the language of these texts fall in with the idea that the Messiahship of Jesus is the Gospel in epitome, and that this was the instrumentality used by the first preachers to bring men into the family of God!

The resurrection of Christ is the crowning proof of his Messiahship, and therefore Peter well says, (1 Pet. i: 3:) " Blessed be the God and Father of our Lord Jesus Christ, who, according to his abundant mercy, hath begotten us again to a hope of life by the resurrection of Jesus Christ from the dead." If, then, Regeneration be not what I have proved it to be by this simple, and, as I think, unanswerable argument, I shall despair of ever understanding the meaning of language, and shall boldly affirm that to make a revelation of the will of God in the symbols of human speech is plainly impossible.

4. *The end proposed in our Regeneration is "that we should be a kind of first fruits of his creatures."* In Deut. xxvi: 2–10, we have the law regulating the affecting ceremony of presenting the first fruits before God; and from it we gather that God required the first fruits of the land as an acknowledgment by the Israelite of the providential care that had watched over Abraham and his posterity from the beginning; that had now given the people an abundant harvest, and for his goodness deserved this tribute at their hands.

The first fruits were holy and dedicated to God; they were the choicest productions of the earth, and they were an earnest of the harvest about to be reaped. When a man is regenerated according to the Scriptures, he is wholly devoted to God. All his faculties and powers, his time, talents, and opportunities, his whole being and life are consecrated to him whose he is and whom he serves. He is a new creature in Christ Jesus, and his reasonable service is to present his body a living sacrifice, holy, acceptable unto God. The principle of Regeneration is one that prompts to entire devotion to God. Changed in state, in life, and in purpose, his affections purified, and his soul freed from the thralldom of sin, the renewed man seeks conformity to his Divine model, and is thus prepared for his master's use. He is, indeed, " a kind of first fruits of his creatures."

II. THE NECESSITY OF REGENERATION.

And first, my brethren, let me say, that in calling the process by which we are introduced into the kingdom and patience of Jesus a birth, the Savior has brought before our minds one of the most appropriate and expressive comparisons imaginable. Let us be here distinctly understood: The change in both state and character of which we are the subjects in Regeneration, is as real as the creation of the world by God, or its redemption by Jesus; but the setting forth of that change under the similitude of a birth, is highly figurative, and is at once appropriate and instructive. Christ is one of the most figurative of teachers; his instructions abound in parables, metaphors, and beautiful analogies: hence the clearness and the charm in what he says. The deep supernatural truths of his kingdom are submitted to our minds and hearts in analogies drawn from the frame of nature; both these constitute but one system of God, and of that system Christ as the Divine Logos is the author and the finisher.

The New Institution may be contemplated in various points of view; it is many-sided, and hence the numerous parables employed by Christ to unfold its nature and excellence. It was foretold by the prophets, under the figure of a kingdom; and therefore, when John came announcing the good news of a "kingdom of God at hand," the Jews were at no loss to understand his meaning, though they were entirely ignorant of its spiritual nature. They supposed it was merely the old kingdom of God established by Moses, now to be made more glorious by the Messiah. It was no longer to be under the heel of the proud Cæsars; it was to triumph over Gentile oppression, and the chosen seed of Abraham were to possess it, because of their fleshly relation to him. Descent from him, according to the flesh, was the ground of their confidence, their boast, and their glory.

John, therefore, laid great stress on the necessity of new principles, a new character, and a new life, as a preparation for the kingdom which he preached; and the seventy disciples were sent out to aid in the good work of preparing men in heart, profession, and conduct, for the kingdom of heaven shortly to be set up. To call the minds of these carnal Jews from their earthly views of the Messiah's reign, the Harbinger directed their attention to the fact that while he immersed them in water, Christ would immerse them in the Holy Spirit.

One of the Jews, a master in Israel, came to Christ himself, and acknowledged him to be an inspired teacher, come from God, as proved by the miracles he wrought. True to the grand design of his kingdom, and in admirable harmony with its nature, the Savior affirms to him the absolute impossibility of any man's enjoying it without being first born again. We are thus shut up by the great Teacher himself, to the conclusion that the birth of which he speaks has respect to a spiritual kingdom, just as we know that the word, in its literal sense, has respect to a literal kingdom. How natural, how apposite, how forcible is all this!

In the New Testament, there are many allusions made to three distinct kingdoms of God; and into every one of these we enter by a birth. There is a beautiful analogy among these, and many passages of Scripture can be understood only as we keep this analogy clearly before the mind. We enter the kingdom of nature by literal birth. Adam was made; we are born. This is according to the will of man. We are born again, according to the will of God, and we thus enter the kingdom of grace; we shall be quickened by the Spirit and born of the grave before we enter the everlasting kingdom of our Lord and Savior Jesus Christ.

We enjoy a life, in each of these kingdoms of nature, of grace, and of glory, suited to its character respectively. In the first, it is natural; in the second, spiritual; and in the third, it is eternal. We derive all from God; but the first is through our parents, the second through the Gospel, and the third through his power in our resurrection. Birth is for the sake of life, and this last is the efflorescence of the germ and bud of our being, the flower that shall know no blight in the paradise of God.

The Spirit of God is the prime agent in all life. Till it brooded in the beginning on the abyss, there was no life; it became an embodiment in the word of the Almighty, and light and life flashed from the darkness and death of chaos, a cosmos of light and life came into being. The

Word was spoken, and through it the spirit of life, the spirit of power, the Spirit of God, generated and brought forth all animate things, and man himself, the crown and lord of all. Animal life is here the result of God's Spirit operating through his word. "His word is spirit and life." At this, "the morning stars sang together, and all the sons of God shouted for joy."

If we look at spiritual life, how perfect the analogy! The Spirit of God is the author of our new life; but that Spirit is again in his word; its re-creating energy is there, and we are regenerated through the word of truth in the Gospel, "for it is the power of God unto salvation to every one that believeth." The word of God was the envelope of his omnipotence in the creation of all things. It is not less so now in quickening us to a new spiritual life in Christ Jesus.

The Spirit that raised up Christ shall again become embodied in a word of God; his voice shall be heard in the charnel house, and those mortal bodies shall throw off the cerements of the grave, and come forth to die no more. We shall enter into what Peter calls "the everlasting kingdom of our Lord and Savior Jesus Christ." It is rightly so called, for it is the grand consummation of all God's purposes of grace and mercy toward his believing and obedient children.

But, we have said, all birth is for the sake of life. Is it not thus? We are born into the world, not that we may simply exist, but that we may live. We eat and drink to sustain life; but that life is in the flesh, and is sustained by the bread and water that perish. We may eat and live thus, grow old and die, and yet be strangers to that bread that came down from heaven to give life to the world. It is in admirable harmony with our analogy of a new birth and a new life that Christ says: "We must eat of the bread that he gives us;" and that "man shall not live by bread alone, but by every word of God." If we do this, "we shall hunger no more, neither die any more." If we drink of the water he gives, "it shall be in us a well of water springing up to everlasting life." The morning of the resurrection shall witness our third and final birth; we shall then enter on an eternal life, to be forever nourished by the tree of life and the river that issues from the throne of God.

We are now prepared to affirm, and to affirm confidently, that the declaration of Christ is in every way consonant with all our conceptions of a kingdom and of life. Who can conceive of the former without subjects? of the latter without birth? And why the former, but for the sake and for the development of the latter? We can not live, in its proper sense, without being born; and, as soon as we are born, we enter a kingdom. "Except ye be born again ye can not enter into the kingdom of God."

This passage, then, teaches one great truth about the new birth, and that is, its absolute necessity. We can not give too much emphasis to this declaration of the Master. In the nature of things, there is no entrance into the kingdom of God; there is no enjoying this new life but by being born again. The sense of the passage is one, and not manifold; there is one, and but one complete judgment of Christ's mind in the language under consideration; that judgment is one and the same to all who know the meaning of words; we do not ask you to admit it, we challenge the world to deny it—that single idea is, that Regeneration is absolutely necessary to the enjoyment of the kingdom of God.

If this truth were appreciated as it ought to be, and if

we were prepared to accept its inevitable consequences, much misconception and wrangling about religion would disappear. Prejudices, such as were a hindrance to the Jew, and are yet so to many a Gentile, would give way. No longer would infant baptism, infant regeneration, infant church-membership, and, I blush to name it, infant damnation, hold a place in Protestant symbols of faith. These, with a score of exploded dogmas in relation to conversion, abstract spiritual operations, and what is improperly called experimental religion, would be known only as the lifeless creed of the dogmatist or the wild fancies of the enthusiast.

We do not mean to say that professed Christians do, in words, deny the necessity of the new birth; we are more than pleased to know that there is a general agreement as to such necessity, but we fear it is more a concession for the sake of orthodoxy, than a conscious truth of the heart. If this be not true, they would hardly repudiate its obvious consequences.

From the nature of the case, then, and from the positive teaching of Christ in this passage, we conclude a new birth to be a necessity in every case to which the language applies. What the Divine Father of all does with those who are incapable of hearing, believing, and obeying the Gospel, is not a question before us, nor is its discussion necessarily connected with our present purpose.

We may now sum up what we have to say on both the nature and the necessity of Regeneration in a brief scriptural statement: It is the Spirit, the Spirit of God, that is the efficient agent in this wonderful transformation; the means employed is the word of God contained in the Gospel, more particularly the truth that "Jesus is the Christ;" which is, in fact, the whole Gospel in epitome.

Through this we are begotten to a hope of life by the resurrection of Jesus Christ. (I Pet. i: 3.) The Father begets us through his Word, inspired into the apostles by the Holy Spirit, and spoken by them in their testimony that Jesus is the Christ; this Word, received into the heart of the sinner, dead in trespasses and sins, is the seed of the kingdom, which germinates there, and of it he is begotten, *and of it only*. When such a one comes forth of the water in which he has been baptized into the name of the Father, the Son, and the Holy Spirit, according to the Savior's command, the process of his Regeneration is completed. He is saved by the washing of Regeneration, and the renewing of the Holy Spirit. (Titus iii: 5.)

From what has been said it follows, as a matter of course, that mystical and abstract regeneration without the word of God, the means and motives of the Gospel, anterior to faith, and in order to faith, is opposed alike to the simplicity of the Divine teaching and the analogy of nature. It is opposed to the simplicity of the Divine teaching, for it leads to confused ideas of the whole plan of redemption; it contradicts the plainest teachings of Christ and the apostles; it nullifies the commands of the Savior, and leads the sinner to depend on an influence of the Spirit not promised, and never to be realized. It makes him the dupe of feelings inconstant and deceptive, and the hero of what would be a farce but for its seriousness and the interests involved. It is opposed to the analogy of nature, for it leads us to suppose that God has two processes of birth into the same kingdom; one ordinary, the other extraordinary; one normal, the other abnormal; one through means, the other without means. Is this true of his natural kingdom? Has God many ways, or one way, of producing animal, vegetable, or any kind of

15

life? Is not his glorious power in the production of myriads of beings in all departments of his physical world manifest in this, that what is necessary for the producing of one is so for all? and that nothing more than he has appointed is necessary?

III. THE BLESSED CONSEQUENCES OF REGENERATION.

The Pythagoreans, who believed in the metempsychosis or transmigration of souls, called the union of the soul with a new body a regeneration. The Greeks called the Spring, when the dormant energies of earth and air are waked to new life and activity, the regeneration of the year. Christ, in one of the only two passages where the word is found in the Scriptures, calls the renovation he came to effect a regeneration. "Verily I say unto you, that ye which have followed me, in the regeneration when the Son of Man shall sit on the throne of his glory, ye also shall sit upon twelve thrones, judging the twelve tribes of Israel." (Matt. xix: 28.)

Christ does two things for those who receive him in the Gospel, which, though co-etaneous and inseparable, are, nevertheless, very distinct. When we believe in Christ, and obey the Gospel, we are freely justified for his sake. According to the terms of the New Covenant, our sins and iniquities are remembered no more. " He that believeth and is baptized shall be saved," are the words of the promise, and the promise, too, of him whose truth never fails. This salvation is not only from former condemnation; it not only obliterates the past, and places us before God justified; but it embraces the implanting in our hearts a new principle of life. We are, henceforth, a new creation in Christ Jesus: " Old things are passed away, and all things are become new." There is something done *for* us, and something done *in* us, by our Redeemer. This latter is the essential idea in Regeneration. It is a new life; but life has respect to a kingdom, and, therefore, we have a regenerated character and a regenerated state. Baptism is the consummation of the Divine process, and marks the point of transition from a state of alienation to one of reconciliation, pardon, and peace. He, then, who, according to the Gospel, puts on Christ, becomes in him a new creature; he is regenerated and born again. This is the spiritual metempsychosis. The new life in Christ is his, and, freed from the condemnation of sin, with the love of it eradicated from his heart, he begins a new existence; the spring of his new life has come; the old man of sin is destroyed, and the new man, created in the image of God, in righteousness and true holiness, lives in him. God has said to him: "Behold, I make all things new." The renovation is effected, and Christ is seated on the throne of his glory.

2d. "Whosoever is born of God doth not commit sin." (1 John iii: 9.) Whereas, before his new birth, sin had power over him, he now has power over sin. "He sinneth not, because his seed abideth in him." What a blessed result is this! The child of God not only has a new life, a new nature given him—he not only lives in a new state, but, when tempted by the world, the flesh, and the Devil, he has the power to resist; he is strong in the Lord, and in the power of his might. He not only has life, but he has it more abundantly. Would we all realized "the fullness of the blessing of the Gospel of Christ" brought to us in our regeneration!

3d. We are adopted into the family of God. We are begotten of him, and, therefore, are his children. The spirit of adoption is sent into our hearts. Thus speaks the

Apostle Paul, (Gal. iv: 6:) "And because ye are sons, God has sent forth the Spirit of his Son into your hearts, crying, Abba, Father." There is not a blessing of the New Covenant that is not included in this. The new-born soul feels its relationship to God, angels, and the redeemed in this world and around the throne of God. There is not a promise it may not claim; there is not a privilege it may not enjoy; there is not an honor in heaven or earth to which it may not aspire.

4th. We become heirs of God by our new birth. The wealth of the universe is ours; the riches of Christ are our patrimony. We may be as our Master was while on earth, poor and needy; but as our Master is, we also become heirs of the world. Thrones, and dominions, and powers are to be subject to us; for, as Christ overcame, and is seated on his Father's throne, so are we to overcome, and to be seated on Christ's throne. In a word, when we become children of God, we come into a new world; the powers and capacities of the soul are free from the thraldom of sin, and a new spirit is given us, and we are made heirs of God and joint-heirs with our Lord Jesus Christ. "All things are yours: whether Paul, or Apollos, or Cephas, or the world, or life, or death, or things present, or things to come; all are yours, and ye are Christ's, and Christ is God's."

Such, my brethren, is the teaching of Scripture on this interesting theme; and may God bless it to our minds and hearts that we may all come to the knowledge of the truth as it is in Jesus. *Amen.*

Yours fraternally and truly
Moses E Lard

MOSES E. LARD.

IF it be true that "just as the twig is bent the tree's inclined," then, if the author of a "Review of Campbellism Examined" did not grow up into a crooked tree, he certainly deserves great credit for overcoming his inclinations. But his life is a fine illustration of the wonderful workings of Providence, as "from seeming evil he is still educing good."

MOSES E. LARD was born in Bedford County, Tennessee, October 29th, 1818. His parents were Scotch, and migrated to Missouri when the son was about fourteen years of age. His father was a man of "quick, strong sense; tall and straight as an Indian, with a flashing eye and black hair; of manly bearing, candid, frank, and generous to a fault; loved his friend with an intense love, and hated his enemy with an intense hate; a man of great courage, quick temper, but cool and self-possessed." He was always very poor, and though respecting religion in others, never became religious himself. The mother was a deeply pious woman, a strict member of the Baptist Church, and thoroughly devoted to the moral training of her children. Soon after settling in Missouri, the father died of small-pox, leaving the widow and six children without any means of support. It was not long before the family was compelled to separate. The parting scene with his mother is thus described by the subject of this sketch: "As my brother and myself stood beneath the little cabin eaves, just ready to take leave of the only objects on earth dear to us, and thus close the saddest scene of our lives, my mother said: 'My dear boys, I have nothing to give you but my blessing and these two little books.' Her soul was breaking, and she could say no more. She then drew from her bosom two small Testaments; and as her tears were streaming, and lips quivering, she screamed as if it were her last, and placed them in our hands. We all said good-by, and that family was forever broken on earth. Yet, gentle reader, think us not poor as we turned from that mean abode. We bore with us a Christian mother's blessing, and the precious words of Jesus. *We were wealthy boys.* To that little book and the memory of that scene my future life owes its shaping. I never neglected the one, thank Heaven, nor forgot the other."

At seventeen years of age he was not able to write his own name; but finally learned to write by tearing down the advertisements stuck up around the village, and using them for copy. From about this time till he was twenty-three, he lived a hard life, and time dragged heavily on. He was deeply religious in feeling, though not so in life; for he did not know how to be so. He heard the various religious parties preach, but could not understand them. Finally, he was driven to infidelity. But after struggling awhile with its unsatisfactory conclusions, he heard one of the Disciples preach the primitive Gospel. He was at once captivated by its simplicity and beauty; and before the meeting closed, he was a Christian. He was twenty-three years of age when he was immersed, and the next year he held his "first meeting," an interesting account of which is given in No. 2, vol. 1 of the "Quarterly." On the 4th of March, 1845, he entered Bethany College. He had then a wife and two children. Under great pecuniary embarrassment he went through college, and graduated with distinguished honors, making the valedictory address. He then returned to Missouri, and entered actively and successfully upon the work of preaching the Gospel— most of his labors being in the evangelical field. In 1857, he published his "Review of Campbellism Examined," a work, which, when considered with reference to its design, simply leaves nothing more to be said. In 1859 he made a successful preaching tour through Kentucky; and returning home, had, in 1860, a debate of several days with a distinguished Methodist Presiding Elder, by the name of CAPLES. In 1863, he removed to Kentucky, and began the publication of the "Quarterly," an able periodical, which he still edits. He resides at present in Lexington, Kentucky.

Brother LARD is about six feet three inches high, has a large, bony frame, dark hair, small piercing eyes, and a mouth that indicates decision and great firmness. He has a strong analytical mind, is a close and vigorous thinker, and stands in the front rank of the Disciples as a writer and speaker. Though an extemporaneous speaker, his style is much the same when speaking as writing. Every sentence is uttered with a correctness and precision to which nothing but diligent, laborious preparation could attain. He is emphatically a student; not that he reads so many books, but that he completely *masters* whatever he undertakes. His preaching is characterized by more *heart power* than is generally supposed by those who have formed their judgments of him from his writings. His whole nature is in deep sympathy with all kinds of suffering; and when thoroughly aroused in the pulpit, he not unfrequently carries his audience before an irresistible tide of the most impassioned eloquence.

CHRIST'S CONVERSATION WITH NICODEMUS.

BY M. E. LARD.

"Except a man be born of water and of the Spirit, he can not enter into the kingdom of God."—John III : 5.

IT is difficult, if not impossible, in the judgment of most professors, to overestimate the importance of the new birth; and when we reflect on the position assigned it by the Savior, this judgment must be felt to be correct. Without it, no man can enter the kingdom of God. Into that kingdom he may desire to enter, may pray to enter, may even think he has entered; but into it he can never go, without being born again. This determines its value.

Now, in whatever the new birth may consist, whatever processes may be necessary to complete it, no matter how many, nor what its component parts, of one thing I am satisfied: its solution must be sought mainly in a well-conducted analysis of the conversation with Nicodemus. If, on examination, this conversation does not suggest its explanation, I shall despair of ever attaining one. Confirmation from other portions of Holy Writ this explanation may receive; but a solution the new birth itself will not receive. The conversation with Nicodemus is the very soil in which the pearl lies buried.

At once, then, I come to consider the great doctrinal statement, in that conversation, which involves the whole subject. It runs thus: "*Except a man be born of water, and of the Spirit, he can not enter into the kingdom of God.*" This statement I regard as presenting us with a complete view of the new birth, as informing us in what it consists, as comprehending, in other words, the two grand *facts* which constitute it. In the declaration, "Except a man be born again he can not see the kingdom of God," the Savior merely propounds the doctrine of the new birth generally, in a statement of the necessity of it; whereas, in the more elaborate statement, "Except a man be born of water and of the Spirit, he can not enter into the kingdom of God," he states definitively in what it consists, reiterating the necessity of it. The former statement propounds the doctrine, the latter statement explains it.

Now, unless it should turn out that the Savior has made provision equally for the salvation of those within and those without the kingdom of God, then the necessity of the new birth becomes absolute and overwhelming. If the blessing of remission of sins be limited to those within the kingdom, then neither flight of fancy nor fertility of imagination can exaggerate the importance of being born again. Should it so happen, moreover, that the Savior has, in the declaration now in hand, afforded us the means of knowing what it is to be born again; if he has put it beyond our power to plead unavoidable ignorance in regard to it, pity, Lord, pity the willful blindness of countless thousands who now call themselves the children of God!

The great statement of which I am now treating naturally distributes itself into two clauses, each clause comprehending an integral part of the new birth, and the two parts exhausting it. These clauses are respectively: *born of water, born of the Spirit*. I shall now attempt to unfold their meaning at length, and in the order in which they occur.

The first question to be settled, and a most important one, is: In what sense are we to construe the expression, *born of water?* in a literal or in a figurative sense? This question will, perhaps, be best answered by resolving the expression into the two simple members which compose it, and by examining each of them separately. These members are *born of* and *water*. To some this division may seem unnecessarily minute. I do not think it so. By thus breaking down the clause into these two simple verbal members, its subjects come singly into view, by which means each can be subjected to a more severe, because a more distinct, examination.

Upon the import of the expression "born of," which all allow to be metaphorical, there exists, I believe, no diversity of opinion, provided only we can settle definitely the import of the term water. Are we, then, to construe this term in its ordinary and literal acceptation, or in a figurative sense? In the latter sense, respond many. Let us now examine the hypothesis implied in this response, which, being concisely expressed in the form of a proposition, is this: *The term water is figurative.*

But this proposition is only asserted; it is not proved. Before, therefore, it can justly challenge our assent, it must be supported by relevant and satisfactory testimony. This testimony we have a right to demand, yet it has never been adduced, though the proposition has often been re-asserted. In proving the proposition, we should expect to see a course pursued something like the following: We should expect an accurate analysis of the

new birth, in which its constituent parts would all be
clearly pointed out; we should expect an orderly enumeration of these parts, *each being complete without water;* we
should expect at least a few apt remarks on the grounds
and propriety of using the term water in a figurative sense;
we should expect to be shown, with remarkable clearness,
what thing the term, in its figurative sense, is intended to
denote—precisely what it expresses; we should expect to
be then shown that this thing, thus expressed, actually constituted one of the previously enumerated parts of the new
birth; and, finally, we should expect the whole argument
to be strongly summed up, and the results shown to correspond minutely with the great elementary doctrines of
salvation as set forth by Christ and his apostles. But
have these reasonable expectations been gratified? They
have not.

Here, then, I might, on grounds strictly just, rest for
the present the discussion of this proposition. I shall,
however, proceed to test its accuracy still further, though,
in logical fairness, under no obligation to do so.

The term water is figurative. This is a tough saying.
Innumerable have been the efforts which have been made
to sustain it; yet not the semblance of success has ever
crowned one of them. On all lies the stain of iniquity.
What, I am curious to know, has ever put it into any
head of man to say of the term, it is figurative? The answer is not difficult. The literal meaning of the term
stands against those who have so said; stands against their
tenets, and shuts them out of the kingdom of God. Hence
to accommodate them it must be figurative. This, and no
other, is the answer.

But is the term figurative? Then is it so for sufficient
reasons, which being assigned, would account for the fact;

and these reasons are discoverable. For if no such reasons exist, then is the term figurative without a reason, which, in the case of a term used by the Savior, is inadmissible; and unless discoverable, though the reasons may exist, the effect is the same with us as though they had no existence. It is presumed, then, that these reasons, unless purely imaginary, will be found in some one or more of the following items:

1. *The nature of the case, of the new birth;*
2. *The laws regulating the use of figurative language;* or,
3 *The sense resulting from a figurative construction.*

First, then, as to the nature of the case. This I conceive to be the ground on which chiefly, if not alone, the figurative construction of the term water is to be defended. For if the nature of the case be such that this term can not be, in a literal acceptation, predicated of it, even in part, then is the figurative construction the alternative we must accept. Are we, then, obliged, by a necessity inherent in the nature of the case, to construe the term water figuratively? If not, then must we construe it ordinarily and literally. Now, if any such inherent necessity exist, it must be owing to the fact that the new birth is, in all its parts and circumstances, complete without water; for, if not thus complete, then we need the term water to express the fact. But before we can infer any thing from the nature of the case, we must, of course, know what the case itself is. Here, now, we encounter a serious difficulty. For, until the import of the term water is settled, the meaning of the new birth remains doubtful. This is one of the terms employed by the Savior to describe the new birth. Until, therefore, we settle its meaning, we remain ignorant to this extent of what the new birth is. Hence from the nature of this thing we can infer nothing.

But should it be alleged that we can know, independently of the import of the term water, in what the new birth consists, and therefore in what acceptation the term is to be taken, I ask how? There are but two possible ways. Either we must be able to know it in and of ourselves, and independently of the Word of God, or from passages of Scripture which contain no allusion to water. No one who is not willing to be the dupe of his own fancy, will assert that he can know any thing of the matter in the first-named way. Neither can he know any thing of it in the second, for the only passage in the New Testament, which describes the new birth fully, contains the term water. Hence, till we know what this term means, we shall never know what the new birth is.

Second: As to the laws regulating the use of figurative language. Most words, as is well known to the reader, are capable of being used in two acceptations: a literal or ordinary, and figurative; some even in three: literal, ordinary, and figurative. In many instances it happens that the ordinary import and the literal are the same, as is the case with the term water; in some, again, the ordinary and the figurative agree, while the literal often differs from both. Hence, in construing a passage, the first thing in order is to ascertain, by the aid of some safe rule, the acceptation in which its terms are to be taken. This rule is, with one consent, allowed to be mainly the sense intended by the writer. But this, though the chief, is not the only means frequently at hand for determining this point. The manner in which a term is introduced often enables us to decide it. When a term is attended by the words *like*, *so*, *as*, with many others, which serve to introduce comparisons and other figures, we at once pronounce the term, so attended, figurative. But where this is not the case, and

where the sense does not imperatively demand it, it is both
arbitrary and dangerous to construe a term figuratively.

Now, is the term water, in the clause in hand, attended
by any verbal sign indicative of a figurative use? Certainly not. Here, then, the inference is conclusive against
a figurative construction. But does not the sense of the
passage require it to be so construed? True, it is so
asserted; but this is precisely the thing which I deny, and
which I do not intend shall be taken for granted. But
the assertion can not be true; for, on the contrary, it is
only when the term is construed literally that the clause
makes any sense at all. Construe it figuratively, and you
forever hide every vestige of meaning in the clause. Indeed, the real question here at issue is not whether the
term is or is not figurative, but whether it has a literal,
or absolutely no meaning. The question is not what
meaning are men willing to receive, but what is the meaning they *must receive*, or reject all meaning. Too many,
I well know, are not willing to receive the literal meaning;
and this is their sole reason for preferring a figurative one.
But this is not to make the will of God, but the preference of man, our rule of action.

But let us concede for a moment that the term water is
figurative. To what class, then, of figurative words does
it belong? Indisputably it is a metaphor; for to this
class belong all those words which are used figuratively
with no verbal sign to denote the fact. Now, a word is
used metaphorically when it is taken from denoting what
it ordinarily means to become, for the present, the name
of something which it does not ordinarily mean. Still,
in all cases, it becomes the name of some *real thing*, never
of *nothing*. A word, moreover, is used metaphorically because the thing which it usually denotes resembles, in more

or less respects, the thing which it is used metaphorically to denote, and because it is wished to suggest that resemblance. Of metaphors there are two classes, determined by the manner in which we discover the meaning of the metaphoric word. To the first class belong all those words which, on being simply heard in their connection, instantly, without any extrinsic aid, suggest to the mind their meaning. To the second, all those words which, on being simply heard, do not instantly suggest their meaning, so deeply is it hid, but have it brought out by some added explanation.

The following may serve as instances of the two classes:

1. The Savior said of Herod: "Go and tell that fox, behold I cast out demons, and I do cures to-day and to-morrow, and the third day I shall be perfected." Here we as instantly collect his meaning as if he had said, Go and tell that *cunning king*.

2. "He that believes in me, as the Scripture has said, out of him shall flow *rivers of living water*." Here the mind is held in complete suspense, unable to penetrate the mystery in which the term water involves the sentence, until it is added: "But this spoke he of the Spirit which they that believe on him should receive."

Now, to which of these two classes—and there are no others—does the term water, now in question, belong? Not to the latter; for no explanatory clause is added. Neither to the former; for, on being pronounced, it suggests, on the figurative hypothesis, just no meaning at all. Hence, again from these premises nothing can be inferred in support of the preceding proposition, but, rather, it is felt to be false.

Third: The sense resulting from a figurative construction. This brings me to notice the most objectionable feature in this whole theory; for, not only has the term water been treated as figurative, without a single reason, but, where it has been assigned any meaning at all, it has been a most fanciful one. Surely, my hearers need not be informed that figurative language has meaning no less than literal; nor that an idea is wholly unaffected by the kind of language in which it is conveyed. A thought remains the same whether communicated in literal or in figurative language. But, clearly, he who asserts a word to be figurative, must know what it means; otherwise, if conscientious, he would not venture the assertion. Hence, clearly, must they who assert that the term water is figurative, know what it means. But have they pointed that meaning out? Never; this they dare not attempt.

True, we are told that water is an emblem—an emblem, too, of purification. But the term water, now in hand, is held to be figurative; hence, of course, there is here no water. It is excluded by the very nature of the case; therefore, since there is here no water, there is here no emblem; and since no emblem, nothing emblemized, and hence no purification. Thus this groundless conceit vanishes.

But is the term water figurative? Granted, for a moment. Still, it has meaning. Let, now, this meaning be determined—definitely determined. Next, let the term water be displaced from the clause in hand, but its meaning retained in some fit word. Then let us read: "Except a man be born of [*the thing which the term water denotes, no matter what it is*] and the Spirit, he can not enter into the kingdom of God." From this there is absolutely no escape. Settle what the term water stands for. Then, of that thing unless a man be born, against him the kingdom of God is forever shut. True, we thus get rid of the water; but whether we thereby ease the way into the kingdom of God, may well be doubted. Still, two things are left, of both of which we must be born. This increases difficulties, not diminishes them; hence, better retain the water. Then only are we true to reason, true to Christ.

Since, then, it is only asserted, not proved, that the term water is figurative; since there is no inherent necessity in the nature of the case for this construction; since the laws of figurative language do not demand it; and since, from such construction, either no sense at all results, or one which does not better the case—since all these things are true, I hence conclude that the term water is construed correctly only when taken in its literal and ordinary acceptation. Hence, when the Savior says, "Except a man be born of water," he means simply and literally water.

What, now, is it to be born of water? On this question I need not dwell long. To be born of, as already conceded, is figurative. Literally, it denotes the event which brings us into natural life; figuratively, then, it must denote an event like it. The two events must resemble each other as type resembles impression, or, if not so exactly, still closely. First, then, we have water given; second, in this a man is buried; third, out of it he emerges. Is not this being born of water? If the reason or the eye may be appealed to in any case to settle either the meaning of a word, or determine the analogy of facts, the question is answered. *This is being born of water.* But this is precisely what takes place in immersion; hence, I conclude that, to be born of water and be immersed are merely two different names—that figurative, this literal—for one and the same act.

A corroborative item or two, and I am done with the first part of my subject. Water is never present in any act connected with the kingdom of Christ, except one. But in that act it is always present, and never absent. That act is immersion. But in the expression, "born of water," *water is present;* hence, it must be in immersion, since it can be in nothing else. Again, it seems that to be born of water and be immersed are identical.

Christ is called the first-born from the dead. This is the statement of a fact, and in it occurs the word born. The fact is Christ's rising from the dead; hence, to arise out of the grave is to be born from the dead. But a man is dead to sin, is buried in the water, and rises out of it. If, now that rising can be called being born from the dead, then is this rising being born of water. If, in argument, analogy be worth any thing, it is decisive here.

If the expression, "born of water," does not signify immersion, its meaning is not determinate. Then, no living man can say whether he is in, or not in, the kingdom of God. But Christ has not left us in doubt on so vital a point; hence, the expression must be determinate, and signifies immersion.

I here terminate my examination of the clause "born of water." The result is submitted to the candid and thoughtful hearer only, but to him with no fear as to the end.

I now proceed to inquire into the meaning of the second division of my subject, namely, "Born of the Spirit." Important as has been the discussion of the preceding division, the discussion of this will be generally felt to be still more so, and I by no means wish to diminish the just interest which may be felt in it.

I shall set out with the assumption, new, perhaps, to many, that the Savior, after stating in what the new birth consists, then proceeds to explain so much of it as is em-

16

braced in the clause "born of the Spirit." One thing, at least, will be conceded, that what is here embraced was least likely to be understood, and, therefore, stood most in need of explanation. Upon the import of the clause "born of water" the great Teacher said nothing. Of this Nicodemus needed no explanation. As soon as he learned from the Savior that he spoke not of a literal re-birth, instantly the meaning of the clause would flash into his mind. He would intuitively take the term water literally; this done, and the meaning of "born of" would be at once perceived. But not so with the phrase "born of the Spirit." Of necessity all would be dark here. Of being born of the Spirit, or of being begotten by it, he had no means of information. To him the subject was absolutely new. Not one incident of universal history could shed a ray of light on it. In his case, therefore, an explanation was especially necessary. Hence the assumption that we have one.

With what is here last said, corresponds, as I deem, the next verse; namely, "That which is born of the flesh is flesh; and that which is born of the Spirit is spirit." Hardly can this verse be held to be free from difficulty; not that its difficulty is insuperable, but only that it is not free from it. In the expression, "that which is born of the flesh is flesh," we have the statement of a simple well-known matter of fact. In this statement every word is to be taken literally; nor can any one acquainted with the fact stated misunderstand the terms in which it is expressed. Flesh produces flesh literally, or the one is the offspring of the other. This we know to be so. But the difficulty lies not here. It is in the expression "that which is born of the Spirit is spirit;" or more strictly, perhaps, in the parallelism which we draw between the two expressions. In the expression last cited the word born is not to be taken literally; for in regeneration no personal spirit is produced; that is, the Holy Spirit does not produce the human spirit in the sense in which flesh produces flesh. In regeneration the human spirit is only *changed*, not *produced*. Hence, in the second expression, the word born is not to be taken literally but figuratively, as denoting, in general terms, simply a change. Now the difficulty, as I conceive, lies here: In drawing the parallel we make Spirit stand to spirit as flesh stands to flesh, in each case the one producing the other. Clearly this is wrong. Certainly flesh produces flesh; but Spirit only changes spirit. Here there is no product, at least no product of substantive spirit. Hence in the first expression the word born is to be taken literally, but in the second figuratively. This causes, unless carefully noticed, confusion, and in this we feel the difficulty. But how, it may be asked, do I know this, or from what do I learn it? I answer, from the very nature of the case. In regeneration the human spirit already exists; it is hence not produced. Consequently the difference in the subjects determines a difference in the terms.

But on the supposition that the Savior is now explaining so much of the new birth as relates to the spirit, this is precisely what we should expect him to say. The word born denotes a change. The Holy Spirit is the agent who effects this change: the human spirit is the subject in which it takes place. That which is born of Spirit—the Holy Spirit, is spirit—the human spirit. The Holy Spirit begets the human; that is, effects the change which takes place in it. The whole process embraces four items, indicated in the four following questions: 1. Who effects the change? 2. What is changed? 3. How is the change effected? 4. In what does it consist when affected? These four questions exhaust the subject. Two of them have now been answered—the Holy Spirit effects the change, the human spirit is changed. Only two, therefore, remain to be answered. Of these the Savior, in the following verses, answers only the third; namely, how is the change effected? The fourth is not answered by him in the interview with Nicodemus, but is answered elsewhere in the New Testament, as will be shown in the course of this sermon.

Here it is proper to determine another point before proceeding further. Should we read *born* of the Spirit, or *begotten* by it? This depends altogether on the view we are taking of the matter in hand. If we are viewing regeneration as completed, completed in both its parts, completed in water, completed in spirit, then it is proper to say born of the Spirit; otherwise it obviously is not. Whenever the two parts of the process are viewed separately, then, clearly, we should say begotten by the Spirit, not born. The Holy Spirit begets the human, or, more strictly, begets a change in it, prepares it for entrance into the kingdom of God. In this preparation, the Holy Spirit, as agent, merely acts on the human spirit, changing it. The human spirit is not conceived of as coming out of, or proceeding from, the Holy Spirit. Hence begotten, not born, is the proper word. Again: being begotten by the Spirit is the first part of the whole process of being born again. It consequently antecedes the other part, being born of water, and is hence more correctly expressed by begotten than born. Further: as the word born applies to the last act in natural generation, so likewise it applies to the last act in regeneration. This act, in regeneration, is coming out of the water. Hence to it we should apply born, to the other, begotten. Accordingly the verse in hand would, perhaps, be more correctly rendered: *That which is begotten by the flesh is flesh, and that which is begotten by the Spirit is spirit.* This much must be correct, more than this might not be; it is hence best to say this much, no more. Certainly, in the fifth verse, we should render the original by born, thus: "Except a man be born of water and of the Spirit, he can not enter into the kingdom of God." Here begotten is wholly inadmissible, since we can not be begotten by water, but must be born of it. Again, it is not by being begotten simply that we enter into the kingdom of God; it is by being born. In the fifth verse the word denotes the act which translates us into the kingdom. It is hence the act of being born, not of being begotten. In the subsequent verses, however, where the word occurs, it is best to render it begotten. I shall accordingly do so, as already in the sixth.

It will be remembered that we are now speaking on the assumption that after the fifth verse, the Savior proceeds to explain how we are begotten by the Spirit. With this assumption agrees the seventh verse more naturally than with any other. The verse reads: "Marvel not that I said to thee, ye must be born again." When I am speaking to a man, and it is obvious to my eye that he does not understand me; and I say to him: Wonder not that I should speak to you thus; for what, most naturally, does my remark prepare him? for an illustration or an explanation? If I have already explained myself, clearly it prepares him for an illustration. But if not, then an explanation is expected. Now, in the case in hand, the Savior had submitted no explanation. Most naturally, then, it seems would his remark induce the expectation of one. I hence still assume that the following verse contains one.

The verse reads thus: "*The wind bloweth where it listeth, and thou hearest the sound thereof, but canst not tell whence it cometh, and whither it goeth; so is every one that is born of the Spirit."*

No passage in the New Testament has been so variously and so inconsistently construed as this. Hardly any two men understand it alike. Hence it is cited to prove any thing or nothing, as may happen to suit the tenets of him who uses it. Generally, by the parties of the day, it is held as containing an *illustration* of the mystery of being begotten by the Spirit. This, I conceive to be the radical misconception which has utterly obscured the sense of this fine passage. Without one solitary verbal mark, in the original, indicative of an illustration, or the slightest ground on which to conclude that one was ever meant, has the verse been assumed to be illustrative, and rendered accordingly. A more unaccountable departure from some of the best established laws of exegesis than its rendering, in some respects, exhibits, I have not met with. And long since, I doubt not, would the present rendering have been utterly discarded, had it not contributed to foster a deep-seated error on the subject now in hand. To any one who is bold enough to think for himself, it is clear that the verse, as it now reads, has simply no appreciable meaning whatever. I shall hence, with no sort of scruple, use whatever means may be at command to free it from darkness.

First, then, in regard to the word which, in our common version, is rendered "*wind.*" This word occurs in the Greek New Testament three hundred and eighty-six times. In three hundred and eighty-four of these it is rendered into English either by the term *spirit* or by its equivalent *ghost.* Once, in the book of Revelation, it is rendered "life," where, beyond doubt, it should have been rendered "a spirit." But in not a single case, in the New Testament, except the verse in hand, is it rendered "*wind*." Now, in translating, one great rule to be observed is this: To translate the same original word *uniformly* by the same equivalent English word, unless the sense forbids it. No translation is deemed good which violates this rule, none very faulty which does not. Now, since the word in hand, out of three hundred and eighty-six instances, is, in three hundred and eighty-four of them, uniformly rendered by the word *spirit*, or by a word of the same meaning, the presumption in favor of a similar rendering, in the two remaining instances, is as three hundred and eighty-four to two. And when it is remembered that the sense does not forbid this rendering, this presumption becomes an imperious necessity. For these reasons, therefore, I render the original by the word spirit, understanding thereby, *the Holy Spirit.*

The leading word thus rendered, and the whole verse is literally translated thus: *The Spirit breathes where it sees fit, and you hear its voice, but know not whence it comes and where it goes; in this way is every one who is begotten by the Spirit.*

On this passage, three questions arise, namely: What act of the Spirit does the word breathe express? Is it true that we of this day know not whence the Spirit comes, and where it goes? And is the sense of the last clause of the verse complete?

1. What act of the Spirit does the word breathe express? Be it what it may, one thing is clear, in the act something is *heard*. This word, then, suggests a probable answer to the question. Only when the Spirit *speaks*, do we *hear* it. Speaking, then, is most likely the act which the word breathe metaphorically expresses. With this, moreover, agrees the word *voice*. The original of this word is a gen-

eric term, expressing sound generally; but, when applied
to persons, it always denotes the voice heard in speaking.
But, in the present case, it applies to the Holy Spirit, a
person. Hence, it is legitimate to infer that it denotes
the voice of the Spirit heard in speaking. But this voice
is never heard, except through prophets and apostles. It
is only when in man that the Spirit speaks to him; hence,
the act is an act of speaking, and the voice heard, the voice
of inspired men. Through these men the Spirit speaks,
and, speaking thus, we hear its voice.

2. Is it true of us in the present day that we know not
whence the Spirit comes, and where it goes, or is the clause
applicable to us? I reply: The clause is not applicable to
us of this day, for the reason that, in no intelligible sense,
can it be said of us that we know not the whence and the
whither of the Spirit. Indisputably it comes from God,
and is sent into the saints. But this, though true of us,
was not true of Nicodemus. We have light on the point,
which he had not. Of him, therefore, the clause was true,
but not of us. As yet, the Savior had taught nothing
respecting the Spirit; the apostles had taught nothing, and
the New Testament was not written. That, therefore,
was true of Nicodemus at the time, which is inapplicable
to us, and which ceased to be true of him, if he lived, as
soon as the Spirit was sent. Hence, in construing the
verse, we must construe it as all applicable to him, but
as applicable to us only with the clause in hand omitted.
In one view only can the clause be deemed applicable to
us of the present day. If the Spirit be conceived of as
roaming up and down on the face of the earth, in some
occult manner unmentioned in the Bible, and unintelligible to man, then may we construe the clause of ourselves. In any other view, it must be held as applying

only to Nicodemus, and only when applied to him has it any determinate meaning. The view of the clause here maintained frees the verse from at least half the confusion which lies on it. It is presented as necessary, and as barely disputable, and certainly relieves a passage of Scripture of no small difficulty.

3. Is the sense of the last clause of the verse complete, namely, *in this way is every one who is begotten by the Spirit?* That it is not, is intuitively felt by every reader. Involuntarily, we ask, in what way? The question implies the incompleteness of the sense; for, were the sense complete, no impulse would be felt to ask the question. Now, in order to render the sense full, and to leave no question remaining, we have to use, in translating, one word more than is in the original. Are we at liberty to do this? Certainly it is often done; but should it be done here? I believe it should ; and my reasons for so believing are concisely these: First, as already said, the sense is incomplete without the word. There is, therefore, a necessity for it. Indeed, without it the verse is an eternal enigma. Second, to supply a word not only completes the sense, but gives a sense in strict accordance with what we know to be elsewhere taught. In a doubtful case, these two reasons for a particular conclusion, with none against it, may be generally accepted as decisive. I, hence, decide in favor of the word. Supplying it, and the clause reads thus : *In this way is begotten every one who is begotten by the Spirit.*

It will be remembered that, in commencing the investigation of the second part of my subject, I assumed that an explanation of *how* we are begotten by the Spirit, was contained in the following verses. I am now ready to show that this assumption was well taken. In order to do this,

I shall omit the clause herein held to be inapplicable to us, merely that I may present, in closer union, the really dependent clauses of the verse. Omitting, as here said, and the whole verse reads thus: *The Spirit breathes where it sees fit, and you hear its voice; in this way is begotten every one who is begotten by the Spirit.* How, then, is a person begotten by the Spirit? *By hearing its voice.* Of the truth of this, I feel profoundly convinced, whether the preceding premises necessitate it or not.

In confirmation, however, of the conclusion, I cite the two following Scriptures.

1. "Of his [the Father's] own will begat he us *with the word of truth*." But the word of truth is what we hear from the Spirit. Now, by this, James affirms we are begotten. The preceding conclusion, therefore, is true. That to be begotten by the Father and by the Spirit is one and the same begetting, is here taken for granted.

2. "Being begotten again, not of corruptible seed, but of incorruptible, *by the word of God*." Here Peter declares, in so many words, that we are begotten by the word of God. This word is from the Spirit, and is what we hear. Hence, by hearing, we are begotten again.

4. But when begotten, in what does the change consist? The following contains the answer: "*Every one who believes that Jesus is the Christ, has been begotten of God.*" (1 John v: 1.)

From this passage, one of two conclusions indisputably results: Either to be begotten of God is to believe, or this includes that, since every believer is begotten. It is here held that to be begotten and to believe are identical. Hence, when a person is begotten, the change consists in believing that Jesus is the Christ. Here, then, I end the second part of my subject.

Finally, from all the foregoing premises and reasonings, I conclude that to be "born of water" is simply to be immersed; and to be begotten by the Spirit, to believe in Jesus Christ. Few conclusions of men will ever rest on safer grounds, or be better entitled to confidence.

And now to show, in conclusion, that when Christ says, "He that believes and is immersed shall be saved," he only asserts, at the close of his earthly career, what he had, at its commencement, asserted to Nicodemus in different language, I submit the following:

He that believes, and is immersed, is saved, and is, therefore, in the kingdom of God. Hence, he that believes, and is immersed, is born of water and of the Spirit, for, otherwise, he can not enter the kingdom of God. The only way to escape the force of this pithy argument is to deny that he who is saved is in the kingdom of God. If a man can not be saved, and be at the same time out of the kingdom, the argument is final.

very truly yours
J. S. Sweeny

JOHN STEELE SWEENEY.

THE subject of this sketch was born near Liberty, Kentucky, September 4, 1832. His father, G. E. SWEENEY, was of Irish descent, and a Baptist in his younger days, but, "when he became a man, he put away childish things," and has since been an earnest advocate for the primitive order of things. His mother, whose maiden name was CAMPBELL, was of Scotch-Irish extraction, and was brought up under Methodist influence, but, for more than thirty years, has been a member of the Christian Church.

His parents were poor, and lived in a country not very well supplied with good schools; consequently, his early education was greatly neglected. After he was fully grown, however, he acquired a respectable education.

Having begun the study of the law, he left Kentucky, in 1854, and went to Illinois, where he continued to prepare himself for his chosen profession, and, just as the most flattering prospects were opening up to him as a lawyer, he became convinced that it was his duty to preach the Gospel. Acting under this conviction, in 1856, he entered actively upon the work of the ministry, and has been constantly engaged in this calling ever since. His labors have been chiefly confined to Illinois, though he has preached considerable in Missouri, Iowa, Wisconsin, Indiana, Ohio, and Kentucky. During this time, he was located two years in Chicago, and a little over one, in Cincinnati. Most of his labor has been in the general field, and his success there has been all that could be desired, having received into the Church, by immersion, about two thousand two hundred persons.

With Methodists, Baptists, Presbyterians, Universalists, and Soul-sleepers, he has held *twenty-five* public discussions, two or three of which have been published. For one so young, this is a rather *pugnacious* record; but when the fact is stated that he has declined equally as many discussions as accepted, and that he never challenged nor sought debate but once in his life, we may be inclined to alter our opinion somewhat. He is not *afraid* of discussion, but does not *seek* it. He thinks that honest investigation is the most certain way to elicit truth; hence, he has generally

(253)

accepted all fair propositions that would be of public interest. His debates have always been largely attended, and have never failed to gain new trophies for the cause of Christ. His home at present is at Winchester, Illinois.

Brother SWEENEY has, in some respects, a peculiar mind. He can not be called a hard student of books; in fact, if you were with him awhile, you would think he never studies them at all. And yet his brain is never idle. He does not read much, but he *thinks*. He is forever working at some problem in theological polemics, or arranging facts and arguments for use in preaching the Gospel; hence, his sermons abound in apt and forcible illustrations. His style of preaching is well adapted to the masses. Every argument is brought out with the utmost clearness, and, however we may be disposed to differ from him, there is never any excuse for misunderstanding him.

While his mind is eminently logical, he has, nevertheless, fine descriptive powers, and is capable of producing superior word paintings. He has seen much of the world, not that he has traveled so extensively—though he has traveled considerable—but he has actually *experienced* about what is the aggregate of human life, and this experience enables him to form very correct judgments of men and things.

He is six feet high, has dark hair, light hazel eyes, and weighs about one hundred and seventy pounds. He has, naturally, a powerful physical constitution, though it is somewhat impaired by ill-usage. He is social and fraternal in his intercourse with men, but somewhat reticent as to his plans of life.

BAPTISM—ITS ACTION, SUBJECT, AND DESIGN.

BY J. S. SWEENEY.

"Go ye therefore, and teach all nations, baptizing them into the name of the Father, and of the Son, and of the Holy Spirit."—MATT. XXVIII: 19.

I PROPOSE, in this discourse, to examine briefly three questions relating to baptism: 1. What is it? 2. Who may Scripturally be baptized? and, 3. What is it for?

I. WHAT IS BAPTISM?

An elaborate argument of this question is not proposed; a fair statement of it, of the positions of parties to it, and of what is claimed and what is conceded by these parties, being deemed all-sufficient for the purpose sought to be accomplished.

The word "baptize" is not strictly English, but an Anglicised Greek word. What is the meaning of this word when expressed in English? Immersionists answer: It means simply immerse. Hence they claim that baptism is immersion; no more, no less. On the other hand, Pedobaptists, so-called, give the question no definite answer at all, but claim that immersion, pouring, and sprinkling are all equally valid "*modes* of baptism," and practice accordingly. They hence do not, at the present day, *define* the word "baptize" at all. And how can they do so, while

(255)

holding and practicing as they do? Suppose they were to say it means immerse, what authority would remain for pouring or sprinkling? And if they were to say it means "pour," then what authority would they have for immersing and sprinkling? And were they to define it "sprinkle," then they would be left without any authority for immersing and pouring. If, therefore, they define the word "baptize" at all, they must give it a definition broad enough to cover their entire practice; and if they define it to mean immerse, pour, and sprinkle—and nothing short of this will cover their whole practice—then they would have to immerse, pour, and sprinkle a person before they could claim to have him fully baptized. Thus we see why it is they never define this word. This is deemed a fair statement of the positions of the parties to the question.

I will next notice what is claimed and what conceded in the controversy. It is claimed by immersionists, that, in classic Greek literature, the word is invariably used in the sense of immerse; that, in every instance of its occurrence in Greek literature, it must be translated into immerse, or some of its equivalents, to make sense of the passage in which it stands. "BAPTISM; ITS MEANING AND USE," a small volume, published by the American Bible Union, contains, it is claimed by the learned author (Dr. CONANT), all the instances of the occurrence of this word in classic Greek literature, by an examination of which the English reader even may satisfy himself as to its uniform meaning. On the other hand, it is very generally conceded by Pedobaptist scholars that the word does usually have this sense in classic Greek. They claim, however, that it sometimes signifies "wash," "dye," "stain," etc. But in classic Greek they never translate it "pour" or "sprinkle." They claim that in the New Testament it is not used in its classic sense. This is deemed a fair statement of what is claimed, and what conceded, as to the *use* of the word.

The Greek lexicons define the word, very generally, in accordance with its use, to mean "immerse," or what is equivalent to it, and very generally give this as its primary meaning, *not one of them ever defining it to mean "pour" or "sprinkle."* They do, however, it is freely admitted, give "wash," "dye," "stain," as meanings of the word, but generally as secondary meanings, some of them being so careful as to say it has such meanings *only by consequence.* For example, BAILEY says: "Baptism, in strictness of speech, is that *kind* of washing which consists in dipping, and when applied to the Christian institution, so-called, it was used by the primitive Christians in *no other sense* than that of dipping."* ALSTEDIUS says: "Baptism, to baptize, signifies only to immerse, not to wash, *except by consequence.*"†

These lexicographers were Pedobaptists, and would be inclined, of course, to favor their own practice as far as they could, and preserve their honor and reputation as scholars; yet, when they give wash as a meaning of *baptize,* they are careful to say it does not have this meaning, "except by consequence." Baptism can only mean "that kind of washing which consists in dipping." And only in this sense can dye, stain, soil, etc., be given as meanings of the word. Any thing immersed may be washed, dyed, or stained, as a consequence of the immersion. Whether dyed, or washed, or stained, depends upon the character of the element in which the immersion is performed. By metonymy, such consequences of an action may be put for the action itself. In this way we often

* Dict., Dr. Scott's ed., 1772.   † Lex. Theolog., p. 221.

17

put wash, dye, stain, soil, etc., for the English word dip. For example: when the dyer dips an article into the dye, we say he dyes it, when, in strictness of speech, he *dips* it, and, as a *consequence*, it is dyed. When, then, the washer dips the same article into water, we say he washes it, when, in fact, the article washed is only a consequence of the dipping in water. But shall we, therefore, conclude that wash is the meaning of dip? Certainly not. So it is of *baptize*, exactly. Wash, dye, stain, etc., are only *consequential* significations of the word. It would be a wonderful word, indeed, to mean primarily to wash, and, at the same time, to mean primarily to dye, which is precisely the opposite. These opposite ideas can only be attached to the word by metonymy. But are we to take the word baptize in the New Testament in this secondary and consequential sense exclusively? Or, shall we not rather take it in its primary, usual, and most known signification? We have no *special* rule given for the interpretation of words in the Bible, nor have we any intimation that this word *baptize* is therein used in any other than its usual and known signification; and hence, if it is not subject to the known and ordinary rules of interpretation, the Bible is more a deception than a revelation. But we must avoid this conclusion; and how shall we do it? Simply by interpreting this word in the ordinary way. Let us, therefore, read an acknowledged rule of interpretation of words: Sir William Blackstone says: "Words of a law are generally to be understood in their usual and most known signification, not so much regarding the propriety of grammar as their *general* and *popular* use."* Common sense floats upon the very surface of this rule. It is one by which all trans-

---

* Commentaries, vol. 1, Introd., sec. ii.

lators, as well as interpreters, must be governed, the only exception to the rule being where the circumstances of its use imperiously demand for any word a secondary signification, to preserve the sense and congruity of the passage in which the word occurs.   As, therefore, the word baptize stands in the New Testament without any express qualification, we must accept it in its current, usual, and most known signification—which, confessedly, is immerse—unless the sense and congruity of the Scripture language are made to suffer.

Let us next notice the New Testament use of the word, and see whether or not the sense, propriety, or congruity of the Scripture language will suffer from a literal translation of it.   In the record of John's administration of the rite, we have the following passages :

"And there went out unto him all the land of Judea, and they of Jerusalem, and were all baptized of him in the river of Jordan." (Mark i: 5.)   "Jesus came from Nazareth of Galilee, and was baptized of John in Jordan." (Matt. iii: 10.) "And Jesus, when he was baptized, went up straightway out of the water."   "And John was baptizing in Enon, near to Salim, because there was much water there." (John iii: 23.)

To read, "were immersed of him in the river," makes good sense.   Between this rendering of the word, and the fact that the baptizing was done "in the river," there is no incongruity; while to substitute either pour or sprinkle for baptize will destroy the sense and congruity of the passage.   "*Poured in the river, of him*"—that is, the people were poured in the river, of John—is rather an awkward, not to say absurd, reading.   Again: to say Jesus "was immersed in Jordan, of John," conveys sense to the reader; and between this reading and the fact that Jesus, "when he was baptized, went up straightway out of the water," there is no such palpable incongruity as is created by the substitution of either pour or sprinkle. And, why was John "baptizing in Enon?" "Because there was much water there." For immersing, "much water" is a necessity; while, for pouring or sprinkling, a *very little* will suffice. This circumstance, then, to say the least of it, rather favors immersion. To evade this argument, it is sometimes said by the advocates of pouring and sprinkling that, doubtless, the "much water" was needed for other purposes than that of baptizing, and, therefore, it was that John was preaching there. But, evidently, no such notion was in the mind of the Spirit. The fact that "there was much water there," is given as the reason why "John was *baptizing* in Enon, near Salim."

In the record of the *Acts of the Apostles* we have this remarkably circumstantial case given: "And as they [Philip and the eunuch] went on their way, they came to a certain water, and the eunuch said, See, here is water, what doth hinder me to be baptized? . . . . . And they both went down into the water, both Philip and the eunuch, and he baptized him, and when they had come up out of the water," etc. (Acts viii: 36–39.)

Here, it is said, that in order to baptize, *they went down into the water*, and when the baptizing was performed, they came *up out of the water*. Do these circumstances of the use of "baptize" demand for it a secondary rather than its usual signification? Certainly not. The word "baptize" means immerse, and the circumstances here recorded strongly indicate it. So strongly and plainly does this language indicate immersion, that we see persons now-a-days frequently go down into the water merely to sprinkle a few drops on the face of a candidate. And why should they *go down into the water for such purpose?* Who can tell?

In Paul's epistles we have the following allusions to baptism, which imply immersion as clearly as any language can: "Therefore we are buried with him by baptism into death." (Rom. vi: 4.) "Buried with him in baptism, wherein also ye are risen with him." (Col. ii: 12.) "Having our hearts sprinkled from an evil conscience, and our bodies washed with pure water." (Heb. x: 22.) No honest person, though unlearned, need be in doubt as to what baptism is with these passages before him. To substitute pouring or sprinkling for baptism in any one of these passages, would make the passage perfectly absurd. And can persons, who have only had a few drops of water sprinkled on their faces, say, we have had our *bodies washed* with pure water? Will pouring or sprinkling answer the demands of this passage in Hebrews? Certainly not. Then, we find that the use of the word in the New Testament, the circumstances recorded as to the performance of the rite, the references to it in the Epistles, as well as the explanations of its significance, require its *primary sense*, and will not admit of a secondary one.

"I indeed baptize you *with* water" is sometimes cited as indicating an application of water to the subject, rather than an immersion of the subject in water; but it is exceedingly difficult to see how any scholar can rely on this passage as favoring pouring and sprinkling. The word "with," in the passage, is not a correct rendering of the Greek word *en*, for it can not be denied that *en* most usually signifies *in*. And would it not be much easier to give it its primary meaning in the passage, and read, "I indeed baptize you in water," than to harmonize all the other passages noticed with the idea of pouring and sprinkling? And, then, if this does prove an application of the water to the subject, we can not translate baptize, pour, or sprinkle, for neither of these is even a *secondary* meaning of the word. It is never so translated or defined.

Down to the middle of the last century, it was admitted by Pedobaptists very generally, that *baptize* means immerse; that our Lord instituted immersion; that the apostles practiced it exclusively; and that the Church knew nothing else for baptism till the middle of the third century; and that affusion of water for baptism was substituted *by the Church*, in favor of *clinics*, and for convenience, where the climate was cold and water scarce. To all this only eminent Pedobaptists shall testify. And in the first place, we will hear one whose ecclesiastical history is a standard among Protestants, and who was himself a Lutheran.

Dr. MOSHEIM: "The sacrament of baptism was administered in this [the first] century without the public assemblies, in places appointed and prepared for that purpose, and was performed by an immersion of the whole body in the baptismal font."* Also, speaking of baptism in the second century, the same author says: "The persons that were to be baptized, after they had repeated the creed, confessed and renounced their sins, and particularly the devil and his pompous allurements, were immersed under water." So much for *primitive practice.*

Dr. WALL, author of the "History of Infant Baptism," says: "In cases of sickness, weakness, haste, want of quantity of water, or such like extraordinary occasions, baptism by affusion of water on the face was by the ancients counted sufficient baptism." The doctor then proceeds to give a few of the "most ancient cases" of such baptism, and gives, as the most ancient case, that of Novatian, who had water poured upon him, on a sick bed,

* Eccl. Hist., vol. 1, p. 46.

A. D. 251. And this was counted sufficient baptism *only by the Church at that day.* [*]

RICHARD BAXTER: "We grant that baptism, then, [in primitive times] was by washing the whole body, and did not the difference of our cold country as to that hot one teach us to remember 'I will have mercy, and not sacrifice,' *it should be so here.*" [†]

GROTIUS: "The custom of sprinkling or pouring seems to have prevailed in favor of those who were dangerously ill, and were desirous of giving up themselves to the Lord, whom others called *clinics.* See the Epistle of Cyprian to Magnus." [‡]

PERKINS: "The ancient custom of baptizing was to dip, and, as it were, to dive all the body of the baptized under the water, as may appear in Paul, Rom. vi, and the councils of Laodicea and Neocesarea; but now, specially in cold countries, *the Church* useth only to sprinkle the baptized, by reason of children's weakness—for very few of ripe years are nowadays baptized. We need not much to marvel at *this alteration,* seeing charity and necessity may dispense with ceremonies and mitigate in equity the sharpness of them." [||]

WESLEY explains Rom. vi: 3, "Alluding to the *ancient manner* of baptizing by immersion." [§]

Next, that we may have the matter still more clearly before us, we will hear from a distinguished Romanist. Speaking of "the foundation of continuing the communion under one kind," as he styled the subject, BOSSUET says: "Baptism, by immersion, which is as clearly

---

[*] See Wall's Hist. Inf. Bap., part ii, chap. ix, p. 463.

[†] Paraphrase of the New Testament, at Matt. iii: 6.

[‡] Apud Poli. Synopsin, and Matt. iii: 6.

[||] Works, vol. i, p. 74, edit. 1608.

[§] Notes on New Testament.

established in Scripture as communion under the two kinds can possibly be, has, nevertheless, been changed into pouring, with as much ease and as little dispute, as communion under one kind has been established. It is a fact most firmly believed by the Reformed (though some of them *at this day* wrangle about it) that baptism *was instituted to be administered by plunging the body entirely;* that Jesus Christ received it in this manner; that it was thus performed by his apostles; that the Scriptures are acquainted with no other baptism; that antiquity understood and practiced it in this manner; and that to baptize *is to plunge*—these facts, I say, are unanimously acknowledged by all the Reformed teachers; by the Reformers themselves; by those who best understood the Greek language and the ancient customs of both Jews and Christians; by Luther, by Melancthon, by Calvin, by Casaubon, by Grotius, with all the rest; and since their time, by Jurieu, the most ready to contradict of all their ministers. Luther has even remarked that this sacrament is called *Tauf*, in German, on account of the depth; because they plunged *deeply* in the water those whom they baptized. If there be in the world a fact absolutely certain, it is *this*. Yet it is no less certain, that, with all these authors, baptism, without immersion, is counted as lawful; and that *the Church properly* retains the custom of pouring." *

What is here so boldly and so frankly said by this Romanist has been often repeated in the faces of Protestant Pedobaptists, and it remains for one of them to make a respectable attempt at refutation. It is not strange that they do not attempt it. The entire history of the Church is against them. Their brethren, men of learning, such

---

* Hist. des Egleses Protest., tom. ii, pp. 469, 470.

as those named by this Romanist, have conceded every thing in the controversy.

Lastly, we will hear the testimony of English Episcopalians. Only two of them shall testify.

Bishop BURNET: "We know that the first ritual of baptism was by going into the waters, and being laid as dead all along in them; and then the persons baptized were raised up again, and so they came out of them. This is not only mentioned by St. Paul, but in two different places he gives a mystical signification of the rite; that it signified *our being buried with Christ in baptism*, and our being *raised up with him* to a new life: so that the phrases of rising with Christ, and of putting on Christ, as oft as 'they occur, do plainly relate to this; and yet, partly out of modesty, partly in regard to the tenderness of infants, and the coldness of these climates, since such a manner might endanger their lives, and we know that God loves mercy better than sacrifice, this form of baptizing is as little used by those [Pedobaptists] who separate from us, as by ourselves. . . . . From all these things, this inference seems just: That according to the practice of those who divide from us, the Church must be supposed to have authority to adjust the forms of our religion, in those parts of them that are merely ritual, to the taste, to the exigencies and conveniences of the several ages and climates."*

This right reverend prelate speaks forth boldly and unmistakably. He believes *the Church* has power to decree and change ceremonies. It was hence little trouble for him to defend pouring and sprinkling for baptism. But Church authority was his sole ground of defense. He believed not only that the Church had the right to make it,

---

* Discourses to the Clergy, pp. 281, 282.

but that the change from immersion to pouring and sprinkling was a wise and prudent one, having respect, as it did, to "modesty," "the tenderness of infants," "coldness of climates," the "danger to life," and to the fact that "God loves mercy better than sacrifice."

Mr. Evans: "There is a confessed variation allowed of and practiced by the generality of Dissenters, both Presbyterians and Independents, from the institution and practice of Christ and his apostles, in the sacrament of baptism; for they have changed immersion, or dipping, into aspersion, or sprinkling, and pouring water on the face. Baptism by immersion, or dipping, is suitable to the institution of our Lord, and the practice of the apostles, and was by them ordained and used to represent our burial with Christ, a death to sin and a new birth into righteousness, as St. Paul explains that rite."*

This testimony—and it might be tediously accumulated—shows that, in the last century even, there was no controversy about the institution of our Lord, or the practice of the apostles. Then pouring and sprinkling rested confessedly upon no higher authority than that of a fallible and corrupt Church. Since such authority has fallen into disrepute, men have begun to claim Scripture authority for the practice of pouring and sprinkling. Some have made such astonishing progress as to deny flatly that the Savior himself was immersed, or that the apostles ever immersed any body; and all this in the face of what we have read from their own authorities, as well as from the Scriptures.

To conclude this question, we have seen that, confessedly, the word baptize was used by the Greeks in the sense

---

* Cases to Recover Dissenters, vol. iii, pp. 105, 106, 3d edit.

of immerse, and never in that of pour or sprinkle; that it is, accordingly, defined by the lexicons to mean immerse, not one of them defining it to mean pour or sprinkle; that, when it is defined to mean wash, dye, stain, etc., it is explained that it has these meanings *only by consequence;* that its use in the New Testament not only justifies, but demands for it the sense of immersion there; and, lastly, that, down to the middle of the last century, it was admitted by Pedobaptists themselves that the word baptize means immerse; that our Lord instituted and his apostles practiced only immersion; that pouring and sprinkling were substituted by the Church in favor of *clinics,* and, in consideration of "modesty," the "tenderness of infants" and "coldness of climates," quoting only for *Divine* authority that "God will have mercy, and not sacrifice." How far the argument, so briefly drawn, falls short of demonstration, let candid people for themselves decide.

II. WHO MAY SCRIPTURALLY BE BAPTIZED?

That believers may properly be baptized, no one denies. All parties that practice baptizing at all are agreed that believers may properly be admitted to baptism. But here those called Antipedobaptists stop, this being the extent of their affirmation. Pedobaptists go farther, and affirm that infants also may scripturally be baptized. Some of them say all infants, and some say only infants of believing parents, may properly be admitted to baptism. This subdivision, however, is one with which we have nothing to do. We deny that any infant can be scripturally baptized. To the extent of the difference on this question, it will be readily seen that Pedobaptists are properly in the affirmative, and, of course, the burden of proof falls due to them. How, then, can they prove that infants of any kind may scripturally be baptized? They do not claim that they can prove it by express precept or example of the Scriptures. On this point, we will hear what the affirmants themselves say.

Bishop BURNET: "There is no express precept or rule given in the Scriptures for the baptism of infants."[*]

Dr. WALL, speaking of John's baptism, says: "There is no express mention of any children baptized by him." Again, he says: "Among all the persons recorded as baptized by the apostles, there is no express mention of any infants."[†]

FULLER: "We do freely confess that there is neither express precept, nor precedent, in the New Testament for the baptizing of infants." And the very best this learned divine could say as to Divine authority for his practice stands in these words: "There were many things which Jesus did which are not written, among which, for aught appears to the contrary, the baptizing of these infants (mentioned Luke xviii: 15–17) might be one of them."[‡]

MARTIN LUTHER: "It can not be proved by the sacred Scripture that infant baptism was instituted by Christ, or begun by the first Christians after the apostles;"[||] and scores of such concessions of eminent men who lived in Luther's time, before and after, might be quoted; but these sufficiently show that, whatever authority was then claimed for the practice of infant baptism, it was conceded that the Scriptures are silent upon the subject. This is still conceded by the advocates of the practice. In proof of this, let us read, from an article on baptism prepared by a committee

---

[*] Expos. of the Thirty-nine Articles, art. xxvii.
[†] Introd. Hist. Infant Baptism, pp. 1–55.
[‡] Infant's Adv., pp. 71, 150.
[||] A. R.'s Vanity of Infant Baptism, part ii, p. 8.

appointed by the General Conference of the Methodist Episcopal Church, in 1860, to take the place of Mr. Wesley's treatise on that subject, in the Doctrinal Tracts, which article is now published with the indorsement of Conference: "That there is no such express warrant for the baptism of infants [as for the baptism of believers] is freely acknowledged."* And again, (p. 255,) this Tract says: "We do not *pretend* to found the right of infant baptism on any supposed precept or example of the Scriptures which expressly declares that infants were, or that they should be baptized." Since, then, the advocates "*do not pretend* to found the right of infant baptism on any supposed precept or example of the Scriptures," upon what is it founded? What are the grounds of it? This question they may answer in their own words. But they are far, very far, from agreement in their answers. They agree that the baptism of infants should be retained. They agree very *generally* as to the profound silence of the Bible on the subject; but when they come to the reasons for the practice, they go apart widely. We will hear a few of them:

Mr. Wesley: "As to the grounds of it, if infants are guilty of original sin, then they are proper subjects of baptism, seeing, in the ordinary way, they can not be saved unless this be washed away by baptism."† So the Methodist Church believed and taught, up to the year 1860, when they refused any longer to publish and indorse Mr. Wesley's treatise. The learned

Mr. Walker said: "Where authority from the Scripture fails, there *the custom of the Church is to be held as a law.*"‡

---

* Doctrinal Tracts, p. 250.
† Doctrinal Tracts, 1832 edit., p. 251.
‡ Modern Plea for Infant Baptism, p. 221.

HENRY WARD BEECHER admits frankly that there is nothing whatever said about the practice of infant baptism in the Bible; and also that no legitimate deductions can be drawn thence in its favor; and, for authority, falls back on what he calls "*Christian liberty*," claiming that Christians have a right to practice whatever experience has shown to be "a good thing;" as, for example, we put a yoke upon oxen, because experience has shown it to be a good institution. Now, when we consider that the Bible is confessedly silent upon the subject of infant baptism (it being only claimed that possibly among the *unwritten* sayings of our Lord some authority might be found, for aught we know to the contrary), and that some found the right of it upon the *guilt* of infants; others upon "the *custom of the Church;*" and still others, upon "Christian liberty;" are we not warranted in calling it simply a *human tradition*? May we not safely say that it had its origin in no higher authority than that of the Church, and in a very dark period of its history at that? Nevertheless, we must confess it is of great antiquity, having been practiced by a majority of professing Christians for perhaps fifteen centuries; and, in consideration of this fact, it is certainly entitled to respect, so far as Christians are at liberty to respect a human tradition of this kind. Is it an *innocent* tradition? If so, its innocence should go far to shield it from attack. We will not require our Pedobaptist friends to prove that it is "a good thing," but only to establish its innocence. But this even remains to be done to our satisfaction. We *know* that our Lord ordained, and his apostles commanded, in his name, that *believers* should be baptized. But infant baptism, so-called, stands in the way of this command. To the extent of its prevalence, it makes void the command of the Lord, to *believers*, to be baptized. This should sink it forever in the estimation of every Christian. The Lord said: "Go *teach* all nations, baptizing them;" "Go preach the Gospel to every creature; he that *believes and is* baptized shall be saved." And so his apostles did, baptizing none others than believers, as has been conceded by the advocates of infant baptism. To our Lord's command, and to the precept and precedent of his apostles, we must be true. Therefore we are bound to require believers to be baptized; and as the tradition in question comes in the way of this, we must oppose it. We say to its advocates, in the language of the Savior, "Ye have made the commandment of God of none effect by your tradition," and we dare not hold our peace. It will not do to tell us "infants are *guilty of original sin*, and must *therefore* be baptized. In the first place, infants are not guilty of original sin. But if they were, and baptism were necessary to their cleansing, the Lord would have ordained it (and it would have been found among his *written* sayings), and his apostles would have practiced it. Nor will any supposed authority, among the "*unwritten*" sayings of the Savior satisfy us. *Why was it not written?* Nor is Christian liberty sufficient ground for it. While we gladly agree that Christians have great liberty, we do not believe that even *they* have liberty to make void the commandments of God, teaching for doctrine the commandments of men. Nor yet will it silence us to say that "where authority from Scripture fails, *there the custom of the Church is to be held as a law*." We respect antiquity, but have not sufficient respect for all the mere customs of the Church to receive them as laws.

Baptism is "the answer of a good conscience toward God." (1 Pet. iii: 21.) But infants can have no conscience in baptism. Therefore infants can not properly be baptized. Whatever else may not be, it is clear that some *conscience* is essential to baptism. It may be said, "But an infant could properly be circumcised, and why not as properly be baptized?" The cases are not parallel. In the former case, parents were commanded to have their children circumcised; in the latter, the obligation rests upon each individual person to be baptized. Circumcision was a mark in the *flesh* for the *natural* seed of Abraham, and hence infants could receive it; while baptism is an act of *faith*, having nothing to do with the flesh, but with the conscience; and hence infants can not properly receive it. Paul, speaking to the Romans (sixth chapter) of their baptism, says: "Ye have *obeyed from the heart* that form of doctrine which was delivered you." But infants can have no heart in baptism, nor can they *obey* in any sense. Therefore infants can not scripturally be baptized. "If thou believest with all thy heart, thou mayest" be baptized, is a rule by which Christians must be governed in admitting persons to baptism.

III. WHAT IS BAPTISM FOR?

The Disciples teach that it is *for the remission of sins.* They are the only religious people among Protestants who, at the present day, hold this position. True, the same is taught in almost all the creeds and standard books of the popular parties, though disavowed by their press and living pulpits. A few definitive remarks, therefore, are deemed necessary in entering upon the discussion of this question.

1. We interpret the Scripture phrase, "for the remission of sins," to mean *in order to the remission of sins;* and, hence, make baptism antecedent to remission. We do not believe, as has often been said of us, that baptism, in

any sense, *procures* remission.   It is simply *a condition*—a
condition precedent to remission; a condition because the
Lord has made it so, by positive law.   This is the extent
and fullness of our affirmation on this question.

2. We make a distinction between conversion, or what
is very generally called regeneration, and remission of sins.
Conversion, as it is popularly understood, is internal, and
pertains to the mind and heart; and, so far as this is true,
it precedes baptism.   And conversion certainly does pertain to the mind and heart of the converted, though not
wholly.   But what is popularly called conversion and regeneration is an internal work to the converted, and precedes baptism.   One is not properly a subject of baptism
till, in the popular sense, he is converted, or regenerated.
Hence, the charge of "baptismal regeneration" sometimes
preferred against us, is entirely without foundation in
truth, growing out of a popular confounding of conversion and remission of sins, which, with us, are two very
distinct things.   And that this distinction is scriptural, is
made obvious by these passages: "Repent ye, therefore,
and be converted, that your sins may be blotted out."
(Acts iii: 19.)   "Lest at any time they should see with
their eyes, and hear with their ears, and should understand
with their heart, and should be converted, and I should
heal them." (Matt. xii: 15.)   The blotting out of sins is
remission, and comes after conversion.   So, in the other
passage, *healing* is remission, and comes after conversion.
The popular error of confounding conversion and remission of sins together as one thing, has caused much injustice to be done us as a people.   We simply teach that
baptism is in order to, and, hence, a condition precedent
to, the remission of sins, remission being something *the
Lord does for* the converted person.

18

3. We teach that this is so *now*, in the Gospel dispensation. We hold that the law of pardon, under the Gospel, went forth from Jerusalem after the ascension of the Savior and the descent of the Holy Spirit; that it was promulgated for the first time by the Holy Spirit, through Peter, at Jerusalem, on the first Pentecost after our Lord's ascension, as is recorded in the second chapter of the Acts of Apostles. This is in accordance with prophecy, and the teaching of our Lord and his apostles: "And it shall come to pass in the last days, that the mountain of the Lord's house shall be established in the top of the mountains, and shall be exalted above the hills; and *all nations* shall flow into it. And many people shall go and say, Come ye, and let us go up to the mountain of the Lord, to the house of the God of Jacob; and he will teach us his ways, and we will walk in his paths: *for out of Zion shall go forth the law, and the word of the Lord from Jerusalem.*" (Isaiah ii: 2, 3.) That this prophecy relates to the founding of the kingdom or Church of Christ, few, if any, will for a moment question. It teaches that the Church was to be established "*in the last days;*" that "*all nations*" were to flow unto it, and that the "*law was to go forth from Zion, and the word of the Lord from Jerusalem.*" And our Savior says (Luke xxiv: 46, 47): "Thus it is written, and thus it behooved Christ to suffer, and to rise from the dead the third day; and that repentance and remission of sins should be preached in his name among *all nations, beginning at Jerusalem.*" Hence, he said to his apostles, whom he had commissioned to preach remission of sins to *all nations*: "But tarry ye *in the city of Jerusalem* until ye be endued with power from on high." Therefore, when the apostles were endued with power from on high at Jerusalem, they began first to preach "repentance

and remission of sins," which was for "*all nations*." Then and thence went forth the law of the Lord—the law of the New Institution—from Jerusalem. Then and there, "at Jerusalem," the place of "the beginning," in the "last days," Peter, directed by power from on high, propounded the law of the New Institution. To heart-pierced believers he said: "Repent, and be baptized every one of you, in the name of Jesus Christ, *for the remission of sins*." This was the first promulgation of this law, which, be it remembered, was for *all nations*. Now, the question to be determined is: Does this language of Peter make baptism a condition precedent to remission of sins? We say it does, and here we will stand or fall. The controversy hinges on the meaning of the word "for." We say it here means *in order to*, while it is contended by our opponents that its sense is *because of*. It will be granted that it sometimes has the meaning we give it in this case; and we are ready to admit that it sometimes means *because of*. And what is here said of "for" may be truly said of the Greek word it represents. Then, can we ascertain what the word means *in this passage?* Happily for the truth, there is a circumstance in the case which enables us to determine this question. It is this: The relation which "for" expresses here between baptism and remission, is the same that repentance sustains to remission, the relation of both to remission being expressed at once by the same word; therefore, that relation is one. The law to the believer is, "Repent, *and* be baptized *for* the remission of sins." Will any one say that we may read, "Repent, and be baptized *because of* the remission of sins?" Does any one believe in repentance *because of* the remission of sins? No one so believes. No one so preaches. The relation of repentance to remission is that of a precedent to a subsequent. But the relation of baptism must be the same, for it is expressed by the *same word*, and *at the same time;* therefore, the relation of baptism to remission of sins is that of a precedent to a subsequent. This argument has never been met. We feel perfectly confident it never can be. Thus far, our opponents have only attempted to evade it, by claiming that, if we allow that *for* remission means *in order to* remission, it makes Peter's teaching on this occasion conflict with his teaching at other times and places, as well as with the teaching of Scripture generally, on this subject. But this has never been shown to be true.

Time will only allow reference to be made to some other Scriptures which teach the same as the one just examined.

In the commission, our Savior makes baptism for the remission of sins in the same sense, in these words : *"He that believeth and is baptized shall be saved."* By "saved" here, it is very generally agreed that remission of sins is meant, to which the Savior's language evidently makes baptism a condition precedent.

"Arise and be baptized, and wash away thy sins, calling on the name of the Lord." (Acts xxii : 16.)

If baptism be not a condition going before remission of sins, this passage becomes a puzzle, and who can tell what it means?

"Baptism doth also now save us." (1 Pet. iii : 21.) If baptism is not for the remission of sins, in what sense does it *"now save us?"*

Many other passages of Scripture might be cited that teach the same thing; but these will suffice the candid, and others can not be reached.

Christianly Your bro
Winthrop H. Hopson

WINTHROP HARTLY HOPSON.

WINTHROP HARTLY HOPSON was born in Christian County, Kentucky, April 26, 1823. His father, SAMUEL HOPSON, was born in Culpepper County, Virginia; his mother, SALLIE CLARK, daughter of Captain JOHN CLARK, deceased, of Calloway County, Missouri, was born in Hopkinsville, Kentucky. His grandfather, Colonel JOSEPH HOPSON, was an officer in the Revolution, under General DANIEL MORGAN. His mother's grandfather, HENRY CLARK, was a patriot brigadier-general of North Carolina in the Revolution of '76.

At an unusually early age the subject of this sketch learned to read and write. He went to the common school of his father's neighborhood until he was eight years of age, when he was sent to Bonne Femme Academy, in the adjoining county of Boone. He commenced at once the study of Latin. With occasional intermissions, he was at school, from home, nine consecutive sessions of ten months.

Portions of 1836 and 1837, he was at school in Jacksonville, Illinois. While there, he boarded in the family of that great reformer, preacher, and eminent Christian, B. W. STONE. Under his preaching, the evening of the first Lord's day in August, 1837, in Jacksonville, the Doctor made the good confession, and, the next day, was immersed in a stream near by.

His father had him educated for the law, and the Hon. EDWARD BATES, of St. Louis, had agreed to take him into his office as a pupil; but, feeling it to be his duty to preach the Gospel, in 1839, at his home in Fulton, Calloway County, Missouri, he delivered his first public exhortation to sinners. This effort was a decided success, and, from that time, he continued to exhort at all the protracted meetings he attended, until, in 1842, at Millersburg, Missouri, he was regularly set apart to the ministry.

On the 30th of April, 1844, he was married, in Gasconade, Missouri, to Miss REBECCA GRISWOLD PARSONS, and, in the following February, his father died. Having now a wife and widowed mother to support, and receiving a very small salary for preaching—the first seven years of his ministry yielding not over fifty dollars per year—he decided to commence the study of medicine, with the hope that he could the better support his family, and, at the same time, preach the gospel.   Accordingly, in the winter of 1846, he attended his first course of medical lectures in St. Louis, and, the next spring, began the practice of medicine in his own neighborhood, in Osage County, within a mile of the Gasconade line.

In April, 1847, his wife died, young in years, but rich in faith and good works.   He now moved to Fayette, Howard County, and preached for the Church, at the same time practicing his profession.   In the winter of 1847 and 1848, he completed the course in the Medical Department of Missouri University, in St. Louis, and received the degree of M. D.   The subsequent March, he was married to Miss CAROLINE HENLY GRAY, of Fulton, Missouri.   She died, September 20, 1849, in the triumphs of the Christian faith.   He now abandoned the practice of medicine forever, and gave himself entirely to the ministry of the Word.

In September, 1850, he was married to Mrs. ELLA LORD CHAPPELL, his present wife.   The next month, at the State Meeting in Fayette, he was requested to act as Evangelist, and in December he commenced his work.

For seven years, he taught a successful female school at Palmyra.   He spent the year 1858 traveling in Missouri, Illinois, and Kentucky.   In January, 1859, he held a remarkable protracted meeting in Cincinnati.   For six weeks the interest was unparalleled, and about ninety were added to the Church.   In December, he took charge of the Church at Lexington, Kentucky, which position he held until April, 1862, when he entered upon the work of an Evangelist.   He is now located in Richmond, Virginia, where his labors are highly appreciated, and his success very encouraging.

Dr. HOPSON is six feet one and a half inches high, very erect, and weighs about two hundred and ten pounds.   He has excellent health, and never tires in preaching the Gospel.   He is one of the ablest preachers among the Disciples.   But he is a speaker, not a writer; a reasoner, rather than exhorter; a good pastor, but better Evangelist.   He is more than an average scholar, and his general reading is quite extensive, though he is often careless in the selection of choice words.   He aims to be understood, and, in the possession of a happy communicative talent, he has no peer.   No one who listens can fail to comprehend him.   Even in a Greek criticism, he makes every thing plain to the people.   Though remarkably dignified and courtly in his bearing, he is, nevertheless, a *people's man*—they feel that they can understand him.   In his advocacy of the truth, he is bold, belligerent, and fearless.   He carries the war right into Africa; consequently, the sects do not love him.   But he is very popular with both the preachers and churches of his own brethren.   He is especially kind to young preachers, and always helps them in whatever way he can.   In money matters, he is liberal to a fault, and never turns a deaf ear to the poor and needy.

BAPTISM ESSENTIAL TO SALVATION.

BY W. H. HOPSON.

"And he said unto them, Go ye into all the world, and preach the Gospel to every creature. He that believeth, and is baptized, shall be saved; but he that believeth not shall be damned."--MARK XVI: 15, 16.

I THINK that the subject selected for consideration in this sermon, should be fairly, faithfully, fully discussed. Hitherto, in my opinion, this has not been done. In the "Quarterly," "Harbinger," and in our other religious papers, every doctrine and practice peculiar to the Disciples of Christ is being subjected to the most thoughtful review. This is right. The pulpit also is engaged, equally with the press, in this thorough reconsideration of the issues between the Disciples and the opponents of "the truth as it is in Jesus." This existing spirit of honest, earnest, searching inquiry into the teaching of the Christ and the apostles on the subject of man's religious faith, obligation, and duty, as relates both to the saint and the sinner, is a most praiseworthy and hopeful condition of things. I propose, in this discourse, in harmony with this commendable spirit of re-investigation of the things pertaining to the spiritual interests of mankind, to contribute my aid, in this direction; and shall, therefore, call your attention to the consideration of one of the earlier, rather than the later, issues of the current religious reformatory movement.

Aiming at no display of scholarship, carefully avoiding all criticism upon Greek particles, and making simply a plain argument, in plain English, to plain, common-sense people, I hope that the sermon will be productive of good in determining the precise conditions precedent to the enjoyment of forgiveness on the part of the sinner against God.

In order to a proper appreciation of the argument on the part of the hearer, I deem a few preliminary explanatory statements of high importance. There must be, in the discussion of the thing before us, no dodging of the precise issue, no misunderstanding of terms, no confusion of speech. To this end, a satisfactory definition of the words used in forming the proposition is necessary, as well as a definite understanding of the extent to which the proposition reaches. Before this is done, let me direct your attention to the law of pardon, as given by the Savior to his apostles. The statement, as recorded in Matthew xxviii: 19, 20, relates more especially to the duties of the apostles as ambassadors of the Christ. This I shall designate the Apostolic Commission. It reads thus: "All power is given unto me in heaven and in earth. Go ye, therefore, and teach all nations, baptizing them into the name of the Father, and of the Son, and of the Holy Spirit: teaching them to observe all things whatsoever I have commanded you: and, lo, I am with you alway, even unto the end of the world. Amen." This statement contains a *declaration* of the Son of God as to his supreme authority; a *command* to the apostles to teach, to baptize, and to teach "all things;" and a *promise* that he would be with them "alway, even unto the end of the world." The statements, as recorded by Mark xvi: 15, 16, and by Luke xxiv: 46, 47, I shall unitize into the following: "Go ye into all the world, and preach the Gospel to every creature. He that believes, repents, and is baptized, shall be saved; he that believeth not shall be damned." This form of the Divine utterance relates more especially to the duties of the sinner. It contains, it is true, a *command* to the apostles to "go into all the world, and preach the Gospel to every creature," but, it will be admitted, nevertheless, by all, that its main feature is a definite *promise* from the Savior, through the apostles, of salvation to the sinner, upon the sinner's believing, repenting, and being baptized. I would, then, designate this "The Savior's Amnesty Proclamation."

Salvation, in the proposition, is equivalent to pardon, remission of sins, or forgiveness of sins. "Essential" is that which is not only very important, but indispensably necessary. The proposition does not include those who have never heard the Gospel in heathen lands. It does not include infants or idiots, who, though they may live in a land of Bibles, where the Gospel is faithfully preached, are, by the consent of all, intellectually incompetent to believe or be baptized of their own free-will and accord. It does include all *who hear*. Hear, in Biblical currency, includes both the opportunity and the mental ability to comprehend the Gospel. Responsibility for the acceptance or rejection of the amnesty proclamation lies just here. Whatever, then, is declared in this proclamation to be a sinner's duty, in order to salvation or remission of sins, I hold to be essential to that end. In the proclamation, remission of sins is made to depend upon faith, repentance, and baptism as equally conditions precedent, and it is absolutely certain that no subsequent declaration of the Savior or the apostles can be found, making a distinction as to their respective importance, and distributing them into essential and non-essential; but, on the contrary, it is certain that the last utterance of the Savior placed them in positive association with each other, and for the same purpose, and that the apostles, in their preaching under the commission, did, always and everywhere, in any fair understanding of their discourses, as reported in the Acts of Apostles, command their hearers to believe, repent, and be baptized, and that they never, in any address to sinners, or in any epistle to saints, gave the most distant intimation that any one of these three conditions could, under any circumstances, be dispensed with.

In the light, then, of the above facts, definitions, and restrictions, I affirm "that faith, repentance, and baptism are essential to salvation." The law of pardon, contained in the statement of the Savior to the apostles on sending them into all the world to preach the Gospel, is, in its own simple utterances, so plain and easy of comprehension, that I am at a loss to conceive how a thoughtful mind could misapprehend its teachings. Faith and repentance are conceded by the Disciples, and by all Protestant sects, to be essential to the salvation of all who come within the provisions of the proclamation. We and they agree that "saved" or "damned" in the proclamation applies to those, and *those only*, who have an opportunity to hear the Gospel, and who, in years and in reason, have the ability to understand it—to accept or reject it. The issue between them and us in the preaching of the conditions of pardon, as we respectively understand the Savior to command and to promise, is confined to the question, "Is baptism essential to salvation?" We affirm that it is.

That the law of pardon enjoins on the sinner faith, repentance, *and baptism*, in order to remission of sins. That all this is required, and that nothing short of this will suffice. Permit me now to submit the proof, after the above lengthy, but necessary, introduction.

I. The law of pardon, as above given, is *the first, the last, and the only* amnesty proclamation in the New Testament offered to sinners by the authority of the Lord Jesus Christ, who is the only Savior of sinners, and to whom belongs "all authority in heaven and upon the earth." We are therefore shut up to a compliance with its provisions as our only hope of pardon. And should any conflict, probable or real, between the provisions of this law and the antecedent statements of the Savior on the subject of remission be found (we admit none), even then such collision would, in no sense, invalidate the above conclusion; for it is a well-established rule in legislation, both human and divine, that the enactment of a law, by competent authority, necessarily annuls and makes void all previous existing laws at variance with it. This rule, as applicable to the law of pardon enacted by the Savior, is most clearly substantiated by the very satisfactory utterance of the Apostle Paul in Hebrews vii: 12, "For the priesthood being changed, there is made of necessity a change of the law." As the priesthood officiates almost exclusively with reference to an atonement and the remission of sins, the change in the law must be in reference to the same things. As, then, in the very necessity and philosophy of things, the last law repeals all laws previously made, not in harmony with it, it becomes, in this discussion, a matter of transcendent importance to ascertain the time when the above-mentioned law came into being and force. If it be the last law on the subject, then to it, and to it alone, must we look for the conditions of salvation. When was the commission given? Not in the lifetime of the Savior upon the earth, when he was a suffering, sorrowing sojourner among the sons of men; not in the valedictory address to his Disciples just before "his hour had come;" not amid the agonies of the Cross; but, after his death; after his resurrection; after he had been with the Apostles for forty days, "speaking of the things pertaining to the kingdom of God," and "opening their understanding that they might understand the Scriptures,"—*after all this*, was the commission given. When, then, is still the question. The *exact time* must be determined. Amid the solemn surroundings of the farewell scene, as the risen Savior turned to take the last fond look of the beloved twelve, who had been his companions and his pupils for nearly three years and a half; who, so oft, had sat at his feet and listened with a breathless silence and an enrapt attention to the words of eloquence and truth that fell from his lips of inspiration; and who, in wonder and astonishment, had witnessed the stupendous miracles performed by him in attestation that he was the Christ—then, *precisely then*—amid the crushing sorrow of that parting hour, just as he was about to ascend out of their sight through the clouds into heaven, to be coronated King of kings and Lord of lords—he said to them : "Go into all the world and preach the Gospel to every creature. He that believes and is baptized shall be saved; he that believeth not shall be damned."

II. What has just been shown to be the *last* law of pardon Jesus gave, is also the *first* one he ever gave as Lord of all, under the New Testament dispensation. Before his resurrection, the Savior himself tells us that he spoke and acted in obedience to the command of his Father.

"Lo, I come to do thy will," was his valedictory in leaving the heavens to come to earth; and "Know you not that I must be about my Father's business," is his first recorded declaration on the earth. Now the Crucified One is crowned King, clothed with supreme power, and the scepter of authority is passed over into his hand. Now, he makes laws in his own right as Sovereign of the heaven and the earth. The first exercise of authority under his reign as absolute monarch, was to enact the conditional amnesty above mentioned, and to commission the apostles to proclaim it to every creature, "among all nations, even unto the end of the world." This law, then, both the first and the last on the subject, is binding, in all its provisions, and as long as the Christian dispensation shall last.

III. This law is certainly the only one in the New Testament that offers pardon, on any terms, to a Gentile as such—the first one, perhaps, in the Bible, since the election of Abraham, and the selection of his posterity to be the children of God. Hitherto, a Gentile could only be in "covenant relationship" with God by becoming a Jew by adoption, through circumcision. The Savior, while a teacher on the earth, notwithstanding his great loving heart, confined his instruction to the "lost sheep of the house of Israel." The Gentiles were never personally included, and, if he taught them or blessed them in performing upon them some miracle of healing, he did it under protest, saying: "It is *not lawful* to take the children's bread and give it unto dogs." When the Savior sent out the seventy and the twelve on their first mission, he positively restricted their preaching to the Jews. Their commission, as recorded in Matt. x, reads thus, so far as it pertains to the point before us: " Go not into the way of the Gentiles, and into any city of the Samaritans enter ye not: but go rather to the lost sheep of the house of Israel." But now Jesus is King, and " the fullness of the time" for the coming in of the Gentiles has come, and the blessed Savior gives the apostles a new, and enlarged, and final commission: "Go into all the world, and preach the Gospel to every creature." Go to Jerusalem, to Samaria, and to the uttermost parts of the earth, and preach " the unsearchable riches of the Christ." Go wherever there is a mind to think, a heart to feel, a soul to save, and tell " the glad tidings of great joy to all people"—salvation from sin, its guilt and power, on the terms of this proclamation. Go, tell the people of every mountain and valley, every hill and dale, every continent and isle of the seas, of every tribe and tongue, that peace, pardon, and joy are offered to every baptized, penitent believer, through the atoning blood of the once crucified, but now coronated Jesus, the Son of God, the Savior of sinners.

Dear friends, most, if not all of you, are Gentiles; and should you not rejoice that, at length, " God has granted to the Gentiles repentance unto life;" and as this is, beyond all doubt, the only law of pardon in which you have ever personally been included, is it not of paramount importance to you to embrace it? and will it not imperil your soul's salvation to neglect it, in whole or in part?

Thus far, in the investigation, we have found that the commission contains the first law of pardon enacted by the authority of the Christ; that it is the only one personally addressed to Gentile sinners; that it is the last law given by Divine authority on the subject of pardon, and, consequently, all previously existing ones are repealed; that its provisions, or terms, are faith, repentance, and baptism; and that this law, neither more nor less, is to be proclaimed, in all time, among all nations, to every creature. It is evident, therefore, that the sinner's only hope of salvation, so far as obedience is necessary at all, is to be found in full compliance with the provisions of this enactment. Jesus is the only atoning lamb, and, as such, if we despise and neglect *him*, "there remaineth no other offering for sin;" so, is this the only law of pardon to sinners, and, if they neglect and despise *it*, there remaineth no other law by which they can be saved; for of Jesus alone can it be truthfully said: "Thou hast the words of eternal life." May every sinner ponder well Peter's query: "To whom shall we go, if we leave thee?"

IV. The great commission contains the New Testament statutory law with reference to the pardon of rebel sinners. It is characteristic of statutory law that all its provisions are expressed, that none are implied; that to it nothing is to be added, from it nothing to be taken away; that to the enjoyment of any blessing promised therein, upon certain conditions, full compliance therewith is invariably required. Non-compliance with any one of them will work deprivation. For instance, the statutory law governing the elective franchise in some of the States of the American Union grants this political privilege to one who is "white, free, a male, a citizen, and twenty-one years of age." The matter for thought is not, whether the law be good, bad, or indifferent. We might raise the questions: Have not women the right to vote as well as men? the negro as well as the white man? a boy at eighteen years of age as well as one of twenty-one? The simple question however, is, "What sayeth the *law?*" Who has the right to vote? I answer: He, and he only, who has the five qualifications mentioned in the statute. Were they five times five, the argument would be the same. This law, when enacted, repeals all others inconsistent with it. It is absolutely binding, in its every provision, until it is itself repealed. The voter, under it, must have all the qualifications; the non-possession of any one of them will constitute disqualification. The subject of the law, having them all, can not be refused the privilege of voting; lacking one qualification, the privilege, *according to the law*, can not be allowed him, for the provisions are all equally essential. The application is easy. The Savior, in his wisdom and goodness—and all his acts are both wise and good—has seen fit to suspend the forgiveness of the sinner upon the three conditions, Faith, Repentance, and Baptism. A full compliance is necessary to salvation, according to the statute governing the case. The willful neglect of a solitary condition will work deprivation of the blessing sought. These three conditions are in the law. The promise is made to depend upon full obedience to the three. They equally possess the element of a condition precedent, and, *in this sense*, are equally essential. He, therefore, who willfully neglects compliance with any one of these simple and easy conditions, can not be saved. He who fully complies, is saved, if confidence can be placed in the declaratory promise of the Savior. Who dare doubt his word? who question his veracity? Let the sinner, then, joyfully accept the pardon on the offered terms. Let him tremble at the enormous wickedness of even the thought of "striking out" or "inserting" here. "What God hath joined together let not man put asunder," though spoken in reference to marriage, is, nevertheless, an enactment applying to every Divine institution, so far as the sacredness of the tie is concerned. The last command of Jesus, given in person, was a command to the apostles to offer salvation to the baptized penitent believer; his last command, by inspiration, is a command inhibiting us from "adding to, or taking from, the words of this book." He, then, that strikes out faith or baptism from this law of pardon, contemns the authority of Christ, and repudiates the last command he ever gave in person, and the last one he gave by the Holy Spirit; indeed, the very last Divine command given to man in the Bible. Can such a man be saved? If so, who need fear being lost?

V. In discussing the law of pardon, it is both pertinent and appropriate now to inquire, What is law—law itself? We have sound enough definitions of law as to physics, metaphysics, and ethics; but these do not apply here. In human government, a law is defined to be a rule of human action. I accept this as correct, so far as it goes. But it is a definition informing us only of what law is as it relates to the party under law. What is it in reference to the Supreme power that ordains it? I answer, it is will. Law, written or spoken, is an expression of sovereign will. A rule of action, prescribed by legitimate authority, is a duty—an act due to the authority that rules and reigns. Law is, then, *will*, in the direction of the lawgiver; *duty*, as to the subject. This will, this duty, is expressed in a command, an enactment, or a law. A father commands his son, a master commands his servant, to do a certain thing; that command is law; that law expresses the will of the father or master, as the case may be, and the duty of the son or servant. The law of God is the will of God; to do his will, when he commands, is our duty. If he commands us to do any thing, he wills us to do that thing. If he commands us to refrain from a certain thing, he wills us to refrain. The New Testament doctrine or enactments is called "The perfect Law of Liberty." Perfect is that

19

to which nothing requisite is wanting. The New Testament reveals the whole will of God concerning us. Our every religious duty is laid down in it. In the revelation there is nothing wanting. To be a dutiful child of God one must do the will of God. In each and every command of God he finds that will expressed. "Not every one that saith unto me, Lord, Lord, shall enter into the kingdom of heaven, but he that doeth the will of my Father, who is in heaven." Does not the Savior command us to be baptized? Is not the giving of the command an unmistakable declaration of his will? Is not obedience to him our imperative duty? Baptism, then, is indispensably necessary to salvation. If not, then a man can be saved who refuses to obey the commandment of his Lord, who persistently and contemptuously neglects a known duty, who proudly slights and despises the clearly-expressed will of Jesus. The whole conduct and *animus* of such a man (acts, it is said, speak louder than words) is an emphatic utterance of—"Savior, not thy will, but mine be done." Such a man can not be saved; his heart is full of rebellion; "he is led captive by Satan at his own will;" "his sins are open beforehand, going to judgment." Argument, scriptural authority, the will of Jesus can not influence him. "Ephraim is joined to his idols, let him alone."

VI. No law of pardon, enacted by Divine authority, in any religion, Patriarchal, Jewish, or Christian, can be found, which does not contain, as a constituent element, a positive institution. Baptism is the positive institution, which occupies this place, in the law of pardon, under the Christian dispensation, and the only one among the positive enactments of the Savior that can sustain this important relation. Positive law is, among Christians,

a stereotyped form of expression, including all commandments that relate to ceremonies, forms, ordinances, etc.
Theologians distribute the law of God into positive and
moral. A better distribution would be, soberness; duty
to one's self; righteousness, duty to your fellow man;
godliness, duty to God. But I accept the first, on account
of its universality, and the familiarity of my readers with
the thought. It is somewhat difficult to define and to distinguish these with exactness. I will do my best to make
the difference prominent and perceptible. A moral law is
intuitively right, right in itself—grows out of our relations to our fellow men; our obedience to it proves our
love for each other; between it and its results there is eminent fitness, as of cause to effect.

Positive law is right, because it is an expression of the
will of the authority that enacts it—grows out of our relation to God; between it and the end to be gained there
is the absence of appreciable adaptedness; obedience to it
is proof of our loyalty, and love of our reverence and
respect for the lawgiver.

The non-essentiality of baptism to salvation is the
outgrowth of the following infidel sentiment, common to
the religious sects of the day: "If a man obeys the moral
law, it is somewhat a matter of indifference whether the
positive law is obeyed or not." I object to this. I most
stoutly protest. It is absurd, it is false, it is wicked. A
moral law is duty to our fellow man. Positive law is
duty to God. Are we prepared, then, to admit (and we
must so admit if the above proposition be true), that in
order to salvation, it is essential to discharge the duties
growing out of our relations to man; but, it is indifferent
as to our salvation, whether we do, or do not, comply
with the obligations growing out of our relation to God?

As our relation to God is the higher relation, our duty to him is the higher duty. Adam in Eden was subjected to the operation of two laws. He was the husband of Eve, must love her, and, in proof, treat her kindly. But as creature, he was subordinate to the creator, God—must love and honor him, and, in proof, abstain from the prohibited fruit. He obeyed the moral law in spirit and in letter, but he disobeyed the positive law, knowingly and willfully. The result we know. "Original sin," that resulted in the expulsion of our first parents from their Edenic home, and from the presence of God, by which man was shorn of his glory, and which sin "brought death into the world, and all our woe," which led to the after-sorrow, sufferings and sacrifice of Jesus, *was no more, no less, than an act of disobedience to a positive law, committed, too, by one whose obedience to the moral law was faultless and perfect.* "To obey God rather than man," is the doctrine of both the Old Testament and the New. It is the duty of a man to do the whole will of God as far as "lieth in him"—his will, in moral obligations—his will, in positive enactments. He must obey God in both. But, if in the history of a human life, it should occur, that a man is commanded of God to perform a positive obedience, that directly conflicts with the moral law, instead of neglecting the positive, and complying with the moral, requirement, duty demands that he neglect the moral, and comply with the positive, enactment. We feel, in our hearts, that such an occurrence, in the Divine legislation, must be rare. Such instance did occur in the history of Abraham. "Thou shall not kill" is a moral law, in strict harmony with all the definitions of it given above. "Take thy son, thine only son Isaac, and sacrifice him to me," etc., is a positive law. "God tried Abraham." Positive institutions are tests of faith. God tries us by and through them. Shall we "be found wanting?" Abraham's trial was severe, but he "staggered not in unbelief." The will of God was his will. He obeyed, and became the friend of God, and the father of the faithful. They who, like him, are full of faith, will not speak slightingly of the ordinances of the Lord, but will "walk in them, blameless."

The proof of our faith in Christ, and of our loyalty to him, is found in an honest, cheerful, willing obedience to his positive institutions. They are proofs of faith, because, seeing no fitness between the thing done and the blessing promised, the obedient man, of necessity, "walks by faith, not by sight;" and, from the same inability to appreciate adaptedness, it is a proof of loyalty, his only reason for obedience being: "The Lord commands; I love and honor him; I will gladly, joyfully please him in doing his will."

A man may obey God in every moral duty, (if such obedience be possible,) and give no proof by it to heaven or earth that he believes in God, or loves him. Who is it that loves God? Who is a Christian? We speak now of honest men, not of hypocrites. Select your best man in the Church, and test him by the moral law, and you will never find the proof sought. What can you say of him? He is an honest man; pays his debts; does not lie, nor steal, nor murder; does not blaspheme God, nor gamble, nor get drunk; is kind to his aged parents, to his wife, his children; is benevolent to the poor; visits the sick, etc. Does that prove his faith in God? Can not all this be predicated of many men of your acquaintance who do not profess faith in Christ, or love to God? It, then, proves too much; therefore, it proves nothing at all. But when you say of a man, he was baptized, he prays, he observes the Lord's day, he regularly celebrates the Lord's Supper, you have entered the region of proper proof. These are positive institutions, and God's own ordained tests of the faith, love, and loyalty of his people. That, in all ages, they have been such tests, is easily shown from the Bible; and that parties were blessed or punished as they proved faithful or faithless when thus tested, is equally true. The throwing down of the walls of Jericho, by the blowing of ram's horns on the part of the people, and by marchings around the walls; the healing of the Syrian leper, Naaman, by "dipping himself seven times in the Jordan;" and the cure of the blind man "by washing in Bethesda," is each a superlative proof of faith in these obedient parties. To the sinner believing in Jesus, deeply convicted of his guilt, mourning over his sins, and truly repenting of them, baptism is ordained to be precisely such a test. How could the things done produce the above-mentioned results? How can baptism wash away sins? "Stagger not in unbelief. Walk by faith, not by sight." Adam lost Eden and the favor of God, Saul his kingdom, and Uzzah his life, in disobeying the positive laws of God. In obedience to one, Abraham became the friend of God; and Jesus, the second Adam, was acknowledged of the Father as "my well-beloved Son." In conclusion, the truth seems to be this: We are commanded to live "soberly, righteously, and godly." This command is addressed to the Church, but applies to the sinner in principle. Godliness or righteousness, in their broader meaning, include the whole of our religious obligation. In their narrowest meaning, as here, they include singly but a part. Soberness (as eating, drinking, etc.,) consists of that class of duties whose operation is upon one's self. Righteousness—that class of duties that affect our neighbor, as, "Thou shalt not lie, bear false-witness," etc. Godliness—to those duties that grow alone out of our relation to God, baptism, Lord's Supper, etc. A man is sober because he loves and respects himself; he is righteous, because he loves and respects his neighbor; he is godly and is baptized, because he believes in the Christ, and loves and honors him, and would do whatever is well-pleasing to him. No man can prove to heaven or earth that he has faith in Christ, repentance toward God, or love to him in his heart, who knows that Jesus commands him to be baptized; that the command has not been repealed, and is, therefore, still binding; who stubbornly and willfully neglects it. The sinner, like the Christian, must "show his faith by his works." His persistent neglect of baptism is rebellious resistance to the authority of the Savior. Such a man, with such a stubborn will and unloving heart, can not be saved.

I will now briefly notice some of the principal objections made to the design of baptism as advocated in this discourse.

"Admitting your argument, thus far, to be sound, and, in the main, I think it is, yet, in my judgment, prayer, and not baptism, is the positive institution ordained for remission of sins to the penitent believing sinner," says an objector. It is strange, with the New Testament before him, that any man should hold prayer to be the remitting ordinance to the sinner. It is a wide-spread error, and I deem it important to give it a thorough sifting.

1. In the commission—proven in this discourse to be the only law of pardon to sinners under the Christian dispensation—baptism is named among the conditions of pardon, *prayer is not*. It has also been shown that it is a great sin "to add to or take from the Word of God."

Is it not, then, a "presumptuous sin" in a man, instead of preaching "He that believes and is baptized shall be saved," to strike out is "baptized," and insert "prays," preaching, that "He that believes and prays shall be saved?"

2. In the Acts of Apostles we have the only authentic record on earth of the apostolic preaching under the authorization of the commission. Their discourses, given only in part, are still full enough to teach us their understanding of the Savior's meaning in giving the law. As they were inspired expounders of the law, their interpretation is infallible. Throughout their entire preaching, as recorded in the book of Acts, they did invariably command their hearers, composed of sinners, to be baptized, and in not one instance did they command them to pray.

3. We read, in this book, that "three thousand" were converted on the first day, "five thousand" the second, and afterward "great multitudes" are reported as being "added to the Lord," who daily "added to the Church the saved." No one will accuse me of exaggeration, when I state the number of the converted, reported as the result of the preaching from Jerusalem to Rome, at one hundred thousand souls. In the history of these numerous conversions, every one of them was commanded to be baptized, and not one commanded "to pray, or be prayed for;" and yet I must be gravely told that "baptism is a non-essential, and that prayer is the heaven-ordained condition of remission to the penitent believer."

4. In the history, also, it is found that the only man who was both commanded to pray, and who asked them to pray for him, was a baptized believer, Simon Magus. But, says the objector: "Was not Paul commanded to 'be baptized and wash away his sins, calling on the name of

the Lord,' and is not 'calling on the name of the Lord equivalent to prayer?" I reply: Saul had been very wicked; had denied and blasphemed the Christ; had been a great persecutor of his disciples; that it was the duty of all believers in the Christ to confess him with the mouth before men. The good confession was omitted in no case. In Saul's case it was pre-eminently a duty. "Calling on the name of the Lord," with him, was the recognition of the authority of Jesus, the confessing him to be the Christ.

But, grant that prayer is commanded in this instance, what of it? It does not invalidate baptism; it does not substitute prayer for it, as you assert, but simply associates prayer with the baptism. This extent hath the admission, no more. What does it teach, if prayer be meant? That the penitent believer is to be baptized, and wash away his sins, praying, *at the time and in the very act of baptism*, to the Lord, that, "in coming to his holy baptism," he "may receive the remission of sins." But the admission was made to show you that, being made, it will not avail you, as you thought. While, then, a sinner is not *commanded* to pray; while it is nowhere spoken of as a term of pardon to him; while it can not be regarded as his duty; still, an unpardoned man, going forward believingly, penitently, lovingly in the pathway of obedience that leads to forgiveness by the Divine promise, would, as the legitimate effect of his faith, his deep sorrow for sin, and conviction of his great guilt, offer up from his heart the silent prayer, if not with his lips the spoken one: "Lord, have mercy on me, a sinner; and grant that, as my body is washed in water, my soul may be washed from sin in thine own blood." Such a prayer, at such a time, as the outgush of a believing, penitent soul, I do not object to. I rather like it. I think it beautiful and appropriate. But when sub-

stituted for a Divine command; when these agonizing utterances of a human spirit under conviction of sin are relied
on as terms of pardon—holding, as I do, the Divine authority pledged to that end—and when, as is always the case,
the preacher and the mourning sinner are knowingly treating baptism with contempt, and regarding it as a non-
essential, then, from the very depth of an honest heart, I
loathe, I hate the doctrine and the practice, and my profoundest sympathies are stirred in behalf of the deluded
mourners whose "blind guides" are leading them "into
the ditch," and out of which, I fear, they will never come.

5. The truth is, baptism and prayer are positive institutions, ordained alike for remission of sins; baptism to the
sinner, prayer to the Christian. To believers not in the
Church, Peter says: "Repent, and be baptized for remission of sins." To the baptized believer, Simon the
magician, who sinned in the Church, the same apostle said:
"Repent and pray." Guided by the apostle, we can not
err.

In final statement on the subject of prayer, I beg leave
to say, that a sinner (by which is meant an unpardoned
man, who has never been a member of the Church), as
such, is nowhere commanded in the Bible to pray for the
remission of his sins, or for any other purpose; and that
every soul that was ever commanded or encouraged to
pray, in the New Testament, by the Savior or the apostles,
was at the time either a member of the Church of God
under the Jewish dispensation, or of the Church of Christ
under the Christian dispensation.

But says another objector: "In the commission, it is
said that 'he that believeth not shall be damned;' and, if
baptism is essential, it seems to me it ought to have
read: 'He that believeth not, and is not baptized, shall be

damned.'" In your own mind, write out the commission, adding your amendment. Then salvation is left where we found it, dependent upon *two* conditions; but damnation, instead of being suspended on one act of disobedience, can now only be executed upon two acts of disobedience. *Then*, he could be damned if he believed not; *now*, he can not. Before he can be condemned under the improved commission, he must also be unbaptized. To be damned, he must be a non-believer, and unbaptized. A baptized unbeliever and an unbaptized believer, having obeyed one command and disobeyed the other, could, according to this commission, be neither saved nor damned.

You have altogether mistaken the value of the omission of baptism from the last clause of the commission. The meaning of the commission—in the light of itself, of the New Testament, and of common sense—is, that the believer shall have remission of sins in being baptized; but that the unbeliever will be damned, whether baptized or not baptized.

Dear hearer, we can not alter that law of pardon. Were we to attempt it, in some new translation, we would recoil at the unmitigated wickedness of the act. What we dare not print in a newly-published Bible we are getting out, it is both a bold and wicked act to teach. Let us try, for experiment's sake, to alter it. We will employ the word "not" as the chief element of alteration. We can alter it in several ways.

He that believeth, and is *not* baptized, shall be saved.

He that believeth *not*, and is baptized, shall be saved.

He that believeth, and is baptized, shall *not* be saved.

No lover of the blessed Jesus would consent to pervert God's holy word. Hence, no honest man could sanction any one of these alterations. Then let the commission stand. Touch not a single part—mar not, by human addition, the fair proportions of the Savior's finished work. "Handle not the Word of God deceitfully;" "diminish not a word;" "declare the whole counsel of God." Let us preach the commission fully, faithfully, and forever.

"But will I be damned if I am not baptized?" Certainly. Why not? It is the blood of Christ that really washes away the guilt of sin. We come to the blood "into the death" of Christ, through faith and repentance, and in baptism. You believe and repent, but say baptism is a non-essential, and, therefore, will not obey it; that is, you will do nothing for the love of Jesus but just so much and no more as is necessary to "escape the damnation of hell." Why should you be damned if you do not believe, and not damned if you are not baptized? Why is faith essential to salvation, and baptism not? Is faith essential? Yes. Why? Is there any intrinsic merit or saving efficacy in faith? None. Is Jesus under any obligation to you because you believe? No. Is there any merit in faith and repentance combined? None. Add baptism, and is there any? None. The efficacy is in the grace of God, and the blood of Jesus. Of three things which equally are void of merit, how can two of them be essential, and the other not? Of three nonentities, can you make two entities, and have a nonentity left? Of three nothings can you make two of them something, and the remaining one still nothing? Why is faith essential? Jesus suspends the pardon of the sinner on it. He commands him to believe, but he commands him to be baptized also; and he gave this command at the same time, under the same circumstances, in the same sentence, to be preached to the same people—for the same purpose as he gave the command to believe. If one is essential, so is the other. If one is non-essential, so is the other. The believer will be pardoned if he will be baptized. The baptized man will be pardoned if he be a believer. There can be no other meaning to the mandatory promise, "He that believeth, and is baptized, shall be saved." "Believe," here used in its broader meaning, includes repentance. The baptized, penitent believer, according to the Savior's promise, will receive the remission of sins. No other man will. I believe and teach that, according to the law of the Lord in the New Testament, a man must believe with all his heart in the Divine Redeemer; must deeply, sorrowfully, truly repent of his sins against God and the Christ, and must be baptized, in the name of the Lord Jesus, into the name of the Father, and of the Son, and of the Holy Spirit, in order to the pardon of his past sins. I further believe and teach, that no one will obtain an inheritance among the redeemed and sanctified in heaven who willfully neglects baptism, knowing it to be a commandment of the Lord Jesus. Is it not strange, passing strange, that the Protestant parties in the land consider the acknowledgment of the Trinity an *essential* element of an orthodox faith, and an *essential* qualification for admission into an orthodox Church; yet will treat as a matter of inferior moment (speaking of it as a *non-essential*) a commandment of Jesus the Christ, which is a clear revelation of his will concerning our duty, and the only one in all the Bible commanded to be done in or into the names of Father, Son, and Holy Spirit? But such is, nevertheless, the fact, and it furnishes an additional reason why we should "contend earnestly for the faith once delivered to the saints."

Yours Truly
W. K. Pendleton.

WILLIAM KIMBROUGH PENDLETON.

WILLIAM KIMBROUGH PENDLETON was born in Louisa County, Virginia, September 8, 1817. He is of English descent, and his ancestors, both paternal and maternal, have, from the earliest history of this country, occupied distinguished positions in the state and the church. His mother was brought up under Episcopal influence, but his father, Colonel EDMUND PENDLETON, was not a member of any church until WILLIAM was about sixteen years of age, when he became a reader of the "Christian Baptist" and "Millennial Harbinger," and, after a full and free investigation of the plea presented by the advocates of primitive Christianity, he determined to be immersed "for the remission of sins." He soon became an active and earnest worker in the cause of Christ, and, through his influence, a church was established in his neighborhood, which was the first Disciples' church in that part of Virginia, and was the nucleus of the Mount Gilboa Church, which afterward became celebrated for being the germ from which sprung many other congregations. The "peculiar doctrines" which the father advocated met with very determined opposition from the various religious sects of the neighborhood. Hence, every position of the new movement was subjected to the severest investigation; and, as his father's house was the center of most of these discussions, WILLIAM had, thus early, every opportunity to become thoroughly acquainted with the principles of the Reformation.

From his earliest boyhood his education was carefully provided for. After attending, for several years, the best schools in that part of the State, he entered the University of Virginia, where, besides the academical course, he studied *the law* two years, and was licensed to practice. During most of this time he had been a regular reader of the "Christian Baptist" and "Millennial Harbinger," and a constant and earnest student of the Word of God. He also acted as amanuensis for his father in conducting some epistolary discussions with a Baptist preacher and others; heard Elder S. HIGGASON and JAMES BAGLEY preach for years, besides hearing occasionally many of the most distinguished preachers among the Disciples; was constantly in company with Disciples at his father's house; and, above all, and before all, was carefully trained from his infancy by a pious mother—"a woman possessing the gentleness and mildness of a child, combined with the firmness and courage of a Spartan mother—*extremely* modest and unobtrusive, yet, when drawn into conversation, showing great depth of thought and clearness of perception, and a mind well stored with information." Such was the character of the religious influences brought to bear upon him, and, under these, having come to a full understanding of his duty, he was, in June, 1840, immersed by ALEXANDER CAMPBELL, at the Mount Gilboa Church, Louisa County, Virginia, being, at the time, in the twenty-third year of his age. In the fall of 1840, he was married to LAVINIA M., daughter of ALEXANDER CAMPBELL, a lady of brilliant intellect and beautiful Christian character, who died in the spring of 1846.

He was appointed Professor of Natural Philosophy in Bethany College, in May, 1841, (the year the college was founded,) and has been connected with it ever since as Professor, and, much of the time, as Vice-President, and now as President. In 1844 he was united to the editorial corps of the "Millennial Harbinger," and has continued in that relation ever since, being at this time its proprietor and senior editor.

In August, 1848, he was again married—this time to CLARINDA, also a daughter of ALEXANDER CAMPBELL. Mr. CAMPBELL's celebrated letters from Europe were addressed to this daughter. She was greatly beloved by all who knew her, and was thoroughly devoted to the cause of Christ. She died in January, 1851, rich in good works, and "meet to be a partaker of the inheritance of the saints in light." In the autumn of 1855, he was again married—to CATHERINE H., daughter of Judge LECEISTER KING, of Warren, Trumbull County, Ohio.

For several years previous to the death of Mr. CAMPBELL, Professor PENDLETON discharged the duties of President of Bethany College, and, on the death of Mr. CAMPBELL, was unanimously elected by the curators to fill the place so long and ably occupied by his father-in-law.

President PENDLETON is five feet eight and a half inches high, and weighs about one hundred and fifty pounds. His nervous system predominates over both the muscular and vital; hence, he is capable of great intellectual force, but has rather a feeble physical organization. As a speaker, he is chaste, logical, and impressive, but, on account of his profession, has never had sufficient opportunities for thoroughly testing his powers before the people. As a writer, he stands unquestionably without a superior in the ranks of the Disciples. But it is as the dignified, courteous, polished, Christian *gentleman* that you *delight* to know him. And, to understand what we mean by this, you *must know* him, for no *description* can ever do him justice.

THE MINISTRY OF THE HOLY SPIRIT.

BY W. K. PENDLETON.

"Nevertheless, I tell you the truth; it is expedient for you that I go away: for if I go not away, the Comforter will not come unto you; but if I depart, I will send him unto you. And when he is come, he will reprove the world of sin, and of righteousness, and of judgment: of sin, because they believe not on me; of righteousness, because I go to my Father, and ye see me no more; of judgment, because the prince of this world is judged."—JOHN xvi: 7–11.

WHEN the Savior said to his apostles, "It is expedient for you that I go away," it must have been to them a declaration *hard to understand*. His presence had been so necessary to their confidence, and so full of comfort and of power, that they could not regard a separation with less than the gloomiest forebodings. They had hung upon his words with the fond and newly-awakened hopes of eternal life; they had forsaken all to follow him; and now, to be left alone, what could it seem but the saddest and darkest disappointment? When "many of his disciples went back, and walked no more with him," and he had asked them, with such pathetic tenderness, "Will ye also go away?" Peter, the prompt and impulsive Peter, had answered, "Lord, to whom shall we go? Thou hast the words of eternal life." There was no light, no strength, no hope to them but in Christ, and how could it be *expe-*

20

dient for them that he should go away? It was a saying hard to be understood, requiring, in fact, a fuller revelation of the Divine economy of redemption than he had yet made to them.

Hitherto, the central power of this economy had been in *his sensible person.* Martha, weeping over the death of Lazarus, says: "Lord, if thou hadst been *here*, my brother had not died." Before Jairus's daughter is raised, Jesus goes to the house of her parents, stands over the bier, takes her by the hand, and says, "Daughter, arise."

The power of Christ to help was centered in his *visible, sensible person,* and that was limited to *time* and *place.* True, in sending out *the seventy*, and healing the centurian's servant, we have instances of power exerted where he was not personally present. But even in these cases there was direct connection with his person by some one before the influence was imparted. Evidently these sensuous limitations were not suited to the omnipresent wants of a spiritual kingdom. An omnipresent agent is needed for a universal kingdom. A spirit-presence must take the place of a sense-presence. The heart must be filled where the eye can not see; and Jesus must go away, that the *Paraclete*, the advocate and comforter, may come. Let us consider the difference. Suppose Jesus to-day at Jerusalem, and seated on the throne of David, in the person he wore when he stood, eighteen centuries ago, arraigned as a criminal before the bar of Pilate. Around the throne there might be the effulgence of glory, and in his presence fullness of joy. But what would he be to us, in this far distant land of the West? Between him and our hearts an ocean-barrier rolls; the radiance of his countenance beams not upon us, and his words come to us through the telegraph, chilled by the distance and void of the vital breath of the King. We can not see him, or hear him. Like Moses, wrapped in the misty shroud of Mount Sinai, he is hidden from our view. What would be left us but, like the children of Israel, to turn to our own devices, and cry: " Up, make us gods which shall go before us." Peter returns to his nets, and the rest go with him.

On the other hand, enthrone Jesus in heaven, invest him with all power, and fill the earth with the presence of the Spirit—the Paraclete—the official advocate and comforting minister of his reign. Here is a power wide as the domain of his truth, breathing with ever-present influence through words of eternal life; working with the same energy that brooded over the primitive chaos, and molding into order, and form, and beauty, and conscious blessedness, the *new* spirit-world, a glorious regeneration of the wreck of the *old*.

Doubtless the apostles felt disconsolate when the Savior said, "I go away;" but when, on the day of Pentecost, the Spirit came, and they were baptized in its power, and began to speak with tongues, and felt the mighty energy of truth burning for utterance, and saw its two-edged sharpness piercing the hearts of their enemies, they could say: " We are not left comfortless; the blessed Jesus has indeed gone away; but, being by the right hand of God exalted, and having received of the Father the promise of the Holy Spirit, he hath shed forth this which ye now see and hear." Truly did he say, " It is expedient for you that I go away," because, as he promised, he hath sent the Comforter.

Thus, in one passage, the Savior very formally announces his purpose to devolve the advocacy of his cause upon the Holy Spirit, to replace his personal presence by the ministration of the Paraclete, and declares it to be expedient for his disciples that he should do so. There is to be a new administration of affairs, and a new ministry. Let us consider—

    I. THE MINISTER.

    II. TO WHOM HE IS SENT.

    III. WHAT IS HIS WORK.

I. THE MINISTER.

He is called the *Paraclete*. The term, in its fullness, means a comforting helper. It is a name by which the Savior calls the Holy Spirit. (John xiv: 26.) In our passage he is presented to us as the successor of Christ in the administration of the economy of redemption. He proceedeth from the Father, and is sent by the Son. (John xv: 26.) He is, therefore, a distinct manifestation of God. For the want of a better term, we call him a *person*, a word which very inadequately represents the idea of a spiritual essence. But the New Testament leaves no ambiguity as to the threefold manifestation of God, in Father, Son, and Holy Spirit; and as the word *person* has been used by the common version to translate both the *prosopon* (προσωπον) of Christ, (2 Cor. ii: 10,) and the *hupostasis* (ὑποστασις) of the Father, (Heb. 1: 3,) we are warranted in applying the same term also to that manifestation of God, which is called, in the Scriptures, the Holy Spirit. That the Holy Spirit is a distinct personal manifestation of God is evident:

First, from the fact that he is designated, like the Father and the Son, by appropriate names. He is called "the Paraclete," and "the Holy Spirit;" and the latter designation is expressly given as his name: "Baptizing them into the *name* of the Father, and of the Son, and of the Holy Spirit." (Matt. xxviii: 19.) The expression is literal, and the distinctness of the *three* marked by a definiteness that could not be more sharply indicated by language. Our baptism brings us equally into relation to the *three* as *persons*, and presents the *three* to us, at the same time, as also *one in nature*.

Second. From the fact that both intelligence and determining will are ascribed to him. "He is a Spirit of wisdom, of understanding, of counsel, and knowledge." (Isa. xi: 2.) "He searcheth all things, even the deep things of God." (1 Cor. ii: 10.) He is the author of spiritual gifts; and the apostle declares that, in distributing these, "he divides to every man as he will." (1 Cor. xii: 11.) But what can thus act with intelligence and free choice but a distinct person? These are not isolated passages, but the general drift of revelation, concerning the Holy Spirit, is to the same effect.

Third. Not only has he intelligence and free choice, but also accompanying power. He descends on the day of Pentecost, as a mighty rushing wind; he imparts the power of working miracles to the apostles, just as Christ had done; he raises up Christ from the dead; he smites the hypocrites Ananias and Sapphira with death in the instant of their falsehood; and many other marvelous works are ascribed to him, which present him constantly before us, in the boldest and most striking aspects of personal grandeur and power.

Fourth. Our passage speaks of him as a person, as one that can *come*, that may be *sent*, that can glorify the Son, and guide the disciples into all, or the whole truth. "He shall take of mine," says the Savior, "and show it unto you." (John xvi: 15.) Can an agent like this be a mere influence? Can language like this be applicable to merely impersonal means, having no distinct energy of their own, and moving simply as they are moved by some other power? Surely words are meaningless, and all reality must be banished from the Scriptures, if these expressions are simply metaphors, shadows of shades, misty utterances about unknown phantoms, that vanish from our view when we attempt to fix them in thought, or give them, in our faith, "a local habitation and a name."

Fifth. Because, in the new dispensation, he is set forth as the promised personal manifestation of God. In Leviticus xxvi: 11,12, God, speaking absolutely, says: "I will set my tabernacle among you, and will be your God, and ye shall be my people." But Paul, in 2 Cor. vi: 16, interprets this as a *promise,* and finds its fulfillment in the actual bestowal of the Holy Spirit to dwell in the hearts of Christians. He says: "Ye are the temple of the living God; as God hath said, I will dwell in them, and walk among them." This he accomplishes in the person of the Holy Spirit. "Know ye not, that ye are the temple of God, and that the Spirit of God dwelleth in you? for the temple of God are ye." While, then, the Holy Spirit is *personally* distinct, he is, in *nature,* God; so that, when he fills the temple of the human heart, it is truly God who dwells in it.

Thus is this minister of the new reign set before us; by his official and his essential name; by his omniscient intelligence and self-determining will; by his omnipotent power; by his glorious and official procession from the Father and the Son, and by his representative dignity as the personal manifestation of God in the new and spiritual kingdom. By all these, and many other tokens, he comes to us, our Comforter, Helper, Friend. He introduces himself wondrously to us in the sublime and overpowering scenes of Pentecost, and opens up the new empire over the hearts of men, with a grand exhibition of his power to perform the work for which he is sent.   Let us inquire:

II. To whom is he sent.

This question need not detain us long; but it is important, in approaching it, to notice the different economies or dispensations of the Father, the Son, and the Holy Spirit.   Before the fall, man enjoyed the full manifestation of God.   The unveiled Majesty stood before him in the garden.   He walked with God, as a son with a father.   Paradise was garnished for him with " herb, tree, fruit, and flower, glistening with dew."

> " Gentle gales,
> Fanning their odoriferous wings, dispense
> Native perfumes, and whisper whence they stole
> Their balmy spoils."

His heart is open to God in all pure worship.   He moves, a peer among the cherubim, and mingles his praises with theirs.   The will of God thrills through his nature as his vital breath.   He trembles with fullness of joy. "God is all in all"—"Omnipotent, immutable, immortal, infinite, eternal King."   This is the dispensation of the Father.   Man is without sin, and God is manifested only as life, light, and love.

The entrance of sin breaks this harmony.   Man is banished from the garden of Eden.   The dispensation of love gives place to the dispensation of law.   Remedial grace holds the world in quarantine.   God operates afar off through his Son.   He does not utterly abandon us, but out of the thick darkness he speaks in tones of thunder, and, at long intervals, by the "angel of the presence." The promised seed of the woman even now has his "delights with the sons of men." (Prov. viii: 31.) He appears to Abraham, and speaks with Moses in the Mount of Sinai, (Acts vii: 38,) adding the law, till he should come in full accomplishment of the promise. (Gal. iii: 19.) Yet when, in the fullness of time, he is manifested in the flesh, his operation is transient, and mostly limited to his personal presence. Even his apostles do not comprehend him. He speaks in parables, and holds the truth under a veil. Until sin is atoned for, and his work of redemption done, there can be no closer or more intimate relation to the sinner. God and man must be reconciled before the lost fellowship of Eden can be restored. This is his work, and it leads him by the gate of death. He must glorify humanity in his own person before he can sanctify it with his Holy Spirit. This is the remedial dispensation—the dispensation of the Son.

Not until it was *finished* could the Holy Spirit be given. True the Spirit, as of the divine essence, appears in every dispensation as an inseparable, co-operating divine agent. As the Savior said: "The Father worketh hitherto and I work;" and, "Without the Father I can do nothing." So it is equally true that there is also an ever-present co-operation of the Spirit. But it is an operation, *ab extra*, from without. The *glorification* of the Son opens up a new era—the dispensation or economy of the Holy Spirit—a manifestation of the Spirit fuller and more permanent and intimate than had ever been enjoyed before. This could not be, our passage expressly declares, until Christ should go away. "If I go not away, the *Paraclete* will not come unto you; but if I depart, I will send him unto you." The disciples had, doubtless, felt the *influence* of the Spirit in looking upon the radiant countenance, and listening to the burning words of Jesus, and when he breathed on them, and said unto them: Receive ye the Holy Spirit, (John xx: 22,) the action and the word must have thrilled them with a sense of divine ecstacy and power. But he is not yet given, as the fountain of an overflowing river of living water, in the heart of the believer, because that Jesus is not yet glorified. (John vii: 38, 39.) The disciples must yet tarry, sorrowful it may be, but yet in hope, tarry at Jerusalem till this new power—the Comforting Advocate—shall come. (Luke xxiv: 49.)

He had brooded over chaos, the quickening power in creation; striven with the antediluvians in their rebellion against the will of God; cheered with bright and hopeful visions the fainting hearts of the patriarchs, and other immortal heroes of God; opened long vistas down through the mysterious future to the wondering eyes of the prophets, and clothed, in rosy light, the dawning day of the good things to come; thrilled the souls of poets with sweet inspirations and power to strike the sublimest chords of song; cherished and kept alive, in pure minds, the deathless memories of God, and "the pure empyrean where he sits high-throned above all height;" stirred in brooding hearts immortal longings for the return of the golden days of Eden, long dimmed in sinful night; and in all, and through all the wise and wondrous providence of God, moved and worked, one with the Father and the Son, but yet, not as a distinct dweller in the temple of humanity, an abiding guest in the heart of the fallen, a comforting helper to the orphaned exile from the Father's face.

This is a manifestation of the Spirit long promised and yet to come, and its accomplishment brings us to the ever memorable Pentecost; to the scene in the upper chamber, where the disciples are waiting; to the miracles of tongues; to the sermon of Peter, and the conversion of the three thousand in a day. The period of the *last days* is now fully come, and the Spirit is poured out in all fullness and power. Jesus has been glorified. Humanity has been lifted up in his victory, and fitted for the indwelling of the Spirit. He may now enter the long-closed temple of the human heart, now reconciled to the Father, through the death of the Son, and take up his abode there to dwell with it forever.

Returning to our question: *To whom is he sent?* we find the answer easy and intelligible. Our passage says: "I will send him unto you"—you, my disciples. Again: "This spake he of the Spirit, which they that believe on him should receive." (John vii: 39.) Again: "I will pray the Father, and he shall give you another Comforter, that he may abide with you forever; even the Spirit of Truth; whom the world can not receive, because it seeth him not, neither knoweth him: but ye know him; for he dwelleth with you, and shall be in you." (John xiv: 16, 17.) Yet again, on the day of Pentecost, Peter, speaking as he was moved by this same Spirit, says: "Repent, and be baptized, and ye shall receive the gift of the Holy Spirit." (Acts ii: 38.) It is the baptized, penitent believer, then, to whom the Holy Spirit is sent; and to him, in contrast with the unconverted, the impenitent, the unbaptized "world" to whom he is not sent. And the reason of this is plain. As his coming is restrained till Jesus shall go away, and his ministry withheld till humanity is first glorified in the person of Christ, so it is incompatible with the dignity and purity of the Divine economy that the Holy Spirit should be sent to dwell in a heart that had not, by faith, received Christ, and washed in the fountain of his blood, opened for sin and uncleanness. (Zech. xiii: 1.) The mission of Christ ends with

---

his fitting humanity, by faith in him, for the reception of the Spirit. The mission of the Spirit commences by his taking up his abode in the temple thus prepared for his entrance.

III. WHAT IS HIS WORK?

This is twofold. *First*, in the heart of the believers, leading them to glorify Jesus, by reproducing in them his life; and *second*, through the disciples, upon the world.

In these twofold operations there is this difference: in the *first*, he dwells *in* and works *with* the believers. In the apostolic age he imparts spiritual gifts to them; then and always, he dwells in the heart of the disciples to help their infirmities, (Rom. viii: 26,) and work in them both to will and to do of his good pleasure (Phil. ii: 13). In the *second*, he operates through the disciples *upon* the world. "*The world*," as such, can not receive him. Upon them he works from without, producing faith, and preparing them, by the reception of Christ, to become fit temples for his entrance as a comforting guest. And this is the great work to which our passage especially points our attention. It is what the Savior emphatically declares the *Paraclete* shall do when he comes. "He shall convince or reprove the world of sin, of righteousness, and of judgment." These are the grand themes of the great advocate. Let us consider them.

1. *He shall reprove the world of sin.* What is the method of the Holy Spirit in working conviction in the hearts of men? How shall he reprove the world of sin? Shall he descant upon the doctrine of the fall; weave fine metaphysical webs about human depravity; decide whether it is total or partial; discuss the ethics of transmitted guilt; draw nice distinctions between original and hereditary sin;

turn all our misfortune and woe over to Adam; or, looking into our own actions, condemn us by the special crimes
of our own personal life? This is man's method—the
bungling diagnosis of our spiritual doctors. Into what a
maze of controversy it leads us, and how it turns the
heart away from Christ, and the great question which the
Holy Spirit raises with the world! "Shall I be damned
because my ancestor, six thousand years ago, imprudently
ate of an apple?" says one; and he stands excusing himself
on the ethics of this question till he is lost. "I live in all
good conscience," says another; "I defraud no one, I give
to the poor, and 'with gentle heart worship nature in
hill and valley,' cherishing

> " 'A sense sublime
> Of something far more deeply interfused,
> Whose dwelling is the light of setting suns,
> And the round ocean and the living air;
> A motion and a Spirit, that impels
> All thinking things, all objects of all thought,
> And rolls through all things.'

"Shall I, thus elevated in soul, and wrapped in Divine
spheres of reason, be ranked with the vulgar herd that
grovel in the dust? What is my crime? What stain
spots the robe of my righteousness?" And thus, self-
fascinated, he puts aside the great question of the Holy
Spirit, and goes to the judgment without Christ. Amazing folly! These, O man, are not the questions which
the Holy Spirit raises with you, by which he reproves you
of sin.

He asks you, "What think you of Christ?" He reproves you of sin, not because of Adam's sin; not because
you stand, a shattered column from the ruin of Paradise;
but because, so standing, marred and defaced by sin, you

refuse his offered help to restore you—to renew in you the effaced countenance of the Father, and fill your heart again with the blessed fellowship of his Spirit. "He shall convince the world of sin, because they believe not on him." The sin that is brought home to us, to each of us, to you and to me, is our own sin—not another's. He says to us: "Look around upon the world's ruin; look within, at the withered glory of the soul; see the work of the enemy; behold, over it my love, like a Niobe of nations, weeping, stoops to regenerate it. Through agony and blood I have travailed to victory. The work is done. Come and share it with me." Who will refuse? What can make us refuse but the love of sin—the sin that caused his death?

Is not this a simple criterion? Christ finds us ruined by sin—held under its bondage; he comes to redeem us, suffers for us, conquers for us, and offers us the fruit of his victory freely—without money, and without price. "What the law could not do, in that it was weak through the flesh, God sending his own Son, in the likeness of sinful flesh, and, by a sacrifice for sin, condemned sin in the flesh." (Rom. viii: 3.) And now to refuse him as our sin-offering, what is it but to cleave to the sin which he has condemned? And is not this *sin in us?* Adam, tempted, and without experience of the damning guilt of sin, yielded to the fatal fascination. He found himself naked, stripped of the glory that had covered him as a mantle, and shrank, abashed at his own deformity, from the purity and beauty of Paradise. He is cast out, a banished exile from the presence of the Father, but with the promise of deliverance. "The seed of the woman shall yet bruise the serpent's head." He sold the life of Eden for the knowledge of good and evil, and received the penalty—death. In the fullness of time, the promised seed comes. The deliverance is achieved. The Holy Spirit is sent to call us to accept it. A free return to the tree of life is offered to us through Christ, and we refuse it. With all the sad experience of six thousand years under sin, we deliberately adhere to the choice of Adam. *We repeat his act in our own freedom.* We say to Christ: We will continue as we are, hug our chains, CLING to our bondage; we will not come back. Adam has chosen, we abide the choice. The tree of life has been forfeited, we stand by the result. We despise your sufferings, we refuse your sacrifice. We will repeat the sin of the first Adam, and die, rather than accept the sacrifice of the second Adam, and live. O friend, is not this deeper sin than that which brought our fall? Is not deliberate and conscious sin worse than tempted and ignorant impulse? impenitence and ingratitude, than passion and appetite? "This is now the condemnation, that light has come into the world, and men prefer darkness to light, because their deeds are evil." (John iii: 19.) This is the reproof of the *Paraclete*, that *Jesus has died and risen again, and men will not believe on him.*

2. *He shall convince the world of righteousness.* This is the second great theme of the *Paraclete*, to convince the world of *righteousness.* This term has a double sense: it points, *first*, to the personal character of Christ; *second*, to his representative character. In both these respects, Jesus must be vindicated before the world.

His personal character was involved in two charges. The Jews accused him of *blasphemy* and *treason*; blasphemy, because he professed to be the Son of God, and thus made himself equal with God (John v: 18); and treason, because he claimed to be a King, and so was a rival of Cæsar. (John xix: 12.) The refutation of these charges was easy. The great argument is that "I go to the

Father." If I am not the Son of God, the Father will not receive me; if I am not King, he will not welcome me to the throne. He will not acknowledge an imposter, nor honor a pretender. Condemned before Pilate, I appeal to the "King eternal, immortal, invisible, the only wise God, with whom are honor and glory forever and ever." (1 Tim. i: 17.) If he acquits, who shall condemn? "I have set the Lord always before me: because he is at my right hand, I shall not be moved. Thou wilt not leave my soul in hell; neither wilt thou suffer thine Holy One to see corruption." (Psalms xvi: 9–11.) This was the sublime confidence with which Jesus went to the bar of Pilate, to the cross, to the tomb, to the judgment of the Father. Who shall witness the trial, and report to us the eternal verdict? Human witnesses can not be admitted to this scene. The *Paraclete* must come, and the demonstration must be worthy of the sufferer.

This is the first great theme of Pentecost. Peter makes it the prominent point in his first argument. The mighty wonder of the out-poured Spirit demonstrates this:—"This same Jesus whom you took, and with wicked hands crucified and slew, hath God raised up, whereof we are all witnesses: him hath God acknowledged as his Son, and exalted to the throne, saying, 'Sit thou on my right hand, until I make thy foes thy footstool.' Let all the house of Israel know assuredly this, that God hath made that same Jesus whom you have crucified, both Lord and Christ." (Acts ii: 32–36.) Thus is he vindicated in his high pretensions as the Son of God, as the King of kings and the Lord of lords, and thus is the personal righteousness of Jesus proved by the Spirit.

But there is another sense, in which the righteousness of Christ is of deepest interest to us. As a matter merely personal to him, his righteousness is, indeed, also a question of vital interest to us, since all his pretensions as our Savior hang upon his Divine nature and official grandeur as both the Son of God, and King. But, in connection with his representative character, his righteousness has a dearer and more comforting significance to us. In his manifestation as the Son of God, he is also the Son of man. "The word was made flesh." He became Immanuel, God with us. In our nature, he fulfilled all righteousness. He carried humanity successfully through temptation, through suffering, through death, and through judgment, up to the very throne of God. He demonstrated the possibility of its becoming and being perfect, "holy, harmless, undefiled, separate from sin, and higher than the heavens." This knowledge is too high for us. It is an announcement of the *Paraclete*, one of the comforting things which the Spirit hath heard of the Father and shown unto us, a revelation of the superlative and transcendent grandeur of humanity in its new and mysterious union with Christ, that passes all understanding. Ineffable honor, that thus we may be lifted up from our degradation and ruin to the honors and privileges of heaven !

> "Nearest the throne, and first in song,
> Man shall his hallelujah raise;
> While wondering angels crowd around,
> And swell the chorus of his praise."

This perfect righteousness of the God-man becomes, again, the sufficient ground of our justification. "By the sacrifices of the law, there was only a remembrance of sins again from year to year; for it was not possible that the blood of bulls and of goats should take away sins: but this man, after he had made one sacrifice for sins forever, sat down on the right hand of God; from henceforth expecting till his enemies be made his footstool; for by one offering he hath perfected forever them that are sanctified." (Heb. x: 3–14.) Upon the altar of his divinity, he offers the sacrifice of a perfect humanity, and is made of God unto us, who glory not in the flesh, wisdom, and righteousness, and sanctification, and redemption. (1 Cor. i: 30.) "He shall convince the world of righteousness, because I go to the Father."

3. *He shall convince the world of judgment.* If there were no evidence of a judgment, there would, perhaps, be but little respect for law. Man is so perverted by sin that he has but little respect for authority that has no adequate sanction attached to its commands. But here, again, the demonstration of the Spirit goes at once to the root of all rebellion. It contemplates man as, by nature, under the power of the wicked one. It does not stop to inquire into the guilt or innocence of individuals; but, with one sweeping generalization, involves all men in the great controversy with Satan, and condemns them because of their relation to "the Prince of this world." It declares to us that the great controversy is one for dominion. By the successful temptation of the Garden, man fell under the power of the tempter. Christ comes to set him free. The conflict is not with man, but with Satan; that tyrannical prince, under whom man is held in bondage. His dominion is right, or it is wrong, legitimate or usurped. If it is right, then we are justified in adhering to it. If it is wrong, then we are involved in its guilt, if we do not forsake it. This is the issue. Jesus makes it, and Satan rises in all the might of a last desperate struggle to meet it. He approaches him with alluring temptations in the wil-

21

derness; lays cunning traps for him in the opposition of
the Jews to catch him in his words; confronts him with
demoniacal possessions, to test the measure of his power;
and, day after day, month after month, year after year,
throws around him the cunning meshes of his strategy,
till he brings him to the bar of Pilate, with specific charges
and infuriated witnesses.   The power of hell is at war
with the Son of God.   The final issue seems to hang upon
this trial before Pilate.   The conflict is of the many against
the *one*, and the majority carry it.   Jesus is humiliated,
mocked, scourged, condemned, led away to be crucified,
carrying his own cross, with fainting footsteps, to the
summit of Calvary.   All men forsake him.   He "looks,
and there is none to help;" therefore, "his own right arm
must bring salvation to him."   He must go down alone
to the citadel of this enemy.   "The war must be carried
into Carthage."   The way is through the valley of death,
and the stronghold is the grave.   These must be invaded;
and Jesus enters them, not as a strong man, prepared for
battle, but with tears, and bitter cries of agony, and burden of sin, at which angels gaze with mute wonder, and
the solid earth shudders to its center.   Oh, this is the
moment of hell's triumph!   Through its fiery caverns
the shout of demons thunders: "*Victory! victory!* The
Son of God is a captive.   Let captivity rejoice, and hell
flaunt her banners over the fallen!"

O, thou bleeding Lamb of God, thou hast not fallen,
but stooped to conquer!   Thy strength returns to thee.
Thine arms are around the central columns of this temple
of Dagon.   Thy mocking enemies are within the crushing
folds of thy omnipotence.   Thou canst not be holden of
death.   Rise, in the might of thy power, and shake off
the shackles of the grave; burst the cerements that bind

thee, and, as thou saidst for Lazarus, so for thyself: "Come forth !"

Let us thank God that he did not suffer his Holy One to see corruption, but that he "declared him to be his own Son, with power, according to the Spirit of holiness, by his resurrection from the dead." (Rom. i: 4.) That in his final conflict he gave the verdict in his favor, and condemned Satan, with an everlasting judgment, to "chains under darkness, to be kept till the punishment of the last day." (Jude: 6.)

And now, what is the short argument of the *Paraclete* with the world? Simply this: If "the Prince of this world is condemned"—already conquered, subdued, and in chains—what is the condition of "*the world*," who still adhere to him? Are not they under sentence with him, shut up in the fate of their "prince?" Does not this argument "stop every mouth, and subject all the world to the judgment of God?" (Rom. iii: 19.) The Spirit does not enter into a personal examination of the moral character of each man, and seek the ground of his condemnation in his personal misdeeds; but he raises the broad and universal question: Whom serve ye? The conquering Son of God, or the conquered prince of the world? These are the two powers. With which do you stand? With the triumphant soldiers of the Cross, or the broken columns of hell? Is not this a plain question? Can not all men answer it? Is it not an important question? Should not all men consider it? Is it not a decisive test of loyalty? Should not all men be judged by it?

And now, how simple, and yet how comprehensive, is the ministry of the Spirit. In his great plea there is the one supreme end ever in view—the regeneration of the world. In all his work, there is the co-operation of the

Father and the Son; for, "while there are diversities of gifts, it is the same Spirit; and differences of administration, it is the same Lord; and diversities of operations, it is the same God, which worketh all in all." (1 Cor. xii: 4, 7.) In his manifestation to believers and to the world, he maintains sharply the distinction between a heart cleansed by the blood of Christ and reconciled to God, and one still under the power of sin, and allied to Satan; entering the one and dwelling *in* it, as a deity in a temple, and operating *upon* the other as an influence from without. In his operation upon the world, working through the disciples—to whom alone he is sent—and employing words and miracles, truths and demonstrations, to convince and reprove them. And in the wide breadth of his plea, comprehending only the three great themes of sin, righteousness, and judgment: "Sin," says the Savior, "because they believe not on me; righteousness, because I go to the Father; and judgment, because the Prince of this world is judged."

Most Fraternally

J. W. McGarrey

JOHN W. M'GARVEY.

FEW men among the Disciples have obtained a more enviable reputation, and enjoyed more generally the confidence of the brethren, than the subject of this notice. Blessed with more than an average amount of practical common sense, and having faithfully done his duty in all the positions he has occupied, it is not strange that he should now be regarded as one of the safest and truest men in the Church of Christ.

JOHN W. M'GARVEY was born in Hopkinsville, Kentucky, March 1, 1829. His father was born in Ireland, and, when grown, came to America, and settled at Hopkinsville, Kentucky, where, with a small capital, he went into the dry-goods business. His mother was a Miss THOMSON, of old Virginia stock, and was born and reared near Georgetown, Kentucky. In 1833, his father died, and, some time after, his mother was married to Dr. G. F. SALTONSHALL.

In 1839, the family removed to Tremont, Tazewell County, Illinois, where he was trained to industry by his step-father, and thoroughly instructed in primary and academic branches by Mr. JAMES K. KELLOGG, a successful educator of that place. In April, 1847, he entered the Freshman Class of Bethany College. While at college he made the good confession, and was immersed, by Professor PENDLETON, in April, 1848. So soon as he became a Christian, he determined to devote his life to the preaching of the Gospel, and it was not long before he gave very conclusive evidence of fitness for the work. In July, 1850, he graduated as one of the honor men, delivering the Greek speech, and receiving marked tokens from the faculty of their high appreciation of his scholarship.

Meantime, his family had removed to Fayette, Missouri, at which place, soon after leaving college, he taught a male school for ten months. In June, 1851, his step-father died of cholera, while on his way to attend the commencement of Bethany College. He was a warm friend of the college, and gave it twenty-five hundred dollars while living, and left it a child's part in his estate.

At the call of the Church in Fayette, Brother M'GARVEY gave up his school, and, in September, 1851, was ordained to the work of the ministry, and afterward preached for the Church at Fayette and neighboring county churches until February, 1853, when he removed to Dover, Lafayette County, Missouri. In March, 1853, he was married to OTTIE F. HIX, of Fayette.

He resided at Dover nine years, and, during this period, he spent about half of the time at home, and, the remainder, preaching extensively over the State of Missouri, holding five public debates with various religious parties; he also collected money to erect a boarding-school in his village, and conducted the school two years.

In the spring of 1862, he accepted the pastoral care of the Church in Lexington, Kentucky, where a large field of usefulness was open to him. During the same year he published his "Commentary on Acts," which had occupied all the time he could devote to it for three and a half years. This is a work of decided merit, and at once fixes his reputation as a fine Biblical scholar.

On the removal of Kentucky University to Lexington, in 1865, he accepted a chair in the College of the Bible, with the understanding that only a small portion of his time was to be devoted to teaching, such as would not materially interfere with his labors in the Church. Under his ministry, the Church had reached a remarkable degree of prosperity, and his labors were highly appreciated by the entire congregation. But, finding that his whole time was needed in the university, in 1866, he resigned his charge of the Church; but, as the Church has not succeeded in obtaining the regular services of a suitable man, he has not yet been relieved. President GRAHAM, however, now shares the labor of preaching with him.

Brother M'GARVEY is a little below medium size, has dark hair, light hazel eyes, and a very youthful appearance for one of his age. He is very strict and regular in his habits, and this fact explains why it is that he has been able to accomplish so much mental labor without impairing his health.

That which most distinguishes him as a writer and speaker is *clearness;* there is never the slightest confusion in his ideas. He has very little imagination, and relies almost exclusively on *facts* for effect. His mind is well stored with these, and, in the construction and management of an argument, he uses them with great ease and success. In debate he is one of the safest and ablest men among the Disciples, and not the least source of power here is his remakable *coolness*—he is never thrown off his guard.

As a teacher, he has very few superiors. Knowledge is what a student needs; hence, the *matter-of-fact* man is always the best teacher—all other things being equal. But Brother M'GARVEY is also an excellent preacher, and, as a pastor, has been eminently successful. He has a kind, generous nature, but is not very demonstrative. He attends strictly to his own business.

THE WITNESS OF THE SPIRIT.

BY J. W. M'GARVEY.

" The Spirit itself bears witness with our spirit, that we are children
of God."—ROM. viii: 16.

IN order to our eternal happiness, we must become
children of God. In order to our happiness in time,
we must know that we are such. He who is in doubt
on this subject, must be not less unhappy than he who
knows he is not a child of God. Indeed, the advantage
is on the part of the latter; for he is likely to cast the
subject out of his thoughts, and put off the evil day to
the last; but the very fact of being in doubt supposes a
man to be awakened upon the subject, and to have made
some efforts to become a child of God, but such efforts
as leave him still uncertain whether his sins, which he
mourns, are actually forgiven. His soul hangs in trembling suspense; now thrilled with hope, the more ecstatic
from its very uncertainty, and now sunk to the very verge
of despair. Such is the experience of thousands of the
orthodox worshipers of to-day. They never attain to
more than a "hope" that they are born again; and to
often entertain serious doubts, is the best evidence that
this hope is well grounded. To hear a man express himself with confidence, would be to them a ground for sus-

picion that he was self-deceived. Their religious enjoyment fluctuates with the phases of their hope; and there
are no songs more popular than those which give expression to these fluctuations. What else has given popularity
to these familiar lines:

> "How tedious and tasteless the hours,
>   When Jesus no longer I see;
> Sweet prospects, sweet birds, and sweet flowers,
>   Have all lost their sweetness to me.
> The midsummer sun shines but dim,
>   The fields strive in vain to look gay;
> But when I am happy in him,
>   December 's as pleasant as May."

Or, why else should men, professing to be Christians,
ever sing these doleful strains:

> "'Tis a point I long to know;
>   Oft it causes anxious thought:
> Do I love the Lord, or no;
>   Am I his, or am I not?"

How unutterable must be the distress, at times, of men
who can sing these songs with the spirit and the understanding! And yet, so common is this experience, that
men look upon it as the common heritage of those who
obey Christ. I dropped in one night at a protracted
meeting, and heard the preacher addressing a company
of some thirty young converts. He was warning them
against certain sins and temptations which they must expect to encounter, and, among others, against what he
called the "*sin of despair*." He defined it about thus:
"The time will often come, my young friends, when you
will seriously doubt whether you have ever been born
again. I suppose I can appeal to the experience of every

Christian in the house to-night for proof of this.   All of us experience seasons when we hang our harps on the willows all the day long, and can not sing the songs of Zion. When these seasons come over you, beware lest you give up in despair, and turn away again to the weak and beggarly elements of the world." I could but feel pain that such a prospect should be held out before young Christians, and I wondered if this is the unhappy lot which our heavenly Father has assigned us.

Turn to the Bible, and let us see whether there is not something better within our reach than this limping and halting gait at which the people go.   The experience of David is that which most of all gives shape to our modern religion, and just as you might expect, here you find the very fluctuations of hope and despair which we have described. Hear him, in the Twenty-third Psalm: "The Lord is my shepherd, I *shall* not *want*. He maketh me to lie down in green pastures : he leadeth me beside the still waters. He restoreth my soul. Yea, though I walk through the valley of the shadow of death, I will *fear no evil:* for *thou art with me;* thy rod and thy staff, *they comfort me.*" What exultation and confidence are here! Who that had listened to these strains, could, for a moment, imagine that the same heart and lips gave utterance to the following plaintive notes : "My God, my God, why hast thou forsaken me? Why art thou so far from helping me, and from the words of my roaring? O, my God, I cry in the day-time, but thou hearest not; and in the night season, and am not silent." Yet, these are David's feelings as expressed in the Psalm next preceding the one just quoted. Truly, our modern experiences have at least one model in the Word of God. But David lived in a darker dispensation, when the sun of righteousness had not yet

risen and thrown his bright light upon the world. When
you turn from his to the experience of the apostles, you
find all the difference that there is between the uncertain shadows of twilight, and the clear light of noonday.
Where do you read of Paul, or Peter, or James, or John
expressing any doubt as to their relations to God? Not
one single note of uncertainty can be found in all their
writings. On the contrary, you hear Paul declare: "We
are *always confident; knowing* that while we are at home in
the body, we are absent from the Lord. We are confident, I say, and willing rather to be absent from the body,
and to be present with the Lord." (2 Cor. v: 6–8.) To
the Romans he says: " Being then *made free from sin,* you
became the servants of righteousness." To the Ephesians:
"In whom we *have* redemption through his blood, the
forgiveness of sins." And to the Thessalonians: "Knowing, brethren, beloved, your election of God." Here all
is the language of confidence, of certainty. And so with
the other apostles. Peter does not look upon the election
of his brethren as a mystery that can not be solved in life,
and that never can be certainly known till the judgment;
but he writes, in tones of confidence, to strangers scattered
throughout the provinces, as being " Elect according to
the foreknowledge of God the Father, through sanctification of the Spirit unto obedience and the sprinkling of
the blood of Christ." And John exclaims: " Beloved, we
are now the sons of God: and it doth not yet appear what we
shall be, but we know that when he shall appear we shall
be like him: for we shall see him as he is."

Now, the secret of all this confidence on the part of the
apostles and early Christians, is found in the passage before us: " The Spirit itself bears witness with our spirit
that we are children of God." If the spirit of God testi-

fied to the fact, how could they doubt it? No wonder, that with such testimony, they were always confident. But, then, you remind me, that our doubters of modern times are the very men with whom this passage is the greatest favorite. In the midst of all their doubts and conflicts, these words are constantly on their lips. Even the preacher, of whom I spoke as addressing some young converts, had, just before that speech, made them all believe that they had the witness of the Holy Spirit itself, bearing witness with their spirits that they were children of God. Yet he was then telling them that they would be certain, in many future days, to doubt this testimony of the Spirit. What was the trouble with the man? Could he and his young converts really doubt what the Spirit of God would testify to? I suppose not. And yet, they are full of doubt while dwelling upon and relying upon the very passage of Scripture which gave the apostles their unwavering confidence. What clearer proof could we possibly have that their understanding of the passage is different from that held by the apostles. And how do they understand it? Why, in the process of their conversion, they have experienced certain emotions, which they are taught to believe are the result of a direct impact of the Holy Spirit upon their spirits, and which they understand as the testimony which the Holy Spirit bears to them that they are children of God. But the trouble is, that they can never be altogether certain that it was the Holy Spirit which they felt. Sometimes they feel as if it certainly must have been; and sometimes they fear that it was merely the workings of their own spirit, mistaken for those of the Holy Spirit. Thus they are tossed to and fro upon the waves of doubt, while the ghostly experience, like a specter in the distance, becomes dimmer and dimmer as time removes farther away,

and the shadows of failing memory fall upon it. The
Lord deliver us from such uncertainty, and lead us into
the clear light that shone upon the path of the early disciples!

It is easy to see the sense in which the apostles understood this passage, or, rather, the sense in which Paul used
it. He supposes an individual asking himself the question, "Am I a child of God?" and sitting down deliberately to find the answer. Now, this is a question of fact,
and is to be determined, like any other question of fact,
by competent evidence. Further, it depends upon two
other facts: 1st. What character constitutes a child of
God? 2d. What character have I? If I can learn with
certainty what a man must do and be, in order to be
adopted into the family of God, and then ascertain, with
equal certainty, what I have done and what I am in those
particulars, the question is settled. If what I am, and
what a child of God is, are the same, then I am certainly
a child of God. If they are different, then I am certainly
not a child of God, and there is no doubt about the matter either way.

Each of these subordinate questions is to be settled by
evidence, and the witnesses are named by the apostle in
the passage. The first is the Holy Spirit. He is the
only competent witness whose testimony we have on the
first question; for the question as to what character a man
must have to be a child of God, depends entirely upon
the will of God; for "the things of God knoweth no man,
but the Spirit of God," and "the Spirit searches all things,
even the deep things of God." The apostles had heard
Jesus testify; but he had not told them all the truth; nor
could they, with certainty, remember all that he had said.
It was left for the Spirit to bring to memory all that Jesus

had spoken, and to lead them into all the truth. Upon the Spirit, then, they depended for all their knowledge of the will of God. If they wished to know what constitutes one a child of God, they learned it from the testimony of the Spirit. They had no other way to learn it, and no other way was needed, for this was infallible. What they learned thus, they spoke with equal infallibility to the world. "God has revealed these things to us through his Spirit," says Paul; "which things we also speak; not in words which man's wisdom teaches, but in words which the Holy Spirit teaches." Others, then, heard the testimony of the Spirit through the lips of those inspired men, and in this they heard the very words of the Spirit. These words, again, were written down, so that those who had not the opportunity of hearing the living voice of the apostles might have the same words in writing, and suffer no disadvantage, as compared with those who first heard them. We stand in the position of this last class. We have no testimony of the Spirit by inspiration of our own minds, neither have we the living voice of inspired men to inform us; but we have, what is just equal to this in value, the written depositions of the Spirit of God; and these testify, in unmistakable terms, what a man must do to be a child of God.

Lest some one should doubt whether it is scriptural to represent the statements of the Scriptures as the testimony of the Spirit, listen to a few examples of Scripture usage. Nehemiah, in the prayer of the Levites, uses this language in reference to God's dealings with the children of Israel: "Yet many years didst thou forbear them, and *testifiedst* against them *by thy Spirit in thy prophets*." Peter says the old prophets searched "what or what manner of time the Spirit of Christ which was in them did signify, when it

testified beforehand the sufferings of Christ, and the glory
that should follow." And, still more to the point, in the
tenth of Hebrews, Paul, after stating that " by one offering Christ has perfected *forever* them that are sanctified,"
says: " Of this the *Holy Spirit is a witness* to us;" and immediately quotes a passage from the 31st chapter of Jeremiah as the Spirit's testimony. These passages show that
the Spirit's communications to the inspired men themselves—those made through them to living cotemporaries, and the same when written down for the instruction
of future ages—are all alike regarded and treated as the
testimony of the Spirit. Paul, in the passage we are discussing, had reference, no doubt, to all these forms of
testimony, for his language is unrestricted, and, therefore,
includes all the testimony that the Spirit has given on the
subject in hand. But to us, the reference must be practically limited to the written testimony, for this is all we
have.

The whole matter of the Spirit's testimony resolves
itself into this: that the Holy Spirit, through the Scriptures, testifies that men who pass through certain changes,
and maintain, afterward, a certain character, are children
of God. Whatever may be men's theories of spiritual
influence, you will find no believer in the inspiration of
the Scriptures who will deny that the Spirit does thus testify, or who will affirm that he communicates ideas on this
subject in any other way. And when you come to the
details of the testimony itself—whatever may be men's
theories of conversion—you will find few to deny that the
man who believes with all his heart in the Lord Jesus
Christ, who really repents of his sins, and who is really
baptized, becomes a child of God. Some will insist that
baptism is no part of the process; but none will deny that

the true believer, when truly penitent and truly baptized, is a child of God.   Here, then, we have the unquestioned testimony of the Spirit describing a certain character, who, unquestionably, becomes a child of God.

But, when a man has heard this testimony of the Spirit of God, he is not yet quite ready to say whether he himself is, or is not, a child of God.   There is another witness yet to be examined before a conclusion can be reached, and though his testimony is given so briefly and so silently as to be sometimes overlooked, it is, on this account, none the less indispensable.   This witness is your own spirit. He is the only witness who can tell you, with certainty, whether you have believed with all the heart, or whether you have really, through sorrow for sin, turned away from it.   And still further, in the present distracted condition of the public mind on the subject of baptism, your own soul must testify for itself—as it will answer to God in the great day—whether you have been really baptized.

In respect to our own spirit's testimony, especially, have our friends of the religious parties generally misunderstood this passage of Scripture.   They understand the text as if it read: "The Spirit itself bears witness *to* our spirit that we are children of God."   This would make but one witness, the Holy Spirit.   But Paul has two witnesses, for he says: "The Spirit itself bears witness *with* our spirit."   This is an exact translation of the Greek. Now, when I testify *to* my brother, there is but one witness; but when I testify *with* him, he and I are both witnesses, and my testimony agrees with his.   This is just Paul's idea.   The Holy Spirit itself bears testimony which agrees with the testimony of our own spirit, that we are children of God.   The point of agreement is just this, that the character which the Holy Spirit asserts to be that of a child of God, agrees with what my own spirit asserts to be my own character.

Perhaps some one is ready to object, just here, that it is rather a strange mode of speech, for a man to represent his own spirit as being a witness to himself.   But this is not the only passage in which Paul speaks in this way. When speaking of the unbelief of Israel, in the ninth of Romans, he uses this language: "I say the truth in Christ, I lie not, my *conscience* also *bearing me witness* in the Holy Spirit, that I have great heaviness and continual sorrow in my heart."   In the Greek we have here the same verb as in our text, so that, more exactly translated, it would read, "my conscience also bearing witness *with* me."   Here are two witnesses, himself in the aggregate testifying to the brethren, and his conscience, which does not in every man agree with the spoken words, asserting within him the same thing.

We now have the subject sufficiently before us, to begin to feel the solid ground beneath our feet.   When the Holy Spirit testified to Paul what character God would adopt as a child, he could not doubt it; and when he honestly inquired of his own spirit what his own character was, he could not doubt the answer that was given.   When these two characters agree, to doubt that you are a child of God is to doubt either your own consciousness, or the words of the Holy Spirit.   While you are in your senses, you can not doubt the former; and until you become a skeptic, you can not doubt the latter.   This is true, not only of your first becoming a child of God, but also of your continuance in the Father's family.   It is of this more particularly that Paul speaks; for the brethren to whom he was writing had all been in the service of God for some length of time.   The Holy Spirit testifies what character a man must sustain, in order to continue in the Father's house, and not, like the prodigal son, wander away and squander what the Father has given in riotous living. My own soul testifies at every point whether these are the traits of my own character. And here it is that I feel most called upon to glorify the favor of God; for at almost every point my own spirit testifies that I come short of the character that the Holy Spirit's testimony prescribes, and were it not for one gracious provision, the answer would always be, I have become a prodigal. That gracious provision is made through the blood of Christ; for a part of the Spirit's testimony is this, that if the children will confess their sins, they have an Advocate with the Father, who is faithful and just to forgive their sins, and to cleanse them from all iniquity. My own spirit leaps with joy at this, while it testifies that in humble penitence I daily confess to God my daily sins, and thus, from day to day, the Spirit itself still bears witness with my spirit that I am even yet a child of God. This is no airy and unsubstantial means of determining this momentous question, such as prevails in the sectarian world. It is incomparably more solid and reliable than that which modern visionaries have blindly substituted for it. It impels a man, by all the force of his desire, to know his prospects of heaven, to study closely the elements of character prescribed in the Word of God for his imitation, and then to look deeply within himself, not for some mysterious whisperings of the Spirit of God, but for those fruits of the Spirit which characterize the child of God. He who intelligently applies this test, can no more doubt his conclusions than he can his own consciousness, on the one hand, or the Word of God, on the other.

It is not usual, in the New Testament, to find these two

22

witnesses brought together in the strict logical connection
which Paul, in our text, makes them assume. Usually the
writer alludes to but one of them at a time, presuming upon
the reader's acquaintance with the other.   One or two, out
of many instances, will suffice for illustration of this statement.   Paul says to the Corinthians: " Examine yourselves, whether you are in the faith."   But how could they
decide, by examining themselves, without some standard
by which to judge themselves?   This standard is furnished
in the Spirit's testimony, and the disciples were well acquainted with it.   Again, John says: "Hereby we know
that he abides in us, by the Spirit which he has given us."
But no man knows that he has the Holy Spirit, except by
its fruits, as they are developed in his life; and for a knowledge of these he is dependent on the testimony of his own
spirit.   In every view of the subject, you find a continual
necessity for the testimony of both the witnesses, and you
always find their testimony sufficient to set the mind at
rest, or to make the soul feel the certainty of its orphaned
or its alienated estate.

And now, sinner—poor, wandering sinner—would you
be a child of God, and an heir of glory? The way is before you.   It is no uncertain way.   I call you not to dreams
and airy visions, but to the highway of the Lord, where
your feet, at every step, will tread upon a rock; where the
clear light of heaven will shine on your path; or, if the
tempest beat upon you, you may never lose your way.
You have sinned against heaven, and are no longer worthy
to be called a son of God, yet he will receive you, he will
fold you to his arms like a tender, forgiving parent, and
the tears of your penitence will drown all your sorrow,
and melt away into eternal peace.   God help you to come,
and to come without delay.

W. Wellstood Sc.

A. S. rar. hand

Beny Franklin

BENJAMIN FRANKLIN.

IT may be safely affirmed, that no preacher among the Disciples is more generally known than the subject of this sketch. He has been so long connected with the Press, and has traveled so extensively, that wherever, among Christians, the *Bible alone* is the rule of faith and practice, there the name of BENJAMIN FRANKLIN is as familiar as household gods.

He was born in Belmont County, Ohio, February 1st, 1812. His early religious training was according to the Methodist faith, though he never belonged to any church until he united with the Disciples. In the year 1836, when he was about twenty-four years of age, he was immersed, near Middletown, Henry County, Indiana, by Elder SAMUEL ROGERS, then extensively known as one of the most successful pioneer preachers of the current reformation.

Soon after his obedience to the Gospel, Brother FRANKLIN began to preach in the name of the Lord, and has been engaged actively in the work ever since. During the first twelve years of his ministry, his labors were chiefly confined to Eastern Indiana, where he was instrumental in establishing many churches, and scattering the good seed of the kingdom generally. He next labored extensively in Ohio and Kentucky; and, of late years, has traveled and preached in more than half the States of the Union, as well as portions of Canada. Under his personal ministry, about eight thousand persons have obeyed the Gospel; which speaks more for his zeal, industry, and fitness for his work, than any thing else that could be said. He is most at home in the general field; possesses little adaptation to pastoral work; and, in this department of labor, has met with little success. He has held some twenty-five public discussions, five of which have been published, and had considerable sale. This fact would seem to indicate that he takes delight in controversy; but it should be remembered, that his method of working is well calculated to place him frequently in positions where he can not consistently avoid collision with the religious parties of the land. And, when he thinks it necessary, he never hesitates to " contend earnestly for the faith once delivered to the Saints." That he is particularly averse to discussion, need not be affirmed; but that he loves discussion for discussion's sake, may be successfully denied. He has lived and labored through the stormy period of the Reformation, when a great deal of unpleasant work had to be done; and he has never shrunk from any duty because it was not calculated to polish him, and fit him for the elegant walks of life. He has evidently been deeply in earnest in the work committed to his hands; and, consequently, has had little time for any thing but *work*—constant, laborious WORK. He is emphatically a self-made man, and has had to labor to his present position through most discouraging poverty.

On the 1st of January, 1843, he began his editorial career—taking charge of the "Reformer," a monthly of sixteen pages, published from Centreville, Indiana. This he continued to publish for about seven years; the last three from Milton, Indiana. He then removed to Cincinnati, and formed a partnership with D. S. BURNET, by which they published, jointly, the "Reformer" and "Christian Age," for one year. The two papers were afterward consolidated, and FRANKLIN was employed as editor; which position he held for nearly three years. During the next two years, he published the "American Christian Review" as a monthly. He then came into possession of the "Christian Age," and commenced the publication of the "Review" as a weekly, which paper is now conducted under the style of "FRANKLIN & RICE," and has an extensive circulation, and several assistant editors.

Brother FRANKLIN is about six feet high; has bold, strong features, large gray eye, prominent mouth, well-developed chest and lungs, and weighs about one hundred and ninety pounds. His whole physical and mental organization indicates that he is capable of an immense amount of work; and this is shown to be the fact in the active, laborious life he has lived. As a writer, he lays no claim to elegance, his articles too frequently bearing unmistakable marks of haste in their preparation. But he is generally forcible, and, as a writer for the masses, has been quite successful. He has written a number of tracts, all of which have been very popular; and the one entitled "Sincerity Seeking the Way to Heaven," has had the largest sale of any tract ever published by the Disciples.

He speaks very much as he writes; or, rather, he writes very much as he speaks, for his extemporaneous style in speaking characterizes all that he writes. He does not depend upon either elocution or rhetoric for effect, but upon the *power of the truth*, which he presents to the people. He speaks as if he believed what he says. There is no hesitating—no doubting in his manner. And as he illustrates and simplifies every thing, so all can understand him, his preaching carries conviction to all honest hearts. Before a popular audience, he exerts a wonderful power.

THE CHURCH—ITS IDENTITY.

BY BENJAMIN FRANKLIN.

"But we think it right to hear from you what you think: for, as it re-spects this sect, we know that it is every-where spoken against."—Acts xxviii: 22. (*Anderson's Translation.*)

THE Lord says, in Matt. xvi: 18, referring to the confession Peter had made: "On this rock I will build my Church." My work, in this discourse, will be to define and identify the community styled by the Savior "my Church." This is evidently the same com-munity styled "this sect" in my text. The former is the Lord's way of speaking of the body in view, and the latter the way men, not in the community, and not understanding it, or its position, but owing it no ill-will, spoke of it. This language comes from "the chief men of the Jews," as we learn from verse seventeen. That which our Lord calls "my Church," they call "this sect." Those "chief men of the Jews" regarded the body, or Church, merely as a "sect," or faction, and certainly a very unpopular one, as it was "every-where spoken against."

This word "sect," is never used in a good sense in the New Testament; nor is the original word from which it comes. *Hairesis,* the original word from which we have "sect," occurs nine times in the New Testament, and is

(341)

translated "sect" five times, and "heresies" four times. We read of damnable *heresies* (2 Pet. ii: 1), and find *heresies* put down with "the works of the flesh" (Gal. v: 20); and find the statement added, verse twenty-one, "that those who practice such things (as *heresies*) shall not inherit the kingdom of God." Heresy is ranked with "lewdness, uncleanness, wantonness, idolatry, sorcery," etc. In the speech of Tertullus, accusing Paul (Acts xxiv: 5), he charges him with being a ringleader of the "sect" of the Nazarenes. Verse fourteen, same chapter, we find Paul's reply, in which he says: "After the way which they call sect, so do I worship the God of my fathers." He does not admit that the body with which he was identified was a sect, but that it was *called a sect*. We can not, therefore, speak of a "Christian sect," or call the Church a sect, without as great an impropriety as to speak of a *Christian heresy*, or call the Church a *heresy*.

There is a community called, in the New Testament, "the kingdom of God" (John iii: 3); "the Church of the living God" (1 Tim. iii: 15); "one body" (Eph. iv: 4).

To be in this body, Church, or kingdom, is the same as to be "in Christ." It is to be in a justified state, or pardoned state. To enter into it, is to enter into a state of justification or pardon. In entering into that body, we come to the blood of Christ, which cleanses from all sin; to the Spirit and to the life of Christ, all of which are in the body. If we enjoy pardon, the benefits of the blood of Christ, the Holy Spirit, the life of Christ, we must be in the body. God and Christ dwell in the Church, which is the temple of God and the "pillar and support of the truth." To dwell with God and Christ, enjoy the cleansing of the blood of Christ, the remission of sins, the impartation of the Spirit of God, and the new life, we must

be in Christ, or in his body—the Church. To be out of
the Church is to be separated from God, Christ, the Holy
Spirit, the blood of Christ, the life of Christ, and justification. It becomes a matter of momentous importance,
then, to know that we are in Christ, or in the Church.

It is not enough to know that we are in *a Church*, but
we must know that we are in "the Church of the living
God," "the kingdom of God," or "body of Christ."
There is not a promise in any other institution or community, but this. The Lord has one Church, and we must
not mistake something else for that Church. How can we
know that we are members of the Church, unless we know
what the Church is? If we do not know what the Church
is, we do not know whether we are in the Church or not,
whether we are in Christ or not, whether we are justified or
not. If we intend to enjoy God, Christ, the Holy Spirit,
the blood of Christ, and, in one word, the salvation of God,
in the kingdom or Church, we must be in that kingdom.
To be in the kingdom or Church, we must know what it
is. How shall we, then, identify the Church or kingdom
of Christ? I lay down the following points for consideration:

I. A body, or community, not built on the foundation
which God laid, is not the community which the Lord calls
"my Church."

II. A community not founded and established in the
right place, is not the Church of Christ.

III. A community not founded at the right time, is not
the kingdom of Christ.

IV. No church can be the true Church not founded by
the proper persons, Christ and the apostles.

V. A kingdom, with any other law than the one given
by the head of the Church, is not the kingdom of Christ.

VI. Any community labeled with a foreign name, or a name not found to designate the body of Christ, in the New Testament, is not the kingdom of God.

A failure at any one of these points is fatal to the claims of any body professing to be the body of Christ. It is due to the greater portion of the religious bodies of our day, called "churches," to state distinctly that they do not claim to be the kingdom of God, or the body of Christ. Excepting a few, the balance only claim to be *branches* of the body, or Church of Christ. Where a church does not claim to be "the Church," but simply a *branch* of the Church, the members are only members of a branch, and the officers are only officers of a branch, and not members and officers of the body of Christ. These branches, and officers in them, are as separate and distinct from the king- dom of Christ and the officers in it, as Great Britain and Russia, and the officers of these respective governments. One of these *branch* communities does not respect the acts of another, or in any way regard them. These different *branch* communities are distinct, separate, and independent kingdoms, with different laws, officers, names, founda- tions, times, and places of origin. They are not built on the same foundation, did not originate at the same time and place, have not the same law and officers, nor the same ecclesiastical organization, and are, to all intents and purposes, independent and distinct communities. If one of them dies, there is no grief or lamentation among the others, in view of the loss, nor an effort *to save another branch of the same church from dying*. They are all willing it should die. They have not one particle of sympathy for it. If a new party attempts to rise, the parties in ex- istence, instead of thanking God that another orthodox church has been born, taking it by the hand and raising it up to manhood, and rejoicing in its appearance, turn their batteries on it from every quarter, denouncing it as a "damnable heresy," and do their utmost to destroy it. When they fail, and find that it will live in spite of all their denunciations and efforts to kill it, they turn round and recognize it as another "orthodox denomination." Not a new religious party ever came into existence on the face of the globe that was not denounced as a *heresy*, when it first made its appearance, and that was not fought and opposed while it was young and weak. But when a party becomes strong, influential, and popular, it becomes an *orthodox branch of the church!* Thus, all the parties now called "orthodox branches" were once styled "heresies;" and that, too, when they were better than they are now; but when they could fight their way, and live, in spite of the old ones, they ceased to *be heresies*, and became *good orthodox branches!*

I. We have said, that no party, or community not built on the foundation which the Lord laid in Zion, is "the Church of the living God." What, then, is the foundation of the true Church? The Lord inquired of the apostles, "Who say you that I am?" Peter replied: "Thou art the Christ, the Son of the living God." The Savior proceeded: "On this rock I will build my Church." On which rock? On this grand statement, which flesh and blood had not revealed, but which the Father in heaven had revealed, and which he compares to a rock—that "Jesus is the Christ, the Son of the living God"—"on this," says he, "I will found my Church." This is the great proposition of the Divine government. In it all the minor propositions are included. In it centers, and on it rests, the entire revelation from God to man. If this grand proposition concerning Jesus, that "he is the Christ, the Son of the living God," is true, the entire Scriptures are true; for this being true, he knew all things, and his numerous quotations from Moses, the Psalms, and the Prophets, as *the word of God*, and *the language of the Spirit of God*, is an indorsement of all these writings. His calling the apostles, sending them and qualifying them, as well as endowing them with supernatural power, gave them an endorsement that no man can in honor evade. This grand proposition is the foundation of the Church, the faith, all true piety, and the hope of heaven. It is not a proposition concerning a theory, a speculation, or subtlety, but a proposition concerning *a person*, who was dead and is alive, and lives forever and ever. This proposition is of such momentous magnitude, if true, that we will be lost forever if we do not receive it. The Almighty Father will cast us off forever, as if we had rejected himself in person, if we reject this fundamental proposition concerning his Son. The moment we receive this proposition, we bind ourselves to receive all that Jesus taught, do all he commanded, and furthermore, we have a right to hope for all he has promised.

How many churches have we in this generation that are built on this foundation, or that will receive a person on this foundation? I regret to know that many of them openly declare this *not sufficient.* They maintain that we must have something more. In doing this, they do not honor our most gracious and adorable Lord, but dishonor him. Is there one church in the world that ignores all articles of religion, written out by *uninspired men*, in receiving the sinner, and that receives him on the confession, that "Jesus is the Christ, the Son of the living God?" There is one Church that does this. This Church is built on this great truth, and receives every

person that comes on this foundation-truth, to the initiat-
ing rite of the New Institution ; and it will receive him
on nothing else.   Those received on this foundation, and
united in one body, are on the rock—the sure foundation.
Those built on any other foundation, or not on this foundation, can not claim to be the Church of the living God,
the body, or kingdom of Christ.   The Romish Church is
not built on *the truth* that " Jesus is the Christ, the Son
of the living God"—the *rock*—but on "the lie" that *Peter
is the rock*.   The central idea, or foundation-thought, in
the Episcopal Church, is its form of church government.
Its very name originated in this peculiar form of government.   This is a side foundation, or another foundation,
and not the one which the Lord laid.   Not being built
on the true foundation—the one which God laid—it is
not the building of God, not the temple of God.

   The fundamental, or central, idea in Methodism, or in
the Methodist body, is method.   It took its name from
the idea of *method*.   It is founded on the idea of *method*.
There is nothing religious, spiritual, or celestial in *method*.
There are as many methods of doing evil as of doing good.
Still, this is the central idea of the largest Protestant party
in the world.   This is not only *another*, but almost *no
foundation*.   No wonder that a people should be dividing
every few years, with a central idea so feeble in its attractive
powers.   The Presbyterian body has for its central, or
fundamental idea, the *Presbyterial form* of church government, or the idea of governing by a *presbytery*.   This
is, so far as it is a foundation at all, *another foundation*,
and not the one which God laid.   The body, or building
on it, is not on the true foundation, and not the building
of God.   The central idea in the Baptist body is *baptism*.
The body takes its name from the initiatory rite of the

kingdom, and not from the head over all, blessed forever and ever. It is founded on *an ordinance*, and not on *the truth* concerning him who authorized the ordinance. This is another foundation. So on, the whole round of sectarian establishments. Not one of them is founded on the true foundation—the truth—concerning Jesus, that " he is the Christ, the Son of the living God." Not one of them has confidence enough in our Lord to make *the truth* concerning him its central idea, its foundation. Not one of them is willing to identify itself with our Lord, commit itself to him as its teacher, leader, and head, and, binding itself to his holy law, declare itself for him, and all he taught.

II. A community not founded or established in the *right place* is not the true Church. I am rejoiced that I need no special effort to show the place where the true Church was founded. All agree that *in Jerusalem* was the place. The Lord said it behooved the Messiah to suffer, and to rise from the dead the third day; and that repentance and remission of sins should be preached in his name to all nations, *beginning in Jerusalem*. It would be easy to refer to the prophets, and to many portions of the New Testament, and show, beyond all reasonable doubt, that the true Church was founded in Jerusalem. But, as all parties admit this, I shall not occupy my limited space in arraying the proof.

If my hearers desire to know whether the body with which they stand identified is the true Church, let them inquire *where it was founded*. If it was founded in Jerusalem, it may be the true Church; but if it was not founded in Jerusalem, it is most conclusive evidence that *it is not the true Church*. No matter how many good people there are in it, nor how many good things are taught and done

in it, it is not the true Church.   One clear difference between a counterfeit and genuine note detects the one that is
counterfeit, especially so clear a difference as a difference
in the place of location.   A difference, then, between any
body of people and the body of Christ so striking, as originating in Rome, and originating in Jerusalem, or the dif-
erence between being founded in Rome, and being founded
in Jerusalem, proves that which was founded in Rome,
London, or Geneva, to be counterfeit.   The Church of
Christ was first planted in Jerusalem, and all churches first
planted or founded anywhere else are certainly *spurious*.
They are not genuine.   Nor is it any matter how many
points of resemblance there may be between the genuine
and the counterfeit, they are not the same; but the counterfeit is only the more dangerous, and likely to deceive.
When trying them, to determine which is the true or the
genuine Church, look for this mark on it : " In Jerusalem."

III. A community not founded at the *right time* is not
the kingdom of God, or body of Christ.   This test is a
severe one.   It is unambiguous.   The community which
the Lord calls " my Church " (Matt. xvi : 18), was certainly not built when he said : " On this rock I *will* build
my Church."   He alluded to what he intended to do in
the future, and not to what he had done in the past, when
he said, " I will build my Church."   He taught his disciples to pray, " Thy kingdom come;" but certainly did
not teach them thus to pray after the kingdom *had come*.
" There be some standing here who shall not taste death
till they see the kingdom of God come with power."
Many Scriptures like these show that the kingdom had
not yet come, or that the Church was not yet established.
In the apostolic letters, we find numerous references to
the Church, kingdom, body, house of God, temple of

God, etc., as then in existence, showing that the Church, or kingdom, was established. This, then, proves that it was founded in the time of the apostles. This is sufficient for my purpose now. The true Church was, then, founded in the time of the apostles. This is a mark of the genuine Church not to be found on any counterfeit in the world. A community not founded in the time of the apostles, is not the one which the Lord called " my Church," or is not the Church of the living God. I care not where the history of a community of people may lead us. If it lead not to *the time* of the apostles, it does not lead us to the founding of that body, purchased and cleansed by the blood of Christ.

When did the Church of Rome originate? It did not originate in a day or a year, but gradually subverted the apostles' teaching, and, in centuries, inaugurated full-grown Popery. But there is not a trace of a Pope or Universal Father, to say nothing of Vicegerent of Christ, or Lord God, the Pope, nor Popery, in the history of the first three centuries of the Christian era. Popery was inaugurated too late, by at least three centuries, to be the true or genuine Church. It is one of the basest and most impudent counterfeits ever imposed on the credulity of man. If Popery was born *too late*, or is *too young* to be the true Church, what shall be said of those communities born in the past three centuries? They are all too young by largely more than a thousand years. No church that came into existence since the death of the apostles can be the Church of the living God.

IV. No church can be the true Church that was not founded by Christ and the apostles. Churches founded by other persons, or originating with other persons, are simply not the Church of Christ. All books, all parties, and all men agree that Christ and the apostles founded the community called "the body of Christ"—the "one body" of Paul. What shall we say, then, of a church that traces its history to George Fox, and finds not a trace of its existence beyond him. There never was a Quaker before George Fox, nor a Quaker Church. The history of the world does not refer to the existence of a Lutheran or a Lutheran Church before Martin Luther lived. The Lutheran Church originated with Luther. The body of Christ existed from the apostolic day till the time of Luther, before there was any Lutheran Church. The Presbyterian Church originated with John Calvin. Before the time of Calvin there never was a Presbyterian, nor a Presbyterian Church. The Church, or body of Christ, existed from the time of the apostles till the time of Calvin, and consequently could not have been established by Calvin. Presbyterianism was, therefore, born many long centuries too late to lay any claims to Christianity. It may have incorporated some Christianity in it, but it is still carefully and very justly labeled "Presbyterianism." The Methodist Church originated with John Wesley. Before the time of Wesley there never was a Methodist Church or a Methodist. But the Church of Christ existed from the time of the apostles till the time of Wesley. Hence, Methodism originated with the wrong person to be the Church of Christ. The body of Christ originated with Christ and his apostles, and not with Wesley. Any body or community that did not originate with Christ and the apostles, but with some more modern person or persons, is manifestly not the body of Christ.

V. A kingdom or community, with any other law than the one given by the Lord, the great Head of the Church, is manifestly not the kingdom of Christ. The law of the

great King is clearly laid down in the Bible.   The Bible
contains the constitution and law of the King for his kingdom.   This was the only law ever authorized by the great
King and Head of the Church, or adopted, approved, and
practiced under in the time of the apostles.   Any church or
body of people, who have substituted any *other law*, no matter how many resemblances there may be between it and the
law of God, is not the body of Christ.   He never authorized a living man even to alter his law, add any thing to
it, or take any thing from it, to say nothing of *substituting
another law for it*.   It may be replied that these other laws
are like the law of God, or taken from it.   This, these parties do not believe themselves.   A Presbyterian does not
believe that the Methodist " Book of Discipline" is of
Divine authority ; has no regard for it ; and probably never
reads it.   A Methodist does not believe that the Presbyterian Confession of Faith is of Divine authority, and has
no regard for it.   There is not a party in the world that
has any regard for the Presbyterian Confession of Faith,
except, the Presbyterian party.   The same is true of the
creed of every other party in the world.   But all good
people have respect for the law of God.   The law of God
is supreme, and those loyal to it, united under it, and
keeping it, are his people—the body of Christ.   But those
formed into parties, under other laws, are new settlements
not indorsed by our King.

    VI. Any community labeled with some foreign name,
or some name unknown to the New Covenant, must be a
new and strange body.   There can be no use in a *new*
name for the *old* body or community.   There must be a
new idea, or something different from the old community,
to create the necessity for a new name.   If we have nothing they did not have in apostolic times, we need no other

names than they had. If we have the kingdom of God, the Church of God, the body of Christ, and nothing else, there is no need of calling it any thing else. But the truth is, new names come from new ideas, and are intended to express something new. A man may read of the Church of God, the body of Christ, the kingdom of God, etc., for a month, and it never suggests a Methodist Church, a Presbyterian Church, or a Baptist Church, unless in contrast. He knows that he is not reading about these latter bodies, as they were not in existence at the time of the writing. The new and foreign name shows that it does not refer to the body of Christ, but something else.

Now, there are so many notions about succession of churches, preachers, officers, ordinations, ordinances, and the like, that I know that many will inquire for a succession in some of these respects. It will, therefore be necessary to make a few observations touching this subject:

1. The attempts at making out a succession of Popes on the part of Romanists—the wicked Popes through which their pretended succession runs, and the successions attempted to be shown in the Greek and Episcopal churches, are sufficient to cover the face of a man of conscience and sense with utter shame and confusion. If there is no grace to be found unless these successions, or any one of them, can be made out, the world is lost. But I am thankful that the New Testament knows as little of any of these successions, or any necessity for them, as it does of a Romish, Greek, or Episcopal Church. The Church of Christ is not built on a succession of any kind, Romish, Greek, or Episcopal, but on the truth concerning Jesus, that "he is the Christ, the Son of the living God." The souls of the saints rest not on the difficult and doubtful task of making out successions of any kind.

23

They turn their hearts to the truth concerning our Lord, which he compares to a *rock*, on which he said, " I will build my Church." They find the Church built on that great foundation-truth, and it receives all its members on that truth, as it did at the beginning, in the *right place*, in Jerusalem; at the right time, on Pentecost; originating with the right persons, Christ and the apostles; having the right law, the law of God; and with the right name, the body of Christ, the kingdom or Church of God, with the original worship and all things as they were at the first. Having come into the school of Christ, they are now his disciples, learners, pupils, and he is their Teacher. They are so busily engaged in the lessons given them by their Great Teacher, and so enraptured with them, that they have no time for examining musty records about successions of churches, men, or ordinances. They depend not on succession, but fellowship with the Father, and his Son Jesus the Christ. They listen to no unregenerated men, prating about a succession which never was, and never can be made out, but to the law of their glorious King. If these successionists ask where the Church was in the dark ages, tell them you know not; that the Lord took care of it, and you are thankful to know that it is here still, full of life, power, and determination, and destined to do a greater work than ever before. Tell them, that, with God's blessing, we intend to restore the sure foundation which the Lord laid, and build on, sweeping away every thing in the way of the work; that we intend to reinstate the authority—the supreme authority of our only Potentate, Jesus the Messiah, head over all, blessed forever and ever, and sweep from earth all opposing authority of men; that we intend to restore the law of God to the people of this generation, reinstate it fully, where the clergy had set it aside by the doctrines and commandments of men, at the same time sweeping away all creeds, confessions of faith, disciplines, etc., in the way of the full and free administration of the law of God. Tell them that we intend a complete restoration of the faith, practice, worship, and all things as they were at the first.

Here is clear and definite work. That body, which the Lord called " my Church," which was "every-where spoken against," in the time of Paul, is here, alive, standing on the old foundation, with the same head, creed, or law, and the same name; nor does it fail to be "every-where spoken against" still; nor is it a matter of importance whether it can trace a succession back through the dark ages or not; it is here and alive, and as determined as ever to live and maintain its rights. If it was dead, during the dark ages, God has raised it from the dead, and breathed new life into it. What we want now, is to know *who its friends are?* We want to see every man who intends to stand for the Head of the Church, the foundation, the apostles' teaching, and all things as they were at the first, to stand out on one side. If there are those who do not intend to stand to this, we want them to stand on the other side. We desire to know who is on the Lord's side, and who is not; who is for us, and who is against us; who is loyal, and who sympathizes with the enemy.

We are occupying the most responsible position of any body of people on the earth. We are bound to the Lord Jesus, in the new and everlasting covenant, sealed by the blood of Jesus, and confirmed by the oath of the Almighty, as well as by all the veracity and honor there is in us, to be true to this great work. Let us, then, make a glorious record, one that we shall be happy to contemplate at death, and that shall be a credit to us in the day of judgment.

To the King eternal, immortal, and invisible, the only-wise God our Savior, be glory and dominion, majesty and power, forever and ever.

Very Truly &c
T. P. Haly

THOMAS PRESTON HALEY.

THOMAS PRESTON HALEY was born in Fayette County, Kentucky, on the 19th day of April, 1832. In the fall of 1833, his father emigrated to Missouri, and settled in Randolph County, of that State. The first Christian Church in the county of Randolph was organized in his father's house, and was composed chiefly, if not entirely, of members of his father's family. Under the care of Christian parents, and the earnest preaching of the lamented ALLEN WRIGHT, THOMAS became deeply interested in the subject of religion, and, at the early age of fourteen, confessed the Savior, and was immersed, under the ministry of HENRY THOMAS, now of Austin, Texas.

When about sixteen years of age, he commenced reading the Scriptures and praying in the social meetings of the Church. In this way, he gradually acquired confidence, and began to give promise of the ability which has since characterized his public ministry.

Having made considerable progress in a rudimental education, and being thrown on his own resources, on account of the moderate circumstances of his family, before he was seventeen years of age, he took charge of a country school, which he conducted for some time in a very satisfactory manner. While engaged in teaching this school, he was in the habit of lecturing his pupils on various subjects connected with their studies and the practical duties of life. This practice further developed his speaking talents, and, under the advice and instruction of MARCUS P. WILLS and T. M. ALLEN, of Missouri, he was induced to give himself to the ministry of the Gospel. Accordingly, after having spent a few years preaching in a somewhat miscellaneous way, he was, on the third Lord's day in November, 1853, ordained to the ministry, at Antioch, Randolph County, Missouri. Since then, he has given his whole time to the work, excepting two years during the late war, at which time he was engaged in teaching. He was married, on the fifth day of May, 1855, to MARY LOUISA M'GARVEY, of Howard County, Missouri.

From 1853 to 1858, he was engaged principally in the general field, traveling extensively in north-western Missouri, and meeting with encouraging success in the proclamation of the Gospel.

In the fall of 1858, he became pastor of the Church at Lexington, Missouri, which position he held until the summer of 1864. He then removed to Louisville, Kentucky, and became pastor of the Chestnut-street Church, in that city, which is his present field of labor.

Brother HALEY has a finely-developed physical organization, being considerably over medium size, and compactly built. He has dark hair and eyes, is very erect, and has a striking personal appearance. His mental powers are evidently well supported by a healthy, vigorous, physical constitution.

As a preacher, he is a good Evangelist, but a much better pastor. In the last department of labor he has been eminently successful. The Church at Lexington, Missouri, was never so prosperous as while under his pastoral care. His labors in Louisville have also been greatly blessed. The Church for which he preaches has grown from a very small and weak congregation to one of the largest and most influential in all the country. These successes have been achieved by constant, laborious, and faithful work.

His social powers are well developed, and these give him great influence in any church for which he labors. While he is dignified and commanding in his manners, he is easily approached, and every one receives from him the most courteous and respectful attention. He is a much more than average speaker, but by no means exerts his greatest power in the pulpit; he preaches his best sermons in the social circle, and at the fireside of the members of the Church.

BUILDING ON THE ONE FOUNDATION.

BY T. P. HALEY.

"According to the grace of God that is given to me, as a wise master-builder, I have laid the foundation, and another builds on this. But let every one take heed how he builds on this. For other foundation can no man lay than that which is laid, which is Jesus Christ." (1 Cor. iii: 10, 11.)

THERE were divisions in the Church of Christ, in the city of Corinth. One object of the Apostle, in the letter from which the foregoing language is quoted, was the healing of these divisions. In the tenth verse of the first chapter we find the following language: "Now I beseech you, brethren, by the name of our Lord Jesus Christ, that you all speak the same thing, and that there be no *schisms* among you; but that you be perfectly united in the same mind, and in the same judgment."

The apostle again affirms (1 Cor. iii): "And I, brethren, was not able to speak to you as to spiritual men, but as to those who are carnal, as to babes in Christ. . . . . For since envy, and strife, and divisions are among you, are you not carnal, and do you not walk as men?"

The apostle thus proceeds to present such considerations as are calculated to correct this evil. He says to them: "You are God's field. You are God's building."

He does not say: You, brethren, are God's *fields*, or

God's *buildings*; but employs the singular number. Having introduced the term *building*, he very naturally proceeds to speak of the foundation; and as God has but *one building*, there is but *one foundation*. The Church of Christ is, then, considered by him under the figure of a building or a house.

What, then, is the foundation of this house?

It has been affirmed that the Church was built in the days of Abraham, and that his family and immediate descendants were in it; that it was built on a "covenant of grace" that God made with Abraham. Of course, if this be true, then the "Church of Christ" has had a visible existence since the days of Abraham, and all his descendants have been members thereof.

When, however, the harbinger, John the Immerser, came, he cried to Israel, saying: "Repent, for the kingdom of heaven—the Church of Christ"—is at hand (Matt. iii: 2), or comes nigh. Now if the kingdom had already come, if the Church had existed from the days of Abraham, how could the harbinger say it is at hand, or, it comes nigh? He could not have said it. Besides, the Savior, in speaking of John, says: "Verily, I say to you, among those born of women, there has not risen a greater than John the Immerser. But the least in the kingdom of heaven is greater than he." (Matt. xi: 11.) If the Church of Christ, the "building," was founded in the family of Abraham, and embraced all his descendants, John, being one of them, was already a member thereof; and the Savior could not have said, "he that is least in the kingdom is greater than he." But the kingdom, or the Church, not being yet founded—being yet in the future—he could, with great propriety, say, that, notwithstanding John was "more than a prophet," the least in the kingdom is greater than he.

Again: If the Church of Christ, or God's building, was founded in the family of Abraham, then, of course, it existed when Jesus commenced his ministry; and yet the burden of his discourse was, "the kingdom of heaven is at hand," or, the Church is about to be established.

Again: "When Jesus came into the regions of Cæsarea Philippi, he asked his disciples, saying: 'Who do men say that I, the son of man, am?' They replied: 'Some say that thou art John the Immerser; others, Jeremiah, or one of the prophets.' He said to them: 'But who say you that I am?' Simon Peter answered and said: 'Thou art the Christ, the Son of the living God.' And Jesus answered and said to him: 'Blessed are you, Simon, son of Jonas; for flesh and blood did not reveal this to you, but my Father who is in heaven. And I say to you, that you are Peter, and on this rock *I will build my church;* and the gates of hades shall not prevail against it.'" (Matt. xvi: 13–20.) It is not difficult to see, from this passage, that the "Church of Christ" was yet future; and equally clear that it was not built, *nor to be built,* on a "covenant of grace." Whatever may have been organized or established in the family of Abraham, it was not the Church of Christ.

It would not be difficult to show that the Jewish Church differed, in many essential points, from the Church of Christ, to which Paul refers in the passage under consideration, under the figure of a building; and while we might readily grant that the Jewish theocracy was founded in Abraham's family, and on a covenant of grace, we should as promptly deny that the "Church of Christ" had an existence at the time in which Christ said, "I will build my Church."

It is affirmed by Papists, with great confidence, that the "Church of Christ was founded or builded on the holy Apostle Peter." When Paul was considering the Church under another figure, he says: "Now, therefore, you are no longer strangers and sojourners, but fellow-citizens with the saints, and of the household of God; having been builded upon the foundation of the apostles and prophets, Jesus Christ himself being the chief corner-stone." (Eph. ii: 20.) With this declaration of the apostle before us, may we not ask, Why should it be affirmed that the Church is builded on Peter, rather than on Paul, or James, or John? It would, indeed, be far more consistent in the Romanist to affirm that the Church was built on Paul, since it is certain that Paul did minister in Rome; and equally certain that Peter never saw the Papal city, which was to be so prominent in perpetuating his memory.

In the language quoted above from Paul, he is considering the Church of Christ under the figure of a house, composed of living stones, each member being a lively stone, as the apostles and New Testament prophets were the first admitted. The Church is said to be "builded upon apostles and prophets, Jesus himself being the chief corner-stone." But, even from this point of view, Peter is the foundation in precisely the same sense as were all the other "apostles and prophets."

Paul has, however, settled the question definitely in the following words: "Other foundation can no man lay than that which is laid, which is Jesus Christ." (1 Cor. iii: 11.) Considered, therefore, as a house composed of living stones, Jesus the Christ is the foundation. "Behold, I lay in Zion for a foundation a stone, a tried stone, a precious corner-stone, a sure foundation. He that believeth shall not make haste." (Isa. xxviii: 16.)   Considered as an organized association or society, the truth confessed by Peter, "Thou art the Christ, the Son of the living God," is the foundation; and "other foundation can no man lay than that is laid."

The question may be asked, How does a "truth," couched in a proposition, become the foundation of an organized association or society?   We can not better answer this question than by presenting several illustrations. We have, in this community, an organized society, called a "Temperance Society."   The *truth* upon which this organization is founded is stated in the following words: "The use of intoxicating drinks, as a beverage, is unnecessary, and injurious."   Every person embracing this truth, and willing to act in conformity therewith, is ready to be admitted a member of the society.   He who denies the truth of the proposition can not be a member thereof. Since all within do believe this proposition, and do act in conformity therewith, the society rests upon, or is founded upon, the truth couched in this proposition.

Again: Mohammedanism is an organized religion, or Church of Religionists.   The proposition containing the supposed "foundation truth" is, that Mohammed was a prophet of God.   When one is convinced that this proposition is true, and is willing to act in harmony with his convictions, he is a Mohammedan.   Since all Mohammedans believe the proposition, and since no one can be such who denies it, we say it is the foundation proposition.

Again, we have, across the waters, organized governments, called monarchies.   The truth, or supposed truth, on which they are founded is, that kings rule by Divine right.   Every man who believes the proposition, and is willing to act in harmony therewith, is a monarchist. He who denies the proposition can not be a loyal subject of such government. All loyal subjects believing the proposition, and living consistently therewith, it may be, with great propriety, affirmed that the government rests on this proposition as its foundation.

So the Church of Christ, as an organized association or society, is founded on the truth of the proposition, "Thou art the Christ, the Son of the living God." Every one, therefore, who believes this proposition, and conforms his life to it, is a Christian. No one can be a member of this body, can be in this building, who rejects this proposition, or who will not "show his faith by his works." Paul says: "As a wise master-builder I have laid the foundation, and another builds on this."

How did Paul lay this foundation? He founded the Church in the city of Corinth, and the Holy Spirit has caused to be written a history of this transaction in the following words:

"After these things Paul departed from Athens, and came to Corinth; and finding a certain Jew named Aquila, born in Pontus, who had lately come from Italy, with Priscilla, his wife (because Claudius had commanded all Jews to depart from Rome), he went to them; and because he was of the same trade, he made his home with them, and worked; for by trade they were tent-makers. But on every Sabbath he reasoned in the synagogue, and persuaded the Jews and the Greeks. And when Silas and Timothy came from Macedonia, Paul was roused in spirit, and earnestly testified to the Jews *that the Christ was Jesus*," or, as the old version rendered it, that "*Jesus was the Christ*."

Paul, then, laid the foundation "as a wise master-builder," not by preaching a "covenant of grace," nor the Apostle

Peter, but by preaching Christ, remembering that "other foundation can no man lay than that is laid, which is Jesus the Christ." In referring to his labors among these brethren, Paul says: "For I delivered you, among the first things, that which I also received, that Christ died for our sins, according to the Scriptures, and that he was buried, and that he rose again the third day, according to the Scriptures, and that he was seen by Cephas, then of the twelve," etc. (1 Cor. xv: 3.) And again, referring to his first entrance among them, he says: "And I, brethren, when I came to you, came not with excellence of speech, or of wisdom, declaring to you the testimony of God. For I determined not to know any thing among you but Jesus Christ, and him crucified." (1 Cor. ii: 1, 2.) Thus we learn *not only how* he laid the foundation, but precisely *what the foundation is which he did lay.*

It is manifest, from these Scriptures, that Paul laid the foundation for the Church of Christ in Corinth, by "testifying to the Jews that Jesus was the Christ," by preaching "Jesus Christ, and him crucified." What a lesson to preachers of this generation! How many would now be content, in establishing a church, to preach as Paul preached—no more, no less? Not many, we fear!

But the apostle says: "Another builds on this, but let every man take heed how he builds on this." How, then, may we ask, did Paul build on this foundation? He did it as a master-builder, a skillful architect. The Holy Spirit tells us in the following words: "But Crispus, the ruler of the synagogue, believed on the Lord, with all his house, and many of the Corinthians, hearing, believed and were immersed." (Acts xviii: 8.) Thus were they builded on the one foundation, and the apostle has solemnly warned every man to take heed *how* he builds thereupon.

Those who thus build now—lay the foundation by preaching Christ and him crucified—and teach the multitudes to hear, believe, and be immersed are surely building as did Paul, and will secure the approbation of God. But, alas! for those who build on this foundation any material not thus prepared! This proceeding of Paul was in precise harmony with "the Great Commission" under which he was acting. "Go preach the Gospel, the death, burial, and resurrection of Christ to every creature. He that believeth and is baptized, shall be saved; he that believeth not shall be condemned." (Mark xvi: 16.)

On the day of Pentecost, ten days after the ascension of Jesus from the brow of Olivet, the Holy Spirit came down, and inspired the apostles to lay the foundation, or to set forth the foundation which God had laid in Zion. They did this by "preaching Jesus." The waiting and anxious multitudes, among whom were the murderers of the "Holy One, and the Just," already conscience-smitten, heard. The natural and necessary result followed. They believed. "They were pierced to the heart, and said, Brethren, what shall we do? Then they that gladly received his word were immersed; and on that day there were added to them about three thousand souls." (Acts ii: 37.)

The foundation, "Jesus is the Christ," was laid. Three thousand were builded upon it by hearing, believing, and being immersed. The single article of faith presented to that audience was the foundation-truth. "Therefore, let all the house of Israel know assuredly, that God has made this same Jesus, whom you crucified, both Lord and Christ." They heard this proposition, with the evidence presented, and the foundation was laid. They then obeyed the commands given, and were builded on the foundation. Thus was the Church of Christ in Jerusalem founded.

The Church of Jesus Christ in Samaria was founded precisely in the same way: "Then they that were dispersed went every-where preaching the word. And Philip went down to the city of Samaria, *and preached the Christ to them;* and the multitude with one mind gave heed to the things which were spoken by Philip, when they *heard* and saw the signs which he did." (Acts viii: 4.) Thus was the foundation laid in Samaria. The people were builded upon it thus. But when they believed Philip, who preached the good news concerning the kingdom of God and the name of Jesus Christ, they were immersed, both men and women.

It will be seen that, in order to found a church of Jesus Christ in apostolic times, it was not necessary to discuss the questions of original sin; of total hereditary depravity; of justification by faith only; of the abstract influence of the Holy Spirit. So far as preaching was concerned, it was only necessary to preach Christ and him crucified. Nor was it necessary, in order to build upon this foundation, that men should understand any of the philosophies mentioned; nor was it necessary that men should "labor under conviction" for a long season—that they should ask the intercession of good men, pray, and be prayed for. It was only necessary that they should "hear, believe, and be immersed into the name of the Father, Son, and Holy Spirit." When they did so, they were recognized by the inspired apostles as Christians, and soon afterward addressed as such. He who accepts Jesus as the Lamb of God, slain for sinners, and yields to his authority expressed in the commandments given to the Gospel, is a Christian.

Whenever these truths shall be perceived by the religious parties in Christendom—when faith in Jesus Christ and submission to his authority shall be the test of Christian character, and the bond of Christian union, communion, and fellowship—then shall that earnest prayer of the blessed Savior be answered: "That they all may be one, as thou, Father, art in me, and I in thee; that they may be one in us; that the world may believe that thou hast sent me." (John xvii: 21.) Consummation most devoutly wished! when all who love our Lord Jesus Christ shall be united in one body—built upon one foundation; when it can again be said: "There is one body and one Spirit, even as you have been called, in one hope of your calling; one Lord, one faith, one immersion, one God and Father of all, who is over all, and through all, and in you all." (Eph. iv: 4–6.)

Then shall Zion arise in her might. She shall put on her beautiful garments, and go forth to battle against sin and uncleanness, "fair as the moon, bright as the sun, and terrible as an army with banners." Then shall the kingdoms of this world become the kingdom of God and his Christ.

"Then shall righteousness prevail, even as the waters cover the channels of the great deep. The lion and the lamb shall lie down together, and a little child shall lead them."

> "How sweet, how heavenly is the sight,
> When those that love the Lord,
> In one another's peace delight,
> And so fulfill his word.
>
> "When each can feel his brother's sigh,
> And with him bear a part;
> When sorrow flows from eye to eye,
> And joy from heart to heart."

J.B. Forrest. Sc.

With kindest regards,

R. Milligan

ROBERT MILLIGAN.

R OBERT MILLIGAN was born in the county of Tyrone, Ireland,
     July 25, 1814. He came with his parents to America in 1815, and
lived in Trumbull County, Ohio, for several years. In 1831, he entered
Zelienople Academy, in Beaver County, Pennsylvania, and, in 1833, entered the Classical Academy at Jamestown, Crawford County, Pennsylvania, then under the Presidency of Mr. JOHN GAMBLE, a distinguished graduate of the University of Edinburgh, Scotland. In this academy, he completed a very thorough course of Latin and Greek, and devoted some time
to the elements of English literature and mathematics.

He was strictly educated in the standards of the Associate Reformed Presbyterians—his father being a ruling elder in the Church—and, in 1835,
became a member of the Associate Presbyterian body, and was greatly
esteemed for his piety and faithfulness by all who knew him.

In 1837, he opened a classical school at Flat Rock, in Bourbon County,
Kentucky, and, while engaged at that point, some of his students were in
the habit of asking him for the exact meaning of sundry passages in the
Greek Testament, and, for the first time, he was thus providentially made
to *realize* the great responsibility of the man who presumes to interpret
for others the oracles of God. He resolved to divest himself of all the
bias and prejudice of his previous education, and to know the will of God
as it is revealed to us in the original Greek and Hebrew, and to make that
will the rule and guide of his life. He accordingly re-examined the whole
grounds of his religious faith, and the result was, that, in March, 1838, he
was immersed by Elder JOHN IRVINE, of the Church at Cane Ridge, Bourbon County, Kentucky.

In 1839, he entered Washington College, Pennsylvania, where, in 1840,
he received the degree of A. B., and, in 1843, the degree of A. M.   In
1840, one session before he graduated, he was elected by the Board of
Trustees of Washington College to the vacant Chair of English Literature. In this department he labored nine and a half years, in the meantime,
however, giving instruction in the Latin and Greek classics, as well as in
English literature. He was transferred, in 1850, to the Chair of Chem-

24   (369)

istry and Natural History, in the same college, and, in 1852, resigned this position, and accepted the Chair of Mathematics in the State University of Indiana; but, at the request of the Board, he was soon transferred to the Chair of Chemistry, Natural Philosophy, and Astronomy. In 1854, he accepted the Chair of Mathematics in Bethany College, and, the following year, was made an Elder of the Church at Bethany, and became co-editor of the "Millennial Harbinger." In all these departments his labors were highly appreciated, and Bethany College and the Church there were never more prosperous than while he was connected with them.

In 1859, he accepted the Presidency of Kentucky University, and the Chair of Sacred History and Mental and Moral Philosophy. In these positions he labored most earnestly and faithfully, managing the University with such prudence that it was not suspended a single day, at a time when almost all other institutions of learning in the State were closed, on account of the civil war. When, in 1866, the University was moved to Lexington, he was, at his own request, relieved from the Presidency of the University, and his labors confined to the College of the Bible. The Board unanimously elected him Professor of Sacred Literature, and Presiding Officer of that college. He still occupies that position, and is doing a great and good work in preparing young men for the ministry. Eternity alone can reveal the value of his services in his present department of labor.

It will be seen, by this brief record of events, that President MILLIGAN's active life has been chiefly occupied in teaching, and, furthermore, that he has taught nearly every branch in the college curriculum. The immense amount of labor necessary to prepare for all these departments has severely taxed his constitution, which, though never very rugged, is now seriously impaired. Nothing dispireted, however, he continues to labor on in the cause of Christ with a zeal and constancy that acknowledge no discouragements.

His connection with the various colleges, already referred to, was of great advantage to him, and gave him an unusually large experience among different classes of distinguished men, and this experience is now of great value to him in discharging the duties of his present position.

President MILLIGAN is a ripe scholar, an excellent preacher, and, as a teacher, has no superior in all the land. He has written considerable for the periodicals of the Disciples, and has recently published a valuable work, entitled "Reason and Revelation; or, the Province of Reason in Matters Pertaining to Divine Revelation." This work is intended for schools, colleges, and private families, and is destined to have an extensive circulation, and will certainly do much good in giving the public proper views concerning the origin, character, and interpretation of the Word of God.

THE SAFETY AND SECURITY OF THE CHRISTIAN.

BY R. MILLIGAN.

"And we know that all things work together for good to them that love God; to them who are the called according to his purpose."—ROMANS viii: 28.

IT is a question which, I suppose, is likely to occur sometimes, even to the most pious, whether the Christian, having done all that he possibly can do to inherit eternal life, will certainly enjoy it; or whether he may not, like many a poor, unfortunate adventurer in the affairs of earth, be finally and for ever disappointed.

It seems to me that this question is very clearly and definitely answered in the words of my text. For, if *all things work together for his good*, then surely the possibility of his failure and final disappointment is utterly out of the question.

True, indeed, the child of God, during his present state of trial and discipline, may, like other men, be subjected to many severe afflictions, temptations, and privations. Like Job, he may have to suffer the loss of all his property. He may lose his friends. And even his very life may be sacrificed by the diabolical hate and malice of his enemies. But, the Bible being true, all these temporal

(371)

losses will result in his eternal gain.   For while God rules
the universe, *all things* must and will work together for the
good of those that love him.   These light afflictions, which
are but momentary, must serve to work out for them a far
more exceeding and eternal weight of glory (2 Cor. iv:
17), so that no *absolute evil* can ever befall any one of
them.

And the reason of this is, that God has so ordained it.
Christianity is not an experiment.   God is not a man, that
he should make experiments.   Our knowledge is limited;
and hence it follows, of necessity, that our schemes of government, finance, education, and internal, as well as external improvements, are all the result of many experiments.
But God makes no experiments.   "Known unto him are
all his works from eternity." (Acts xv: 18.)   He knows
not only what is, and what certainly will be; but he also
knows what would result from any and every conceivable
change of circumstances. (Deut. xxviii; and 1 Sam. xxiii:
10–12.)   And hence it follows, that every thing pertaining
to the scheme of Redemption was well understood, and
clearly defined and arranged in the Divine mind, before the
foundations of the earth were laid.   Before the morning-
stars sang together, and the Sons of God shouted for joy,
God perfectly understood who would, in the course of future
ages, be disposed to love, serve, and obey him.   And for
the benefit of all such, he provided, in his remedial plan
and purpose, every thing that was necessary in order to
their being called, and justified, and sanctified, and glorified. (Rom. viii: 29, 30, and Eph. i: 3–14.)

To some persons all this may seem very much like the old
and, we hope, almost obsolete theory of unconditional election and reprobation.   Indeed there is, perhaps, no passage
in the whole Bible that has been more frequently quoted in

support of this doctrine than that which we have now under consideration. But, nevertheless, I am persuaded that a little calm and sober reflection will suffice to convince at least all honest doubters on this subject, that there is not, in this whole connection, the shadow of a foundation for such a hypothesis. For observe, these decrees of security and final triumph rest wholly on the assumption, that the persons to whom they refer shall have *first* become *lovers of God*. Take away this characteristic or moral attribute from any man, and the aforesaid decrees have no reference to him whatever. This is evident from both the text and the context. "And we know," says the apostle, "that all things work together for good *to them that love God;* to them who are the called according to his purpose. For whom he did foreknow," as about to become his humble, faithful, loving, and obedient children, "he also did predestinate to be conformed to the image of his Son, that he might be the first-born among many brethren. Moreover, whom he did predestinate, them he also called," in his purpose; "and whom he called," in his purpose, "them he also," in like manner, "justified; and whom he justified, them he also glorified."

Evidently, then, these decrees and assurances have reference only to the *lovers of God*. But we all know that love can not be the result of any arbitrary decree or enactment. All the decrees of heaven and earth can not make any man, constituted as he is, love that which is unlovely, or which he is not disposed to love. We love that in which we perceive the attributes of loveliness. And hence it is said, "We love God, because he first loved us." (1 John iv: 19.) And when love is thus generated in our hearts, it leads us to a perfect and unreserved obedience. For "love is the fulfilling of the law." (Romans xiii: 10.)

And as long as we love God with all our hearts, and souls, and minds, and strength, and do his commandments, so long God is faithful, and will not allow any *absolute evil* to befall any one of us.

All this, then, is very plain, and simple, and rational. The argument of the apostle, in this case, is just such a one as you would severally employ, if you were endeavoring to persuade your friends and relatives of other lands to become citizens of this Republic. In such a case, you would, of course, say much about the fertility of our soil, the salubrity of our climate, the vast resources of our country, the enterprise, intelligence, and moral character of our citizens. But you would dwell particularly, and with special emphasis, on *the liberal provisions of our Constitution*, on the *chartered rights and privileges* of every faithful American citizen. You would assure your friends that if they would renounce their allegiance to all other governments, and become citizens of these United States, that in that event, all the powers and resources of this vast and mighty Republic would then be pledged for their security and protection.

Now, suppose that your arguments should prevail, and that many of your friends should really leave their foreign homes, and become American citizens; would any one in his senses even imagine that there was any thing compulsory in the case? that this change of citizenship was owing to any decrees of necessity or fatality passed by the framers of our Constitution? Would any one suppose that these persons were deprived of their free agency, and made the mere tools and chattels of our Government? That their being once citizens of our Republic implies, of necessity, that they shall always remain so? that henceforth they have no power whatever to expatriate themselves; and that even if they should do so, our Government would still be under obligations to extend over them the shield of our Republic? that they could rightfully claim the honors and protection of our flag in a foreign land, even after they had renounced their allegiance to our Government, and become the sworn and naturalized citizens of another nation? No one would so reason. No one would so imagine. The most that could be claimed for these persons, in any case, would be the protection of our Government so long as they remained in the relation of its faithful citizens and subjects.

And just so it is in the kingdom of heaven. There is nothing in its constitution, or its laws, or its administration, that in the slightest degree interferes with the personal liberty and voluntary agency of any man, whether he be a citizen or an alien. But, so long as he is loyal to its King, and faithful to its laws, all the powers and resources of the universe are pledged for his safety and security.

The object of the apostle, in this section of the epistle, is to encourage his Roman brethren to endure patiently their many trials, sufferings, and afflictions. For this purpose, he draws an argument; first, from the lightness and insignificance of these, their present tribulations, compared with the glory that is afterward to be revealed, and of which all who now suffer patiently for the sake of Christ, will be finally made partakers. His second argument is drawn from the assistance and consolations of the Holy Spirit. It lays hold of our burdens, helps our infirmities, and makes intercession for us, even by and through our inarticulate groanings; and finally, in the language of our text, and the following context, he calls the attention of the saints—to and for whom he is writing—to the *Consti-*

tution of the kingdom, and to the unbounded philanthropy and resources of their reigning Sovereign. He unrolls the volume of God's decrees; and there he finds it clearly and indubitably recorded, as the immutable purpose of Jehovah, that all the riches, and treasures, and resources of the universe shall be made tributary to the present and eternal well-being of his children, and that all things shall work together for their good, so that neither death, nor life, nor angels, nor principalities, nor powers, nor things present, nor things to come, nor height, nor depth, nor any other creature, can ever really injure or separate from God's infinite love, the weakest and humblest saint that confides in him.

> "In every condition, in sickness, in health,
> In poverty's vail, or abounding in wealth;
> At home and abroad, on the land, on the sea,
> As their days may demand, so their succor shall be."

I am fully aware that we are slow of heart to believe these great and precious promises. We look out upon the world, and we see that the good, as well as the bad, are subject to heavy losses and severe afflictions. And hence, we are prone to become skeptical, and to say, with the practical atheist, that the government of the world is all a matter of chance; and that Dame Fortune is still, ever and anon, from her rolling pedestal, dispensing her gifts without regard to either the character or the destiny of mankind.

But this is all a delusion—a delusion that arises from a still more alarming and fundamental delusion. We are all, alas! too prone to look upon this world as our home; and upon its riches, and its honors, and its pleasures, as the portion of our souls; and hence we are, perhaps, all too much inclined to estimate our fortunes and our happiness by our success in our efforts to accumulate these things for ourselves and for our children.

But the Scriptures teach us—and our own experience and observation teach us—that God himself is the only satisfying portion of the human soul; and that to attempt to fill it, or to satisfy it, with any thing else, is like attempting

> " To fill the ocean with a drop,
> To marry Immortality to Death;
> And with the unsubstantial shades of time
> To fill the embrace of all eternity!"

They teach us, moreover, that if we would enjoy God as the life and portion of our souls, we must be like him; we must become holy as he is holy. (Heb. xii: 14, and 1 Peter i: 16.) And hence, it follows that all of God's gifts to man are to be estimated in the ratio of their tendency to this end; that is, in proportion as they serve to bring us to God, to make us like him, and to unite us to him, as the only eternal and unwasting fountain of life and happiness. If the riches, and honors, and pleasures of the world have, in any case, such a tendency, they are a blessing to their possessor. But if they have the opposite tendency, if they serve to blind the understanding, and to draw away the heart from God, they are just so far a curse, and an occasion of evil.

Now, that they often have the latter tendency is, alas! but too evident to every man of observation and experience. All that we see, and all that we know of such matters, is but an impressive commentary on the words of our Savior, that a rich man, or a man devoted to the honors and pleasures of the world, can *hardly* enter into the kingdom of God. (Matt. xix: 24; John v: 44.) And hence it follows that poverty may sometimes be better than riches; that the frowns of the world may be better than its honors; and that even sickness, and extreme suffering, and destitution of physical comforts, may be far greater blessings than an abundance of all things that minister to our sensual gratifications and animal enjoyments. (Luke xvi: 19–31.)

Suffering is a *necessity*, and, if you please, a *terrible necessity*, designed and ordained by God as a means of purifying our hearts, and of enabling us to overcome the lusts of the flesh, the lusts of the eye, and the pride of life. (Heb. xii: 6–11.) And hence, David could truthfully say: "It was good for me, that I was afflicted; that I might learn thy statutes." (Psalm cxix: 71.) And hence, too, Paul could say, in behalf of all his Christian brethren: "We glory in tribulations also; knowing that tribulation works patience; and patience, experience; and experience, hope." (Rom. v: 3, 4.)

But all these tribulations and afflictions are in the hand of God, and under his control, just as fully and as perfectly as are the means of our present physical comforts and enjoyments. "Is there evil," says he, "in the city, and the Lord has not done it?" (Amos iii: 6.) And again, he says to Cyrus: "I form the light, and create darkness; I make peace, and create evil. I, the Lord, do all these things." (Isa. xlv: 7.) And hence it is that he measures out to us, day by day, *our necessary portion of discipline*, as well as our necessary portion of food. He willfully grieves and afflicts no one; but, as our great and benevolent Educator, he simply directs, and governs, and controls *all things*, so as to make them work together for the *good* of his chosen.

If any of my readers should ask *how* God accomplishes all this—*how* it is that he allows no absolute evil to befall any of his children—I must, in that event, plead ignorance. I can answer the question but in part. It is not to be expected that the finite should comprehend the infinite. It is not to be expected that such beings as we are, who live in houses of clay, whose foundation is in the dust, should, in any case, or under any circumstances, comprehend the vast schemes, and purposes, and resources of Jehovah. Mystery is written on all the works and ways of God. It is seen in the heavens above us. It is seen in the earth beneath us. It is seen in our own constitution. It is seen on every page of the three great volumes of creation, providence, and redemption. Such themes, therefore, as the one proposed, are too high for us—too wonderful for us to comprehend perfectly.

The subject, however, is not entirely beyond our knowledge. We may all understand it in part: perhaps, indeed, as far as is necessary for our comfort and our happiness. Something very similar to it is seen in the care that every parent exercises over his children. Owing to their ignorance, inexperience, and waywardness, they are constantly exposed to danger, accidents, and harm. But their father loves them, and cares for them. His knowledge becomes their instructor; his experience, their monitor; his wisdom, their guide; and his power, their shield and protection. Now, we have only to suppose that the attributes, capacity, and resources of the father are infinite, and then, on this hypothesis, all is well with the children. Then, indeed, they will not only be saved from a thousand ills and misfortunes, but all things will also work together for their good, under the government and administration of such a guardian.

But this supposition is fully realized in the Divine character and infinite resources of our heavenly Father. All
the laws, and forces, and ordinances of nature are at his
disposal; and, if these are not sufficient, he has but to
command, and ten thousand times ten thousand angels
are at once present to minister to the heirs of salvation.
(Psalm xxxiv: 7; Matt. xviii: 10; Heb. i: 14.) And,
if any thing more is wanting to consummate their safety,
their security, and their happiness, he has only to draw
on the infinite resources of his own Divinity, and their
wants are all supplied. He has but to speak the word,
and their tribulations are all ended; their graves are
opened; their bodies are clothed with light, as with a garment; and their souls are filled with the joys and trans-
ports of life and immortality! "If," then, "God be for
us, who can be against us? He that spared not his own
Son, but delivered him up for us all, how will he not
with him also freely give us all things? Who will lay
any thing to the charge of God's elect? It is God that
justifies: who is he that condemns? It is Christ that
died for us; yea, rather that has risen; who is at the right
hand of God, and who also intercedes for us. Who shall
separate us from the love of Christ? Shall affliction, or
distress, or persecution, or famine, or nakedness, or danger, or sword? . . . Nay, in all these things we are
more than conquerors through him that loved us." (Rom.
viii: 31, 37.)
The ability of our heavenly Father to so manage all
the infinitely diversified interests of his government, as to
cause all things to work together for the good of his children, has been very clearly and very beautifully illustrated
in the fulfillment of many other great and precious promises. Take, for instance, the first implied promise of

mercy to fallen man. "I will put enmity," said God to the serpent, "between thee and the woman, and between thy seed and her seed: it shall bruise thy head; and thou shalt bruise his heel." (Gen. iii: 15.)

How very improbable, to the eye of sense and reason, did the proper fulfillment of this promise appear, for a long time. The very first of woman-born was a murderer—a slave of the old serpent. And, after the lapse of about sixteen hundred years, we find millions under his banner, arrayed against the government and interests of the promised seed. Time rolled on; and, soon again after the flood, nearly the whole world was given up to the idolatrous worship of the old serpent. The service of Jehovah was confined to a little district in Western Asia. And even there, how often was the land stained with blood, and polluted with every species of abomination; until, finally, the sin of even God's chosen people culminated in the betrayal and crucifixion of the Promised Seed.

True, indeed, viewed from the proper stand-point, this was a mighty triumph over the old serpent. Christ, in this case, but stooped to conquer; and hence, for a time, his cause triumphed gloriously. But soon again the forces of Satan were rallied. The Church was driven, like a poor disconsolate widow, into the wilderness, for the long period of one thousand two hundred and sixty years. And at the close of this period, in A. D. 1793, when the persecuting power of the Man of Sin was broken by means of the French Revolution, there really seemed to be but little of pure Christianity left in the world.

But since that ever-memorable epoch, how great has been the change, and how mighty have been the triumphs of truth over error! Every thing pertaining to Christian civilization is rapidly advancing. The Church is coming up out of the wilderness, fair as the moon, clear as the sun, and, to her foes, terrible as an army with banners. The apocalyptic angel is even now "flying through the midst of heaven, having the everlasting Gospel to preach to every nation, and kindred, and tongue, and people." (Rev. xiv: 6.) And every thing in the signs of the times, as well as in prophecy, seems to indicate that the time is at hand when "the kingdom, and the dominion, and the greatness of the kingdom, under the whole heaven, shall be given to the saints of the Most High, whose kingdom is an everlasting kingdom; and all dominions shall serve and obey him." (Daniel vii.)

How true it is, then, that all the promises of God are yea and amen in Christ Jesus. (2 Cor. i: 20.) And how exceedingly great is the security, the consolation, and the happiness of those who have fled for refuge to our glorious Immanuel, and laid hold on the hopes and the promises that are in him. Nothing can ever molest them to their real injury. They may, indeed, for a time, like the Church, be driven into the wilderness; or, like their Redeemer, they may have to pass through the furnace of affliction. But, in the end, it will all be for their good. And, with Job, they will each have reason to say, "Though he slay me, yet will I trust in him." (Job xiii: 15.)

There is just *one* thing, therefore, and but one, about which we should all be extremely solicitous. It is not necessary to be anxious about what we shall eat, and what we shall drink, and wherewithal we shall be clothed. If God takes care of the sparrows, and even clothes with beauty and loveliness the lilies of the field, he will not forget his children. But that which is now to us of paramount importance, is *to know certainly*, that we are his chil-

dren; *to be perfectly sure* that we do really love the Lord
with all our hearts, and souls, and minds, and strength.
If we do this, we may safely leave all the rest to God.
Our bread will then be given us, and our water will be
sure.

On this important question, then, the evidence of the
Scriptures is very clear and satisfactory. "*If ye love me,*"
says Christ, "*keep my commandments.*" (John xiv: 15.) And
again, in the same discourse, he adds: "*He that hath my
commandments, and keepeth them, he it is that loveth me.*"
(John xiv: 21. See, also, 1 John v: 3.) Obedience, then,
is made the test of our love, as it is also made the only
sure criterion of our faith. (James ii: 14–26.) And hence
it is, that in the final judgment, the destiny of every man
will be made to depend, not directly on the degree and intensity of his faith, but on the *evidences* of his faith; not
directly on the purity and strength of his love, but on the
evidences of his love.

Hear, on this point, the testimony of the Great Judge
himself: "When the Son of man shall come in his glory,
and all the holy angels with him, then shall he sit on the
throne of his glory. And before him shall be gathered
all nations: and he shall separate them one from another,
as a shepherd divides his sheep from the goats: and he
will set the sheep on his right hand, but the goats on the
left. Then will the King say to them on his right hand,
Come, ye blessed of my Father, inherit the kingdom prepared for you from the foundation of the world: for I
was hungry, and ye gave me meat; I was thirsty, and ye
gave me drink; I was a stranger, and ye took me in; naked,
and ye clothed me; I was sick, and ye visited me; I was
in prison, and ye came unto me. Then will the righteous answer him, saying: Lord, when saw we thee hun-

gry, and fed thee? or thirsty, and gave thee drink? When saw we thee a stranger, and took thee in? or naked, and clothed thee? or when saw we thee sick, or in prison, and came to thee? And the King will answer, and say to them: Verily, I say to you, inasmuch as ye have done it to one of the least of these my brethren, ye have done it to me. Then will he say to them on his left hand: Depart from me, ye cursed, into everlasting fire, prepared for the devil and his angels: for I was hungry, and ye gave me no meat; I was thirsty, and ye gave me no drink; I was a stranger, and ye took me not in; naked, and ye clothed me not; sick, and in prison, and ye visited me not. Then shall they also answer him, saying: Lord, when saw we thee hungry, or thirsty, or a stranger, or naked, or sick, or in prison, and did not minister to thee? Then will he answer them, saying: Verily, I say unto you, inasmuch as ye did it not to one of the least of these, ye did it not to me. And these shall go away into everlasting punishment; but the righteous into everlasting life." (Matt. xxv: 31–46.)

Dear hearer, where will you be on that great day? And what sentence will you hear from the lips of the Omniscient and Omnipotent Judge? Do you love God with all your heart, and soul, and mind, and strength? If so, are you keeping his commandments? Do you believe, with all your heart, that Jesus is the Messiah—the Son of the Living God? Have you repented of all your sins? Have you openly and publicly confessed the name of Jesus as your only and all-sufficient Savior? Have you, by his authority, been baptized into the name of the Father, and of the Son, and of the Holy Spirit? And are you now giving *all diligence* in adding to your faith, virtue; and to virtue, knowledge; and to knowledge temperance; and to temperance, patience; and to patience, godliness; and to godliness, brotherly kindness; and to brotherly kindness, love to all men? If so, all is well. For just as sure as the Lord God Omnipotent reigns, if you continue in these things, and abound in them, you will at last receive an abundant entrance into the everlasting kingdom of our Lord and Savior Jesus Christ. (2 Peter i: 5–11.) There God himself will lead you to fountains of living water; and there he will himself wipe away all tears from your eyes. That this may be your happy and glorious destiny is my humble prayer, for Christ's sake.

The grace of our Lord Jesus Christ, and the love of God, and the communion of the Holy Spirit be with you now, and remain with you forever. *Amen.*

25

Eng. by H. WRIGHT

John Shackleford,

JOHN SHACKELFORD.

JOHN SHACKELFORD was born in Mason County, Kentucky, on the 27th of October, 1834. His paternal ancestors were from Wales; his maternal, from Ireland. His paternal grandparents came from Virginia, and his maternal, from New Jersey. His immediate parents were both born in Mason County, Kentucky.

At the time of his birth his mother was a member of the Presbyterian Church, but did not believe in infant baptism; consequently, he was never sprinkled. His father and mother united with the Christian Church when he was about ten years of age. His father soon became a leading member in the Church, and his mother was a deeply pious woman, who gave special attention to the religious training of her children. Surrounded by these influences, and having an earnest and impressible nature, JOHN soon became anxiously interested in his spiritual welfare. After carefully studying his Bible, and listening to much parental instruction, on the 5th of March, at the age of fourteen, he was immersed in the Ohio River by Elder JAMES CHALLEN.

His early school days were spent in Maysville, Kentucky, where he obtained a good rudimental education, and, at the age of eighteen, he entered Bethany College, Virginia. He remained there until July 4, 1854, when he graduated, and returned home, and taught a school in Mason County for two years.

During this time, he had constantly in view the calling to which he has since devoted his life. Those were years of calm but earnest preparation for the ministry of the Gospel, and, so soon as he felt the time had come to enter upon his chosen work, he at once gave up every thing else, and devoted himself exclusively to the preaching of the Word.

His first labors were in Mason County, and, for some time, he had charge of the Church in Maysville, the place of his father's residence, where he was greatly esteemed for his faithfulness and earnestness as a pastor and teacher. After having been instrumental in doing a good work in his native county, he removed to Paris, Kentucky, to labor for the

Church at that place. He remained there two years, and then accepted an invitation to the pastoral care of the Church corner of Eighth and Walnut streets, Cincinnati, Ohio. His health failing, in the spring of 1866, he gave up his position, and, for a few months, traveled for the American Christian Missionary Society, and, at the annual meeting of this society, the subsequent October, he was appointed its Corresponding Secretary, which position he has held ever since.

A few words in reference to his success in this last department of labor can not be regarded as improper or out of place.

When he took the Secretaryship, his friends had many misgivings concerning his adaptation to the work. The prospects of the Society were by no means flattering, and the labor necessary to make it a success fell mainly upon the Corresponding Secretary. Few persons had much faith in the ability of any one to turn the discouraging prospects of the Society into permanent success. One year of faithful labor has been expended, and we need only state the result: A larger amount of money was raised than ever before, while the prospects of the Society are better than at any other time since it was organized. A success like this is not achieved except by earnest, constant, and prayerful work.

Brother SHACKELFORD is of medium stature, has a delicate, feeble constitution, a highly nervous temperament, and a nature, on the sympathetic side, as tender and susceptible as a woman's. He has light hair, large blue eyes, a mouth which indicates great firmness, and a forehead, though high, less commanding than expressively benevolent. Every feature expresses what he really is—a man of large conscientiousness, deep spiritual longings, and great purity of thought and action. He has very little of the sensuous in his nature, and, so vivid are his intuitions, that he is almost a prophet. As a speaker, if we except his active sympathy with all kinds of suffering, he has few of the elements of a popular orator. His illustrations are generally apt and forcible, but his powers of rapid generalization are not equal to the requirements of a first-class extemporaneous speaker. When, however, the subject of discourse is one that deeply touches his sympathies, he is always impressive, and often truly eloquent.

THE PRIESTHOOD OF CHRIST.

BY JOHN SHACKELFORD.

"For it is evident our Lord sprang out of Judah; of which tribe Moses spake nothing concerning priesthood. And it is yet far more evident: for that after the similitude of Melchisedec there ariseth another priest, who is made not after the law of a carnal commandment, but after the power of an endless life."—HEB. vii: 14-16.

THE letter to the Hebrews treats of the priesthood of Christ. Our Lord sprang out of Judah, of which tribe Moses spake nothing concerning the priesthood. The priests were selected from the tribe of Levi. This Jewish objection to the priesthood of Christ, the apostle answers by the prophecy in the one hundred and tenth Psalm, of a priest, who should not be called after the order of Aaron, but after the order of Melchisedec—a priest not by the law of a carnal commandment, but after the power of an endless life. The Jewish priests were constituted such by their descent and blood; the High Priest of the Christian profession by the eternal fitness of things; because he alone could fill, truly and faithfully, the unchangeable priesthood, of which the Jewish high priesthood was an imposing, yet feeble and inadequate type. Whoever Melchisedec was, it is evident that he was called to his high office by no arbitrary law or consecrated custom, but in consequence of the purity of his life, and the pre-eminence of his gifts and virtues. So with our great High Priest who has entered into the heavens. He is a Priest forever, after the power of an endless life.

My argument in this discourse is to enforce and illustrate this truth. Every people have their priests. This fact bespeaks a universal want. Man longs for an intercessor with God; and Job uttered a purely human cry when he said: "I have no daysman to stand betwixt me and God, that he might lay his hand upon us both."

This desire for priestly intercession may spring from a sense of our weakness, and helplessness, and sinfulness; but, whatever its source, it is inherent in our nature, and can not be quenched. In what is the great power of the Roman Catholic Church? Its priesthood and confessional. It meets this want of the soul inadequately, imperfectly, and impurely; but, nevertheless, meets it directly and tangibly. If a famished man is not supplied with proper food, he will seize any thing within his reach; and if the wants and longings of the soul are not lawfully and purely satisfied, they will seek unlawful and unholy gratification, the consequence of which is always a perverted and diseased life. Nature abhors a vacuum; so does the soul. If Christ does not fill the heart, some monstrous idol or human priest will. An insincere and wanton priesthood may proclaim a false peace to the soul dependent on it for religious life, but it can never truly bless and strengthen. Only the perfect Priest can lead the soul to perfect peace and a true life. Christ is the only perfect Priest, the *one* Mediator between God and man. Speaking on this subject, the apostle says: "The law made nothing perfect, but the bringing in of a better hope did, by which we draw nigh unto God."

There are three qualities which a priest must possess—power, purity, sympathy.

1st. He must have power or ability to save. He must be invested with the Divine authority. Destroy the confidence of the Catholic girl in the power of her priest to mediate for her and secure the pardon of her sins, and you overthrow her religion; she will abandon the confessional. That the priest must have Divine authority, is a truth that has the force of an axiom. Who has this power? Not the Jewish priests; they were compassed with infirmity. Not the priests of pagan or papal Rome. Who, then? Listen: "But this man, because he continueth ever, hath an unchangeable priesthood. Wherefore, he is able to save to the uttermost all that come unto God by him, seeing he ever liveth to make intercession for them." He alone is able to save to the uttermost. The Son of Man has power to forgive sins. All authority is his, both in heaven and upon earth. His right arm will never fail him, though it bear across the tide millions of weak, helpless, heavy-laden, but trusting souls. The mercy and faithfulness of our God are with him. He is his firstborn, higher than the kings of the earth.

2d. The soul demands that its priest shall be pure. This manifests itself in the desire for the prayers of good men in our times of trouble. Even a dying man would summon all his energies to spurn the prayer of a hypocrite proffered in his behalf. Such a prayer is an abomination to God and man. This desire, this vital necessity, expresses itself in the universal demand that preachers of the Gospel shall be pure men. A preacher is not a priest, except as every Christian man is a priest; but he is called upon to discharge certain priestly functions, to comfort the sorrowful, support the weak, pray with the dying; and

the demand for his personal purity is as righteous as it is
instinctive and universal.

The Jewish high priest wore on his forehead a plate of
pure gold, on which was graven, "Holiness to the Lord,"
God thus declaring the holiness of the office.

Now, our High Priest alone meets this demand for purity perfectly. "Such a high priest became us, who is holy,
harmless, undefiled, separate from sinners, and made
higher than the heavens." Mark these words of the apostle: "Such a high priest *became us.*" Not that we have
such an infinitely pure high priest; not that it is fortu-
nate that we have, but it is necessary, "such a high priest
became us." No other could fill the office of the eternal
priesthood.

Consider, my brethren, the High Priest of the Christian
profession. Living on earth, yet undefiled with sin; keeping company with the outcast, but only to bless and save
them. Our purity is soon lost; we leave it in our cradles.
We lay off our innocence with our child garments. But
the Son of Man lived a holy and undefiled life. How
beautiful! how wonderful! that human life of pain, hunger, sorrow, thorns, temptation, and death, without sin!
"Such a high priest became us, who is holy, harmless, undefiled, separate from sinners, and made higher than the
heavens."

3d. Sympathy. We need a priest who can be touched
with a feeling of our infirmities. He must be pure, to
appear before God. He must be filled with all human
sympathies, to win our love and bear our burdens.

The mother is the natural mediator between father and
child. Sometimes the case is reversed, and the woman has
the man's nature, and the man the woman's. But the almost universal law is, that the mother has a sympathy with

her child that no other being has. And the child will say to the mother, "You ask father," when it has any request to prefer. Or, in case of an infraction of the paternal law, the child will flee to the covert of the mother's arms, and trust to her mediation for mercy.

Not only in childhood is it so; but when ambition, and passion, and self-will are developed, and the boy is rebellious, and the father is just, it is the wise, gentle, tender, sympathetic mother that makes peace, and wins the wanderer back. It is the human heart of Jesus that qualifies him for the eternal priesthood.

"His heart is full of tenderness;
His bosom glows with love."

"For verily he took not on him the nature of angels, but he took on him the seed of Abraham. Wherefore, in all things, it behooved him to be made like unto his brethren, that he might be a merciful and faithful high priest in things pertaining unto God, to make reconciliation for the sins of the people. For in that he himself hath suffered, being tempted, he is able to succor them that are tempted." Mark these words: "*It behooved him* to be made in all things like unto his brethren." These words declare, not simply that he was made in all things like unto his brethren, but that it was *necessary* that he should be made in all things like unto his brethren, that he might be a merciful and faithful High Priest.

Again, the Scriptures say: "For we have not an high priest who can not be touched with a feeling of our infirmities; but was in all points tempted like as we are, yet without sin." Our sympathies are contracted. Men sympathize with their class. The rich often can not sympathize with the poor, the learned with the ignorant, men with

children. But Christ can sympathize with all. He understands the heart of every tempted and suffering mortal.
He understands the peculiar trials and perils of a child's
life.   He has borne to the heavens the memory of a childhood spent on earth.   The perils that beset a boy's life
are many and imminent.   Untried, unskilled, pressed by
passion, and tempted by the great enemy, the early years
of our earthly journey are, perhaps, the most dangerous.
Blessed be God, children have a tender and almighty
Friend, who can enter into all their sorrows, and succor
them in all their temptations.   There is no more sublime
and beautiful sight than the struggle of a child to be true,
and pure, and good.   But we behold it with a fearful joy,
lest the victory should be lost at last.   The passions have
a power and urgency to evil much sooner than most parents .think, and the knowledge of good and evil comes
to us in our very infancy.   Let every tempted and struggling child be taught to go boldly to Christ, and find mercy
and grace to help in time of need.   We need not be afraid
to trust the faith of the child because he can not appreciate the evidences of the divine origin of the Gospel.   Salvation is in the Gospel, and not in its evidences.   Life is
in the air we breathe, and not in any knowledge of its
causes and chemistry.

While our Savior can sympathize with a child, he can
sympathize with the great and gifted, who, by the very
pre-eminence of their gifts, are removed from the sympathies of ordinary minds.

When Satan showed Napoleon the kingdoms of this
world and their glory—seas whitened with the sails of com-
merce—beautiful cities—splendid temples—waving fields
—vast armies, marshaled for battle, swords and bayonets
flashing in the light—and said: ''All these will I-give thee

if thou wilt fall down and worship me," in that hour of doubt, and temptation, and conflict, between conscience and ambition, the great soldier might have triumphed if he had sought him who, in "that he has suffered, being tempted, is able to succor them that are tempted." With the guidance and strength of Christ, he might have been a minister of righteousness; without Christ, he was a minister of darkness, and offered a bloody sacrifice to the king of hell.

Christ was the Savior of Martin Luther. The reformer had the passion and power which belong to all kingly souls; but in the fierce tempests that swept over his spirit, he sought a throne of grace, and found "mercy and grace to help in time of need." So, too, with a grander still, Paul the apostle. He was crucified with Christ, and the life which he lived in the flesh he lived by the faith of the Son of God. So, too, with our dear friend who sleeps at Bethany. Jesus was his friend and deliverer. ALEXANDER CAMPBELL was saved from ambition's crime by the grace of Christ.

Let men, then, strong, brave, self-willed, tempted men, know that they can have the sympathy and guidance of a nature greater than their own, who suffered their temptations, and is able to succor them in their peril. God gives men great minds and passions, not to ruin them, not for the service of Satan, but that they may strike heroic blows for him and his truth; that they may stand in the breach, and, when men tremble with fear, bear their testimony for righteousness, and smite to the earth iniquity and oppression. Christ has need of great souls, and has left his promises for them, as well as for us. He is the friend and deliverer of men, as well as children—of the mighty, as well as the feeble. Christianity robs a man of no strength, but consecrates it all to the great battle of the Lord against the powers of darkness.

Christ can sympathize with women in their trials and temptations. When here on earth, the tempted, weary, heavy-laden, found in him a gentle friend and a wise counselor. He had that wonderful dignity which amazed men, and sometimes silenced all questionings; which prompted Simon Peter, like a child, to beckon John to ask him a question. But he had that quick sympathy which drew to him all sorrowing and broken hearts. When Lazarus was dying, Mary and Martha longed for the presence of their friend Jesus; and when he came, (O, blessed history!) he wept with them at the grave of their brother and his friend. He was deeply moved, not at the death of Lazarus, but in sympathy with the sisters. How gentle he was with the sinful woman. Remember, all ye frail and erring, Christ is your only hope and salvation.

I once baptized a repentant wanderer, a child who had been betrayed and led into a dark and polluted life. She was baptized for the remission of her sins, holding, in a simple faith, that she had God's pledge and covenant of pardon. As she came out of the water, she exclaimed: "Bless God for this hour!" And now how can she triumph, how can she leave that dark, sinful life behind, and reach the light and peace of heaven? Blessed be God, through Christ, who has granted her mercy, and will give her grace to help in time of need.

The struggle of the drunkard with his appetite seems, sometimes, almost hopeless. Worn out with his debauch, mortified, humbled in spirit, he resolves to abandon his evil habit. But when nature recuperates, and his mortification is past, in an evil hour he looks upon the wine when it is red, when it giveth its color in the cup, and, tempted by some siren voice, he falls. His history is a repetition of broken resolutions. Christ is his only hope. If he can learn to rely in simple faith on him, he will conquer. The reason why so many professed Christians, and sometimes even ministers of the Gospel, fall into intemperance, is that, in their weakness, they do not seek Him who is able to save to the uttermost. Our Christian life is enfeebled by our hesitating confidence in the great and wonderful promises of our God. He knows all our sorrows. When dying, he had words of comfort for his mother. Ah, dear woman! who can tell her agony on that dark day, as she beheld her child, the purest and noblest of earth, scourged, tormented, insulted, crucified, as a malefactor, between two thieves? How fully she realized the prophecy of old Simeon, spoken when she came to the temple with her two turtle-doves, to offer sacrifice, according to the law, and to present her child to the Lord. And Simeon said to Mary: "Behold, this child is set for the fall and rising again of many in Israel; and for a sign that shall be spoken against; (yea, a sword shall pierce through thine own soul also)."

The dying Savior entered into all the anguish of that crushed heart, that gave him the love of a mother, and the reverence of a worshiper.

Mother, in your great trial, when watching your dying child, and afterward, when you have laid the sleeping body away, and return with a broken heart to a desolate home, remember you have a great friend in the heavens, who is touched with your sorrow, and who will give you mercy and strength. And in the article of death, when all the living fail us, each of us can look for sympathy and support to him who was dead, and is alive again, and, like Stephen, cry, "Lord Jesus, receive my spirit."

The Epistle to the Hebrews breathes hope and consolation to the weary and the tempted. It rises, too, to the height of a great argument for the divine origin of Christianity. It discloses the wonderful perfection of our religion. There is, in the infinite power, purity, and sympathy of Christ, that which satisfies our weary human hearts, as the sunlight delights and satisfies the eye. The Bible is a self-illuminated book. The light of infinite love gleams from its pages. The heavens declare the glory of God. Christ reveals the mercy and compassion of the Father of all. It is not more true that there is one God than that there is one Mediator between God and men, the man Christ Jesus.

Seeing, then, that we have a great High Priest, that is passed into the heavens, Jesus the Son of God, let us hold fast our profession.

I am very truly

J. S. Lamar

JAMES S. LAMAR.

THE subject of this sketch was born in Gwinnett County, Georgia, May 18, 1829. He was soon after removed to Muscogee County, (then newly settled,) where he was brought up amid the surroundings and under the educational disadvantages peculiar to a new country. He acquired, however, an early fondness for learning, and managed, at the age of seventeen, to enter an academy, where was laid the foundation of a good education. In 1850, he was admitted to the bar in the city of Columbus, but, being providentially introduced, about that time, to a knowledge of the primitive Gospel, and baptized, upon a profession of his faith, by an enlightened Baptist preacher, who did not require him to go before the Church, or to narrate an experience, and who considered the example of Philip and the eunuch as a sufficient authority, he was so deeply impressed by the simplicity and beauty, and, above all, the importance of the primitive Gospel, that he was earnestly desirous of devoting his life to the ministry. But he was all alone, having no Church, no fellowship, no Christian sympathy in his community. Besides, he was not willing to assume the responsibility of preaching without a finished education, and a regular appointment to the work. But all these obstacles were happily removed. By the kindness of friends, he was enabled to enter Bethany College, in January, 1853, where he was graduated in July, 1854, and ordained, about the same time, in the Bethany Church, as an Evangelist. Soon afterward he was called to the church in Augusta, where, with one brief intermission, he has been ever since.

In 1859, he published a work entitled "The Organon of Scripture; or, the Inductive Method of Biblical Interpretation." This work is written in an easy and graceful style, and is a very creditable production for one so young to write. If, however, he had spent several more years in perfecting it, the work would, doubtless, have been of much greater value. As it is, it is worthy of careful study, and certainly encourages us to hope that the author will not let his pen remain idle.

Brother LAMAR has a beautiful mind. He is incapable of any thing

(399)

uncouth or vulgar. His thoughts are chaste and fresh, and always expressed in a polished, forcible style. He is a hard student, but reads a very select library. He seeks for perfection in every thing, and, consequently, his literary labors are always carefully performed.

As a speaker, he is clear, pointed, earnest, and impressive. He is very choice in his selection of words, and generally says the right thing in the right way. He has scarcely enough passion for an orator, and his voice, though well modulated, and perfectly under his control, has not sufficient volume for fine effect. His gesticulation is graceful, and his manner pleasing, but his preaching is better adapted to a select audience than the masses. He is an excellent pastor, but does not succeed so well as an Evangelist.

THE HISTORY OF REDEMPTION REPRODUCED IN THE REDEEMED

BY J. S. LAMAR.

" How shall we, that are dead to sin, live any longer therein? Know ye not that so many of us as were baptized into Jesus Christ, were baptized into his death? Therefore we are buried with him by baptism into death; that like as Christ was raised up from the dead by the glory of the Father, even so we also should walk in newness of life. For if we have been planted together in the likeness of his death, we shall be also in the likeness of his resurrection: knowing this, that our old man is crucified with him, that the body of sin might be destroyed, that henceforth we should not serve sin. For he that is dead is freed from sin."—Rom. vi: 2–7.

THE leading doctrine taught in this Scripture, and which it shall be my object, in the present discourse, to prove and illustrate, may be summed up in a single proposition, namely: *That what the Lord did and suffered in order to enter into his glory, must, in some sense, be done and suffered by every one who is to participate in that glory.*

Before entering upon the argument and elucidation of this proposition, it may be well to remark that it embraces the whole of duty and salvation. There is nothing for us to do or bear that is not exemplified in the history of our Great Captain and Leader. At the same time, it is important to remember that, in seeking to follow his ex-

26   (401)

ample, we are not to commence with his birth, or baptism, or temptation, or any of the labors of his active life. All these we pass by, and begin with the *last* scenes *first*. And it is not until after we have followed him through all these, and been made thus the sons of God; not until we can say, "Christ liveth in us," that we can begin to live the life of Christ, or hope to imitate the example of that life. Hence the Scripture from which we shall draw our discourse, points us to the last events of his earthly career as the first for our imitation, thus teaching us that if we would be "glorified together" with him, we must, first of all, *re-enact the history out of which his glory sprung.* A part of this history is implied, and a part is expressed, in the text. Let us refer to it in its regular order, and make the application as we proceed.

It was just after Judas had gone out to betray him, that he exclaimed, with triumphant exultation : "Now is the Son of Man glorified ;" by which he doubtless meant that he was now about to enter upon those sufferings for which he was to be crowned with glory and honor. But so completely was his heart enraptured by the blessedness beyond, that he overlooked or disregarded the intervening sorrows of the Garden, the pains of Calvary, and the darkness of the tomb. And yet it was *out* of these the glory was to arise, and *for* these the crown was to be conferred. And is it not true of every man, that, when heaven is, first of all, appreciated, and its holiness perceived to be the chief good ; and when the freeness and fullness of Gospel promises give assurance that all may be his, he forgets the crucifixion and burial, which must necessarily antedate his resurrection to life and bliss, and learns, not till afterward, that no man can reach the Crown without first coming to the Cross ; and that no man will come to the Cross who has not first passed through the Garden?

It is the teaching of revelation, confirmed by every Christian's experience, that he who comes to Christ has previously felt "weary and heavy-laden;" has realized the agony of sin; his soul has been made exceeding sorrowful—the "godly sorrow for sin which worketh repentance." And how often has such a man retired into the darkness, to struggle with his burden, and to pray all alone; and so, "pierced to the heart," weeping, and in anguish, and, doubtless, strengthened in his weakness by some messenger of God, he comes at last to say, nay to desire, "Thy will, O God, be done?" Thus he "learns obedience by the things which he suffers." He realizes the *necessity* for it. His own misery teaches him the consequences of sin, and he determines henceforth to obey; and from his heart he cries, "Lord, what wilt thou have me to do?" It is then, in the hour of darkness, and tears, and agony, that he gives the first solemn pledge to God, to be, to do, and to suffer all that he wills.

When such a man hears the command, "Follow the Lord Jesus," he will not be careful to analyze it into its external and internal elements, nor to test it by some alchemy of human philosophy, to see whether it be essential or non-essential; enough for him that it is the voice of God. Hence, he goes boldly forward. It may be in the presence of scoffers and infidels; he cares not. He has a settled purpose that he will identify himself with Jesus Christ, and confess with his mouth the confidence he has in him; and he does it, rejoicing that he is permitted, even in this, to imitate him "who, before Pontius Pilate, witnessed a good confession."

But it should not be forgotten that, though this is "the

good confession," and though "with the mouth confession is made unto salvation," it can only result in this blessing when the subsequent conduct is consistent with it. If we pause with the bare profession with the mouth, it is but lip service; and hence, while the Savior has graciously promised to confess those before his Father who confess him before men, he does not fail to warn us that many *call* him Lord who *do* not *obey* him *as* Lord; by which he would teach us that the confession which secures salvation is one which ultimates in obedience. All would be willing to be Christians in name, doubtless, if they might be allowed to live on in the lusts of the flesh and the pride of life; but the plain intimation of the text, and which perfectly accords with the example of the Savior, is, that this confession necessitates *death;* and just here is, for most men, "the stone of stumbling and rock of offense." They are willing to pronounce eloquent, and, it may be, heartfelt panegyrics upon the Cross of Christ. They can speak in melting tones of Calvary, and point to the "marred visage" of the Crucified with evident emotion. They can tell us, too, in well-selected phrase, of the infinite merits of that atoning sacrifice, sufficient to take away the sins of the whole world; but they are slow to learn that, as a matter of fact, it really *does* take away the sins of those only—not who *admire* him—but who are "*crucified with him.*"

"Take up *thy cross*," says the Savior, "and follow me." How prone we are to explain away this "cross," by making it no more than some public confession, some speaking or praying before men, or the performance of some cther duty that is simply disagreeable, as though it were the symbol of mere embarrassment, or as though Christianity held modesty as sin, and self-distrust at discount.

No; the word means *death*, as is explained by the passage, which says: "Whosoever will *save his life*, shall lose it; and whosoever will *lose his life* for my sake, shall find it." And certainly this means that *only* he who loses his life shall find it; or that the old life *must* be destroyed before the new *can* be superinduced.

A point so important and so practical deserves a fuller illustration. Let me quote, then, some passages from the epistles, which will settle the matter, as I think, beyond question: "Our old man is *crucified with him*, that henceforth we should not serve sin; for *he that is dead* is freed from sin." But suppose he is *not* dead! "If Christ be in you, *the body is dead* because of sin." "I am *crucified with Christ;* nevertheless I live; yet not I, but Christ liveth in me."

How this illustrates the words of the Savior! The Apostle took his cross, was crucified, "lost his life," and, according to the promise, "found it." But he does not hold his case as peculiar, for he says: "They that are Christ's"—*i. e., all* that are Christ's—"have crucified the flesh with the passions and lusts." Certainly, then, they that have not done so are not Christ's. It is, therefore, "a faithful saying; for, *if we be dead with him*, we shall also live with him."

I presume, of course, that no one will understand these Scriptures to refer to a strictly literal "death" and "crucifixion." But let us beware. Because they are not *literal*, it does not follow that they are not *real*. We have no right to set aside the included, veritable *truth*, because it happens to be presented enveloped in a figurative expression. Hence, it is certain that "he that *lives* in pleasure;" he that is *alive to the world*, to the *lusts* of his flesh, to his *carnal passions*, can not be said to be *dead* or *cruci-*

fied with Christ, or to have " put off the old man with his deeds."

But even this "crucifixion"—this "death to sin"—to the flesh, and to the world, is not all. That would, indeed, be a very inadequate exhibition of Christianity which should leave us with a *dead Savior*, and ourselves merely as *dead to sin*, but not *alive unto God*. We can not pause with the crucifixion, therefore, without losing the very blessing for which it was endured. It is a part of the Gospel of salvation, not only that "he died for our sins," but that " he was *buried*." In this, too, as in all things, it is our exalted privilege to follow him, to be " *buried with him*." But what can this mean? How are we buried with him? On this question, there might have been room for doubt and perplexity, if the Scriptures had not been so explicit in furnishing a solution. As the death to sin is not strictly a *literal* death, it might have been thought— if we had been left to our own reasonings—that the "burial" is not a *literal* burial, but, may be, some monkish retirement from the world, a "burial" in the caves or dens of the earth; or that, possibly, it has some "spiritual," and, of course, indefinite sense, such as fanaticism has dictated for so many other requirements of the Scriptures. Happily, however, we are not left in doubt. A word is added which relieves the matter of all uncertainty, *and forbids us giving any other explanation:* " We are buried with him *by baptism*." This is, then, the only way in which we *can* be buried with him, and any explanation which leaves out this act of burial, is sheer infidelity. God has spoken in the premises: let all the earth keep silent before him.

Another question, however, may arise here, and that is: The meaning being settled, is it *necessary* that we should be thus buried with him? To which we simply respond:

The new life emerges from the tomb! The Savior did not rise from the *cross*, but from the *grave!* These are facts which no logic can ratiocinate out of existence. They constitute a living demonstration that Christianity contemplates not simply life from the dead, but life from the tomb; and, at the same time, they confirm the assurance that those who have been crucified and buried with him, shall rise *from their burial*, to walk in newness of life with him.

Again, let us see what the Scriptures say upon the subject: "*Therefore*, we are buried with him by baptism into death; that, like as Christ was raised up from the dead by the glory of the Father, even so we also should walk in newness of life." If, now, the question be, *why* the burial, the answer is given, "*therefore* we are buried"—for this very reason—with this identical object in view—that we may walk in newness of life. The one is the natural antecedent of the other; nay, the one is clearly *conditional* of the other. Once more: "Buried with him by baptism, *wherein* also ye are risen with him." The apostle immediately proceeds to address these parties as those that are "risen with Christ," and tells them, "ye have put off the old man with his deeds, and have put on the *new* man." As much as to say (what, indeed, he did say in other places), "As many of you as have been baptized into Christ have put on Christ;" and, "if any man be in Christ, he is a *new* creature." With what clearness and force do these passages illustrate and confirm the doctrine of the text, viz., that "our old man is crucified"—"dead with Christ"—"dead unto sin;" that, as such, it is "buried with him by baptism"—"planted in the likeness of his death;" and that from this baptismal burial we are "raised up" to "walk in newness of life;" the "old man," still "dead, indeed, unto sin," but the "new man" evermore "alive unto God through Jesus Christ our Lord." And hence the appositeness of the conclusion, "yield yourselves unto God as those that are *alive from the dead.*"

We have now followed the Great Captain of our salvation through death, and burial, and resurrection—coming, thus, into the enjoyment and manifestation of a new and spiritual life. "I live, yet not I, but Christ, liveth in me; and the life which I now live, I live by the faith of the Son of God." "If Christ be in us, the body is dead because of sin, but the *spirit is life,* because of righteousness." If we, then, be risen with Christ, if he is our life, while our old dead body may remain upon the earth, the spirit, the heart, the affections, must *ascend with him.* In this sense, "we *have come* to the heavenly Jerusalem, to an innumerable company of angels, to the spirits of just men made perfect, and to God, the Judge of all." "Our citizenship is in heaven;" we are no longer of the world; our heart, and life, and home, and treasures are all above, laid up secure, beyond the reach of corruption or danger.

And, finally, we are *glorified with him.* This is the *terminus ad quod* of all the past. Yes, we *are* glorified, though still encompassed with infirmity, and walking through great tribulation, subjects of toil, and sorrow, and pain, and tears; for "whom he justified, them he also *glorified.*" In one sense, certainly, this glory is still future. And in this view, we joyfully "suffer with him that we *may be* also glorified together." We are, in this respect, like the Savior in his humiliation—*our glory is not manifested.* We are living his divine life, we partake of his divine nature, we are filled with his divine Spirit; but "the world knoweth us not, even as it knew him not." It is "the *manifestation* of the sons of God," for which the "earnest expectation of the creature waiteth;" and this is not the *impartation* of glory, but the "*revelation* of the glory that is *in* us." Consequently, the Christian, having *reproduced the great facts of redemption* in his conversion to Christ, is now remanded to the *example of Christ's life upon the earth*, to reproduce *that*, in order to his final glorification. In other words, being made *a son of God*, he is now to lead the life of *the* Son of God upon the earth.

It will be observed that this is not, as in the former case, to be done in *particulars*, but in *generals*. Ours is to be, like his, a life of love and mercy; of gentleness and forgiveness; of prayer and humility: of labor for the good of others; and, in one word, of *self-sacrifice for the salvation of the world*. Such a life will be continually blessed by the presence and grace of God; and, in closing such a career, we shall, like our glorious leader, simply "lay down" the divine "life" which is in us, to be taken again. We shall, of course, go with him once more to the tomb, but we can now look forward to that *broken prison* without a fear, knowing that "if the Spirit of him that raised up Jesus from the dead dwell in us, he that raised up Christ from the dead shall also quicken our mortal bodies by his Spirit that dwelleth in us." And after this—beyond the resurrection—"it doth not yet appear what we shall be, but we know that we shall be *like him*;" "we shall be glorified together"—"manifested" to the universe as the "sons of God;" and if sons, then heirs, "heirs of God and joint heirs with Christ."

Such, in brief, is the wonderful scheme of salvation. It is simply being *with Christ*, from first to last, from the darkness to the glory. But O! it must needs be, if we are *with him*, that *he also is with us;* with us in our exceeding sorrow for sin; with us in the good confession; the shame and derision; the crucifixion and burial; with us, aye, *in* us, in the resurrection; and with us and in us evermore, in all our toils, and temptations, and sufferings, and tears. Yea, though we walk through the valley of the shadow of death, we will fear no evil, for still he is with us. And beyond the grave, in the glorious world of immortal life, where the Savior reigns the exalted Lord and Christ, the prayer which he breathed in the days of his humiliation is still heard and answered: "Father, I will that they also whom thou hast given me *be with me where I am.*" O, blessed consummation! This is the fruition of all hope, the reward of all labor, the satisfaction of all desire, the very fullness of the blessing of the Gospel of Christ—"EVER WITH THE LORD!"

Fraternally.

David Walk

DAVID WALK.

———

DAVID WALK was born, December 9, 1833, in Reading, a suburban village of Cincinnati. In early life he united with the Methodist Episcopal Church, and, in his nineteenth year, was licensed by that body to preach, and entered upon the work of the ministry. He continued his ministerial labors in the Methodist Church for nearly nine years, but, having read and reflected much on his church relations, and being convinced that his religious position was not in harmony with the Word of God, he resigned his pastoral charge, withdrew from the Methodist Church, and was immersed—all the same day—in Cincinnati, January 3, 1862, by Benjamin Franklin. He claims to be more indebted to Brother Franklin for his present position than to any other man, and remembers, with the liveliest gratitude, the many expressions of kindness received from him.

Soon after his immersion, Brother Walk began to labor in the general field, and spent about three years traveling and preaching in some dozen States, reaching from Central Pennsylvania to beyond the Mississippi River; and, as an evidence of the amount of work done by him while thus engaged, it may be stated that he traveled, in one year, seven thousand miles, and preached three hundred and ninety-five sermons, besides the other labors that naturally devolve on an evangelist. During the three years spent in this way, he was instrumental in doing great good in many places: the weak churches were strengthened, while a considerable number of sinners were turned to the Lord.

Since he ceased to travel as an evangelist, he has been, and is now, pastor of the Christian Church in Paris, Kentucky, where his labors have been greatly blessed. He has been there not quite three years, and, during that time, the Church has more than doubled its membership, and has become one of the most active and influential churches in Kentucky.

Brother Walk is full six feet high, has perfect health, great physical strength and powers of endurance, dark hair and eyes, and all the features of the face are strongly marked. As a speaker, he is logical, pointed, and forcible. He states his points well, and presents his arguments in a clear light. You can scarcely fail to understand him. He has had three public discussions, in which he is said to have been very successful.

Though not a graduate of any college, his scholarship is, nevertheless, quite respectable. His literary attainments are very considerable, and his appreciation of the beautiful in composition both active and discriminating. He has written some for the periodicals of the brotherhood, in which he has shown that he can wield a ready and forcible pen. Every thing that he says and writes clearly marks him as an original, vigorous thinker—one who is not satisfied with a view of the surface of things. He is a diligent student, and prepares his discourses with great care. He never goes into the pulpit without first having well matured the subject upon which he is to speak.

While he has been a successful evangelist, he has shown more fitness for pastoral work. He takes special delight in this kind of labor, and has certainly shown himself "a workman that needeth not to be ashamed." As a pastor, his success is largely owing to his constant attention to the wants of the flock. He is industrious and vigilant, and to these necessary qualifications of a successful pastor, he adds good administrative talents; hence, if he does not *win* the affections of the people so readily as some men by *heart-power*, he compels respect by *will-power* and the force of an example of devotion to his work.

DEATH AND LIFE.

BY DAVID WALK.

"The law of the Spirit of life, in Christ Jesus, hath made me free from the law of sin and death."—ROM. viii: 2.

LAW and government are necessary conditions of man's existence. Man is naturally a subject of law. Whether he will or not, he is compelled to yield to its imperious behests. This is true, both of his moral and physical constitution. If man refuses to yield to the law of physical necessity, he will die physically; and, failing to obey the law of his moral nature, he will die morally. Man, then, must ever be viewed as the subject of law; for, when God made him, he placed him under its dominion.

As to his physical nature, a constant supply of nutritious food is the law of its existence; and, as it respects his moral nature, perfect obedience to the will of his Creator is the law of its existence. Nor is it legitimate to raise the purely speculative question why it is so. For all practical purposes, it is sufficient for us to know that it *is* so. God, who made man, ordained that it should be so. It is impossible to conceive what our condition would have been under any other circumstances than those in which it has pleased God to place us. I am here. I did not bring myself here. I am subject to law. I did not

(413)

make the law.   Be the law good or bad, I can not change
it.   Crediting revelation, I conclude that God made me.
I am distinctly conscious that I did not make myself.
Nay, I know that I did not make myself.   But I exist;
therefore, I believe that God caused me to exist.   Now,
he who made me chose that I should be the subject of
law, he chose that I should be amenable to the authority of moral and physical government.   At least, I know
myself to be subject to such dual government.   But it is
no part of my present purpose to consider the question
of physical law, and I.must not, therefore, suffer myself
to be betrayed into that which is irrelevant.   Thus far,
I have referred to it simply for the sake of illustration;
simply to show that, from the very nature and constitution of his being, man is a subject of law.   The range of
my present discourse, therefore, will not include any question of physical law as bearing upon man's present existence.   But the two laws of which I propose to speak are,
first, THE LAW OF DEATH; and *secondly*, THE LAW OF LIFE.
In the text, these laws are contrasted.   The one ministers death, the other life.

When God made man, he placed him under a specific
law.   For the violation of that law, the penalty was death.
Hence, it is called the law of death.   The laws of death
and life were originally symbolized by two trees which
grew in the Garden of Eden.   The one was the tree of
the knowledge of good and evil; and this tree stands decidedly in the foreground of the picture.   Observe, it was
not the tree of good and evil, but the tree of the *knowledge* of good and evil.   It only remains to be mentioned
that the other was the tree of life.

All we know of these two trees is, that if a man partook of the fruit of the one, he immediately became cog-

nizant of the quality of moral actions; that is, he immediately became conscious of a difference in moral actions.
He at once perceived that some actions are good, and
some bad. Had man not eaten the fruit of this tree, he
would not have known that such difference existed; therefore, to him all actions would be alike. Being ignorant
of this difference, he would not have been, as he otherwise became, obnoxious to the penalty of the law.

The extent of our knowledge concerning the other tree
is, that if a man partook of its fruit, he would live forever, independent of either moral or physical considerations. That is, whether his moral nature were good or
bad, if he ate the fruit of this tree, the effect would be to
render him immortal. The one tree, then, symbolizes the
principle of death; the other, the principle of life.

Now, according to the laws governing here, respectively,
the moment that man partook of the fruit of either tree,
that moment he experienced the blessing or the curse inherent in that act. If of the tree of the knowledge of
good and evil, death; if of the tree of life, life.

I can not be obnoxious to the penalties of a moral law
of whose existence I am unconscious. I will not, hence,
groan; because, in such a case, I will not be burdened
with a knowledge of the penalties of a law which I have
unconsciously violated, and to whose penalties I do not
know myself to be obnoxious. Consequently, though
Adam was susceptible of death, yet, as he did not know
it, his perfect happiness and tranquillity would remain un-
impaired. It was not till this knowledge formed a part
of his own experience, that he became wretched and unhappy.

Now, this is precisely the condition of all his descendants before they arrive at the years of accountability.

They are free from any moral exercises concerning tne stupendous interests of life and death, for the simple reason that they are unconscious of any laws regulating those questions. True, all the posterity of Adam die; but this is exactly the penalty which they have inherited in consequence of the disobedience of their federal head.

Death was to Adam the remote, and not the direct consequence of sin. Had he gained access to the tree of life, he would have lived in spite of his sin. Sin could not, of itself, kill the body. It could, and did, poison the fountain of spiritual life, and kill the moral nature of our first parents; but after this, it could do no more. When, therefore, I speak of death as the consequence of sin, I mean that it is the remote, and not the direct consequence. If one man could live forever in a state of sin, so could every other man under the same circumstances. It is folly, then, to inquire *what kind* of death God meant Adam should die *in consequence of his disobedience,* for there was but one death that *such a cause* could produce, namely, the death of the soul. And, while physical death is set down as the remote consequence of Adam's sin, it by no means follows that all who die physically are, by inheritance, sinners. Adam became mortal only because God withheld from him the means of perpetuating his life, and not because he sinned. This mortality we have inherited. An immortality of physical existence was the precise thing we lost in our illustrious progenitor; and an immortality of bliss, as it respects the whole man, is what we gain in Christ. The certainty of physical death to all his descendants is the one necessary consequence of Adam's transgression, and that, too, independent of all moral considerations; and the certainty of a resurrection from this death, also independent of all moral considerations, is the one thing which we gain in Christ.

As for the rest, Adam could sin, and we can sin; nor can I see any difference between his condition and ours, as it respects this question. Paul says, that "*as* in Adam all die, *even so* in Christ shall all be made alive." The fact and the promise are alike unlimited in their application. Here is the truth in few words: Independent of our own volitions, and irrespective of moral considerations, we die because Adam died, and on precisely the same terms we will all be made alive in Christ.

All men will gain through Christ that which they lost in Adam. In Adam they all, independent of their own volitions, lost life; and through Christ they all, independent of their own volitions, find the life thus lost. If they lost spiritual life in Adam, they will find it in Christ; and if they lost physical life in Adam, they will find it in Christ. In short, whatever man lost in Adam, independent of his own volitions, he will, in like manner, find in Christ.

If you assume the orthodox hypothesis, that we all died spiritually in Adam—that we are sinners *because* Adam sinned—then I will assume the apostolic hypothesis, that the precise thing which we lost in Adam, we will find in Christ. If all die spiritually in Adam, all will live spiritually in Christ; and if all die physically in Adam, all will be made alive physically through Christ. Till man sins, he is just such a being, morally, as Adam was before he sinned. Sin is the transgression of the law: but where there is no law, there is no transgression, and hence, of course, no knowledge of sin. Unconscious infants are not amenable to moral law; they are not cognizant of its existence; they can not infract it; they are not, therefore, obnoxious to its penalties. But they lose the animal life

27

in Adam without volition; they find it in Christ without volition: they are, hence, fully reinstated in all that they lost.

We must not be guilty of the error of confounding animal life with spiritual life, and, as a consequence, physical law with spiritual law. Man comes into a state where certain moral and physical forces are in operation. The moral he can control, the physical he can not. As a result of these uncontrollable forces, he suffers certain inconveniences, and finally death. But, for these inconveniences and death, ample and satisfying restitution is made. The child, grown to the years of what is called moral accountability, can control and shape his spiritual interests. He may make the best or worst of men. But, no matter how virtuous or vicious he may now be, he can not control the physical forces that doom him to decay and death. Therefore, Paul observes: "Until the law" (that is, until the law was written out by Moses) "sin was in the world; but sin is not imputed" (is not charged) "where there is no law." Nevertheless, death reigned from Adam to Moses, even over those who had not sinned after the similitude (in the likeness, in the same manner that Adam sinned; *i. e.*, by violating a known law) of Adam's transgression."

This law was not published; did not become a part of the world's code—or, rather, did not become *the* code—for twenty-five hundred years after Adam sinned; but all this time people continued to die who had not sinned *as* he did. They found themselves, whether they knew the reason why or not, obnoxious to the penalty of a law that had been enacted when man was created—a law coeval with his existence—but a law that had not yet been published.

After the long lapse of two thousand five hundred years, God commissioned Moses to write out that law in all its details, that the people themselves might be placed in possession of THE REASONS WHY they were subjected to suffering and death, and why they were unable, in any degree, to control the evil circumstances by which they were surrounded.

Now, after this law was set forth in all its minutiæ, and its binding force and obligations in all the departments of life fully pointed out, what results followed? Was their condition improved? *Not at all.* Why, then, was the law given? What good purpose could it subserve? To these questions, I desire to return a specific answer. It is this: In this law, they had a full development of all that was typified by that tree whose fruit opened Adam's eyes, and enabled him to see the difference between good and evil. That was all. The law showed them their lost and ruined condition; but it was powerless to put forth its arm and save them. The law, then, when published, stood to the people in precisely the same relation that the tree, after the transgression, stood to Adam. It showed them their sins, but provided no remedy. Or, in other words, the law did for the people what the eating of the fruit did for Adam—*it showed them the difference between good and evil.* Without the law, entering, as it did, into all the ramifications, and affecting, as it did, all the relations of life, they could never have known what sin was. The law itself was not sin, though it is called the law of sin. It was not death, though called the law of death.

As the tree, of whose fruit Adam partook, is not called the tree of good or evil, but the tree of the knowledge of good and evil, so this law, while it is neither sin nor death, brings to our minds a knowledge of sin and death. For this reason, primarily, the law was given. But, in addition to this primary reason, and intimately connected with it, the law had in view an ulterior object. Without the knowledge of sin, which it was the primary object of the law to impart, the ulterior object of the law would never be gained. In brief, without being able to see the exceeding sinfulness of sin, without a plain demonstration of our utter inability to keep the law under which we are placed, we never will accept the mediation of the Lord Jesus Christ. The law, then, did not introduce sin; it only discovered it. The law simply unveiled sin, and showed us the putrid carcass to which we were chained, without, by any possibility, being able to extricate ourselves. It now proposes, having showed us our sins, to take us by the hand and lead us to him who has power to redeem us from their thralldom.

A beam of light, admitted into a room, shows us thousands of motes. But these motes were not introduced by the light; they were in the room previously, only there was not sufficient light to make them manifest. Thus, the law showed man his depravity—showed him how all flesh had corrupted itself before God. Sin was in the world; but, without the law, men could not see it. Hence, Paul says: "I was alive without the law once: but when the commandment came, sin revived, and I died."

Unless a man is first killed by the law, he will not seek to be made alive in Christ. The law, then, was given, *first*, to show us our sins—to slay us; and, *secondly*, to lead us to Christ. "Therefore," says Paul, "the law was our pedagogue to bring us to Christ." The reasoning of this apostle enables us to see still further the practical operations of the law. "We know that the law is spiritual." It takes cognizance of the spiritual nature; it sits in judgment upon spiritual actions; it appertains to the spirit. "But I am carnal, sold under sin." I am the slave of sin. The law is so pure and holy ; it points out so many tempers, actions, affections, as sinful, that I would not else have known to be such, that by it I am bound, enslaved, and slain. " For I know that in me (that is, in my flesh) dwelleth no good thing." How careful he is to use the limiting clause, " in my flesh !" Why did he not decry against the sins which his soul had inherited from Adam ? Because the assumption would have been false. Sin is an act ; and Paul knew that an act of the body, or a volition of the mind, could not be transmitted or inherited. Paul knew that, like Adam, he became a sinner when he sinned. "O wretched man that I am ! Who shall deliver me from this dead body ? I thank God that I shall be delivered through Jesus Christ our Lord." " There is, therefore, now no condemnation to those who are in Christ Jesus, who walk not after the flesh, but after the Spirit." Why is there *now* no condemnation ? Because " the law of the Spirit of life IN Christ Jesus hath made me free from the law of sin and death." Here we reach the second law—the law of life. We talk about the tree of the knowledge of good and evil, till we forget that there was another tree in the Garden—the tree of life. The first is the prototype of the law ; the second, of the Gospel. The law of sin and death was the development of the one ; the law of the Spirit of life in Christ Jesus is the development of the other. The fruit of the one kills ; the fruit of the other gives life, and its leaves are for the healing of the nations.

Let us reverently look at this tree of life. Adam's posterity, as we have seen, without any volition of their own, were subjected to a law that ministered sin and death. The name of this law is justice. But, that God might be just while he justifies, he enacts another law. The name of this law is mercy. The provisions of the former are all just; of the latter, all merciful. Through the latter the righteousness of the former is fulfilled in those whom else it had slain. The law of mercy dishonors not, but rather magnifies the law of justice. Thus justice and mercy hold the scales of Divine government in equipoise.

Much time has been wasted in a mere logomachy as to what God meant by death. "In the day that thou eatest thereof thou shalt surely die." This confusion might be avoided, and the exact truth elicited, by considering the terms of the law, and noting just what was done when it was violated. In imagination we will place ourselves in the Garden. We hear the law from the lips of God, and we will suppose that we know the meaning of every word, with a single exception. That exception is the word death. We never heard this word before, and to us it conveys no meaning. We understand the prohibition, but as to the punishment threatened—if, indeed, we can understand it as punishment at all—we know nothing. Upon this latter we have the serpent's comment; but, in his view, it is something to be coveted rather than shunned. With intense anxiety we wait the issue. Presently we see the man take the fruit and eat it. He does the very thing that God commanded he should not do. A clearer instance of disobedience the world can not furnish. An issue was never more fairly made. Let it now be settled that God meant what he said, and performed what he threatened. Whatever he does, then, in the premises, will be his meaning of death. What, now, does God do? Does he inflict death upon Adam in the common acceptation of the word? He does not; for Adam lived more than nine hundred years after this day. What, then, I again inquire, does God do? *He drives the man from his presence, and hides his face from him.* This, then, is God's meaning of death. And this *is* death. Nay, this is hell! A deep and impassable gulf has been made between God and man. That gulf must be bridged, or man is lost to all eternity. And now, as God whispers one word of hope to his fallen child, he summons a cohort of cherubim to guard the way of the tree of life. And there those cherubim stood for four thousand years. And for four thousand years no mortal had access to that tree. Not till the weight of the law's dread penalty fell upon the head of the Beloved did those watchful spirits take their flight, and leave the way to the tree of life open to all the world. Adam was driven forth from the presence of the Lord. He bore in his heart a deep sense of his sin, and the consequent condemnation. Now, when a man hears the law, understands the law, and then knowingly violates it, he becomes, from that moment, obnoxious to its penalty. In that moment of sin he dies; dies just as Adam died. But, unlike Adam, no shining ranks of cherubim interpose between the sinner of to-day and the tree of life. Thanks be to God for the unspeakable gift!

I sum up, then, as follows: The moral law of God, under which we are all placed, requires true holiness and perfect obedience. But man, in his fallen condition, can not meet these requirements. What, then, is to be done? At this precise point, the law of the spirit of life in Christ Jesus stretches forth its omnipotent arm. This law, or, to speak more strictly, the dispensation of which this is the law, presents a Sacrifice who evaded not a jot or point of the law that had been dishonored. He kept that law perfectly, that he might become the Savior of man, who could not keep it. And as man never would, in this world, be able to keep it, Christ made provision for his escape from its penalties, whether he came to Him as a believing, penitent alien, or as one of His own erring children. And now Christ, our righteousness, through the system of pardon, presents man with a new and living way, through the rent vail of his flesh. That law killed our sacrifice— who suffered without help from God, or angels, or men— just as it would have killed us all but for his mediation.

Our gain and our victory consist, then, in this glorious fact: that Jesus Christ, our Sacrifice, although he suffered the full penalty of the law, finally triumphed over the grave. And now, having risen from the dead, and being clothed with all authority in heaven and on earth, he declares, with immense significance: "I am the WAY, the TRUTH, and the LIFE. No man *cometh* to the Father (from whom he had, by transgression, been *driven*) except through me." Let man, now, attempt to gain access to God through any other medium, and the sharp edge of flaming swords, wielded by the strong arm of warrior angels, will descend upon his head. Just as certain as God's throne is immutable, that man who refuses to submit to the authority of his Son, is lost forever. True, man has naturally no more moral ability now than formerly. He is, of himself, as incapable of rendering perfect obedience to God now as at any former period of his history. Does God, therefore, require *less* of man now than formerly? Has he relaxed the rigor of that law under which he originally placed him? Is God less holy, or does he demand less holiness now than in ancient times? Not at all. To all these queries I respond, not at all. The difference— the sole difference—consists in this fact: God has accepted the obedience of Christ, has accepted the offering which he made of himself, that man, through the obedience of faith, may be made righteous *in* Christ Jesus.

The government has, for the time being, passed into

the hands of the Son; but while there is a change in government, there is no change as it respects moral obligations to God; unless, indeed, these latter have been heightened. Because man is absolved from the slavish observance of the law of commandments contained in ordinances—Christ having taken them out of the way, nailing them to his cross —it by no means follows that he is not now under law. There is a vast difference between legal righteousness and the righteousness which is by faith. A man, to be legally righteous, must be absolutely guiltless in thought, word, and deed: but this no man ever was. Nor in the meantime, as has been intimated, has God lowered the tone of his moral law. This is impossible, for that law is nothing less than a transcript of his own Divine perfections. But now the Lord Jesus Christ, who knew no sin, comes into the world to *put away sin* by the sacrifice of himself; and whoever is washed in his blood is, in the sight of a pure and holy God, held to be righteous. Through the mediation of God's dear Son, the righteousness of his law is FULFILLED IN US: and this is done only through obedience to the law of the Spirit of life in Christ Jesus. This is the law which absolves, or makes us free from, the law of sin and death; and this is the law under which we are now placed. It was first proclaimed by him who alone had authority to fix upon the terms of man's salvation; by him who alone had the right to say what he would accept of man *now*, in lieu of the perfect obedience and true holiness required of him *then*. This law, as it respects the alien, is set forth in the following words: *"He that believes, and is immersed, shall be saved;"* that is, *pardoned*. This, then, is the law of the Spirit of life in Christ Jesus. You will observe that it is not the law alone, not the Spirit alone, but the law of the Spirit of life; and that only as it is IN Christ

Jesus. It, then, derives its sole efficacy from the blood of Jesus. But what is the precise thing which obedience to this law—for all men can obey the law of pardon—does for us? Does it make us actually, literally, free from liability to sin, and from spiritual imperfection; or does it simply free us from all our sins that are past, with the promise of grace to help us in time to come? Do we never again sin after we yield obedience to this law? The apostle does not say so. What, then, under Christ, is our exact moral status? I judge it to be that of holiness through pardon, and not through perfect obedience to the moral law of God. Never in this world will we be free from the liability to sin. What, therefore, do we gain? We gain the *pardon of our sins* through the blood of the Lord Jesus Christ, and absolution from the *law* of sin and death. We no longer groan under a law that contented itself with showing us our depravity, while it was unable to save us from the curse of sin; a law under which we could be neither legally nor spiritually holy; for, on the one hand, man could not render perfect obedience to that law; and, on the other, Jesus Christ had not yet appeared to put away sin. While the law now, as then, shows us our sins—indeed, while it magnifies sin—it, at the same time, shows us how we may obtain remission. But are we made free from death? Do not men still die? Yes, men still die. What, then, is gained? We are now made free from the *law* of death. That law promised *only* death. There was no life in it. This law not only denounces the judgments of God against all unrighteousness, but with this denunciation IT PROMISES LIFE through the blood of the new and everlasting covenant. Consequently, the *fear* of death is gone. I have to die, but I do not fear death. Why do I not fear death? Because the Savior has broken its power and extracted its sting. We are not, then, made free from liability to sin; nor are we made free from death; but we are made free from the *law*—from the *dominion*—of them both. Let me fully illustrate my meaning: You murder a man, and thereby violate a law, the penalty of which is death. As you are led forth to die, executive clemency interposes and pardons you. But are you not a murderer still? The governor's pardon will not enable you to bring back the dead. Could you do this, you would not need pardon; you would be legally acquitted: there would be no law to execute you. But the executive can not free you from the fact of murder, for there lies the lifeless victim of your hate. He can only pardon you—release you—from the *law* of murder. Mercy triumphs over justice. In all other respects, the governor leaves you as he found you. You can not make restitution. An ocean of tears will not wash out the stains of the blood which you have shed; time will not fade out the damning evidence of your guilt; an eternity of penitence will not call back the life which you have taken. There is but one hope for you; that hope lies in pardon, and pardon is just what you receive. Though guilty, you are henceforth treated as though you were not guilty. The application is easy. As a sinner, I am placed under a law which I have violated every hour of my responsible life. The penalty of this law is death: "The soul that sinneth, it shall die." Now, what shall be done to atone for past infractions of this law, though I should be able to keep it in the future? It still clamors for my blood. Pardon is what I want, and pardon—as it respects my past sins—is the one thing which the Savior promises me on the sole condition of my becoming obedient to his will. The moment that I, from the heart, yield my will to his will, and submit myself to his authority, I am pardoned. That moment I am released from the *power* of the law of sin and death, and am freely accepted in the Beloved. Having pardoned me, he now lives and reigns to make intercession for me. But I am weak, and the motions of sin are still in my body; therefore, I shall need constantly to bathe my soul in the fountain of Divine mercy, until the conflict with sin is ended, and my ransomed spirit shall rest in the paradise of God.

Yours Truly
Wm Baxter

WILLIAM BAXTER.

WILLIAM BAXTER was born in Leeds, Yorkshire, England, July 6, 1820, and emigrated, with his parents, to the United States, in the year 1828.

His parents were members of the English Church; consequently his early religious training was in accordance with the Episcopal faith. His natural inclinations, however, did not lead him to sympathize with the church of his parents. He sought church connections where his warm, impulsive, and generous nature would find more scope and freedom. Hence, when about sixteen years of age, he became a member of the Methodist Protestant Church in Alleghany City.

But this position was destined to be only temporary. He found the Methodists a zealous and active people, and, so far, he was satisfied with his religious connections. But, as he became more and more acquainted with the Bible, he was fully convinced that he had not obeyed the Gospel according to the teaching of the New Testament. This conviction soon led him to demand a Scriptural baptism, and he was accordingly immersed, in 1838, by the lamented SAMUEL CHURCH, who was then pastor of the church in Alleghany City.

In the year 1841, he entered Bethany College as a student, and, after remaining four years, graduated in 1845, having, in the meantime, given considerable promise as a preacher of the Gospel. After leaving college he entered at once actively upon the work of the ministry. He preached one year for the brethren in Pittsburgh, Pennsylvania; then three years at Port Gibson, Mississippi; next, Wilkinson County, Mississippi, seven years; next at Baton Rouge, Louisiana, and Fayetteville, Arkansas, four years; and finally, at Cincinnati and New Lisbon, Ohio. At the former place he labored for the Sixth-street Church about two years, and at the latter he is at present located, where he is doing an excellent work in building up and strengthening the cause of Christ in that part of the State. He has also been quite successful as a teacher, having filled, in a satisfactory manner,

the Chair of Belles-Lettres in Newton College, Mississippi, and, more re-
'cently, the Presidency of Arkansas College, at Fayetteville, Arkansas.

Besides publishing a volume of poems in 1852, he has been, for many
years, a regular contributor to several public journals. Among these may
be mentioned the "Ladies' Repository," "Southern Literary Messenger,"
and "Millennial Harbinger." In 1864, he published a volume entitled
"Pea Ridge and Prairie Grove; or, Scenes and Incidents of the War in
Arkansas."

Brother BAXTER is rather small of stature, but compactly built; has strongly-
marked features, with a nervous, excitable temperament. Although in years
past he has been in feeble health, he looks now as if his health was quite
vigorous. But his constitution is one which needs constant, careful watching.

Both as a writer and speaker he is chaste and easy in style, while his
thoughts are always pure and elevating. He has deep and tender sympathies, with large and active benevolence; consequently the poor and distressed never came to him in vain. As a pastor of a church, he is attentive
to the *real* wants of his people, and labors earnestly for their spiritual
advancement. In this department of labor he has been eminently successful.

THE LOVE OF GOD.

BY WILLIAM BAXTER.

"For God so loved the world that he gave his only-begotten Son, that whosoever believeth in him should not perish, but have everlasting life."— JOHN iii : 16.

NEVER were words more deeply fraught with meaning than those which the Savior uttered in the hearing of the learned Rabbi of Israel, words of deep import to you, to me, to the whole family of man. They make known the most benign attribute of the Divine Father; present before us its loftiest exhibition, and declare to dying men its blissful result. That attribute is the love of God; the exhibition of it, the death of his Son; the result, the eternal salvation of all those who, by holy obedience, manifest their trust in the Lamb of God that taketh away the sin of the world.

The angels who beheld the marvels of creative power when God called our world into being, saw not, until the fourth day, the regal sun, the queenly moon, and the starry host. Nor did hoary patriarch, mitred priest, or inspired prophet, ever behold such glories as met the gaze of the fishermen of Galilee when Jesus appeared to them on the holy mount, as he appears to the immortals now. For four thousand years God had been giving the world proofs of his love; but how deep, how tender, how exhaustless that love, the world never knew, until the Savior's words to Nicodemus were fulfilled.

In contemplating the love and compassion of God, there is danger of a trust and confidence that borders upon presumption; while too great attention to the severer attributes—such as justice and holiness—may lead to doubt, and even despair. Viewed in connection, the beauty and harmony of the whole is to be seen. As in the deluge, while there is anger and justice, so there is an ark, a dove, an olive-leaf, the smoke of sacrifice ascending, and, over all, the rainbow hues of love and peace; the fierce, surging waters, like the frown of God—the rainbow, like his smile of love.

Thus, we may contemplate the power of God as displayed in creating and sustaining this vast universe; behold it, in the fierce tornado, and the wild commotion of the ocean storm; see it reflected in the glare of the forked lightning, as it darts across the darkened heavens; hear it proclaimed by the muttering thunder, as if he were speaking in tones of wrath to a guilty world; and we shall find there is nothing in all this calculated to awaken any other feeling save that of terror and trembling awe.

When we remember that God fills all things—that he is every-where present—that thought is calculated to arouse our fears, and rivet upon our minds the conviction that we can not go where he is not; we feel that God is above, beneath, around us; with us in the crowded city and the solitary desert; in the pursuit of pleasure, and the hurry of business; in the bustle of noonday, and the silence of midnight; in the hall of revelry, and the temple devoted to his service; with us at home and abroad, in and around our daily paths; and, with the minstrel king, we are led to exclaim: "Whither shall I go from thy Spirit, or whither shall I flee from thy presence. If I ascend into the heavens, thou art there; if I make my bed in hell, thou art there. If I take the wings of the morning, and dwell in the uttermost parts of the sea, even there thy hand shall lead me, and thy right hand shall hold me." And the boldest will tremble when he remembers that he is in the presence of the Ever-present One.

If we remember that God knows all things, from the thoughts of the loftiest intelligence that burns near his throne, to the instinct of the most insignificant creature that he has made; that he looks on us not as man looks, but that his piercing eye sees through all our disguises and concealments, penetrates the flimsy vail of hypocrisy, discerns the very thoughts and intents of the heart, we quail before the searching glance of the All-seeing One, to whom the secrets of all hearts are known, and who will disclose them before the assembled universe, for our approval or condemnation, in the judgment of the great day.

We call to mind the declaration of holy writ, that justice and judgment are the habitation of Jehovah's throne, and his righteous laws, which we have so often broken, rise up and condemn us; a fearful day of retribution in the future threatens, and our guilty souls find no refuge, no hiding-place from the storm in the justice of God.

We turn to his holiness, the stainless purity of his character; we look at the defilement which sin has brought upon us; we feel that, like the leper, we should place our hands upon our mouths and cry, "Unclean! unclean!" His purity, contrasted with our sin, his holiness, with the corruption which we feel in our own nature, leaves us no foundation for hope in the holiness of God. Had God manifested no other attributes of his nature than these,

28

the condition of man would have been hapless in the extreme; hope would have long since died in the human
heart, and our race would have toiled on in despair, from
the cradle to the grave: but it is recorded on the sacred page
that "God is love;" that "God so loved the world;" and
these glad words drive away all our fears; they bid us draw
near with filial confidence, and, from full hearts, cry,
Father! father!

As the loveliest and sublimest objects in nature, under
certain circumstances, rather alarm than delight us, so some
of the attributes of God, contemplated singly, fill the soul
with dread; but, when viewed in relation to each other,
they glow in the hues of loveliness alone. Thus, if we
wander at nightfall in the depths of the forest, there is
naught around us to give delight; the night wind sweeps
through the overspreading branches like a wail of woe,
and strange shapes are dimly seen through the gloom; a
horror of great darkness fills the mind with vague and un-
defined terror, and we long to escape from the fearful place.
But, lo! the moon rises in queenly splendor, and pours
her mild radiance over the scene; the dew-drops glitter
upon the leaves like diamonds set in emeralds; the wind's
sad sigh now becomes a lofty hymn; and the scene, late so
desolate and drear, as if by enchantment, is changed to one
of surpassing loveliness.   How awful, in the midnight
gloom, is the thunder of Niagara! how awe-inspiring the
fierce rush of its fearful leap into the gulf below! The
soul is hushed in its solemn presence, while fancy shapes
its rising mists into unearthly forms.   But day comes on
apace, and all its terrors depart; like pure crystal seems
the torrent now; the sunbeams irradiate the falling spray,
and the late dreadful cataract wears a rainbow, like a crown
of glory, on its brow.   And thus it is, when the heart is de-

pressed by the thought that God is all-seeing, ever-present, holy, just, and true; then the thought comes, that he is full of compassion and tender love, and, like the moonbeams to the darkened forest, or the sweet sunlight to the cataract, so is the light of love to those attributes that once inspired terror alone. The power of the Almighty, under the guidance of love, will be exerted for the protection of the object of that love; his presence, which made us tremble, will become, of all things, the most desirable; his universal knowledge will make him acquainted with all our wants and all our woes; holiness will glow brighter in the light of love; the severity of justice will be softened; for in the great exhibition of love which God has made in the death of his Son, justice and mercy truly have met, righteousness and peace have embraced each other.

God has ever loved our race. From the time that his mandate called our first parent from the dust, his kind care and tender love have been extended over us. The sentence of exile from Eden had scarcely been pronounced, when God made known his love to man by giving the gracious promise, that one born of woman, like a mighty conqueror, should bruise the head of the arch enemy, and win for man a brighter Eden than Adam lost. God manifested his love by permitting man to approach him through the medium of sacrifice; by his speaking, through angels, to Abraham, Isaac, and Jacob; by the rights and ceremonies of the Mosaic institution; by sending prophet after prophet, and teacher after teacher, to instruct our race and draw it back to himself. But all these exhibitions of love failed to recall lost man from his wanderings. He treated his messengers with scorn, and, by his perversity, forfeited all claim to his merciful forbearance; yet God forsook him not, but gave him the strongest possible proof of his love, to win him from sin and sorrow, to holiness, to happiness, and Heaven. Love consists not in word, but in deed. Men prove their love by their actions, as did the Roman Decias, who, in order to secure victory on the side of his country, in accordance with the prediction uttered by the oracle, drew his robe around him, and rushing into the thickest ranks of the opposing host, yielded himself a willing victim, that Rome might be free; or as Winkelried, who gladly threw himself on the Austrian spears, to open the way for liberty to Switzerland; or as Leonidas, who, with the noble three hundred, met the rushing myriads of the Persian despot, and bravely died, that Greece might not wear the yoke. Thus God, stooping to the usages of men, to prove his love to our race, gave his only-begotten Son, that whosoever believeth in him should not perish, but have everlasting life.

But let us examine the meaning of the saying, "Gave his Son." Does it mean that God sent his Son as an ambassador, attended by shining legions of angels, to treat with our revolted race, and bring them back to their allegiance? No; he came in lowly guise; no stately palace received him; no princely couch sustained his infant head; no national rejoicing hailed his birth; an obscure village is the place where the Son of the Highest makes his appearance; and he is cradled where the horned oxen fed.

But was the obscurity of his birth and the coldness of his reception, the privations and dangers of his infantile years, all that was meant by God giving his Son? Ah, no; for, though when he first appeared among men, he stooped from heaven to earth, this vast descent came far short of exhausting its meaning, and we must seek it in his future history.

Behold him, in the desert, undergoing fierce trial.

The adversary of our race assails him on every point, while demons and angels look with deep anxiety for the issue of this superhuman conflict. He triumphs, but it is only to encounter new trials, to undergo new sufferings; for, though he were maker of all things, yet did he suffer need; and, on one occasion, we hear the homeless wanderer exclaim : "The foxes have holes, and the birds of the air have nests; but the Son of Man hath not where to lay his head." Contrast his friendless destitution with the glory he had laid aside, on our behalf, and then ask, Is not even this a wonderful display of our Father's love?

But let us follow his eventful life, through priestly hate and pharisaic invective—a life stigmatized as evil, though spent in doing good—to that scene of sorrow which transpired in Gethsemane Garden on the night of his dark betrayal. He had just eaten the last supper with the twelve; he had seen Judas depart; and well did he know the foul purpose which filled his traitorous bosom. The echoes of the hymn which closed the feast had died away, and, with his disciples, he sought the retirement of the Garden, whose calm solitude had often invited to solemn contemplation and earnest prayer.

"Tarry ye here, while I go and pray yonder," he says, and soon he is alone. The work he came to perform is nearly accomplished, but, as the closing scene draws near, his nature seems to shrink from the dread encounter; deep sorrow, like a mountain weight, presses on his heart, and his soul becomes exceeding sorrowful, even unto death. He prostrates himself on the cold, damp earth, and, in the most touching tones, he makes his petition to the Father. He pours out his soul to God in strong cries and tears, but no other deliverer can be found, and he treads the wine-press alone. He rises and seeks his disciples; but they had forgotten their sorrows in sleep. He leaves them, and again prays in anguish of spirit. He even asks the third time, and, while prostrate in the dreadful agony of that fearful hour—such was the burden of our guilt, so intense the pain and mental agony which he endured, that his sweat was as great drops of blood falling down to the ground—and the meek sufferer, in that hour of mortal anguish, cries: "Father, if it be possible, let this cup pass from me; nevertheless, not my will, but thine, be done."

We now begin to perceive the meaning of the words "God *so* loved the world that he *gave* his only-begotten Son," as we gaze on the sorrowful scene which transpired near the hour of midnight in that Garden's shade. Oh! it was a fearful and a gloomy hour. Angels, doubtless, were near, weeping, too, if angels ever wept, and gazing with intense interest upon the sight, and wondering when this scene of sorrow, this scene of love, would end. Demons, too, looked on with scowling hate, or rejoiced in the apparent defeat of the Great Champion of our race; while man, alone of all created intelligences, for whom, too, all this was transpiring, was unobservant and unmoved. It might be thought that the scene might, with propriety, close here; that a sufficient proof of the love of God had been given; that it was enough that his Son had descended to earth in humility; that he had dwelt amid scenes of sorrow and privation; that, under the load of our guilt, while we had no tears for our own crimes. they had caused the bloody drops of agony to fall from the body of God's beloved Son. But, no; God has another exhibition of love, than which he himself could give no greater. Without the shedding of blood, there could be no remission. Man must die, or the Son of the Highest must bleed. God gives the just for the unjust, and the spotless Lamb of God is slain for us.

We now come to the grand climax of the love of our heavenly Father, in which all the rich fullness of his affection is displayed; and, if man be not convinced of his love by this crowning act, he must forever remain in utter and hopeless skepticism. This is heaven's last argument; for, when God gives his Son to die, there is no greater gift in the treasury of the skies, to demonstrate his great, his exceeding love to man.

It is a solemn, and often a fearful thing, to die. There is something in death's approach which makes the best and bravest tremble; the severing of all earthly ties; the cold, clammy sweat, the failing breath, the struggle of the spirit for life, and the unspeakable anguish which often attends the closing scene, makes us shrink instinctively from the dying strife. Some, however, who have fallen on the battle-plain, in their country's cause, have been known to die exultingly in the moment of victory, exclaiming: "'Tis sweet, oh! 'tis sweet for my country to die!" The Christian martyr has been seen to yield up his life amid devouring flames, in proof of his attachment to his Lord and Master. Nay, many, very many, have triumphed on the bed of pain and languishing, and, upborne by a living faith, have looked upon death with an unfaltering gaze. But, when death comes attended with open shame and ignominy; when the infuriated mob pours out its reproaches on the object of its hate, and clamors furiously for his blood; when no tear is shed for the sufferer; when his eye looks around for a single look of pity, and sees it not; when his ear listens for one kind word to soothe his last agony, and hears it not; then, indeed, is death terrible. And yet to such a death did God give his

Son. He gave him freely for us all, that he might taste
death for every man. He met it in its most repulsive
form—partook of the death appointed for the vilest malefactors, in token that the benefits of his death might be
enjoyed by the vilest of our race. Betrayed by a false
friend; seized by rude foes in the Garden, hallowed by his
prayers; deserted by his disciples, he is confronted with
those who long have thirsted for his blood.

It is night; yet, with indecent haste, they begin the
trial. False witnesses fail to fasten any crime upon him.
The Roman governor declares "I find no fault in him."
Yet, when all the vile arts of flattery, intimidation, and
perjury fail—for confessing the truth, that he is the Son of
God—he is condemned to die. It is day—high day—and
now the scene of shame, the scene of sorrow, begins. The
multitude, excited by their leaders, demand his execution;
and, in answer to their blood-thirsty clamors, the victim
is led forth. His body, lacerated with cruel stripes, seems
one gushing wound; yet that bleeding body and thorn-
pierced brow awakens no pity in the breasts of his relentless persecutors. Ten thousand eyes glare fiercely upon
him—ten thousand voices rend the heavens with the shout
of, "Crucify him! crucify him!" as, with fiendish exultation,
they behold him delivered to their will. And now the living tide presses to the city gate; the priest, the scribe, the
publican, the Pharisee, soldiers and civilians, rich and poor,
are all in that throng, all animated by the same thirst for
blood, all joining in bitter execrations, all striving to fill,
with unmingled bitterness, the cup of agony he is called
upon to drink; and yet no malediction falls from the lips
of that meek sufferer; no bright-armed legions are called
from the skies, to spread destruction through that ungodly
throng; but, as a sheep led to the slaughter, with painful

step and slow, he urges his way up the rugged steep of Calvary. The goal of his earthly course is reached; his unresisting form is nailed to the cursed tree; the cross is upraised, and the spotless victim hangs on high; and for a season the powers of darkness seem to triumph. The turbaned priest mocks him in his bitter agony; the Pharisee smiles in scorn, the rabble revile and insult the dying victim.

> " Still from his lip no curse hath come,
> His lofty eye hath looked no doom,
> No earthquake's burst, no angel brand,
> Curses the black, blaspheming band."

No; but from those pale lips, quivering with anguish, issue the kind, compassionate words: "Father, forgive them;" and thus, in agony, he hung, bleeding, suffering, dying; he bowed his head, cried, "It is finished," and died for us; and it is in this scene that we must look for the full import of the words "God so loved the world that he *gave* his only-begotten Son."

But why all this Divine compassion, all this love, and all this woe? The answer is: "That whosoever believeth in him should not perish, but have everlasting life." Not that all our race will be saved because Jesus died; not that the unbelieving and disobedient will be forced to the heaven they have striven to avoid; not that the proud scoffer and despiser of God's Son will be saved by that blood he now spurns and tramples upon; but that whosoever *believeth*, may come to Christ and live. But does a mere acceptance of the truth set forth in the text save? No; the sinner must trust in the Crucified One; must love him who laid down his life for his sake; must prove his love and trust, by obeying his commandments; for the faith that leads not to love and all holy obedience, is not the faith of the Gospel. But what is meant by the phrase "Not perish?" Does it mean, "Shall not die?" Surely not, for believers and unbelievers alike taste of death, and are laid in the narrow mansion appointed for all the living. The *perishing*, from which the believer is to be rescued, is more than the death of the body. It is the despair, the remorse, the unutterable woe, the bitter pang of the second death, which all shall know who despise the gift of God's great love, and, by their unbelief and consequent disobedience, exclude themselves forever from the paradise above. The believer in the Son of God, however, has more to expect than a mere escape from the woes consequent upon disobedience; for it is not only declared "that he shall not perish," but the gracious promise is added, "that he shall have everlasting life"—a life not of endless duration only, but a life of eternal blessedness in the presence of Him who makes heaven glorious and the angels glad. The society of the prophets, the apostles, the martyrs, and all the pure in heart; a place near the crystal stream that flows from beneath the throne; the fruit and the shade of the tree of life; exemption from sickness, sorrow, and tears; the harp of praise, the crown of glory, the palm of victory, everlasting joys, eternal songs, all the heart can wish—nay, more than the loftiest thought can conceive of blessedness, are all included in the promise of everlasting life—the inheritance of the believer in Jesus.

A word to those who have not availed themselves of the merciful provisions of the Gospel of peace, and we have done. You have seen the wonderful display of love which God has made, and all this was done for you. You have seen the Lamb of God bleeding, groaning, agonizing, dying, not to save friends, but to secure happiness for his foes. Will God permit you to slight all this love, and all

this sorrow, and yet hold you guiltless? Will you steel
your hearts against all that God has done and Christ has
suffered? Amid all those manifestations of tender compassion, will you force your way down to ruin, and madly
seek that perdition from which the Redeemer died to save
you? Will you still trample under foot his loving-kindness
and tender mercy, and expose yourself to all the unspeakable horrors of death eternal? Stop, I entreat you! Be
persuaded by your soul's peril, by the Savior's blood and
tears. If you shrink from the responsibilities of a follower
of Christ, think, for a moment, of the fearful responsibilities of his enemies. If you shrink at the difficulty of obedience, think of the danger of disobedience. If the weight
of the cross appall you, think, O think, of the brightness
of the unfading, the immortal crown! God loves you;
can you doubt it, when you look upon the cross, and its
bleeding victim? Christ loves you; can you doubt it,
when, for you—

> " He left his starry crown,
>   And laid his robes aside;
>   On wings of love came down,
>   And wept, and bled, and died?"

Can you doubt it, when, through his Gospel, he is ever
crying: "Come unto me?" Can you stay away, when he
says: "He that cometh unto me, I will in no wise cast
out?" Turn, then, from all your sins away, "for the
wages of sin is death." Turn to the Savior, believe in
him, love him, obey him; "for the gift of God is eternal
life through Jesus Christ our Lord."

CHARLES LOUIS LOOS.

CHARLES LOUIS LOOS was born, December 22, 1823, at Woerth-sur-Sauer, Department of the Lower Rhine, France. His father's name was JACQUES G. LOOS, and he was also a native of France; his mother was a native of Bavaria, consequently, German.

The early life of CHARLES, in France, was spent, after his fourth year, in attending the academy in his native place, until his departure for the United States, in 1834. His father, who was an enthusiastic Republican, left France for America, in 1832, to find a home for the family. The family followed in the fall of 1834, and, when they reached the United States, found the father sick at New Franklin, Starke County, Ohio, where, in a short time, he died.

While he was in France, CHARLES had been educated in both the French and German languages, and his knowledge of these enabled him soon to become acquainted with the English. His family belonged to the Lutheran Church, and he was trained religiously by a pious grandmother, in whose family he was reared. He has never ceased to recognize the blessed influence of his early religious training, and thinks he is largely indebted to it for becoming a preacher of the Gospel.

In the fall of 1837, he was confirmed in the Lutheran Church; in a few months afterward he became acquainted with the Disciples, of whom there was a Church at Minerva, five miles from his home. He at once began to examine their religious position, and, having become satisfied that it was in accordance with the teaching of the Word of God, in 1838, at a meeting held by J. WESLEY LANPHEARE, he was immersed by JOHN WHIT-ACRE. This caused great bitterness and opposition among his Lutheran relatives; but he had taken the step under an earnest conviction of duty, and did not stop to consult with flesh and blood.

He taught school at sixteen years of age, and, at seventeen, began to preach in the vicinity of his home, and gave great promise of future usefulness.

In September, 1842, he entered Bethany College, where he graduated

(445)

in 1846, and remained in the college three years, as a teacher in the primary department. He was married at Bethany, July 6, 1848, to ROSETTA E. KERR, daughter of Rev. JOHN KERR, a Presbyterian minister, of Newry, Ireland. She had been in America four years.

In 1849, he was ordained to the work of the ministry, and removed to Wellsburg, Virginia, and preached for the Church at that place one year. In October, 1850, he removed to Somerset, Pennsylvania, where he remained five years, and, while there, in addition to his pastoral labors, edited a monthly periodical, called "The Disciple," for two years, and was principal of an academy for the same length of time. In January, 1856, he took charge of the Church corner of Eighth and Walnut streets, Cincinnati, also assisting in editing the "Christian Age." Having been elected President of Eureka College, Illinois, he moved there in January, 1857, and remained till September, 1858, when he returned to Bethany College, having been elected to the Chair of Ancient Languages and Literature in that institution. He still occupies that position.

Professor Loos is just five feet ten inches high, has dark hair, light hazel eyes, and weighs about one hundred and forty pounds. His personal appearance and manners indicate his French origin, while his speech is decidedly German. The influence of these two races is still more clearly marked in his mental characteristics. The studious thoughtfulness, the philosophical acumen, the plodding industry, and the generous hospitality of the German are happily blended with the volatile spirit, fire, and enthusiasm of the French. He is a deep, earnest thinker, and generally takes a broad, comprehensive view of things. As a public speaker, his style is very original. His gesticulation is rapid, and, when warmed up, his thoughts flow like a torrent. His whole soul seems to be absorbed in his theme, and sometimes, in his happiest moods, he speaks as if he were inspired.

GLORYING IN THE CROSS ONLY.

BY C. L. LOOS.

"But God forbid that I should glory, save in the cross of our Lord Jesus Christ, by which the world is crucified to me, and I unto the world."— GAL. vi: 14.

WE have selected this passage, as the thought which it contains, so nobly uttered by Paul, has ever been, and ever will be, a leading one for guidance in the right way—for confidence and joy, for strength and victory, to every true Christian heart. It is a bright torch in our hand, illuminating the path of our studies and contemplations in the field of Christian doctrine and Christian history. It interprets to us the evangelical voices of the prophets; reveals to us the glorious mysteries of our Savior's earthly history, and of the apostolic life and labors; and sends its illuminating beams across centuries and millenniums, to lead men, in every age, to a true understanding of the advancing history of the Church in doctrine and in life.

The strong deprecatory language of the apostle in our text, reveals to us that there are other objects than the Cross in which men glory; that all such glorying is not only "vain," and opposed to the spirit of the Gospel, but in the highest degree fatal to the fidelity and purity,

(447)

the joy and power, of the individual Christian life in the apostle, and to the work of God in his hand. So we are to understand and accept his words. It is strong, decisive language, most comprehensive, and that can not be mis-understood, uttered from an earnest heart, under the promptings of the Spirit of God. It is one of those great declarations of the apostle that often, in one word, reveal to us the great law of his own and of all Christian life, individual and associate. It stands before us not only as an oracle of the Holy Spirit, and, as such, demand-ing our acceptance; but, beyond this, it has a special sig-nificance and value to us, in revealing the law of life that controlled Paul as an individual Christian man, and made him what he was, and has been, for all ages, as a monu-ment of the grace of God; a " man of God," rising loftily in his marvelous devotion to Christ, in his life of labor, suffering, and victories for Christ's sake; for he speaks this directly of himself: " God forbid that I should glory, save in the cross of our Lord Jesus Christ, by whom the world is crucified unto me, and I unto the world."

The history of such a man is given to us as a rich in-heritance, and should ever be to us a special study, that we might not only rejoice in what he was in his wondrous life, but that we also might learn the mystery of such a life. It thus becomes a great *demonstration* of what the power of God is in the Gospel—that " power of God unto salvation," as he himself has called it—in so marvelously transforming the lion-like, fiercely-persecuting *Saul of Tar-sus* into Paul the Christian apostle, through a long life of unexampled endurances the lion-like hero, in his complete devotion in the Gospel as a " servant of Christ."

With such thoughts, then, we come to meditate upon the declaration of Paul that constitutes our text, looking at it in its double significance, on its negative, and on its positive side; what it forbids and deprecates, and what it rejoices in and commands as the true and chief object of our glorying.

It is our purpose, however, especially to discuss what is embraced in the *negative* side of these words, what Paul so strongly condemns, as it is this condemnation of all false glorying that gives such peculiar force to the declaration, and so strongly arrests our attention. The importance of this part of the study of our text must be evident to the thoughtful Christian mind. The very force of the language suggests it, and the careful tracing out of the field which it covers will fully reveal and justify this force of words. And let us keep steadfastly in mind that Paul's language is most exclusive. It allows no object of "glorying" whatever, in the strong sense which Paul gives to this word here, except the Cross of Christ. His denunciation, therefore—the denunciation of the Holy Spirit—covers all that lies outside of this. What, then, are these false objects of human glorying? To inquire into this shall be the special purpose of this discourse.

A few preliminary reflections are necessary to give the proper designed weight to what we intend to say.

Since man, in his first disobedience, by a direct inspiration of Satan, threw off the supreme and complete dominion of God over him, and conceived the rebellious, fatal thought of being his own master and god—his soul, in its disordered wanderings, has been, for the lack of this sovereign control from on high, the sport of sinful passions, by which, as evil powers, it has been urged on all sides to sin against God, and to work out its own ruin. There have been manifested by the universal implantation of the seeds of disobedience and sin universal *tendencies*

29

away from God, the central power of all that is true, and
good, and blessed, and toward all that is false, evil, and
destructive of human happiness.   These *tendencies* of our
evil nature—as they are alone the direct offspring of sin,
and as " all have sinned"—are as universal as humanity,
inherent in our "flesh," and as enduring as the ages of sin
on earth.   It is of great consequence well to note this
truth.   Wherever one being is that wears the form of
Adam, the sinful, the earthy—that is clothed in the flesh,
dwelling on *this* earth, and so surrounded by the world of
sin, these *common tendencies* to evil will be found as his
perpetual attendants.   They are neither Asiatic, African,
European, nor American; they are Adamic.   They belong
exclusively, neither to the past, the present, nor the future;
they belong to all time.   They are limited to no class;
and from them no party—whatever its creed, religion, or
its philosophy, whatever its attainments in knowledge or
life—is free.   They are the motions of sin, and will cling
to us all, whatever, in any respect, we may be, as long as
the liability to sin is with us ; as long as " we dwell in
houses of clay, and have our habitations in the dust;" as
long as that solemn and most significant saying of Christ
will be true of us: " The spirit indeed is willing, but the
flesh is weak!"—as long as this "burden" of life, of this
body and this world, is upon us.

Humiliating as it may be to human pride, yet it is most
needful, without ceasing, to impress this truth upon the
minds and hearts of men ; for such is our proneness to pride
and self-righteousness, such our trust in and boast of creed
and party perfection, amounting often to idolatry, that we
perpetually forget that we, as all others, are yet but men, are
yet in the flesh—this sinful flesh ; are yet under the motions
of sin, and liable to all the frailties and aberrations inherent

to our common Adamic nature, and that for the best there is no entire and final release until we are freed from this body. Advancement, indeed, there may be in the mighty conflict with these manifestations and powers of a sinful nature; glorious victories, by the grace of God, may be gained by those who are strong "by faith," with "strength in the Lord and the power of his might" "to overcome the world." But only when the battle of life is ended, and "mortality is swallowed up of life," will the great deliverance come. Especially can this immunity never be the lot of any class or party, however pure and perfect its creed. For whatever eminent attainments and progress in the Divine life individuals here and there may make, and do make, such attainments are never true in a like degree of *entire bodies of people*, representing every form and class of humanity. For any religious people to claim it, is a foolish and sinful vanity, that reveals an ignorance of the Bible, of the history of humanity in the Church, and especially *of themselves*. That the pure doctrine of Christ, so rarely understood and accepted, and an earnest, divinely-supported effort to live in conformity to it, gives us the surest and greatest triumphs over all these common evil tendencies of a fallen nature, is a truth so clear, so well accepted, that it need not for a moment be questioned. Purity of doctrine—of creed, if you choose—is to be insisted on for this very reason, with "all diligence," and is not for a moment to be compromised or lightly treated. It is an essential Divine means to salvation from sin. Let this never be overlooked. But—let us repeat it—the purest and fullest conception of Bible truth does not grant to us a perfect freedom from the liability to these evil tendencies, as it does not, and can not, grant us an immunity from sin. "If we say we have no sin we *deceive* ourselves, and the truth is not in us." This is a solemn saying. This is true of individuals; how much more of whole bodies. Let every Christian man ponder it well.

In direct application, now, to the subject before us, we say that among the most immediate and pernicious of these motions of sin—these *evil tendencies*—is that which, in direct opposition to God's command, leads us to false objects of "glorying." We use this term in our discussion in the sense in which it is employed by Paul in our text, denoting that to which we give the supreme devotion of our hearts, and which is the highest object of joy and glory to us. If "glorying" be employed in any weaker and more subordinate sense, it is not that which Paul here employs. This declaration of Paul is made particularly and directly in opposition to the Judaizers in the Galatian churches, who "gloried in the flesh." "As many of them as desire to have a fair show in the flesh, compel you to be circumcised, only (for the purpose only) that they might not suffer persecution for the Cross of Christ. For neither the circumcised themselves keep the law, but desire you to be circumcised that they may glory in your flesh. But for me," (and by way of contrast—for such is the literal force of the passage,) "God forbid that *I* should glory save in the cross of our Lord Jesus Christ, by which the world is crucified unto me and I unto the world." Observe well the grand reason which he attaches—the power of the Cross to emancipate him from the dominion of the world.

We look at this question only as it relates to our religious and spiritual life, and as it affects and is illustrated in the Church of Christ. With the history of the question as it lies outside of these limits, we have, at present, nothing to do.

The great significance of the words of Paul in our text is fully verified in the entire history of God's people. The endless aberrations from primitive truth, from the law and spirit of the Gospel, that characterize the annals of the great apostasy, and are signalized more or less in the records of every sect and party, are largely due to the violations of the great law of Christian life here announced by Paul—to glorying in false objects of devotion, in lesser objects than the Cross of Jesus Christ; so robbing our Lord of the glory due only to him, shutting out our souls from the power of the Cross, and thus perverting and debasing, by this idolatry, our own nature. To us, especially, who are laboring for a repristination of the Church after the pure law and spirit of the New Testament, it is of special moment to study well the character of this prolific source of evils in the Church.

The limits of our discourse allow us to speak only of some of the chief manifestations of this "carnal glorying." We select those that have been most prominently historic, and whose extended evil workings are obvious to all.

"Let no man glory in men," says Paul. Yet *to glory in men* is a constant tendency of our corrupt nature. We speak not now of this passion of hero-worship outside of the Church, that has made men make demi-gods of their fellows, and has led millions often willingly to subject their souls in base, slavish bondage, to the dominion of their idols. Every-where, among the most enlightened, as among the most degraded, the passion of men for this servile idol-worship is seen. But it were well if such a sinful proneness to idolatry had been limited to the secular world. This could not, however, be expected. It is an *Adamic* sin, inherent to the *human*. In the bosom of the Church of Christ we see it also manifested, and that

through the entire course of its history.   Let us consider
it for a moment in its charaĉter and evil workings.

In the first place, *it is positively prohibited by the Holy
Spirit:* "Let no man glory in men."   To do so, then, is
to violate, in a direĉt and positive way, an express law of
God.   The Holy Spirit would not so severely and exclusively denounce this sin, were it not a sin, and were its effeĉts
not pernicious to the cause of God.   These evil effeĉts are
manifold.   *This glorying in man enslaves the minds and souls of
men.*   It clothes the very objeĉts of this hero-worship with
perfeĉtions not theirs, and hides or sanĉtifies their defeĉts
and errors.   It makes men ready willingly to receive as authoritative, the opinions, expositions of doĉtrine, and spiritual control of their *masters,* often to the rejeĉtion of the
highest and most salutary truths.   It enchains, with the
ipse dixit of the master, the precious liberty with which
Christ has endowed his people.   This liberty, this glorious
gift of God, permits and commands us to push our inquiries, uncontrolled but by the limits of the law of God, onward and onward evermore, into the infinite treasures of
the wisdom and knowledge of God, and so to satisfy our
souls' hungering and thirsting after the light and life, the
truth and love, the joys and the glories, of Heaven.   But
this base idolatry confronts us perpetually with the demands of submission to the law of the *master's* attainments
and opinions, commanding abjeĉt homage to these—making these a hitherto, beyond which no man must proudly
venture; thus basely seeking to enslave the noblest inspirations and aspirations of the free Christian soul, to which
it has been awakened by the freedom with which Christ
has made it free, to the finite, the *human,* when it should
bow to the infinite, the unerring *Divine* alone.   This
erring *human,* beset as it is, in every possible case, with

weaknesses, prejudices, and errors, even in the highest examples of wisdom, of knowledge, and piety, can never, must never, be allowed to control this lofty freedom of the Christian soul—a freedom, the glorious consciousness of which is a supreme joy that *the slave* can never feel, and gives the soul unwonted strength that he can never know. It bears it upward, as upon wings, in the consciousness of *right*, and of a sublime energy to ascend in the pathway of truth. This grand highway of the Bible, opened to man, to lead him ever onward, and ever upward, to the throne of the Eternal, must not be obstructed by human idols, made so by foolish men.

Such false homage to the human *debases* the soul. The freest and fullest development of all that is great and good, pure and lofty, in man, is possible only where the fullest freedom, limited only by the sovereign law of God, is found. But to subject the soul to the human, cripples it in its strength, cultivates narrow-mindedness, prejudice, and the love of ignorance. It also inspires a spirit of wicked tyranny; for none are such tyrants as those who are willing and degraded slaves themselves. To see this, look but for a moment at the soul-and-mind-emasculated Catholic, monkish devotee, who, in dark and vacant spirit, crouches before his superior, in the abjectness of his slavery, spiritless as a corpse—and *there* is a tool of tyranny, fearful and terrible, as he is ignorant and degraded.

There is another evil effect that this "glorying in men" but seldom fails to produce on the objects themselves of this servility. In spite of all the better promptings of wisdom and true piety, this perpetual praise and adulation, this constant incense-burning and submission before them, will often beget in them an extravagant, false notion of their wisdom, their knowledge, power, and authority. It makes them, in the end, expect, and not sel-dom *demand*, the homage as a right which they have so long been accustomed to receive. It is a dangerous and evil thing to make men taste the power of authority, so sweet to our unfortunate nature. Be not surprised at this. We are all but men; and as a habitual life of slavery generally ends in making really a *slave* out of a *man*, so also, in like manner, a long-enjoyed, easily-yielded homage and domin-ion, finally begets the love and assertion of it.

Finally, this "carnal glorying in men"—an error undy-ing as sin, with millenniums on its brow—is yet vigorous for evil, in its Protean shapes, to-day as of old! It would have made the Nazarene prophet a king, from the falsest of motives, entirely ignorant and regardless of his real character as the true Messiah. It made fierce assaults on the infant Church in the very day of the apostles, and with the most specious pretenses. One gloried in Paul, another in Cephas, another in Apollos. It has made man, from age to age, in servile abeyance to the tyrannous behests of this passion of slavery, subdue in his own heart, and at-tempt to subdue in the hearts of others, the best convic-tions of truth that, in a loud voice, demanded utterance for God and humanity. It is a prolific fountain of injustice to men often the purest and the best, and is the origin of strifes and ugly-hearted factions. It often fastens the chains of mental and spiritual slavery on generations; and, above all, turns men away from Christ, to "worship the creature rather than the Creator!"

Man must bow to God alone! How the soul, that hungers and thirsts after God and his truth, revolts at these base attempts of weak man to fetter it in its progress to a fuller knowledge, and to higher enjoyments of the blessed Gospel of Christ!—these attempts to awe into silence and slavish, creeping fear and submission, free and noble spirits, by the idolatrous, tyrannous utterance of other names than God and his Christ!   Let the soul be early taught and disciplined—especially in all that concerns its religious life, in all that concerns its relations to God— to bow in deepest homage and submission only to the *Divine*—never to the *human!*   And when foolish man is disposed thus basely to bow to the human, even in its highest perfections, say to him: "See thou do it not!   These are but thy fellow-servants.   Bow to God only."

It is the voice of the Holy Spirit, in the Word of God and in the heart of every regenerate man, to thank God for the men who have been, in every age, his true chosen servants; to esteem them highly for their works' sake, and to seek to emulate their eminent examples.   He that is most enlightened by the law and Spirit of Christ, and who has drunk deepest into the inspirations of the words of Paul in our text, will feel this most, and do the best. Above all others, will he rejoice at those great men of God, who, foremost in the ranks of God's people, "have fought the good fight" against a gainsaying, apostate generation; and who have boldly taught and defended the truth of the Gospel; called men back to the pure doctrine and life of the New Testament; and who will, in the eternal world, "shine as the stars forever and forever."   All this it is our joy and our duty to do.   But to place our souls in bondage to their words; to "glory" in them; to do homage to them, with a glorying and a homage due only to Christ the Crucified, is slavery, idolatry, and sin.

Another form of false devotion, which is also one of these *common tendencies* of our sinful nature, is *to glory in party*.   This sect devotion, this selfish party pride and bigotry, is one of the rifest vices all over Christendom, and deserves to be especially noted in its evil influences. *It keeps our eyes blinded to our own defects, in doctrine, faith, and life.* "*Our* views, *our* faith, *our* conduct," as a party, must be justified, as they *now* are. No man must raise even a doubt, or suggest any improvement or progress. If any one among us does not so "glory," and burn perpetual incense, as we do, to this party idolatry, let him be marked as false, and be denounced at once; shake the party lash over him; conjure up before him the fearful phantoms of party vengeance. This evil spirit dooms a people to narrowness, stuntedness, weakness—to all the fatal effects of mental and spiritual slavery. And among every people there are always, in abundance, these devotees to mere party, and they are always among the greatest *human* enemies religion has. It requires the least mind, the least intelligence, piety, and goodness, to be such a poor sectary.

It prevents us from looking in the proper light at our fellow-beings. We can not, with this bad spirit, do justice to them. It fills us with the evil passions of jealousy and hate toward men that "are not of us," and makes us commit endless wrongs against them, and to sin against God, and against the Spirit of the Gospel. *It makes men indifferent to the means adopted to advance the party.* The mere sectary glories in numbers, in numerical predominance, in ecclesiastical, triumphant superiority; and, as the motive and the end are purely carnal, so the means adopted must necessarily be chiefly so. All is justified that advances "our Church;" all is denounced that opposes it. It is not a chief matter to the sectary to have souls converted to Christ, saved, and purified, redeemed from the world, and fitted for heaven. His highest aim and glory is in the outward triumph of seeing men join *his* Church. All his ambition is utterly carnal. Yet all this time this poor, blinded victim of this carnal passion imagines that he is fighting for God, and "for the faith once delivered to the saints;" and it is often beyond the power of God and man to make him see his error.

But, above all, it keeps us from Christ, and makes us sin against him; for, this false object of our pride, this evil spirit toward mankind which it inspires, this blindness to our own defects and sins, and the general self-righteousness it begets and nourishes—all prevent us from knowing and feeling the need, the object, the power and blessings of the Cross of Christ, which ever reveals to us our own imperfections and sinfulness, calls us to love God and man, and teaches us that a "*new creature*" alone avails before God.

The devotion to Christ and his Cross, expressed in the text, alone will save us from this debased form of idolatrous glorying. Let us beware of this fatal error, so delusive in appearance, but whose real form and life have ever been so ugly and repulsive, and whose ripe fruits so destructive to the true interests of the cause of Christ. Wide and fearful has been its power over the souls of men, and very stubborn its life and endurance. And let us remember—and this especially for our own sakes, that it is a *human, Adamic* sin, having its origin and home in our common nature; and, therefore, let us be wisely and jealously on our guard, lest we also be tempted and led away after the same manner of sin.

We must not mistake this unhallowed party bigotry for the pure love and devotion due from every true Christian to his brethren and the Church and cause of Christ. The partisan glories only in external prosperity; but the true child of God in that which is real, the spiritual prosperity

of the Church.   His great joy is to lead men to Christ,
to see his brethren become daily wiser and better, "growing in grace, and in the knowledge of our Lord and Savior
Jesus Christ."   To this end he prays and labors that they
may see their imperfections and sins; that these may be
remedied and put away, and the Church put on her beautiful garments of truth, holiness, and love, and, in the
strength of the Lord, go forth to conquer, "fair as the
moon, clear as the sun, and terrible as an army with banners."

Again: let not an ill-natured, hateful, carping fault-find-
ing, that is devoid of all love and hope, and of all attachment to God's people; an all-despising, evil-speaking
against the Church, be mistaken for a pure purpose to
see and correct the errors in our midst, that God may be
glorified among us.   Paul, however clear his eye, and ready
and bold his voice, to see, rebuke, and correct the defects
and sins of the brethren and churches, yet always revealed
the fidelity and nobility of his heart in a generous appreciation and love of God's people.   This we demand
in every man among us; and the censor that does not show
these noble qualities must expect a just and prompt rejection of his censorship.

Another *common evil tendency* is to *glory in doctrines*.   This
very ready error is to be found boldly on the surface every-
where throughout the whole history of the Church.   It is,
indeed, one of the *most* common of the unfortunate aberrations of the human mind manifested in Christian history.
Men very early, in the first years of the Church, began
to grow in very devoted love with favorite doctrines, and
mistook thus, altogether, the true object proposed in our
religion, of our faith and our love, our trust, joy, and
glorying.   *It is substituting the means and the statement of*

the object, for the final object itself to be reached by these means.
This tendency shot into revolting, desolating maturity in
one form in ancient Gnosticism. It makes men single out
some doctrine or dogma as the object of their blind, idolatrous adoration and apostate glorying. We truly call it
idolatry and *apostasy*; for men's hearts, by it, stray away
from Him as the only true object of our devotion. *It makes
the heart vain, intolerant, and impious.* How often do we
see men rudely, and almost impiously, carry on a carnal
warfare among men, not out of love to Christ and humanity, not glorying and rejoicing, like Paul, in a crucified
Redeemer, but in a *doctrine*, having nothing but this doctrine and its triumphs in their eyes and hearts. These
men only aim to convert men to their doctrines, and not
to Christ. With them the favorite doctrine, and not
Christ, is the first and the last, the alpha and the omega,
the beginning and the end; that which was, and is, and is
to come for evermore. The salvation of *souls*, the rescuing
of men from *sin*, as brands from the eternal burning; the
preparing of the spirits of men for the eternal holiness of
heaven; the love of God and men in Christ, that "con-
strains" men to the glorious work of the Gospel—all these
are things to which these doctrine-idolaters are strangers.
Therefore, also, it is not seldom the case that when their
glorying in doctrines has burnt out its earth-born flame,
their faith, their joy, and hopes are at an end, and their devotion and labors are over. With the novelty of the doctrine, which was their only source of life and inspiration,
their zeal, too, passed away. That deep, exhaustless fountain of everlasting life and power which is found only in
Christ, they knew not, and had never drunk from. Such men
are those mere creed-devotees, who often, for their creeds,
written or unwritten, long or short, will hate and lie, cal-

umniate and scandalize, crucify and burn, all the time far away from Christ, his truth and his love. See, for example, those two men in the pulpit, in discussion. Observe in their eyes, and on their lips, the play of every carnal passion; note the low trickeries, the vulgar legerdemain, the shallow and dishonorable fallacies, the unmanly insinuations against each other, the debasing appeals to party prejudices and hatreds—all so gross and revolting that the generous soul turns away with loathing and sorrow. And what, think you, are these two gladiators debating about? Do not be startled; they are vigorously discussing the question, *How the Holy Spirit operates in the conversion and sanctification of men!*—and both these valiant doctrine-defenders utter strangers to the Spirit of God and its blessed influence!

Doctrines do not save us; we are saved by Christ. Doctrines do not cleanse us from our sins; it is the efficacious blood of Christ. We are not converted to doctrines, but to God. We do not believe in doctrines, but in Christ. We are not baptized into them, but into Christ. We do not hope in them, trust in them, glory in them, but in Christ Jesus the Lord.

He that makes a doctrine the object and end of his glorying errs, whether that doctrine be true or false. But it is the testimony of all experience, and a logical result, that such glorying soon perverts and corrupts a true doctrine into a false one. We say, Give up not one jot or tittle of heaven's holy truth. Contend earnestly for it. Make ever a broad, impassable distinction between the truths of the Bible and human errors. But remember, all these Divine *lights* are only designed to illuminate your pathway to Christ and his Cross; they are but the Divine forces to bring you to him. Reserve the worship and glorying of your redeemed, joyful soul for him alone, as the *End* of all. Rest not with the doctrine; bow not before it. Never stand still till you have arrived at the feet of Jesus on the Cross; and thence, by the power of the Cross, press forward to the eternal throne of Him who is the "King of kings and Lord of lords."

And there is yet another prominent form of this carnal glorying, another one of these *common tendencies* of a sinful nature, and than which none is more fatal to the spiritual life in the individual Christian man, or to the general cause of Christ on earth. It is that which glories in *human reason*; that "enemy of Christ and all righteousness," denominated, in modern days, *Rationalism*. It sets up in Religion, in the Bible, and in the Church, human reason as the sovereign monarch, as the human idol before whom all must bow, "of things in heaven, in the earth, and under the earth," of things in time and in eternity. Proudly it has sought to enthrone itself in the temple of God, showing itself that it is God." (2 Thess. ii: 4.) Before its sovereign dictates and decisions all things must give way. In the interpretation of the Word of God, all things that are not in harmony with *its* carnal wisdom must be branded as false, and blotted out. Nothing so sacred, nothing so awfully Divine, nothing so direct and plain in the words of the Holy Spirit, that its impious, destructive criticism, its *proud human judgment* can not degrade, dishonor, and rob of all its sacredness, its Divine power, and drag down to its own low conceptions of truth and *reasonableness*. It is, by way of pre-eminence, *the power of impiety*. It is, historically, in the directest manner, of Satanic origin, having the spirit of the pride of the fallen archangel as its essential life. It was the inspiration and burden of the first temptation. "God alone is not the supreme, sovereign judge of right and wrong, of 'good and evil.' You yourselves, as *men*, have within yourselves this sovereign wisdom. You yourselves, as *men*, can 'be as gods,' knowing good and evil; and what God has said, you must interpret in harmony with *your reason, and the dictates of your lusts*, even if it be to the exact *inversion of his words.*" Such was the burden of the tempter's words, and such has ever been, in essence, in spirit, and often in exact form, the voice of this Rationalism.

Its voice is that of the siren, flattering to the easily-deluded ear of man. Its approaching step is covert and stealthy, as of the serpent, its prototype in Eden. Its purpose is concealed, but deadly. The fruit it offers to human taste is "fair to behold," and pleasant to the carnal, sinful appetite. Woe to him that heeds not the voice of warning; that makes not God, and his direct word, in its plain, obvious meaning, his defense, as did Christ in *his* temptation! Woe to him who, with evil lust, tastes of the fatal fruit! It will turn to gall and wormwood within him, and kill off the life of Christ in his soul.

Of the terribly destructive history of Rationalism within the last century it is not our purpose here to speak. It is not necessary. This history is now read, and known, and acknowledged of all men. We stop only to note, as precisely in place here, one important and most significant fact in the history of Rationalism. And that is, *its fierce enmity to the Cross of Christ*. This has been the special point of its most violent and most incessant attacks. All that characterizes the Cross; all that belongs to its history and significance—the hopeless sinfulness and depravity of man; the perfect Godhood of Jesus Christ; the true character of sin; the Biblical doctrine of the motive and of the necessity and purpose of the atonement;—all this, that together constitutes the doctrine of the Cross, and alone gives it its meaning and power, has been, and is now, the object of especial offense to the spirit of Rationalism. As it was to the Jews and to the Greeks of old, an offense and a foolishness, so it is to this spirit of proud glorying in human reason to-day. Nothing in all the history of the Church, not the Pope himself, has set itself more proudly in opposition to God and his Word, in the very bosom of the Church itself, than this proud idolatry of Reason. But as of old, so now Paul would say, that "What to it, and to them that perish, is a stumbling-stone and foolishness, is to him, and to all that truly believe and are saved, the power of God and the wisdom of God." And what *they* despise, is to *him* the one chief object of glorying.

But will our *denouncing* these errors be a sufficient guarantee against our falling into them? By no means. It is the singular blindness that accompanies these *common* errors that they often who are loudest in their denunciation, are the first to run the deepest into them. So the apostle speaks of those boasting of and promising liberty, who are themselves, all the while, the meanest slaves of the basest passions. The Quaker, while solemnly denouncing the vanity and obsoleteness of all external forms, is, for generations, notoriously and servilely in bondage to the very cut and color of his garments, the shape of his hat, and the obsolete forms of his speech, so that he can be easily discerned, even from afar, by his "outward appearance." The deluded or depraved victims of the spiritualism of our land and of our day, have, long since, demonstrated to all that their pretension to the *spiritual* is only an excuse and a cloak for a swifter and more immediate descent to the vilest carnality. And so in other cases innumerable.

30

Mistaking the *denunciation* of an error for freedom from it, is one of the most every-day facts and follies of human life. Let us not forget this. The closest and most candid self-scrutinizing; the most earnest and constant appeals for Divine aid; and the fullest acceptation and realization in all our soul of the words of our text, accompanied by a never-ceasing watchfulness over ourselves, alone will save us from these and other like fatal errors.

Christ alone is the light and life of men; therefore, to them to whom he is not, as in our text, symbolically represented, the only source of light and life in religion, this religion is only a cold world of darkness and death. Falsest of false, a vanity of vanities, a bitterest deception, that blots out the celestial glories, and tears out the life-giving, life-disseminating heart of the Gospel of our redemption—is every pretense of Christianity, however fair its voice and carnally attractive its form, in which Christ the crucified is not the sole joy, strength, and glory, the beginning and the end, the first and the last!

And let us not be misunderstood as to what we mean by "the Cross," by "Christ the crucified;" for here again, as every-where else, fatal errors are made. Do we mean by it only, or chiefly, a noble example of life and death given to humanity; one who, by his pure life, his teaching of sublime, heavenly wisdom, and his martyr sufferings, is worthy of the highest admiration, the most ardent love, and the most generous emulation of men, and that saves men by his example of life and death, and the inspirations it affords? Is this the sum and burden of our joy, our glorying, and our hope? No! a thousand times, no! None of these cheating acceptations of Christ, that rob him of his chief glory, and us of our chief joy and hope—is what Paul means, and what we rejoice in, though never so beau-

tifully and delusively expressed. It is Christ the crucified, as the God-man, the Savior of men, "the Lamb slain
from the beginning," who shed his *atoning, expiating, sac-
rificial* blood for the sins of the world, as *the only price that
purchased our redemption*, and thus to man the only hope
in life and death. With the proud, Christ-degrading ne-
gations of Unitarianism, in every possible shape and form,
from that highest type of ancient Arianism to that lowest
of modern Socinianism, the words of Paul, in our text,
and our acceptation of it as our joy and confidence in its
teaching and spirit, are forever utterly irreconcilable.

Let this Divine and blessed Redeemer—as we see him
and hear him on earth, "going about every-where doing
good," by his heavenly teaching and his heavenly works
of love and power; as we behold him on the Cross, suffering for a sinful world ; and as we see him in heaven triumphant—ever be our only joy, honor, strength, and
hope, our exceeding great reward, our present and everlasting glory. And may this holy and single devotion to
him, filling all our soul, be the star of our life, to guide
us, finally, to his own eternal dwelling-place in the Father's
presence, "where there is fullness of joy, and to his right
hand, where there are pleasures for evermore."

"God forbid that our souls should ever glory, save in
the cross of our Lord Jesus Christ, by which alone the
world is crucified to us, and we to the world!" *Amen.*

Ever Truly Your
Isaac Errett

ISAAC ERRETT.

A MONG the preachers and writers of the nineteenth century who have
plead for a return to primitive Christianity, the subject of this notice
stands pre-eminently among the most distinguished. For more than thirty-
five years he has been connected with the Disciples, and, during the greater
portion of that time, has been an earnest, able, and successful advocate of
their plea for reformation.

ISAAC ERRETT was born in the city of New York, January 2, 1820.
His father was a native of Arklaw, county of Wicklow, Ireland, and his
mother was a native of Portsmouth, England. His paternal grandfather
was shot down in sight of his own house during the Irish rebellion of
1798. His immediate parents were both of Protestant families, and became identified with the Disciples in New York City as early as 1811—
the father being an elder in the original Church in that place. Hence, the
son was trained from infancy in the principles which he now cherishes,
and, in the spring of 1832, at Pittsburgh, Pennsylvania—where his mother
had moved soon after the death of his father, who died in 1826—when
only a little over twelve years of age, at a time when the Church was without preaching, under the instruction of his mother, he, in company with
an older brother, went forward and asked the privilege of baptism. He
was baptized by ROBERT McLAREN, one of the elders of the Church.

He now became a diligent student of the Word of God, and, under many
embarrassing circumstances, made constant and encouraging progress. From
the time he was ten years old, he has been dependent upon his own personal
exertions for a living; hence, his respectable education has been gathered,
in the midst of toil and care, by dint of untiring, industrious application.
While laboring as farmer, miller, lumberman, bookseller, printer, school-
teacher, and editor, he has never ceased to augment his stock of useful
knowledge, and to use whatever opportunities he had for the development and discipline of his mental powers.

He commenced preaching in the city of Pittsburgh, Pennsylvania, in
the spring of 1840, and soon gave promise of the distinguished position
which he has since held as a preacher of the Gospel. He enjoyed the

advantages of frequent and intimate association with WALTER SCOTT, THOMAS CAMPBELL, ALEXANDER CAMPBELL, and most of the early advocates of primitive Christianity in the West; and his association with these men was of incalculable advantage to him, for they not only gave him valuable instruction in the principles of the Reformation, but he was enabled, by coming in frequent contact with them, to draw inspiration from their lives and characters for the great work upon which he had entered.

His ministerial labors have been divided between the work of an evangelist and pastor. He was pastor of a church in Pittsburgh three years; New Lisbon, Ohio, five years; North Bloomfield, Ohio, two years; Warren, Ohio, five years; Muir and Ionia, Michigan, eight years; and Detroit, Michigan, two years. At all these points he was eminently successful, and, besides his regular pastoral labors, did considerable work in the general field. He removed to Warren, Ohio, in 1851, and, while there, was Corresponding Secretary of the Ohio Missionary Society three years; and it was he who first put that society into systematic and active operation. In 1856, he removed his family to Ionia County, Michigan, and, while laboring to build up a congregation at that point, he was prevailed upon to take the Corresponding Secretaryship of the American Christian Missionary Society, which position he held three years, and succeeded in bringing the society to a degree of prosperity which it had never before reached. When he resigned the Secretaryship, he was appointed first Vice-President, and afterward presided at the annual meetings of the Society until 1866, when he was elected President. This, however, he at once declined. In the spring of 1866 he removed to Cleveland, Ohio, where he now resides, and edits the " Christian Standard," a religious weekly published in that city.

Brother ERRETT's personal appearance is striking and prepossessing. He is about six feet one inch high, has dark auburn hair, light gray eyes, and a well-developed muscular organization. As a public speaker, he has few, if any, superiors. His language is chaste and copious, containing an unusually large per cent. of Saxon words; his gesticulation easy and natural, but his voice, though well under control, has not volume enough to give full force to his beautiful and stirring thoughts. His writings, like his sermons, are full of strong and rugged points, and are frequently interspersed with brilliant passages of exquisite beauty that will compare favorably with many of the finest word-paintings in the English language.

In the social circle he is companionable, but not a very good conversationalist. He needs the inspiration of an audience, or the quiet solitude of the study, to bring out his full strength; hence, while he is pleasant in company—full of wit and humor—he does not appear there to the best advantage.

THE LAW OF PROGRESSIVE DEVELOPMENT.

BY ISAAC ERRETT.

"And he said, So is the Kingdom of God, as if a man should cast seed into the ground, and should sleep and rise, night and day, and the seed should spring and grow up, he knoweth not how. For the earth bringeth forth fruit of herself; first, the blade; then the ear: after that, the full corn in the ear. But when the fruit is brought forth, immediately he putteth in the sickle, because the harvest is come."—MARK IV: 26–29.

THE Law of Progressive Development is operative alike in nature and in grace. I have no confidence in the development theory which seeks to trace up all the forms of animated nature from monads, by regular development or spontaneous generation, and even to give the history of worlds and universes of matter, from a nebulous infancy through a patient growth into the solar and stellar magnificences that now gem the heavens. This stupendous effort to banish a personal Creator and to subdue all things—even the workings of mind, the movements of nations, and all historical developments, to the operation of blind and resistless forces of materialism, is at war with the fundamental idea of a Divine revelation, and can have no sympathy where faith rests in a Divine Creator, who spake, and it was done; who commanded, and it stood fast. Yet the fact that such a theory commands the advocacy of

(471)

distinguished and honored names in science and literature, shows that there is a sufficient groundwork of facts to invest it with plausibility. What geology has unfolded of a sublime series of creations and destructions in the history of our earth, and the just analogies of nature, which proceed from this starting point, render it probable that this law of progressive development pervades the universe. However this may be, we are certain in regard to its operation in and on our own globe, in the realms of matter and of mind. Life is growth, development, from a germ of existence through successive stages of infancy, childhood, youth, to manhood's perfection: "first the blade, then the ear, after that the full corn in the ear." And the kingdom of heaven, in the text, is likened to this; thus teaching us that the laws of the kingdom of grace are analogous to those of the kingdom of nature; that religion does not outrage the established laws of matter or of mind; that the volumes of nature and revelation are from the same author, in the same handwriting; and that the same principles of rational investigation, which we carry with us in the interpretation of the former, are equally legitimate and necessary in the interpretation of the latter.

It has long been a mischievous delusion that the operations of grace are, if not lawless, at least out of sympathy and out of harmony with the known laws of mind; that religion is not a science to be learned, or a life to be developed; that religious faith has nothing in common with other faith; that religious peace and happiness ignore all the established conditions of peace and happiness; that a touch of magic or of miracle flashes light on the mind, peace on the conscience, and joy on the soul; and that, like Minerva from the head of Jupiter, the child of God springs from the bosom of the supernatural, full-armed, into life.

It may be well, therefore, to examine the law of progress announced in the text, and, in its light, obtain more
satisfactory and profitable views of the ways of God to
man. We propose to examine the operations of this law

I. In the Gradual Unfolding of the Purpose of
God in the Plan of Redemption.

II. In the Development of Individual Life and
Character.

III. In the Historical Development of the Church.

Our purpose in this is not a complete elaboration of our
theme—for this the limits of a sermon will not allow—but
to furnish such outlines and landmarks as will enable the
reader to pursue the investigation for himself; giving him
such an insight into some of the laws and methods of the
Divine government as will assist him more intelligently to
survey, and more rationally to enjoy, the salvation of God.

I. The Gradual Unfolding of the Purpose of God
in the Plan of Redemption.

It has been with unbelievers a standing objection to the
plan of salvation, and a source of embarrassment to many
believers also, that the fullness of the Gospel was not communicated immediately on the fall of man. "Why," they
ask, "must four thousand years elapse before the Savior
appears? Why, for two thousand years must the favor of
God be confined to a single family and nation, while all
the rest of mankind are left to perish in their sins?" And
why, we ask in return, does this law of progressive development obtain at all? Why must man begin in puling infancy, and *grow* into manhood, slowly developing not only
his physical frame, but his mental and moral characteristics
likewise? Why is not knowledge flashed instantaneously

into the mind, rather than left to be acquired slowly and painfully through a thousand struggles and repeated failures? Why must we have toys for infancy, and object-lessons for childhood, and carry the learner patiently through elementary instructions before he can grasp broad generalizations, or master the mysteries of any science? Why do nations grow, and ages move in cycles? Why did nations, without a revelation from God, struggle so long in vain with the problems of duty and destiny? At the very time when this objection was most loudly urged, unbelievers were looking to geology, to find such revelations in the stone-book as would forever silence the pretensions of the Bible. But, lo! when these revelations were made, the same lesson of progressive development was written on every page; the same calmness and patience were everywhere traceable in the Divine Architect's plan of building a world. If we could say no more, we could be content in saying that this gradual unfolding of redemption is of a piece with the gradual unfolding of creation.

We are far from saying, however, that we are ignorant of any reason for this slow progression. Nay, we see reasons for it in redemption, that we could not plead in behalf of progressive development in creation. It is consistent with our best ideas of Omnipotence that a world or a universe of matter should be spoken into instant perfection of existence. But it is not consistent with our knowledge of the rational nature of man that Omnipotence should instantaneously redeem it from error and guilt. Omnipotence might, perhaps, instantaneously annihilate such a nature, but certainly can not instantaneously save it; because the salvation of a rational nature implies that the nature itself desires to be saved; that it is weary of sin; is conscious of its curse; has trust in a Savior; and penitentially returns to submission to the will of God. These are not the results of mere omnipotence. Some of them are results which can only flow from man's own experience. To know the whole bitterness and curse of sin; to know man's inability to redeem himself from its power and guilt; to attain to such a knowledge of human helplessness and hopelessness that a sinning race shall be willing to come, sin-sick and heart-broken, to cast themselves imploringly on the mercy of God—these are results which can only be reached through long and varied experiences, through repeated demonstrations, in human history, of man's depravity and helplessness, and of God's compassion and mercy. Therefore, when men did not like to retain God in their knowledge, he gave them up to their own ways, (Rom. i: 21–32,) until, like the prodigal son, their heritage wasted in riotous living, and every step plunging them into deeper want, they should be prepared to say, "*I will arise and go to my Father.*"

Meanwhile, Divine Wisdom set on foot such remedial measures as the condition of the race demanded, and developed these, step by step, during a long period of Divine forbearance, while the human experiment of self-government and self-redemption was pending. Let us glance at the landmarks which indicate this progressive development of Divine mercy.

1. A promise is made to the first sinful pair that the seed of the woman shall bruise the serpent's head. (Gen. iii: 15.) Here the seed of the Divine purpose is cast into the ground.

2. Abraham is chosen as the founder of a nation, with the promise, *In thy seed shall all nations be blessed.* (Gen. xii: 3.) Here the seed is germinating.

3. The Jewish nation appears, and is taken into cove-

nant with God, as a peculiar people. Here the blade
springs forth.

It was not for themselves, but for the sake of the apostate nations, that the Jews were elected to be a peculiar
people, that through them truth might be preserved and
disseminated, and the way be prepared for the ultimate
return of the prodigal wanderers. Hence their location
in the geographical center of the earth, as then known.
Hence God's movements, through them, on the most
powerful and enlightened nations of antiquity. It is
worthy of remark, that Jehovah's movements were at the
great centers of learning, religion, and authority—the ra-
diating centers of the world. Through Israel he moved
on Egypt and her idols, and radiated thence over the earth
the knowledge of the true God; and similarly on Nine-
veh, Babylon, Ecbatana, Susa, and thence on all the provinces of vast empires. The books of Esther, Ezra, Nehemiah, and Daniel, as well as many other portions of the
Old Testament, show how, through the Jews, alike in their
victories and defeats, as a powerful nation at home, or as
helpless captives abroad, knowledge was disseminated, sin
denounced, idolatry overturned, justice asserted, mercy
displayed, hopes of a coming Deliverer awakened, until, to
a much greater extent than a superficial reader of the Bible
would suppose, the leaven of Divine truth was deposited
with the nations. The blade is growing. Jewish and
heathen authors attest that, before the Messiah appeared,
a general expectation of a Divine Redeemer had been
awakened. Equally true is it, from all authentic testimonies, that at this time men were every-where weary of their
own experiments, and had been driven to the conclusion
that a Divine hand must save, or the race be hopelessly
abandoned.

A complete view of this subject would require us to notice the respective missions providentially assigned to other nations, all subservient to the one great purpose of preparing the world for the coming of the Savior—the golden thread stretching across the ages, on which all influential events were divinely strung; but our space forbids us to undertake the task.

4. Jesus is born. He comes when the world is waiting for him with eager expectancy; when the spread of the Roman empire has so far unified the interests of the nations as to prepare the way for the universal spread of the Gospel; when the Roman civilization is sinking in its dotage, and with it is departing the last hope of success in solving the problem of human regeneration; when human religions and philosophies have lost their inspiration, and over the ruins of ancient systems a shuddering skepticism dismally broods; when, from all quarters of the globe, men are looking with vague desire to the land of Judea for deliverance, and the wretched prodigals from all lands are sighing for a return to their Father's house.

The purposes of God are ripening. The stars in the Jewish firmament are paling. John the Harbinger, the morning star, joyfully heralds the approaching sun, in whose beams are to be found life and health for all peoples. The Son of God is made known. Gentile sinners and Samaritans seek him for the blessings of his love. The corn is in the ear; and, in a full knowledge of the speedy approach of the time when he shall draw all men unto him, he says : *Lift up your eyes and look on the fields, for they are white already to harvest; and he that reapeth receiveth wages and gathereth fruit unto life eternal, that both he that soweth and he that reapeth may rejoice together.* (John iv: 35, 36.)

Thus, while the Divine forbearance allowed ages to

come and go, waiting till a rebellious race should weary of its selfhood, and come back in submission to its Sovereign, Divine wisdom selected and employed individuals, families, tribes, nations, through whom to communicate his intentions and reveal his will. And step by step can we trace, through the history of four thousand years, the unfolding of the eternal and unchangeable purpose of God to save men by his Son, Jesus Christ.

This sketch, we are aware, is too brief to be satisfactory, except for starting inquiry. But it is sufficiently clear to prepare us for one conclusion of immense importance to all who would understand the Bible, namely, *the Old Testament is no longer a book of authority*. The stars shine no longer in presence of the sun. The blade and ear are no longer trusted in, after the full grain in the ear has been obtained. The revelations and ordinations of former ages were preparatory. They belonged to the infancy and childhood of the race. They were pictorial, ritualistic, adumbrative. The law was a pedagogue to bring men to Christ. But now that faith is come, we are no longer under the pedagogue. (Gal. iii: 24, 25.) The same God, who, at sundry times and in divers places, spoke unto the fathers by the prophets, has now spoken by his Son, not the words of a temporary law, but of the "everlasting Gospel;" and has established, not a kingdom to be shaken and destroyed, but a kingdom which can not be shaken. (Heb. xii: 28.)

Leaving this ante-christian development of the kingdom of heaven, we proceed to notice—

II. The development of Individual Christian Life and Character.

In this application of the text—and we do it no violence in thus applying it, for the principle is still the same, whether applied to individuals, societies, or nations—there are three things worthy of note.

1. There is a *seed*, containing the germ of all spiritual life, without which the fruits of righteousness and holiness can not be grown.   That seed is the word of God—the truth of the Gospel. (Luke viii: 11.)

2. There is a *soil* in which that seed must be deposited, to cause it to grow.   That soil is the human heart; and as "the earth bringeth forth fruit of herself"—automatically, by virtue of her native capacities, and through the certain, though mysterious, chemistry by which the ever-present God elaborates life, and bloom, and fruitfulness from the dull clod of the valley—so is the spiritual nature of man possessed of capacities for automatic development of the truth it has received.   The truth of God is adapted to our nature, and the soul "brings forth fruit of herself," by virtue of her own capacities and powers for receiving, digesting, and appropriating truth.   *It is this that clothes our rational nature with fearful responsibility.*

3. Men plant and water—God gives the increase.   We are at last dependent on Him who gives the seed-time and the harvest; who gives sunbeams, and showers, and all needful heavenly blessings to crown the labors of man with success, to multiply the seed sown, and increase the fruits of our toil.

4. The life that springs from this germ, through this soil, is feeble in its beginnings, and *grows* into completeness; "first the blade, then the ear, after that the full corn in the ear."

How sadly mistaken are our conceptions of religious life!   We have been taught to rely so much on religious experiences, and have listened to so many extravagant narrations of the miraculous transformations instantaneously

wrought, that we are constantly looking for the kingdom
to come "with observation," with signs and wonders, and
outward display.   We fail to learn that the kingdom of
God is *within* us, in the truth which an honest heart has
welcomed, in the faith to which that truth has led us.   We
look for the earthquake, tempest, and fire in which God
is not, and fail to hear the "still, small voice," in which
God is.

There will always be great variety of psychological manifestation attendant on conversion, because of the great
variety of physical organization, temperament, and education.   Yet, as a general rule, especially in Christian lands,
where we grow from infancy into the knowledge of the
Gospel, there will be found a silent working of truth in the
heart and conscience, and a growth into life, silent and gradual, but beautiful and progressive.   The New Testament
Scriptures every-where contemplate spiritual life as a
growth from small beginnings; as involving necessarily the
weakness of infancy, and the struggles of childhood, ere we
are prepared for the ripeness of manhood.   The child of
God, when born of water and Spirit, is but a babe.   The
faith and baptism that bring him into Christ but enable
him to *begin* to live in "newness of life."   And this life,
like all other life, depends for its perpetuation and development on food, air, and exercise.

1. Truth is the Christian's food, milk first, meat afterward.   *As new-born babes earnestly desire the pure, spiritual
milk, that you may grow thereby.* (1 Pet. ii: 2.) *Thy words
were found, and I did eat them; and thy word was unto me
the joy and the rejoicing of my heart.* (Jer. xv: 16.)

2. The atmosphere of the kingdom of God is a pure
atmosphere; we "live in the Spirit," and "walk in the
Spirit."   It is essential that we keep our place within the

limits of the kingdom ; for, outside its walls there are marshes of unbelief and carnality, whose malarious exhalations wither the life of all who inhale them.

3. The exercise to which we are called consists of the delightful activities of faith and love to which the example of Christ and of the primitive Church leads us.

All these are essential to the fullness of life. We may eat, and not thrive, if we live in a bad atmosphere. We may live in a pure atmosphere, and languish, if we refuse to eat, or if we eat forbidden fruit. We may have good food and pure air, and still be dwarfed, if we fail to exercise ourselves unto godliness—to employ all our ransomed powers to do good to man, and to give praise to God.

With these premises before us, we deduce some conclusions of practical importance.

1. Many fear that they were never converted, because there has been nothing extraordinary to mark their transit from death to life. But this arises from the use of human standards of conversion, and a foolish comparison of ourselves with others. The apostolic tests were different. *He that believeth that Jesus is the Christ, has been begotten of God.* (1 Jno. v: 1.) *Every one that works righteousness has been begotten by him.* (1 Jno. ii: 29.) *Every one that loves has been begotten of God.* (1 Jno. iv: 7.) *We know that we have passed from death to life, because we love the brethren.* (1 Jno. iii: 12.) If the kingdom of God is within us, and is like to a man that sowed seed in his field, we must have our eye on small beginnings, and test the genuineness of our *life* by the character of its *growth.* The first converts to Christ began with slender capital. They learned simply to put their trust in Jesus as their Lord and Savior, and, for his sake, to renounce their sins. They were then baptized into Christ, and placed in the Church—the

31

plantation of grace—where, from this germinal faith, they might, in God's own sunshine, watered with the dews of his love, and sustained by the Spirit's inspiring breath, develop the blade, the ear, the full corn in the ear.

2. Many doubt their acceptable standing, because they fall, in actual life, so far below their ideal. They have many imperfections, many conflicts with evil, and even many sins. This, they think, could not be if they were Christians; especially in view of the inspired declaration, *He that has been begotten of God does not commit sin.* (1 Jno. iii: 9.) But if Christian life is a *growth*, of course our attainments must fall below our ideal. Why doubt that the tender spear, that first breaks through the clod, is wheat, because you see no "ear" on it such as your ideal grainstalk has? It is *growing* to that. Are you *growing* in grace and in knowledge? Are you gaining additional victories over weakness and impulse? Is your hand growing steadier and more skillful in holding the helm to guide your vessel through the storm? Then remember that it is *first the blade, then the ear, after that the full corn in the ear.* Remember, too, that childhood is a period of struggle and of peril, and that the symmetry and strength of manhood are gained only through toil and conflict, overcoming opposition and failure. True, he that is begotten of God does not *work* sin; it is not his *vocation;* he pursues it not as his calling; that which he works at is righteousness. Yet he may be a feeble worker, and sometimes a failing one; but the greatest of all questions to settle is, *does he grow* in the right direction?

3. Many are living in the past. They have no growth. They had an overgrown infancy—a precocious piety—and now they are spiritual dwarfs. They have grand stories to tell of their conversion, and it is all they have to tell.

The abundant blossoms of their spring-time have brought
no fruitage. There was a blade of great promise, but it
never yielded grain in the ear. Beware of these preten-
tious beginnings. Mourn not if thy faith is like a grain
of mustard seed; only let it grow until it becomes a tree.

But we hasten to consider, in the last place, the operation of this law,

III. IN THE HISTORICAL DEVELOPMENT OF CHRISTIANITY.

The Jews, ignorant of this law, were looking for a kingdom to appear, in full-grown might and splendor, to command the instant submission of the nations. Yet Daniel
had predicted it as *a stone cut out of the mountain without
hands.* (Dan. ii: 34.) *Not by might, nor by power, but by
my Spirit,* (Zech. iv: 6,) was the decree of Jehovah, touching the erection of this spiritual edifice, which "*groweth*
unto a holy temple in the Lord." *The kingdom of God
cometh not with outward display,* (Luke xvii: 20,) said the
Teacher. Its sole original herald was an obscure Naza-
rite, in coarse garments, lifting up his voice in the wilderness, and soon arrested, imprisoned, and beheaded. Then
comes the lowly Nazarene, attended by a feeble band of
poor people. He spends a few years in works of mercy,
and in peregrinations through the land of Judea, to instruct the people. Then, without leaving a written speech
behind him, or a page of written history, or an organized
society, he yields himself meekly to a dishonorable death.
The shepherd is smitten, and the sheep are scattered.
Next, we see one hundred and twenty disciples assembled
in an upper room in Jerusalem. They are poor. They
are unlettered. They are unpolished. They are without
public influence. They are on their knees, in prayer and

supplication, waiting for the promised Spirit of Truth. The germ of all the life, dominion, and grandeur of the kingdom of heaven is in the keeping of that little band. When we remember that this was in the Augustan age, when Rome's imperial power and greatness filled all the world with awe; and then reflect that Rome's imperial grandeur, and the military prowess that supported it, and all that made that vast dominion the terror of foes, and the pride of citizens, has long since passed away, leaving to us only the hopeless wrecks of her greatness, and the melancholy history of her decline and fall; while the kingdom, whose fortunes lay sleeping in the hearts of that little assembly in Jerusalem, survives the decay of empires, of races, and of religions, sways the destinies of nations, and is to-day the most puissant of the moral forces at work in the world; we may well divorce our souls from the cheating splendors of material greatness and the triumphs of brute force, and bring our votive offerings to the King of Truth, whose victories are bloodless and immortal.

It was indeed a small seed—a diminutive lump of leaven— a little stone; but it has grown to be a great tree whose roots strike into every soil, and whose branches shelter nations and continents; it has leavened the literature, science, jurisprudence, and commercial, social, and domestic life of the most powerful and enlightened nations of the earth; it has broken in pieces the once worshipful tyrannies and superstitions of universal empires, and from a little stone is becoming a great mountain.

This, it is true, has not been speedily accomplished. The first springing of the blade was speedy and promising. But, as with the seed which the farmer sows in the autumn, which springs at once into beautiful life, the frosts of winter lock it up, and the snows of winter hide it away, and the storms

of winter howl over its grave, as if in dismal prophesy of
utter ruin, so that any one ignorant of the wonderful ways
of God would regard the labor and hopes of the husbandman an utter failure; so here, after the beautiful upspring-
ing of the seed of the kingdom in the first century, came
on the reign of a fierce winter of adversity, when the kingdom was hidden from the view of men, and the persecuting
rage of the nations swept over it, until to one unskilled in
the workings of Providence, the cause of Christ was a failure. But the spring's sweet influence comes, in nature's
regular course, and melts the ice-bands, and breaks the fet-
ters of frost, and opens the bosom of earth, so long locked
up in sullenness, to the sun's directer ray; and the quickened pulses of life thrill through all her frame, and her
hidden treasures of bloom, and fragrance, and fruitfulness
are brought forth to enrich and adorn the desolate surface
of the earth, and it is found, at last, that stern winter was
performing a necessary work, and helping on, in strange,
mysterious ways, the glories of the harvest-time. And so
in the moral world, after a long reign of wintry desolation,
during which it seemed as if truth had perished, the vernal
season of rejoicing came at last, heralded by such warblers
as Wyclif, Huss, and Jerome, who, like robins, came with
the first gleams of rosy light and the first breath of spring,
out from the darkness and the cold, sweet harbingers of
better times. There were, indeed, a few of God's min-
strels who had never ceased to sing. Away in the mountain solitudes of the Alps and the Appenines, hidden in the
deserts, caged up in the caves, God gave them "songs in the
night" which they never ceased to carol. Some of their
lays were sweet memories of the past, and some of them
gay prophecies of the coming glory of the kingdom. And
many a brave heart that lay bleeding in despair, weary of

watching for the morning, faithless of any returning spring-time, and ready to ask, on the brink of utter faithlessness, "Who will show us any good?" had been charmed into new hope and courage, and had risen for new toils and sufferings. And the spring-time came; and the blade, so long hidden, grew into vigor and fruitfulness. The Bible reappears; the Christ is again proclaimed Lord of the conscience and Savior of the soul. His quickening voice again goes forth, and nations spring into new life, and go after him, out of darkness into light—out of slavery into freedom—out of a dismal stagnation of soul into heroic activities and gloriously free adventures—out of weakness, and sin, and inglorious vassalage, into strength and righteousness, and the priceless treasures of civil and religious liberty. The Protestant Reformation, with all its blessed fruits of intelligence, liberty, and progress, was the spring-time of the Kingdom of God. The blade grows and the ear appears.

But "the full corn in the ear" has not yet been seen. Between spring and harvest there is a season of peril for the grain. It is subject to upheavals by frosts and thaws; to raids of insects, which burrow into the very heart and root of its treasures; to the sweep of storms and the tramp of beasts; out of all these perils we clutch with joy at last the golden sheaves. Analogous to this has been the history of the kingdom since Luther's Reformation. We can not trace a steady and prosperous growth. There have been many drawbacks, many sad failures, many heavy disasters; but still the fields wave in golden beauty and richness, and glow with promise of a coming harvest. The brightest day of promise is yet to come. We have seen the stone break the image, and roll on with accumulative magnitude; but we have not yet seen it "fill the whole earth." We have seen the witnesses of God, that prophesied in sackcloth, slain, and have witnessed their rising; but we have not yet heard the seventh trumpet proclaim: *The kingdoms of this world are become the kingdoms of our Lord and of his Christ, and he shall reign forever and ever.* (Rev. xi: 1–15.) We see "the man of sin" consumed by the spirit of the Lord's mouth, but we have not yet seen him destroyed by the brightness of the Lord's coming. (2 Thess. ii: 8.) The kingdom is not yet given, "under the whole heaven," to "the people of the saints of the Most High."

We can not enter here on the question of the millennium farther than to say that we look for no such materialistic and sensuous, if not sensual, paradise as many seem to expect; we leave all such carnal dreams to Mohammedans and Mormons; nor yet do we look for such a universal spiritual triumph as many others hope for. This world can not, while it lasts, be other than a scene of trial—of probation; but we do look for "the full corn in the ear," for such a spread of truth and triumph of righteousness as has never yet been seen; for such an overthrow of beasts and false prophets, such a splash, and gurgle, and roar of waters when Babylon, like a millstone, is cast into the sea; such an overthrow of tyrannies, oppressions, superstitions, and impostures, and such a recognition of the supremacy of the Lord Jesus, on the very earth which was the theater of his suffering and shame, as shall vindicate the long-suffering, the wisdom, and the justice of God. And we feel like saying to our blessed Lord, so long insulted and rejected, as the fields grow white to the harvest—as the morning-star glows with unusual brilliancy in the heavens—as the dim twilight of the past gives way to the roseate hues of a gay morning—as we listen to crash after crash of falling errors and wrongs, and catch the notes of one and another song of deliverance—we feel like saying, in the beautiful language of Cowper:

> "Come, then, and, added to thy many crowns,
>   Receive yet one, the crown of all the Earth,
>   Thou who alone art worthy!   It was thine
>   By ancient covenant, ere Nature's birth;
>   And thou hast made it thine by purchase since,
>   And overpaid its value with thy blood.
>   Thy saints proclaim thee King; and in their hearts
>   Thy title is engraven with a pen
>   Dipped in the fountain of eternal love.
>   Thy saints proclaim thee King; and thy delay
>   Gives courage to their foes, who, could they see
>   .The dawn of thy last advent, long desired,
>   Would creep into the bowels of the hills,
>   And flee for safety to the falling rocks.
>   The very spirit of the world is tired
>   Of its own taunting question, asked so long,
>   'Where is the promise of your Lord's approach?'
>   The infidel has shot his bolts away,
>   Till, his exhausted quiver, yielding none,
>   He gleans the blunted shafts that have recoiled,
>   And aims them at the shield of Truth again.
>   *   *   *   *   *   *
>   Come, then, and, added to thy many crowns,
>   Receive yet one, as radiant as the rest,
>   Due to thy last and most effectual work,
>   Thy word fulfilled, the conquest of a world!"

From this phase of our subject we deduce some practical reflections, with which this discourse will be concluded.

1. Whatever triumph is yet to come, is to be the result of *moral power.*   "The full corn in the ear" is but the full development of the germ in the seed sown, and has the same source as the blade and the ear.   We must not grow skeptical, then, as to the conquering power of the

truth.   There are many whose faith in the triumph of
truth is paralyzed; and, in sheer skepticism as to the
deathless force of the word of God, they are seeking comfort in the wildest imaginings of earthquake, and fire, and
tempest, to close the scenes of time.   They indulge in the
most dolorous croakings over the hopeless degeneracy of
the times, and overwhelm with evil vaticinations every
hopeful enterprise for the world's salvation.   Dante has
placed in one of his hells such as predicted future events.
Their punishment is to have their faces reversed, and set
the contrary way on their bodies, so that they are compelled to look and walk backward.   It seems to us that
many of our modern prophets have had their heads reversed even here, so that their lugubrious gaze is led into
the past rather than the future; and they find more material for reflection in the wrecks of past struggles than in
the promises of coming triumphs.   We should carefully
guard against such a paralysis of faith.   The triumphs of
our King are assigned, in the Scriptures, to moral power.
As a King, he is King of Truth.   It is in this that his
kingdom is declared to be "not of this world."   Were
the raging passions of men to be subdued until harmony
would reign over the scenes of former discord and cruelty?
The reason given is: *For the earth shall be full of the knowledge of the Lord as the waters cover the sea.* (Isa. xi: 6–9.)
Is Babylon to fall?   That fall is preceded by the mission
of an angel having the everlasting Gospel to preach to
every nation, and kindred, and tongue, and people. (Rev.
xiv: 6–8.)   Are wars to cease, and peace to brood, dove-
like, over all the earth?   The reason given is: *For the law
shall go forth from Zion, and the word of the Lord from Jerusalem.* (Isa. ii: 1–4.)   It may seem like a slender reliance;
but it lives to plant its standard over the ruins of colossal

empires that once sought to destroy it with the sword! It is not alone. Its author lives and reigns to guide it to victory. His providences open for it a free course. If men and nations erect themselves in pride and stubbornness against the Lord and his anointed, He that sitteth in the heavens knows to abase the proud and exalt the lowly. If nations become incorrigible, Divine judgments can annihilate them, and give their places to others. The Great Engineer has been for ages tunneling the mountains, bridging the chasms, spanning the floods, forcing a highway through flinty rocks, along precipitous heights, and over barren deserts. The track is partly laid, and trains are running over sections of the road. A day may consummate at last what it required ages to prepare the way for, and we shall reach the desired terminus. Deep down beneath the tumults and wrecks of the surface of Time's stormy sea, in the eternal calm of His own purposes, God is stretching the wires that shall connect this world with the next, and bring heaven and earth into unison.

To the eye of sense it seems as if the Church is a feeble instrumentality to work out these great results; and so it is. The Gulf Stream is, in comparison with the ocean, a small stream, and one would think, to look on that river of warm water, that the cold waters of the ocean would swallow it up right speedily. Yet there it is—in the ocean, but not of it—an everlasting river, never failing in drouths nor overflowing in floods, flowing steadily and resistlessly on from the Gulf of Mexico to the Arctic seas, bearing the warm treasures of the tropics to frozen regions—changing climates—giving channels to winds—spreading grateful blessings of warmth over regions that otherwise would be locked in eternal frosts, and receiving back the cold currents of the north only to be elevated to a more desirable temperature, and sent back again in gratefulness of blessing to the unfriendly regions whence they came. Such a stream does history reveal in the ocean of human life—the Church of the living God. Flowing from the tropical regions of Divine Love, it goes out a river of life, bearing to the icy regions of human selfishness and sin the warm streams of truth and love from God, and, by a thousand gentle influences, as it flows along rocky coasts, or amidst the desolation of icebergs, subdues the severities and conquers the desolations of sin's wintry reign, and gives the bloom of spring and the fruits of summer to lands which else were locked in the everlasting embrace of death. It never ceases to flow. Men may not know it; navigators may look on it with suspicion; fogs may enwrap its beneficial currents and hide them from the gaze of the mariner; but as growing intelligence dispels the mysteries of the past, and unfolds the beneficent purposes of Him who is "wonderful in working," the world will bless the giver for this river of life, and gratefully acknowledge the blessings which it brings.

2. Let it not be forgotten that the noblest fruitage of Christian life is yet to be seen. We sometimes speak of primitive Christianity as if the noblest perfection of character belonged to the first age; as if the blade, in its first springing, was superior to the full corn in the ear. The full revelation of truth belongs to the first age—for that was the harvest-period in the revelation of truth; but it was the seed-time, so far as the fruits of the Gospel are concerned. No one can read the first and third chapters of Romans, and expect to see hewn out of such quarries of Jewish and Gentile humanity blocks of Parian marble. We *inherit* a Christian civilization which they had not; and,

in view of the blessed heritage of faith, and hope, and love which we possess, God has a right to demand of the Church now, a strength, symmetry, and fruitfulness beyond any thing that glorified her early history.   More than the miracles which we have lost, is the strength and certainty of the faith which has been tested through the storms and conflicts of eighteen hundred years.   Perhaps the passive virtues adorned the lives of the patient sufferers of the early ages more than ours; but the *active* virtues of Christian character ought, in the blessed sunlight of this nineteenth century—in this land of freedom, with our surroundings of a high Christian civilization, with our unparalleled facilities for conquering space, and time, and nature, and for condensing into an hour more of real life than used to belong to a year; invested by science with an almost godlike command over the elements, and a godlike dominion over the treasures of the soil, the waters, and the mountains—the active virtues of Christian life ought to shine in us with unmatched luster!   The fruits of Christian philanthropy should abound in unparalleled richness and variety, and the blessings of a triumphant faith and cheerful piety should spread their light and power over all the earth.   We can not take time here to sketch our ideas of the triumphs yet to be won by the Church of God.   A Spiritual Brotherhood, redeemed from all human authority, united only in Christ, with no test of admission but submission to Christ, and no test of membership but obedience to Christ's commandments—such a brotherhood, enjoying, in the closest spiritual unity, the highest spiritual freedom, and consecrating all their powers, in holy enthusiasm, to the world's regeneration, would soon banish infidelity, superstition, and tyranny from the earth, mold the governments of the world into humaner forms, drive out selfishness, oppression, aristocracy, and caste, before the light of Christ's ideas of the Fatherhood of God and the Brotherhood of Man, and plant in all lands, and in the islands of the sea, peace and good-will among the families of mankind. The Spirit of God would brood lovingly, in dove-like sweetness and gentleness, over such a scene, and heaven stoop down to bless, with unwonted lavishness of bounty, the reconciled earth. The glorious harvest of the full corn in the ear would be gathered in with joyful shouts of harvest-home, and the sower who went forth with tears, and the reaper who gathered in the sheaves with joy, would rejoice together before the Lord.

W. Wellstood Sc.

Your truly
A. S. Hayden

AMOS SUTTON HAYDEN.

THIS well-known, faithful minister of the Gospel was born, September 17, 1813, in Youngstown, Trumbull County, Ohio, to which place his father, SAMUEL HAYDEN, had emigrated from Pennsylvania, in 1803.

In a family of eight children, seven of whom were sons, SUTTON was the youngest. In boyhood, he sought every opportunity to indulge his inclination for study, and used such books and facilities for education as lay in his way. He was especially fond of religious books, and read with great delight "Hervey's Meditations" and the "Pilgrim's Progress" at a very early age. Other works, mostly of a religious character, fell into his hands, some of which required close application and study, to which he diligently applied himself, and, by this means, made considerable progress in the acquisition of useful knowledge. From the age of fifteen to seventeen, he laid the foundation of a classical education in his own native village. He rose rapidly in his classes, surpassing older students in the study of the classics, for which, rather than mathematics, he had a taste.

His religious convictions were early, and marked. His parents were honorable members of the Baptist Church, and he was trained in the doctrinal views and practices of that body. Previous to his obedience to the Gospel, he passed through the usual Baptist experience, so common at that day, of "getting religion," and often wondered why it was that God was so long in coming to give relief and bring joy to his soul. At last, he had the Gospel plan clearly explained to him by that gifted and eloquent servant of God, WALTER SCOTT, by whom he was immersed, March 20, 1828, in the fifteenth year of his age.

He soon began to exercise his gift in exhortation, traveling considerable with other preachers as associate and aid, especially with his brother WILLIAM.

In the summer and fall of 1832, when nineteen years of age, he began to hold meetings, and his labors were every-where crowned with encouraging success. He was married, May 31, 1837, to SARAH M. ELY, of Deerfield, Portage County, Ohio.

(495)

In September, 1840, he settled in Collamer, Cuyahoga County, Ohio, then known as Euclid, as pastor of the Church; and, in 1850, on the founding of the Western Reserve Eclectic Institute, at Hiram, Ohio, the Board unanimously elected him Principal of the seminary. Under his administration, seconded by able assistants, the institution rose to great strength and prosperity. After holding that position seven years he resigned, and returned to Collamer. The next year he was elected Principal of the McNeely Normal School, at Hopedale, Ohio, and accepted, laboring there for one year in the double capacity of Principal of the school and preacher for the Church. He resigned in August, 1859, and returned to his Church in Collamer, which had been constantly urging him to resume his labors among them. He has been located at that point ever since, where he is greatly beloved by the entire community. Excepting the periods already mentioned, that has been his principal field of labor for twenty-seven years, presenting a rare but instructive example of permanency in the work of the ministry.

He has also been quite successful as a musical composer and publisher. He is the author of the first compilation of church music published among the Disciples. It appeared when he was only twenty-one years of age, and was much sought after. It was a great benefit at the time, in furnishing tunes for the use of the infant churches. He has published several musical works since, one of which, the "Sacred Melodeon," has run through many editions, and had an extensive sale. He was also one of the committee that compiled the new edition of the "Christian Hymn Book," and, in the preparation of that work, rendered valuable assistance.

Brother HAYDEN is distinguished for large conscientiousness, intense delicacy of feeling, earnest religious convictions, and great purity of life. He is a model Christian gentleman, an excellent pastor, and a scholar of no mean attainments.

CONSCIENCE AND CHRISTIANITY.

BY A. S. HAYDEN.

"Which show the work of the law written in their hearts, their conscience also bearing witness, and *their* thoughts the meanwhile accusing, or else excusing one another."—ROMANS II: 15.

THE New Testament reveals a grand and glorious salvation. The angel that announced the birth of the Lord Jesus announced him as a Savior: "He shall save his people from their sins." (Matt. i: 21.) The Divine grace is poured forth, in boundless profusion, "to purge our sins"—to recover us, absolutely and eternally, from our ruin in depravity and guilt. Salvation is the herald-note of the Gospel—its voice of proclamation to the whole human family. This is the burden of the apostolic mission. Repentance and remission, in the name of the crucified, exalted Prince and Savior, were, through the obedience of the Gospel, to be brought to every son and daughter of a lost and ruined race. He who studies the Christian religion, therefore, must, first of all, contemplate it as a great salvation.

But it is also a boundless benevolence—full and free, and surpassing all utterance. This thought is itself the result and outflow from another which lies above and back of it as its cause—the Divine philanthropy. "God so

32   (497)

loved the world that he gave his only-begotten Son, that whosoever believeth in him should not perish, but have everlasting life." (John iii: 16.)   God *so* loved.   This speech "*so loved*" admits of no degree above it.   It is the highest form of speech—the superlative of superlatives. No conception of philanthropy can transcend this.   Angelic powers could rise no higher.   The humblest saint is equal—in enjoyment, is superior—to the highest seraph, in respect to this unparalleled and unlimited benevolence. The Gospel, issuing from this full fountain of goodness, begets in all who receive it the like emotion; so that the work of redemption is not complete in us even when we have heartily embraced it, and secured to ourselves the possession and enjoyment of the great salvation.   It works in us to kindle the fires of that supernatural benevolence which sought and found a way to rescue and glorify lost man.   The saved sinner will feel after his lost brother till he find him; and, having found him, he will exclaim, with one of old: "We have found him of whom Moses in the law and all the prophets did write, Jesus of Nazareth, the son of Joseph." (John i: 45.)   The second, perhaps the higher, study of the Christian religion, is the view of it as a grand and superlative philanthropy.

But the third—the grandest, the highest—is its justice. It is an eternal, an inexorable righteousness.   "Mercy and truth go before the face of the Almighty, but justice and judgment are the habitation of his throne." (Psalms lxxxix: 14.)   In the unfolding of his character in the work of redemption, justice and mercy meet; righteousness and peace kiss each other.   (See Psalms lxxxv: 10.)   The union of these ineffable attributes is the highest thought in the revelation which God has made to man.   To realize and embody it in the work of redemption is the richest and

loftiest display of infinite wisdom. The oracle which reveals Jesus Christ as a *priest on a throne* unfolds more fully
than any other the counsels which originated man's recovery. It sets him forth in the highest possible glory, com-
bining the royalty with the priesthood—a kingly priest, a
sacerdotal monarch, ruling the universe in reference to the
salvation of the human race. Consider attentively the
whole passage: "He shall bear the glory; and shall sit
and rule upon his throne; and he shall be a priest upon
his throne: and the counsel of peace shall be between them
both." (Zech. vi: 13.) Peace to the soul comes from both
the royalty and the priesthood. Both offices are united in
him who bears the glory, and who sits and rules, a priest,
upon his throne.

Now, CONSCIENCE discerns the *right*. Without this
power, or faculty, man would be incapable of any discern-
ment of moral rectitude. Conscience is the moral eye of
the soul—an eye single to righteousness. Then the con-
nection-level between God and man is where conscience
apprehends God's righteousness. The Gospel, as a system of justification, reveals God's righteousness—that is,
his system of justification—through and by the cross.
And it is no less its purpose to establish God's righteousness, while he stoops to recover and save the sinner, than
it is to bring salvation to man, who is *justly* condemned in
his sins. It deserves emphatic mention, that the completeness of the work of salvation is not accomplished until the
conscience sees the Divine justice displayed equally with
God's mercy, and feels satisfied in the glorious work of restoring sinful man to a state of pardon, acceptance, and
holiness. Then the justified sinner rests, for he is reconciled. Then he is satisfied, for he sees the ground of immutable security in the justice of God—the very founda-

tion of his throne. Then he can understand that justice, as well as mercy, is his friend, and offers him pardon. Accordingly, the holy apostle says: "If we confess our sins, he is faithful and just to forgive us our sins, and to cleanse us from all unrighteousness." (1 John i: 9.)

We see that conscience is the link of communion between man and God in the highest development of the Christian religion. It is the avenue through which flow into the soul all the high, reconciling, and exalting sentiments which are awakened by God's justice, holiness, and truth—powers which secure to the soul its firmest trust, and kindle to flames the feelings of praise, devotion, and adoration.

Nature and Subordinate Position of Conscience.

Conscience is neither innate, in the sense of a perfect guide of itself—an image or representative of God in the soul—as some imagine, to prompt and guide, always infallibly, in the right way; nor yet is it the "creature of education"—an expression very faulty, and of uncertain sound. In respect of the first position, those who believe in innate total depravity can not believe it; for then would there be at least one power or faculty, and that a moral power, which, so far from being totally depraved, would not be depraved at all! Nor can any reflecting person believe it, who considers the infinitely differing and conflicting decisions which conscience, as a judge, is making in precisely the same cases. And in respect to the second position, that conscience is the creature of education, it may be sufficient to remark, that education creates no faculty. There must be some thing to be educated before education can commence its work. It is time this loose style of speech were abandoned.

Conscience, then, is a faculty or power among the original endowments implanted in us by the Creator; not to take the place of God in the heart, but it rejoices in its dependency, and looks up with reverential humility for the word and will of God to prompt all its impulses and guide in all its decisions. No one of all our faculties is so prompt as conscience, when in a healthy state, to respond to the Divine appeals, and to say, in the language of Samuel, "Speak, for thy servant heareth." More than this, it seems to be intrusted with a subordinate dominion, a viceroyalty, to summon to duty the whole garrison of our moral powers, to keep them in the line, armed and equipped, ready for defense, or for invasion upon the enemies of the Supreme Sovereign.

Conscience is an eye; but the eye needs light. The best eye discerns nothing in darkness. Conscience without a guide is Sampson without eyes. It must be led; it wants a hand to lead it to the pillars. There is no clearer example of the confusion yet prevailing in Christendom, than is found in the strangely inconsistent views entertained on the question of the supremacy of conscience. While it is a faculty in our nature, like all other faculties in man, it needs illumination. Or, to accept the definition which Locke gives of conscience, "The power of judging of the rectitude or the pravity of our own actions," it is still manifest that, as rectitude has respect to right rule, and pravity implies a departure from one, conscience needs a rule, or standard of judgment. If she "accuses," her accusation must rest on fact and law. If she "witnesses," her testimony relates to conformity to a right rule, or to dereliction and disobedience. The conclusion is plain, that there must be a rule or standard *for every act of conscience.*

The Romanist has his rule of conscience—the creed and practices of the Romish Church. Compliance with that rule satisfies his conscience. But the Greek Christian's conscience would never be satisfied with the Romish rule. The Musselman's conscience conforms to the Koran. Thus consciences differ as the standards differ throughout the multiform variety of rules which men have adopted. As—

"Education forms the common mind,"

so, in a very emphatic sense, the religious teaching which a man adopts becomes, invariably, his conscience-standard.

It is assumed throughout this discourse, and ought to be, doubtless, in all sound reasoning, that while conscience is the supreme moral guide in us, its dictates and decisions are neither different from the light we possess, nor beyond it. A good conscience, in the sense of one faithful to its moral convictions, will act unfailingly in harmony with the moral bias of its possessor. From these reasonings the following propositions appear to flow:

1. Conscience reflects, or uses executively, the degree and character of instruction the possessor of it has received.

2. If his teaching be erroneous, conscience will be tainted with the same error, and to the same extent.

3. If the instruction be from the Word of God, it will be correct, and conscience will give a correct testimony.

4. Conscience is not an infallible guide, unless it be infallibly led.

5. But the Divine revelation is such an infallible guide, by which the conscience, when duly instructed, is infallibly led; which, in turn, leads man infallibly by the knowledge of God.

Conscience belongs only to Man.

While it is the highest of our faculties, linking us to the Creator through the highest display of his revelation, his eternal holiness, it is worthy of special remark, that conscience is a faculty which pertains to man alone. Some of the lower orders of animals seem to share with him in at least a semblance of the intellectual powers, as also in some of the moral qualities possessed by men. Some of them manifest a degree of fidelity in their attachment very touching and almost human. Some of the *knowing* capacities appear, in measure, to shine among some of them. But while there is an overlapping of certain affections and capacities between man and the irrational creation, it is apparent that those affections and capacities are possessed in the strongest degree which are of the lower grade. As we rise in the scale, as respects the nature of the qualities thus mutually possessed, they become dim and weak in them, till man is left alone in the supremacy and enjoyment of all the higher grade. Animals have strong affections—a mere dim reflection of intellect—and no conscience. Thus it is equally shown that man is supreme in excellence on the earth; and also that conscience is supreme among and over all the grand endowments implanted in us by the Creator.

It is man's moral personality—without it, no moral character. As is his conscience, so is his character. Character and conscience are correlates. The one is the embodiment of the other. Conscience forms character, and character is the index of conscience. Men differ, all things considered, in moral character, according to the differences in their consciences. Here is the point of observation from which to study the pictures men are making. Every man assumes his own attitude and position—works on the canvas from his own angle. He colors and shades according to the moral hue and force of his conscience. Whatever else enters into the dye wherein he dips his brush, conscience is the background, shading all, setting all in prominence or relief.

Susceptibility of Cultivation.

Conscience is susceptible of greater cultivation than any other of our powers. It is also capable of a greater degree of depravity. In this man is equal unto the angels, and a companion also of demons. Delectable above all things of beauty is a well-educated and upright conscience, ruling like an empress, and regulating with equity and prudence the whole empire of the soul. Here is perfection—the only perfection of which man is capable. Every intellectual power and moral quality in his nature is susceptible of indefinite, almost limitless, improvement; but this alone may reach absolute perfection. Conscience may prompt perfect obedience to a perfect law, for conscience, like an architect, works by rule; but the power to obey may be far in the rear of the perfect intention. Here a conflict ensues between the demands of the will, which requires perfect obedience, and the tardy passions, which are untrained and rebellious. Conscience mourns to find the obedience so far behind her standard. She rallies her forces, chides delays, reproves, admonishes, and tries every means to bring the recusant "members" to duty. Sometimes she makes us cry out in despair: "O, wretched man that I am! who shall deliver me from the body of this death?" This was her forlorn hope all along under the law. Thus do we understand Paul in the seventh chapter of Romans: "For to will is present with me, but how to perform that

which is good I find not." Conscience sought and prompted the right way. It was good in its impulse and decision;
but the power to control the refractory members, the aid
to the obedience it demanded, was not in the law. But
when the needed aid appeared, the Gospel, with its blessed
hope, its cheerful and free spirit, its assurance of pardon,
and its gracious mercy, the relieved conscience exultingly
exclaimed: "Thanks be to God who giveth us the victory,
through our Lord Jesus Christ." (Rom. vii: 24, 25.)

The Court of Conscience.

The offices of conscience appear, in the light of the Holy
Scriptures, to be summarily as follows:

1. It acts as an *accuser*. "Being convicted by their conscience, they went out one by one." (John viii: 9.)

2. It is a witness. "Their conscience also bearing witness." (Rom. ii: 15.) Also (chapter ix: 1), "My con-
conscience also bearing me witness in the Holy Ghost."
"Our rejoicing is this, the testimony of our conscience."
(2 Cor. i: 12.)

3. It is a judge or arbitrator in morals. "Why is my
liberty judged of another man's conscience." (1 Cor.
x: 29.) "Commending ourselves to every man's conscience in the sight of God." (2 Cor. iv: 2.) See also
1 John iii: 20, where, under another term, the same notion
of an arbitrator among our moral powers is distinctly asserted: "If our heart condemn us, God is greater than our
heart, and knoweth all things."

The word of God speaks of a "good conscience."
That is good which fully and constantly answers the ends
of its creation. The conscience that is healthy and vigorous, acting spontaneously and without bias, receiving no

bribe—which is tender, quick, and true—is a good conscience.

There is, also, an evil conscience. A conscience is evil when it refuses service, or is incapable of duty; or when it has been trifled with till it has become callous and past feeling. Of some, it is said their conscience is seared as with a hot iron. The flesh, when thus seared, is insensate. This is a strong figure, and of easy understanding in its application to the conscience. It has lost its sensibility. It no longer files in its accusation. It no longer arbitrates in the great questions of duty. Such persons are hopelessly lost, as it is only through the conscience the soul can be reached.

A conscience may be weak, and yet good. It may be watchful—even over-careful to avoid the wrong. Its tension may be high through mere delicacy. Such a conscience demands the tenderest treatment. No greater mistake, or more painfully serious in its consequences, is committed by pastors and elders of churches, than to disregard the cases under their care of overwrought tenderness of conscience. Some of the purest and most delicate souls—of highest and acutest sensitiveness, yet sincere to the last degree— are bluntly addressed and coarsely treated by persons incapable of appreciating them. They languish for relief on some troublesome case of duty omitted, or some act performed. They sigh in darkness, and long for some one to whom they may commit freely their troubles. Here, thou spiritual adviser, here be thy skill displayed. To trifle here is to ruin a soul. The slightest contempt may sink their remaining hope immeasurable fathoms down into the depths of the most dismal despair. It is painfully certain that this class of scrupulous sufferers are in most of the churches, and none with eye to discern, heart to appreciate, or tongue to relieve them.

An evil conscience also exists when its possessor feels a sense of unpardoned guilt. It differs from a defiled conscience. An evil conscience, in the sense here considered, carries the conviction of guilt. It is penitent, but unpardoned. A defiled conscience is corrupt, impure, impenitent. A pure conscience is free from the consciousness of sins cherished. A good conscience, as here spoken of, is free from a sense of guilt.

Here a distinction of great importance may be mentioned between the *change of heart* and the *forgiveness of sins*—two states of the heart, or conscience (for sometimes these terms may be used interchangeably) which are frequently confounded. When the heart is changed, the conscience is purged from defilement; the heart is purified of its love of sin; it delights in holiness; and in its reconciliation it cries out, with Saul, "Lord, what wilt thou have me to do?" The conscience is now pure. It longs for the pardon of the sins which it now mourns. In other words, to that state of heart, correctly termed a *pure* conscience, is now to be added the joy of that state called in Scripture a *good* conscience—one made free from guilt by forgiveness. Then a change of heart prepares the sinner for pardon; and the knowledge of pardon, obtained in obedience to the Gospel, clothes him with a good conscience, "through the resurrection of Jesus Christ."

A few passages of the Holy Scripture, considered together, throw much light on this part of the subject. We introduce merely the sentences to be considered, requesting the reader to examine them carefully in their connection.

Hebrew ix: 14: "Purge your conscience from dead works."

Hebrew x: 2: "Worshipers once purged should have no more conscience of sins."

Hebrew x: 22: "Hearts sprinkled from an evil conscience."

1 Peter iii: 21: "Answer of a good conscience."

From a careful study and comparison of these passages, the following remarks appear to be plain and pertinent:

1st. An *evil* conscience is one that feels the sense of guilt. The worshipers under the law were never relieved of that burden. Paul argues that if they had enjoyed that freedom from sin their offerings would not have been repeated. (Heb. x: 2.) And, from verse 22, we learn that the relief, or sense of pardon which they sought, and for which the offerings of the law were inadequate, was gained through the sprinkling of the blood of Jesus Christ; and that unpardoned state of heart is there called an "*evil* conscience." Then, an evil conscience is a guilty conscience; and a good conscience is one which has been relieved from that guilt by a knowledge of pardon.

2d. That the law was unable to confer that blessing. "It is impossible for the blood of bulls and goats to take away sins." "Every priest standeth daily ministering, and offering oftentimes the same sacrifices, which can never make the comers thereunto perfect as pertaineth to the conscience." "The worshipers once purged should have no more conscience of sins." (Heb. x.) Then the unspeakable joy of sins forgiven, a conscience which witnessed to its possessor to the act of forgiving mercy, which pronounced a full and formal absolution from the guilt of sin, was a blessing to which the Jewish heart was a stranger—a blessing enjoyed only by the sons of God under

Jesus Christ. And hence the accompanying spirit of adoption belongs, as Paul shows extensively elsewhere, only to Christians, to the members of the new covenant.

3d. That what the law could not do in this respect, the Gospel of Jesus Christ doth fully and happily accomplish. "How much more shall the blood of Christ, who through the Eternal Spirit offered himself without spot to God, purge your conscience from dead works to serve the living God." (Heb. ix: 14.) "Let us draw near to God with a true heart, in full assurance of faith, having our heart sprinkled from an evil conscience, and our bodies washed with pure water." (Heb. x: 22.) This forgiveness is neither typical nor formal, merely, but actual; so that the worshipers, once purged, *have no more conscience of sins.* And the consequence of this blessing is the enjoyment of the Holy Spirit, which, as sons of God, we now receive; being adopted as the sons and daughters of a Holy Father. And thus we become the adopted brothers of the "only-begotten Son," and share the honors and joys of the Divine family. Christians should, then, not go mourning all their days, but lift up their heads and rejoice in hope, and be careful to walk worthy of the vocation with which they are called.

4th. That this sense of relief, or knowledge of pardon, is conveyed intentionally and formally to the converted sinner in baptism, through the promise which the merciful Savior vouchsafes to those who obey him. Thus the sprinkling of the blood of Jesus Christ and the washing of the body in pure water are associated. (Heb. x: 22.) And the seeking of a good conscience and baptism are connected for the same purpose, through the resurrection of Jesus Christ, who bore our sins in his own body on the tree, and who rose the third day for our justification.

The Freedom of the Conscience.

The language of the Apostle Paul may be justly adopted and applied here: "I am free from all men." And again: "Not without law to God." This expresses accurately, and with high authority, the nature of the freedom which of right belongs to the conscience. It is too sacred for man to interfere with. It is man's own moral personality. Into this sanctuary he retires to settle his accounts with his God, and prepare for the judgment; a business too awful and too peculiarly his own to admit of any intermeddling from without. A "hitherto shalt thou come, and no farther," peremptorily forbids the approach of any third party.

Of very necessity, and of its own inalienable right, the conscience is and must be free. The moment it is coerced or compelled, it is destroyed. No indignity so great can be offered to human nature. The surrender of this right is the surrender of our highest manhood, and the holiest prerogative of our nature. Half the wars, revolutions, and convulsions of society have come from the exacting and unnatural attempts of some power in accidental supremacy to dictate law to the conscience. Bless God for the liberation of men from the terrors of the *auto da fé*, the impious cruelties of the Star Chamber, and the awful and diabolical tyrannies of the Inquisition. The sufferings of the million, who, dying in prison, in exile, or by torture, are the impressive and emphatic protest of God's martyr host against the enormous wrong.

"No martyrs now!" Not quite, perhaps, but nearly. Read with inward thought. The church requires its pastor to preach the prevailing "doctrines" embodied in its compend of the faith. He failing in the imposed obligation, they place him under the ban of silence, cut off supplies from his table, or make him so uncomfortable in his position that he is forced to depart hence. Or they open upon him the thunders of the higher anathema. So, held in "durance vile," under the threats, very significantly suggested, of a withdrawal of support, or removal from office, or, it may be, expulsion from church communion, he stifles conscience, sells his manhood, and ceases from that hour to be God's FREE man. Is his conscience free? It may not be the sublime, *ex-cathedra* denunciations of the Vatican, but the equally arrogant and illiberal decisions of the session or the presbytery.

In many ways the conscience is held in chains. The spirit of bigotry and dogmatic intolerance still prevails. The cry, "He followeth not with us," still goes up to the Master's ears, and calls for vengeance on the dissenting object of theological odium. The confessional, or the spiritual court of death awaits non-conformity to the reigning order of faith and practice. The victims of this dry, blasting simoom of ecclesiastical despotism lie thick along the highway of modern church history. The victim of Romish intolerance, when she sought to make laws for the conscience, was impaled, eviscerated, tortured; now his brother in sufferings is scourged with the cords of sarcasm, has the key of fellowship turned against him, or, by secret management, is made odious to "the elect." O, when will the emancipation of conscience be complete? When will this benign power, the eye of Divinity within us, be disenthralled from every incumbrance, and be left where God left it, responsible only to him?

It was a noble utterance of the assembly of divines at Westminster, which they made: "God alone is Lord of the conscience." (See the Presbyterian Confession of Faith.)

Our government is the only known government which, looking vigilantly after all the social interests of the people, has ventured on the responsible and untried experiment of letting the conscience alone. It has let us gloriously alone! God preserve it forever!

The importance of appealing to the Conscience in Conversion.

The Church should be laid in righteousness. A scepter of righteousness is the scepter of Messiah's kingdom. So every member of it should bow with an intelligent surrender to that scepter. It is not doubted nor denied that motives which appeal to the sense of fear, and which move the soul with a desire of safety and personal salvation, are legitimate. More, they are Scriptural. "Save yourselves from this untoward generation." "Flee from the wrath to come." "Beware, lest that come upon you which is written in the prophets. Behold, ye despisers, and wonder and perish." Many such are in the Word of God. So also the wide range of motives of benevolence. The goodness of God invites to repentance. Let the goodness of God, then, be pressed pointedly and eloquently. Yet the conscience should not be neglected. It should be thoroughly aroused and fully enlightened. Conversions would be more thorough, and apostasies fewer. The excited fears will subside. Impassioned appeals are highly important; but follow them up with the stronger reasons which lie at the foundation of permanent reformation.

Many appeals for conversion by partisan pleaders do but corrupt the heart. They encourage selfishness, rather than self-denial, in it. Men are persuaded to come in because they are of use to the Church. They have talents. Their influence is great, and many are looking to them. They are very good men now, and need nothing to complete their character but the Christian profession. Thus they are flattered, coaxed, besought with protestations of friendship, and of the happiness to us if they will but take their place with us. Ah! the desecration of the Gospel! Impious flattery! Does Jesus Christ need sinners for his sake? Do they not, rather, need him for their own sake? It is shameful to set the Lord begging thus for followers. Thousands have been "beat up" into the ranks of the Church by spirited charges upon their honor, their manhood; their bravery has been challenged, and all the selfhood of the heart aroused, and plied dexterously to swell the host of nominal church-members. Then the numbers were carefully footed up and sent forth to the world by bulletin, herald, and proclamation. Alas! the Church militant! Wars come of passion. With passion and pride untamed and unhumbled, such converts quickly relapse, or remain to bear the bitter, crabbed fruits of such a planting.

Men should not be pressed into the Church faster, or beyond the desires of their own repentant hearts. If the preacher would not have his work prove "wood, hay, and stubble," let him see to it that he apply the motives which will lead the soul to conviction for sins; that he should make chief his aim to lead up the conscience to Christ, and lay the crucified Redeemer in the conscience of the sinner.

In respect of children, this is, probably, still more important. How admirable and worthy of all imitation the course of the holy apostle: " Children, obey your parents in the Lord; for this is right." (Eph. vi: 1.) Note well the motive. He descends not to the plane of selfishness. He lifts the heart of pliant childhood quite up to the highest of motives. It is right. He touches and teaches

33

the conscience. Here is a lesson deserving the careful study of teachers and preachers, and, above all, of parents, whose office in this behalf can not be alienated from them, nor delegated to any other person whatever.

Motives form character. Then lay the foundations aright. Many lives are false throughout, not because their course of action is evil or erroneous, but because the motives are all wrong from which flow the actions of such lives. Multitudes are never undeceived by others. They never detect the fundamental error themselves, and their whole life is a well-managed deception, with nothing in it of Christ, of sacrifice, of self-sacrifice, of self-abnegation, of self-devotion. "I am crucified with Christ; nevertheless I live: yet not I, but the grace of God liveth in me. And the life which I live in the flesh, I live by the faith of the Son of God who loved me, and gave himself for me." (Gal. ii: 20.)

Truly

T. Fanning

TOLBERT FANNING.

TOLBERT FANNING was born in Cannon County, Tennessee, May 10, 1810. When he was eight years of age, his parents moved to Lauderdale County, Alabama, and he remained in that State until he was nineteen. His father was a planter, on a small scale, and young TOLBERT was brought up mainly in the cotton field. He was allowed to attend school from three to six months in a year, and it was his good fortune to be placed under the care of excellent teachers. He soon became fond of study, and made considerable progress in acquiring the rudiments of an education. At this time, his father, though highly respected in his county as an honorable gentleman, was not a member of any church, but his mother was an Old Virginia Baptist, and a woman of fine intellect and great purity of life. From her, and from Baptist, Methodist, and Presbyterian preachers, whom he occasionally heard, he received his early religious instruction. At times his young heart was deeply impressed with the necessity of a religious life; but he was taught that "all men are in a state of total darkness, and must remain so till illuminated by special communications of the Spirit." From the time he was ten years of age he had read the Bible, but supposed he could not understand a word in it without a special illumination from above. Seven precious years of his life were spent in this gloomy and hopeless condition. When sixteen years of age, he began to pay attention to the preaching of EPHRAIM D. MOORE and JAMES E. MATHEWS, who called themselves Christian preachers, and were great and good men. From their teaching, he was encouraged to read the New Testament, with the view of really acquiring spiritual light. Soon all was plain, and his gloomy doubts gave place to an intelligent faith in the Lord Jesus Christ. About the first of October, 1827, he attended a meeting on Cypress, seven miles north of Florence, Alabama, and heard JAMES E. MATHEWS preach a masterly discourse on the Gospel and its Conditions, and, at the conclusion of the discourse, he walked forward, and, with a perfect understanding of the truth, made the confession, and was immediately immersed into Christ.

The next two years were spent chiefly in studying the Scriptures, at-

(515)

tending school, and visiting the brethren in Alabama and Tennessee. On the first day of October, by the advice of the Church at Republican, where he made the confession, he bade adieu to his family, for the purpose of trying to preach the Gospel. Though young and inexperienced, such was his earnestness and zeal, and such the power of the truth which he preached, that every-where thousands attended his meetings, and large numbers were brought into the kingdom.

In November, 1831, he entered the Nashville University, and graduated in 1835. During his college course, he preached considerable at different points in Tennessee, and made a tour with Brother A. CAMPBELL to Ohio and Kentucky. While at Perryville, Kentucky, he held a successful debate with a Methodist preacher by the name of Rice.

In 1836, he spent the spring and summer in a preaching tour, with Brother A. CAMPBELL, through Ohio, New York, Canada, New England, and the Eastern cities. In 1837, he was married to CHARLOTTE FALL, and, the same year, opened a female seminary in Franklin, Tennessee. On the first day of January, 1840, he removed to his present location, five miles from Nashville, and conducted a female school till 1842, when he spent most of the year in a successful preaching tour through Alabama and Mississippi. In 1843, he began to build Franklin College, and, in October, 1844, the buildings were completed, and TOLBERT FANNING was elected the first President of the college. In 1861, he resigned the Presidency to W. D. CARNES, President of the East Tennessee University, with the view of raising money to greatly enlarge the institution; but the war defeated all his calculations, and, in 1865, the college was destroyed by fire. He is at present conducting "Hope Institute," for the education of young ladies, and is senior editor of the "Gospel Advocate."

Brother FANNING's life has been one of great activity. He has been an editor for twenty years, taught school for nearly the same length of time, and traveled and preached in fifteen States, where he has been instrumental in establishing many churches, and scattering the good seed of the kingdom generally. As a speaker, he is remarkably self-possessed, and presents his points in a logical and forcible manner. His mental and physical characteristics are strongly marked, and his whole organization indicates that he is a man of strong will, great physical endurance, and powerful intellect.

THE MISSION OF THE CHURCH OF CHRIST.

BY TOLBERT FANNING.

"Now therefore ye are no more strangers and foreigners, but fellow-citizens with the saints, and of the household of God; and are built upon the foundation of the apostles and prophets, Jesus Christ himself being the chief corner-stone; in whom all the building, fitly framed together, groweth unto a holy temple in the Lord: in whom ye also are builded together, for a habitation of God through the Spirit."—EPHESIANS ii: 19, 20, 21, 22.

TO impress the heart of the erring with the wondrous truth that "the Church of Christ" is heaven's divinely constituted organization for the salvation of the lost, is the first and principal labor of the minister of peace. With the fervent desire, therefore, that I may successfully picture forth this incomparable structure, in colors that will enable sincere inquirers to become "wise unto salvation," I have undertaken the present service.

Plain answers to a few very simple questions, we trust, will embody what should be considered the most valuable lessons in the sacred Scriptures, regarding the Church and her mission. Let us, then, prayerfully and earnestly consider.

(517)

I. Why was it necessary that an organization promising salvation should exist?

Not feeling competent to look into the hidden things of God, I am not sure that I can satisfy the speculative in my answer to this momentous question.

We know not why God did not create a different world from this, or that any creation whatever was essential to his matchless honor. But we are to deal with what has been revealed in the Sacred Oracles, and not with idle conjectures. Man, who had been created sinless, and constituted lord of the earth, hearkened to the bewitching rhetoric of the seducer, and, in stumbling at the words of wisdom, fell, and was delivered over to the buffetings of the usurper. The generations of four thousand years had passed from earth without hope ; the government of the world, in consequence of sin, had been delivered to Satan, and man, alienated in heart from his Maker, and banished from his Eden-home with his race, yielded undisputed loyalty to his treacherous leader. Still, God's compassion to his creation was boundless ; and although the world had sinned, and been led captive by the devil at his will, our kind Father, in great wisdom and tenderest love, condescended to offer a release from the iron grasp of the destroyer, through the mediation of his beloved Son. The rescue was determined, and, for the execution of the grand purposes of heaven, the Son of his love was sent, with "glad tidings of great joy" to the dying. The government of Jehovah having been put at defiance, it was resolved in the counsels of heaven to offer release to death's captives in an organization at war with the powers of darkness.

To establish this institution and secure eternal redemption, cost the sacrifice of God's beloved Son, who "made his grave with the wicked in his death," but who rose a triumphant conqueror, bearing aloft the scepter of life to a sin-stricken race. In this, anxious angels could see how "God could be just, and the justifier of all who believe" and seek protection under the mild reign of the Prince of Peace. The simple statement that God, our Father, *chose* to offer salvation to a lost world through the kingdom of his Son, must suffice as to the *necessity* and *fitness* of such an institution, and I therefore inquire—

II. How, where, and when, did the Church of Christ originate?

It is not only mortifying, but exceedingly humiliating, to know that, in the nineteenth century—in "this enlightened age"—it becomes necessary to reply to such inquiries. In reference to these matters, however, there are at least three classes of inveterate disputants.

In the first, we find those who possess no appreciable idea of such an organization as the Church of the First-born. They speak, to be sure, of "the invisible kingdom within," and regard religion as mere passion-feeling emotion, which we are to "seek and get," and, indeed, which may be lost; but which depends not in the least upon any exercise of the understanding heart. Spiritual life, in this view, is but an abstraction, independent of all organizations and forms—is merely subjective, not objective, and churches and ordinances but hinder the free operation of the spirit within.

In the second class are seen such as hope for a coming dispensation of mercy, and pray, "Thy kingdom come." They preach a dead Gospel, and practice "forms of godliness, but deny the power." The idea of a spiritual body competent to save from sin, and qualify the saved for immortality, has not entered their hearts; but they still look for a Christ to divide lands and govern bloody monarchies.

Those of the third class maintain that, in the days of the apostles, the Church was built upon the rock laid in Zion; that she has withstood the rough waves of eighteen centuries; and that she will, finally, triumph gloriously over all the principalities and powers of earth.

It will become us well to call to our aid the prophets of the Old Testament in regard to "*the how*" of the Church's origin. David, the king, though a man after God's own heart, in consequence of having "shed much blood," was not permitted to build a house in which to record the name of his Maker; but a kind Father promised, with an oath: "I will set up thy seed after thee, and I will establish the throne of his kingdom forever." (2 Sam. vii: 12.) To this promise, Solomon, the son and heir, made reference, in his dedicatory prayer, of the house which he built, (1 Kings viii: 25,) to adumbrate the spiritual temple in David's line, of which it is written, in the 132d Psalm, "The Lord God has chosen Zion for his habitation."

But the house of God built by Solomon has gone to decay, and David's throne is no longer occupied by an earthly descendant. The simple and only question now to determine is: Does Christ, in the full meaning of the prophecies, sit on David's throne, or is he to ascend it at a future coming? As this is a question of fact, our appeal should be to the sacred records alone. The prophet, in allusion to "a child born and a son given," declared that "the government shall be upon his shoulder: and of its increase there shall be no end upon the throne of David, and upon his kingdom, to order and establish it, from

henceforth even forever." (Isaiah ix: 6–8.) Again, he
said: "In mercy shall the throne be established, and he
shall sit upon it in truth, in the tabernacle of David."
(Isaiah xvi: 5.) We can scarcely imagine that any one
can doubt these declarations point to Christ in his kingdom. By another prophet, it is written: "In that day
I will raise up the tabernacle of David which is fallen."
(Amos ix: 11.) This passage is quoted by an apostle, in
direct reference to the call and salvation of the Gentiles
by Christ. (Acts xv: 16.) Gabriel, at the miraculous conception, said: "Fear not, Mary: thou shalt bring forth a
son, Jesus, and the Lord shall give unto him the throne
of his father David; he shall reign over the house of Israel, and of his kingdom there shall be no end." (Luke
i: 30.) Zacharias, in quoting the 132d Psalm, applied
the words: "The Lord God has raised up a horn of salvation in the house of his servant David," directly to
Christ. (Luke i: 69.) But Peter, in referring to the
promise to David, said: "God hath sworn to David that,
of the fruit of his loins, he would raise up Christ to sit on
his throne;" and added: "This Jesus hath God raised
up. Therefore, being at the right hand of God exalted,
he hath shed forth this which you now see and hear."
(Acts ii: 25.) If God raised up Jesus Christ to sit on
David's throne, and crowned him at his own right hand in
the heavens, to be a Prince and Savior, we can see no room
for doubting that his kingdom was established as predicted by the prophets.

But David himself, at the ascension of Christ, said:
"Lift up your heads, O ye gates, and let the king of glory
come in." (Psalm xxiv: 7.) And the Father, at his reception, announced to a listening and anxious world: "I
have set my king upon my holy hill of Zion." More

upon the subject of Christ's having "raised the fallen tabernacle of David," and his sitting upon his throne, we consider would be quite superfluous. But are we required to show that the Church and kingdom are identical? Jesus said: "On this rock I will build my Church," and, with the word still hanging upon his lips, added, "I will give unto thee (Peter) the keys of the kingdom of heaven." Further proof of the identity of Church and kingdom can not be necessary.

Having, however, directed sufficient attention to "*the how*" the Church originated in the line of David, by Christ's raising his fallen tabernacle, and ascending David's throne, when crowned by the Father, it will be requisite, in order to maintain connection, to notice "*the when* and *the where*" of the origin of this spiritual tabernacle.

To the prophets we must again appeal for light. Daniel (ii: 44) said: "In the days of those kings" (in the days of the kingdoms represented by the ten horns of the wild beast) "the God of Heaven will set up a kingdom that shall never be destroyed. It shall break in pieces, and consume all these kingdoms, and shall stand forever."

John the Baptist said: "The kingdom of heaven is at hand." Jesus Christ repeated these words, and added: "Pray thy kingdom come;" encouraged his disciples to "seek the kingdom," "knock and it shall be opened;" and said: "Fear not, little flock, it is your Father's good pleasure to give you the kingdom." To Peter, he said: "On this rock I will build my Church;" and, just before he suffered, he assured his disciples that "there were some of them who should not taste of death till they should see the kingdom of God." But as the Father kept "times and seasons" to himself, neither the angels of Heaven nor our Lord knew the day on which the tabernacle would be reared. John and Jesus, with the apostles, had been preparing materials—making ready a people for the Lord's house; but till the ascension it had not been reared. Just before he left his disciples, they said: "Lord, restore the kingdom to Israel." "Go to Jerusalem," he replied, "and wait for the Spirit to guide you into all truth."

In Matthew, Mark, Luke, and John, we have nothing of the existence of the Church but in promise. But, as to place and time, we may learn an important lesson, by reference to the house built by Solomon.

The materials were made ready, and, when brought together, the edifice rose in beauty and majesty, without the sound of a hammer, or iron instrument, or the least confusion.

When the key was placed in the arch, "the glory of God filled the house," as a token the work was complete. The preparation of materials, bringing them together, and rising into an edifice, with such perfect symmetry, and the overshadowing glory, all pointed most significantly to the temple to be reared by Christ as David's son. Still, the kingdom was not to be seen; it was not to come by "observation," but was to rise miraculously. The materials were prepared, were conducted to Jerusalem, whence "the word of the Lord was to go out," and the disciples having assembled, the Spirit descended. Peter, by the Spirit's diction, delivered the law; three thousand submitted upon the first hearing, and were added to the one hundred and twenty, and, altogether, they constituted the Church of Jesus Christ; and, for the first time, it is said "The saved were daily added to the Church." (Acts ii: 47).

Hence, Jerusalem was the chosen site of the heavenly temple; and the first Pentecost, after the resurrection of the Messiah, was the day upon which the Church was planted. Peter, indeed, called it "the beginning." Beginning of what? The Christian dispensation? The middle wall of partition had been taken down from between Jews and Gentiles; the door of faith had been opened to the Jews on Pentecost, and the remaining key was employed in opening the temple to the Gentiles, some seven years after, at the house of Cornelius, and the work being finished, the Lord proclaimed the door open, which men could not shut. As further evidence that the kingdom now exists, we may add a few plain passages of New Testament Scripture.

Paul declared that the Colossians "had been delivered from the power of darkness, and translated into the kingdom of God's dear Son." (Col. i: 13.) How this transition from the power of darkness into the kingdom could have taken place in the days of the apostles, if the kingdom is yet in the future, we really think no man can explain.

To the Hebrews he said: "Ye have come to Mount Zion, the city of the living God, the heavenly Jerusalem, to the general assembly and church of the first-born, who are written in heaven;" and adds: "Wherefore, we receiving a kingdom which can not be moved, let us have grace whereby we may serve God acceptably." (Hebrews xii: 22–28.)

Again, he said: "God hath called you into his kingdom and glory." (1 Thess. ii: 13.)

The beloved John addressed the saints in the seven Asiatic churches as "his companions in tribulation, and in the kingdom and patience of Jesus Christ." (Rev. i: 9.)

More testimony to show how, when, and where the Church arose, the identity of Church and kingdom, and the present existence of the spiritual temple, it occurs to me, should not be demanded. I trust that we are prepared to next consider the question—

III. WHAT IS THE TEACHING OF THE SPIRIT UPON THE SUBJECT OF CHURCH ORGANIZATION?

It is possible there is no subject connected with the Christian economy shrouded in greater perplexities than the organization of the Church; and yet we are persuaded that, in the light of the New Testament, there are no incomprehensible mysteries involved. In our candid judgment, a fair statement of the question will very much contribute to unity of mind and action among the saints.

In the prosecution of our investigation, it will be proper, in the first place, to call attention to the meaning of organization. In natural history the word denotes *a structure*, with all the parts or organs wisely adjusted for action. Thus, a plant or an animal is denominated an organization, because the organs, parts, or instruments are fitted, arranged, and marvelously adjusted to enable all the machinery to act harmoniously. The mutual action and co-operation of all the parts of the organization are the necessary conditions of its health, growth, and efficiency. Take from the organization the least of its members, and the body is not complete; and it is impossible for one organization to perform the work of another. Not even a single member of one can be made effective in another. Hence, each organization in this vast universe is a sovereignty in itself, as perfect of its kind as the Great Author of all organizations. They all, to the spiritually enlightened, reflect the surpassing wisdom of their Great Author.

The Church of Jesus Christ is called his "body;" "God's husbandry;" "God's building;" "the Temple of God." And hence it is, in the proper meaning of the word, an organization. We read of the "head, mouth, eyes, feet, hands, ears, the feeble and less honorable members," but each is indispensable to the perfection of the "one body."

The apostle informs us that Christians "are builded together for a habitation of God through the Spirit;" and, consequently, God lives in the members, and we in him. He is our light and life.

Next, we may inquire "When," and "How," is a church organized? This question is answered in various forms by the Spirit, and yet the idea is always the same. From the very large amount of instruction we will select but few Scriptures. Each branch ingrafted into the "true vine" is, by virtue of its ingrafting, an organ, instrument, and essential part of the body; and at the instant the branches or members are "tempered," mixed, or fitted together by the Father, and give themselves to each other as the spiritually-born kings and priests to God, they, to all intents and purposes, constitute a perfectly organized church of the saints.

The new-born babe, at the moment of birth, is as perfect an organization as it can ever become; but the organs are feeble, and need suitable nourishment and care. The church, also, the day of its planting, is a perfect organism; but copious draughts of "the sincere milk of the word" are essential to the spiritual health and growth of the members.

These matters will appear clearer when we examine a little more carefully a few Scriptures with reference to this very simple conclusion.

The converts on Pentecost, with the one hundred and twenty, were not only pronounced "the Church," but the new-born organs exhibited spiritual life in "continuing steadfastly in the apostles' teaching and fellowship, and in breaking of bread, and in prayers." This being the first appearance on earth of an organized body of Christ, it might be taken as a model for church organization.

In the further prosecution of this subject, it will be necessary to keep in mind that *God* organizes the Church by the Spirit, and when the "building is fitly framed together, it grows into a holy temple in the Lord." Or, as the apostle says: "All the body by joints and bands, having nourishment ministered, and knit together, increases with the increase of God." As mortar is tempered and made fit for use by wisely adjusting the elements, God has tempered, knit, and compacted the body together, "that there should be no schism, but the members should have the same care for one another." (1 Cor. xii: 24.) In the same connection the apostle says: "God has *set* the members every one of them in the body, as it has pleased him." (1 Cor. xii: 18.) This is the key to the whole subject of church organization.

Are we asked how "God *sets* the members in the body?" how he *tempers* (*mixes*) them together for harmonious action and growth? The Spirit points to Christ as the "Head and Savior of the body." Therefore, no election or ordination by the members, can set a head to the body. God says to the senior members: "Take heed to yourselves, and to all the flock over which the Holy Spirit *has made* (set or placed) you overseers. If God has set the experienced members, as "Stephanas, the first fruits of Achaia, and others with him, who addicted themselves to the service of the saints," as his chosen shepherds, to whom the members, in consequence of their "help and labor," were to "submit," we have forever settled the vexed question of official appointments. God does it. Hence, Elder Peter said to experienced members: "Feed the flock of God, taking the oversight, not by constraint, but willingly; not for filthy lucre, but of a ready mind; not as lords over God's heritage, but as ensamples to the flock: and when the chief shepherd shall appear, ye shall receive a crown of glory that fadeth not away."

The senior women, also, God has "set," appointed, and ordained in the Church, as the natural and only competent "teachers of the younger women."

The younger are commanded to "submit to the elder;" and, finally, "all are to submit one to another," and to "esteem each other highly in love, for their work sake," and on no other account whatever. Therefore, all officials are the natural and legitimate outgrowth of the Church.

This Divine organization, as intimated, began at Pentecost; but many things "were wanting" to perfect the body in the days of the apostles. It may be pronounced the day of the Church's childhood, in which, although the Spirit directed in all things, the members "looked through a glass darkly," till the "perfection" came.

The saints were perfected for the work of ministering to the nations, for building up the body of Christ, and came to the unity of the faith at the completion of the revelation. They attained to the knowledge of a perfect man in Jesus Christ. Henceforth, they "were no more children, tossed to and fro, and carried about by every wind of doctrine," but, by the members, "speaking the truth in love," were to *grow up into* him in all things, and to *make increase* of the body unto the upbuilding of itself in love."

I now feel at liberty to pronounce this the Lord's
ORGANIZATION, and, as I hope to show presently, "THE
LORD's PLAN," for all spiritual service.

' If these things embody the instructions of the New
Testament, upon the great subject of spiritual organization, how are we to regard the conduct of professed Church
organizers, when they assume the right to *appoint* heads,
overseers, pastors, and other officials over God's household? This, though it is the practice of Rome and all
her daughters, to say the least, has not the slightest semblance of Divine authority.

The fancy of preachers that they organize and reorgan-
ize churches, by professing to make elders, deacons, overseers, or other officials, is wholly unscriptural, and a reproach to any people professing to be led by the Spirit.
I would be pleased to answer every possible objection to
these conclusions; but, in the circumstances, I can only
pray our friends to give the subject a *calm* and *impartial*
examination.

If I have comprehended the meaning of the body of
Christ, it strengthens and grows *ab intra*, and not *ab
extra*, from the poor husks furnished by the world and
its wisdom; and thus we are brought to ask—

IV. Is the Church a carnal, mixed, or spiritual
ORGANIZATION?

The sin of the present religious world seems to consist
in giving the Church no higher position than the governments of the earth. Hence, we know no party that has
not either formed alliances with the State, or, in some
manner, sought the protection and friendship of governments under the direction of the prince of this world. It
is the glory of most religious parties in America, that their

34

organizations are modeled after the government of the United States.

But it is the fatal error of these churches, with most prophetical writers—from Baxter, in his Napoleonic Antichrist, to Baldwin, in his millennial and world-wide democracy—to fail to discover the spiritual organization, called "God's house." Perhaps, a very brief examination of the Church and world-powers may be in place. These may be clearly seen, by even a bird's-eye glance, at the elements of each. It has, however, been said of us, that our conclusions are not clear in regard to the Church and world-powers. At this friendly intimation we are not at all suprised. It is said that objects, seen through colored glasses, never appear as they really exist; and we apprehend, that persons so wholly devoted to earthly governments and worldly-wise institutions, for the work of God, as the great masses of the people of this age, would not likely discover the spiritual organization of the New Testament. Worldly wisdom for worldly labor; but into the Spirit's temple, the wisdom of man can not penetrate.

How could we expect such as look through Roman and Protestant mists, to see the fair proportions and Divine symmetry of the body of Christ?

But to the elements of the respective orders of institutions we are contemplating, we must carefully look for satisfactory light.

Worldly governments are not for the righteous, said Paul; and, therefore, God has ordained the men of the world as his ministers to create and direct all institutions worldly. In his spiritual household, our heavenly Father has reserved the right to govern without the admixture of the least human wisdom, which the apostle says is "foolishness with God." The prince of this world is the head

and governor, in all kingdoms and organizations constructed in the wisdom of men. His subjects are such as
are devoted to institutions not Divine. Force is the great
controlling power.

In Christ's body, on the contrary, the Head is spiritual;
his subjects are spiritual; his laws are spiritual; and love
is the only motive power. To us these institutions, therefore, differ across the whole heavens. May we not call to
our aid a few very plain passages of Scripture, as evidence
that we are not mistaken.

Our Lord said: "The field is the world; the good seed
are the children of the kingdom; but the tares are the
children of the wicked one." To the Jews, he said: "Ye
are of your father the devil, and the lusts of your father ye
will do. He was a murderer from the beginning, and
abode not in the truth, because there is no truth in him."
(John viii: 44.)

From these statements, we learn that, while the wheat
and tares grow together in the world, the good seed, representing Christians, are "the children of the kingdom;"
and though in the world, "are not of the world," while the
tares are the devil's sowing and plants. In that solemn
declaration of the Savior before Pilate—"My kingdom is
not of this world; if it were, my servants would fight that I
should not be delivered to the Jews; but now is my kingdom not from hence"—possibly is embodied all that need
be predicated of the spiritual character of the Church for
our present purpose. In the Christian institution, then,
"swords are beaten into ploughshares, and spears into
pruning-hooks," and God's people "study not war." No
violence was necessary to give success to the government
of Christ, and his people employ it not in their journey
to the skies. God is their shield and high tower. If,

through these great words of the Spirit, our friends can not see the broad line between the Church and the world, it is not in my power to describe it.

V. What is the legitimate work of this Spiritual Organization?

Cæsar, in his memorable dispatch to the Roman Senate, embodied a volume in the simple words, "I came, I saw, I conquered;" and of our beloved Savior it may be said: He came to earth, to save the lost; he provided the means in his Church, and he will not be foiled in his purposes.

If men are dead to God, if they are in the broad fields of "the wicked one," we can not see how they can be pardoned or saved till they renounce their old master, "turn from darkness to light," and become loyal to Jesus Christ, by "obeying from the heart that form of doctrine through which they are set free from sin, and become the servants of righteousness." (Romans vi: 17.) Hence, when the wicked turn to God, they are said, as we have seen, to be "delivered from the power of darkness, and translated into the kingdom of God's dear Son." (Col. i: 13.) Jesus said: "Come to me, take my yoke, and you shall find rest to your souls." This is fully illustrated by the "householder who went out early in the morning to hire laborers *into* his vineyard;" and having agreed with them, "he sent them into his vineyard to work."

If it was an essential condition, in order to perform the service of the householder, to enter into the vineyard, we may readily conclude that the works of God can not be performed in the kingdom of the wicked one. Not only does the entrance into the body of Christ secure the remission of sins, the adoption into the heavenly family, "life from the dead," and the full enjoyment of the Holy

Spirit—but, at the close of our pilgrimage, our Lord will deliver up his kingdom—his chosen people—to his Father, that " God may be all and in all." With this agrees the declaration of the wise man, that "The sacrifice of the wicked is an abomination to the Lord; but the prayer of the upright is his delight." (Proverbs xv : 8.) Hence, the proposition that there are really two, and but two, kingdoms or orders of government on the earth—the one under the prince of this world, the devil, and the other under the Prince of Peace—is true beyond controversy. Under the guidance of the God of this world, who is supreme in all worldly governments and organizations originating in the wisdom of men, we consider it entirely safe to conclude that spiritual life can not be engaged. But, thanks to God, whoever will has the right to forsake the kingdom of darkness, and become an heir of God through Christ.

In this connection, it can but be considered an act of simple justice to at least advert to what must, sooner or later, be acknowledged in the world's history as "*The Reformatory Movement of the nineteenth century.*"

We consider it becoming to state, in plain terms, the position which clearly distinguishes the body of Christ from all other religious organizations.

From the apostasy of the Romish and Greek Churches to this day, there can not be found, in the history of denominations, Papal or Protestant, an earnest effort to return to the spiritual purity and authority of the Church of God. True, Luther, Calvin, and Wesley made war upon the accumulated church corruptions of the ages; but it never entered into their hearts to doubt the capacity of institutions originating in apostasy to save the world. Hence, we hear not a word from them in favor of return-

ing to the ancient order of things. Each became perfectly satisfied with the formation of a new sect, on the
model of Rome; and, at the close of the eighteenth century, the *ne plus ultra* of partisan degradation seemed to
have been reached.

Early in the nineteenth century, however, it pleased God
to raise up witnesses, quite as humble as our Lord and
his apostles, to plead for a pure speech and a pure religion.
The effort has been successful in calling from the world,
and the very depths of spiritual Babylon, into religious
union, hundreds of thousands, who fear not to give an
authoritative reason for their hope.

These great men of God split with Romanism, Protestantism, and all other forms of human organizations, simply upon the ground that they had lost all confidence in
institutions originating in the wisdom of men to save the
lost and elevate society to the state of purity required in
the New Testament.

We have not assailed Romanism, or Protestantism,
with the idea of forming a new sect, but solely from the
solemn conviction that religious parties are inadequate for
the work intended by the Church of Christ. If, in our
hearts, we could conclude that denominations, societies,
and organizations not known in the New Testament were
capable of the spiritual labor ordained by Christ and the
apostles, not a word against them would escape our lips.

While we disclaim all connection with Romish and Protestant sects, we solemnly deny ourselves the right to add
another faction to the six hundred and sixty-six which completed the degradation of the apostasy. It is our rejoicing
that we have no denomination, party, or creed to defend,
and no plans, expedients, or organizations that have arisen,
in our wisdom and discretion, to foster. Still, our distinct-

ive position is not negative. Nay, verily; we humbly claim to be the Lord's freedmen; and, confidently believing that the Church built upon the rock—"the pillar and support of the truth"—has so far weathered the storm of factious opposition, that it will finally triumph over his Satanic majesty's expedients, we therefore aspire to nothing beyond membership in the body of Christ. All who believe through the apostles' words we claim as our brethren; and we will have fellowship on no other terms. Believing that all things which pertain to life and godliness are furnished in the Scriptures, we take the Bible, in good faith, as our only creed, and ask no one to believe or do any thing of a religious character for which we have not "a thus saith the Lord." Not only do we regard the Church of God as competent for all spiritual work, but that the adoption of any other organization for such service, as most displeasing to heaven and injurious to man.

Hence, we can but urge our cotemporaries to be Christians in the Scriptural sense of the word; for, without citizenship in the kingdom of God's dear Son, and a faithful adherence to the creed furnished by the Spirit, eternal life is not promised.

VI. THE CONFLICTS OF THE CHURCH.

The war between Michael and Satan is still raging. The destroyer has diligently labored, but in vain, from the planting of the Church at Jerusalem on Pentecost, to overthrow the cause, for the protection of which the veracity of the Father's throne is pledged. The deceiver still employs the principalities, powers, and expedients of the world to overthrow the kingdom of the Savior. Hence we can not hope for conflicts to cease until the Lord shall have put the last enemy under his feet.

VII. WILL THE CHURCH OF CHRIST FINALLY TRIUMPH?

If God is true, his purposes can not fail; and if the Spirit's teaching affords the only authority to which we can confidently look, it is our exalted privilege to believe that the time is not far distant when the problem of self-government, civil and ecclesiastical, will have been worked out—when, from the utter failure of worldly-wise organizations for spiritual labor, the Church of Christ will shine forth "fair as the moon, clear as the sun, and terrible as an army with banners." Then, and not until then, will her true mission be acknowledged.

Yours truly
W. T. Moore

WILLIAM THOMAS MOORE.*

WILLIAM THOMAS MOORE was born in Henry County, Kentucky, August 27, 1832. His paternal ancestors were Irish; his maternal, Scotch. His immediate parents were from Virginia. When nine years of age, his father died, leaving a widow and six children, and, for a number of years, WILLIAM was the chief dependence of the bereaved family. Thus early were the boy's energies of body and mind called to grapple with toil and care; but, doubtless, it was during these years that the foundation of his subsequent successes was laid. From the necessities of his position, his education was neglected, and, at eighteen years of age, his scholastic attainments comprehended reading and writing—no more; but, having an innate thirst for knowledge, he had read whatever books had come in his way—especially had he read the Bible.

At eighteen, Mr. MOORE entered an academy at Newcastle, Kentucky, and, having passed through a preparatory course of study there, and having improved his financial affairs by teaching for a season, he entered Bethany College, Virginia, in the autumn of 1855. In July, 1858, having been chosen from a class of twenty-four to deliver the Valedictory Address, he was graduated Bachelor of Arts. In October of the same year, he was chosen pastor of the Church of Christ in Frankfort, Kentucky, and remained its pastor till the spring of 1864, when he resigned, on account of failing health. In June, 1864, he was married to Miss MARY A. BISHOP, second daughter of R. M. BISHOP, of Cincinnati, Ohio. On the first of January, 1865, his health having greatly improved, Mr. MOORE accepted a call to the pastoral work in the Church of Christ in Detroit, Michigan. Although his labors there were being attended by the most encouraging success, yet, having been elected to a Professorship in Kentucky University, he left Detroit in February, 1866, and entered at once on the labors appointed him in the University. Meanwhile, he had received a call from the Church of God, Eighth and Walnut streets, Cincinnati, Ohio, and, having ascer-

---

* In justice to the Editor of this work, it is proper to state that this sketch of his life was written, at the request of the Publishers, by Dr. L. L. Pinkerton, and appears just as he wrote it.

tained that, for the present, the duties of his University Chair could be met by a brief course of lectures in each session, he accepted the call of the Church. He holds both offices at the present time, October, 1867.

Besides his almost continuous labors as pastor and evangelist, W. T. MOORE has prepared and delivered a number of public addresses on a variety of topics, some of which have been published, and widely circulated. He has also edited a portion of A. CAMPBELL's "Lectures on the Pentateuch," and this volume of Discourses and Biographical Sketches. Amid these constant and varied engagements, he has found leisure to toy slightly with the Muses; nor have these coy nymphs rudely repelled his woorings. Several short poems, chiefly lyric and elegiac, have found their way into print and into public favor. His love of poetry and of music, and his appreciation of the excellencies of both, rendered his services of incalculable value in the compilation of the "Christian Hymn Book"—the best extant collection of sacred sonnets in the English language.

The lessons of persevering toil learned in boyhood in the hill country of Henry County, Kentucky, have not been lost, nor has the love of reading that characterized the boy disappeared in the man. He believes in progress, from the high even to the still higher, and illustrates his faith by his works. Withal, he never seems to be busy; in fact, does not seem to be doing any thing when out of the pulpit, nor *intending* to do any thing; and yet he can be seldom, if ever, idle, as this brief record abundantly attests. With no bustle or apparent motion, there is execution— progress. Few men have accomplished more, in the same time, and under similar circumstances, than has W. T. MOORE.

His manner in the pulpit, whether of action or utterance, indicates deep earnestness. His style sometimes borders on the vehement, but never on the declamatory. The points in his discourses are generally well chosen, forcibly argued, and clearly illustrated, and, when practical, powerfully enforced. But his success as a minister is owing much less to his logic than to the warm and wide sympathy which pervades and vivifies it. His is heart-power—a power without which the logic of Paul and the eloquence of Apollos combined would fail to awaken the conscience of the impeni tent sinner, or arouse the energies of the careless believer.

With whatever is beautiful, and good, and true; with every thing that is pitiable, or distressed, or down-fallen, or oppressed; with all that is elevating, ennobling, hopeful, God has given to W. T. MOORE a quick, a deep, an irresistible sympathy, so that he is ready to rejoice with the happy, and to weep with those that weep. He is ever forward to engage in whatever promises true advancement, and to share his last resources with those he esteems worthy, but who have grown weary and lame, and have thus fallen or faltered in the struggle of life.

FAITH AND SIGHT.

BY W. T. MOORE.

"For we walk by faith, and not by sight."—2 COR. V: 7.

IN our present state, we are necessarily connected with
two worlds—the natural and the supernatural—and
from these we derive all the means of our temporal and
spiritual life. The natural satisfies the senses, and is,
indeed, the soil on which they grow; but only the supernatural can satisfy the conditions of the spirit, for its immortal longings reach far beyond the confines of sensuous
and earthly things. These two worlds constitute man's
entire area of thought and action, affording ample opportunities for the exercise alike of his physical and spiritual
natures. In one, we walk by Sight; in the other, by Faith.
Let it be distinctly stated, however, that there is no *necessary* conflict between the natural and the supernatural.
These are complements of each other, and are both essential to meet the requirements of our organization, as well
as to fulfill the purposes of God in us. It is time that
the crude, irrational, and unphilosophical conclusion, that
God, in his moral government, is forever contradicting
the laws of the physical, had become obsolete—a fossil of
a by-gone, semi-christian civilization. God does not con-

tradict himself, but is perfectly consistent in all his works. Hence, there is no necessary antagonism between spirit and sense; neither is there any between Faith and Sight. But, while this is true, it is equally true that Faith and Sight are exceedingly jealous of each other. No encroachments upon the boundaries of either must be made, for when it is otherwise, a conflict at once begins, which not unfrequently ends in the destruction of happiness, and the ruin of the soul. Each has its distinctive province, and this is sacred against all interference. It becomes, therefore, a matter of grave importance to correctly define the boundaries of these, and whatever other relations they may sustain to each other. Hence, in order to treat the whole subject in a manner somewhat commensurate with its importance, I propose to observe the following plan:

I. Show the difference between Faith and Sight;
II. Trace the analogy between them;
III. Illustrate the Superiority of Faith.

In presenting and developing these points, I shall avoid, as far as possible, every thing like abstract or metaphysical reasoning, though, in the very nature of things, I shall be compelled to go somewhat out of the ordinary path of pulpit discourse. I will endeavor, however, to be as simple in my treatment as the character of the subject will permit; and trust that, by Divine assistance, I may be able to present every thing in such a way as that all may understand and be benefited by the investigation. Let us, then, consider—

I. The Difference between Faith and Sight.

It will greatly facilitate our progress in this inquiry, if we keep in memory what has already been stated in ref-

erence to the distinct province occupied respectively by
Faith and Sight. It must never be forgotten that they
do not belong to the same territory, and that it is only by
keeping them *entirely separate* that harmony between them
is preserved.

The term *Sight*, in the text, may be defined as embracing every thing *outside of Faith*. Whatever belongs to the
Senses, or the Reason, is clearly included in it. Hence,
Sense, Reason, and Faith cover the whole ground of the
natural and the supernatural, the visible and invisible, the
temporal and eternal; and to understand the relation of
these to each other, and to know how to appropriate the
knowledge derived respectively from them, is the end of
all study, the consummation of all effort.

I shall now attempt to illustrate these matters in such
a way that no one can fail to understand my meaning.
If you look upon an object, the soul will be affected according to the qualities of that object. If the object is a
beautiful landscape, the impression made will be *agreeable*
—the soul will *enjoy* the view; but if the object is an un-
gainly thing—something possessing repulsive qualities—
it will be *disagreeable*, and you will experience a very unpleasant sensation. Hence, it may be affirmed that all
sensuous knowledge—that is, knowledge derived directly
through the senses—is either agreeable or disagreeable,
pleasant or unpleasant; and that, therefore, it is the province of Sense to determine the *qualities* of things.

If, however, you demonstrate that the " square described on the hypothenuse of a right-angled triangle is
equal to the sum of the squares described on the other
two sides," it can not be said that there is any thing agreeable or disagreeable, pleasant or unpleasant in that. True,
there is a sense of enjoyment when the conclusion is

reached; but this is no part of the demonstration. The feeling experienced is *after the problem passes from the Reason to the Senses.* But the demonstration itself is a step higher than the Senses. It is in the domain of the Reason, and the knowledge which you derive from your effort may be denominated *rational*, because it comes from the *relation* of things, and not their *qualities.* This is a new field upon which you have entered, and you no longer behold the enchanting sunsets, the meandering rivers, and the beautiful landscapes which every-where meet the view in the world of qualities; nor do you any longer hear the ravishing music of singing birds, laughing rivulets, and dashing waterfalls, as they mingle their strange and wonderful harmonies into a grand oratorio, the sound of which inspires all the region of the sense-land. You have forgotten all these, and are now at work in the world of causes and wherefores, the possible and impossible, where sensation gives place to demonstration, and light comes only through the pure Reason.

We have now briefly surveyed the dominion of Sight; but there are many things yet to be learned. We have done little more than cast a pebble into the great waters of the unknown. The past, with all its joys and sorrows, buried beneath the weight of six thousand years; and the future, with its hopes and fears, stretching out before us like a shoreless ocean, whose treasures can not be gathered, and whose mysteries can not be explained by either Sense or Reason, are yet unexplored. But, thanks to our heavenly Father, we are not left in darkness here. Over all this invisible land, Faith holds undisputed sway. *Just at the point where Sight ends, Faith begins.* When Sense and Reason become helpless and blind, then Faith spreads her wings, and leads on through the regions beyond. Did such a man as the first Napoleon live and act the part ascribed to him in history? If so, how does it become a part of our stock of knowledge? Is it because it is agreeable or disagreeable? Or can it be demonstrated from the relation of things? Can either Sense or Reason reach back into the past, and bring this fact into the knowledge of the present? Who does not see that it is a subject entirely out of the range of either of these, and that, no matter how they may be affected by it, the *fact* is not changed in any way whatever? It is equally independent of the likes and dislikes of mankind, and the boasted power of human reason. All that you can say about it is, that it is either *true* or *false*. If false, nothing can make it true; if true, nothing can make it false. *Matters of faith, then, are matters of fact; and these can be determined only by the weight of testimony.*

If what has been already stated be true, it must be evident that there are but three ways in which knowledge can be derived, viz., through the senses, the pure reason, and by faith. And, for the sake of a convenient classification, we may call the first, sensuous knowledge; the second, rational knowledge; and the third, the knowledge of testimony. These comprehend all knowledge, and exhaust the area of the natural and the supernatural. In harmony with this classification, we have three systems of religion, viz., Paganism, Rationalism, and Christianity; and, upon investigation, it will be found that the characteristics of these correspond respectively to Sense, Reason, and Faith. Let us now examine these systems briefly, and see what their ruling principles are.

1. *Paganism is the religion of Sense.*

It proposes nothing higher than the Senses as an object

of worship, and is constantly controlled by an unrelenting, sensuous philosophy. The appetites and passions become the gods of this Godless religion. Under its teachings, men seek that which satisfies the lusts of the flesh; while every grace of a higher civilization is either destroyed or driven into eternal banishment. Virtue is insulted in the arms of Bacchus; Righteousness is burned in the Temple of Moloch; Truth is lost in the Pantheon; Innocence is chained to the Car of Juggernaut; Love lies bleeding under the heel of Mars; and Peace hears nothing but eternal strife. And yet, all this exhibits but a faint picture of the blighting curse of Paganism in its influence on the civilization of the world. But, if any thing further is needed to illustrate the diabolical spirit of this sensuistic religion, it is only necessary to hear what the apostle says concerning its workings when the people were fully under its control: "Being filled with all unrighteousness, fornication, wickedness, covetousness, maliciousness; full of envy, murder, debate, deceit, malignity; whisperers, backbiters, haters of God, despiteful, proud, boasters, inventors of evil things, disobedient to parents, without understanding, covenant breakers, without natural affection, implacable, unmerciful: who, knowing the judgment of God, that they which commit such things are worthy of death; not only do the same, but have pleasure in them that do them." (Rom. i: 29-32.) These people were certainly the chief of sinners; and, after such an enumeration, can we wonder that the apostle gloried in the Cross by which he was crucified to the world, and the world to him?

But what is modern Ritualism but a refined Paganism? Is not the principle of both precisely the same? What mean all the forms and ceremonies of Ritualism, if they be not to charm the Senses? From this stand-point it does not require much reflection to determine the secret of the success of Catholicism. Take away its liturgy, its ritual service—strip it of every thing except what is legitimately Christian, and it will not be long before the pontifical throne is vacated, and the mistress of the world is humbled in the dust. Catholicism, as opposed to Rationalism, is a religion of superstition; but as opposed to Christianity, it is a religion of flesh.

2. *Rationalism is the Religion of Reason.*

As such, it is only a step higher than sensualism. It is simply more respectable. While one glories in the "lusts of the flesh," the other glories in the "pride of life." Rationalism may deplore the fearful consequences of sin as seen in the progress of sensualism; but it can neither account for that sin, nor offer an adequate remedy for it. It stands, in the presence of the world's greatest need, a condemned pretender, a vaunting hypocrite. It has yet to learn the palpable truism, that *religion is philosophy, but philosophy is not religion.* What care I for the boasted powers of human reason, the wonderful revelations of science, and the splendid trophies of genius, *while all these perish with their using,* and offer nothing to the sad, sick, and weary soul beyond the things of time and sense? What a cheat this Rationalism is! And how impotent to meet our real wants! It has recently somewhat revived in Europe and this country, and, under the leadership of such men as Renan, Colenso, Leckey, and Emerson, it promises great things. But it is the same old story of philosophy against religion, the natural against the supernatural, Sight against Faith, which has been the irrepressible conflict of ages. The Apostle Paul found the same

35

thing at Corinth; and the reason he gave for it then will account for it to-day: "The preaching of the cross is to them that perish foolishness, but unto us who are saved, it is the power of God." (1 Cor. i: 18.)

3. *Christianity is the Religion of Faith.*

No higher encomium could be pronounced upon Christianity than is contained in this statement. Christ's kingdom is not of this world. Hence, the religion which he established is not carnal, but spiritual. Christianity, then, rises far above the sensuous and rational, and rests its claim on Divine authority. WHICH? is the question Paganism or Ritualism asks. It seeks after only the agreeable and pleasant—those things which satisfy the demands of the senses—while Rationalism is equally persistent in pressing the everlasting WHY? looking only for the cause or reason of things, and attempting to solve the mysteries of our present state by the revelations of science. But the question which Christianity asks is WHAT? and has respect, not to pleasure or philosophy, but to *duty.* With all its qualifying words, it stands thus: LORD, WHAT WILT THOU HAVE ME TO DO?

It should ever be remembered that Christianity is not a religion of pleasure, but of self-abnegation, of self-crucifixion. We are constantly exhorted to "deny ourselves," to "keep the body under," to "crucify the lusts of the flesh," and to "suffer for righteousness' sake;" showing clearly that the enjoyment derived from the service of Christ is not sensuous, but spiritual. As followers of Jesus, we may expect to meet innumerable crosses; and if this were not so, we might question our final triumph, for it is only by the Cross we reach the Crown.

This peculiarity of the Christian religion seems to have

been very generally overlooked by our modern system-makers, who would like to have the charities of the Gospel include all the follies and pleasures of mankind; but, He who spake as never man spake, said: "Wide is the gate, and broad is the way, that leadeth to destruction, and many there be that go in thereat: because straight is the gate, and narrow is the way, which leadeth to life, and few there be that find it." (Matt. vii: 13, 14.)

It becomes, therefore, a matter of great importance to determine by what principles we are guided in our religious acts. Is our service the "obedience of faith," or the obedience of sight? Are we seeking to gratify the senses, or to adorn and beautify the spirit? Is our service mere lip-service, or do we worship in spirit and in truth? A proper answer to these questions will do much toward determining our true relations to Christ.

If you wish to see how wide-spread and how desolating the religion of Sight is, go to the people, and talk to them about obeying the Gospel. You will constantly hear such expressions as these: "Every body should belong to some church;" "I *prefer* the Presbyterian Church;" "The Episcopal service *suits me* best—it is so beautiful;" "I *like* Dr. A., and I will join *his* church," etc. All these clearly indicate that SELF-SATISFACTION is the principal thing aimed at. Esthetics, and not Christ, is the object of the worship of thousands. Poor sinners, this is not the kind of obedience Christ demands. What you like or dislike has nothing to do with your salvation, and is not the question for you to consider. You must walk by Faith, and not by Sight. The all-absorbing, all-important question is, *What does the Lord say?* When this is satisfactorily answered, you can go forward, with the blessed assurance that you can "do all things through Christ, who strengthens you."

But again: What business have you with the *reason* of the command? Can you expect to fathom the deep purposes of God? Why, you can not explain the most familiar thing. If, when surveying the legitimate realms of philosophy, you frequently stumble and fall, can you expect to walk by Sight a single moment in religion? Should you entertain such an idea, let me assure you that Faith alone can lead you through the darkness of the present to a bright and glorious future.

II. THE ANALOGY BETWEEN FAITH AND SIGHT.

The New Testament abounds in analogical teaching, but the great Teacher more especially excels in this method of presenting truth. Nothing could be more striking, and certainly nothing more instructive, than this method, when properly used. Besides the *particular* truth it unfolds, in any given case, it teaches us the *general* truth that material things are to be valued, not as an *end*, but as a *means;* and that, therefore, the Senses and the Reason are but instruments by which the soul travels toward the regions of Faith, and are only useful while operating in their proper spheres. Hence they must not be allowed to trespass upon the dominion of Faith, for it can hold no partnerships, make no compromises; it must have undisputed and unlimited control over its own. Let us now examine the analogy between Faith and Sight. Sight clearly implies three things:

1. The organ of sight—the eye.
2. The medium of sight—light.
3. An object upon which to look.

Now when these three things are perfect there will be perfect vision; but remove one—no matter which—and there can be no vision at all. Precisely so is it with Faith. Three things are necessary to it also:

1. *There must be the organ of Faith—the capacity to believe.*

Have we this capacity? Are we capable of believing truth when it is presented before us? Certainly no one ought to hesitate in answering these questions. But, strange to say, some men have doubted our capacity to believe—men, too, who are regarded as lights in the Church, and whose opinions carry with them great weight. Surely, such men do not understand what they teach.

I do not propose to discuss this question. In fact, it is not a question within the range of legitimate discussion. It is a question of experience, and can be decided only by an appeal to every man's consciousness. Every man must decide for himself; no one can do it for him. True, the aggregate testimony of men can be taken, but the question then becomes a matter of Faith, the ridiculousness of which will appear when an *individual* attempts to express himself in the language which this position forces him to use. "I believe that I can believe," is not very passable English, and certainly does not sound out with the same assurance as "I know that I can believe." The question, then, is not one of faith or philosophy, but of actual knowledge. In order to make my meaning more fully understood, I will illustrate: For several hours, upon a pair of scales, suspended by a rope, you have been weighing a thousand pounds at a time. A gentleman steps up, and, after examining the rope, and making a long and intricate calculation, he gravely informs you that he thoroughly understands the philosophy of ropes, and that this one is not now, and never was, capable of bearing up more than five hundred pounds? What would you think of this man's philosophy? And how long would you stop to reason with him about the matter? If you were to consume time with him at all, you would simply say to him, "That you did not care what his philosophy taught; that you had tried the rope sufficiently, and knew, from actual experience, that he was mistaken." So say to every man that doubts your ability to believe the Gospel.

2. *There must be the medium of Faith.*

The apostle says: "Faith comes by hearing, and hearing by the word of God." (Rom. x: 17.) This, then, settles the question as to what is the medium of Faith. Clearly, it is the Word of God. And this at once elevates our view of that Word, and gives us better conceptions of the preciousness of Faith. We bless the hand that bears us the gift. In what reverence, then, should we hold the Word of God, which brings to us such a glorious gift as Faith!

3. *Faith must have an object—something upon which to rest.*

What is this object? Let the Holy Scriptures answer: "God so loved the world, that he gave his only-begotten Son, that whosoever *believeth in him* should not perish, but have everlasting life;" "This is the work of God, that ye *believe on him* whom he hath sent;" "He that *believeth on me* hath everlasting life;" "Ye believe in God, *believe also in me;*" "*Believe on the Lord Jesus Christ*, and thou shalt be saved." Many other passages could be quoted, but these are deemed sufficient to show that the object of our Faith is the precious Savior. And what a blessed fact this is! How consoling to the heart that is tired of the endless controversies about creeds and doctrines! And with what joyful trust does the poor, houseless wanderer come to this sure foundation-stone which God has laid in Zion! The Christian's Faith is not *doctrinal,* but *personal;*

not belief in a *theory*, but in a Divine and glorious *character*; not the reception of a cold, lifeless *dogma*, but a hearty, earnest trust in one whose love is *stronger than a brother's;* who is "touched with a feeling of our infirmities;" who "knows our frame, and remembers that we are dust."

But let us notice in what particulars Christ addresses our confidence. *Is he worthy?* Certainly he who has been appointed "heir of all things;" "by whom the worlds were made;" who is the "brightness of the Father's glory, and the express image of his person;" who is "seated at the right hand of the Majesty on high;" whose "throne is for ever and ever;" who "loves righteousness and who hates iniquity;" and "whom all the angels worship," is worthy of our most unqualified trust and our highest adoration.

Has he done any thing for us that entitles him to our confidence? Read his history. Follow him from his birth to the last scenes on Calvary. His life was one of toil, sorrow, and self-denial, that he might teach us "how sublime a thing it is to suffer and be strong." But who can witness his last dying agony on the Cross without exclaiming—

"Were the whole realm of nature mine,
That were a present far too small;
Love so amazing, so Divine,
Demands my soul, my life, my all."

Will he certainly save us if we put our trust in him? What penitent believer did he ever turn away? "He would not have any to perish, but all to come to the knowledge of the truth." Do we want a Savior who is willing to save? *Jesus is ever willing.* Must he have the official character of a Savior? *Christ is anointed to save.* But do you say he must have power to save? *The Lord is* "*able to save to the uttermost all that come to God by him.*" Sinner, believe on the Lord Jesus Christ, and THOU SHALT BE SAVED.

III. THE SUPERIORITY OF FAITH OVER SIGHT.

Numerous examples illustrating the truth of this proposition may be found in both the Old and New Testament Scriptures. In fact, from that memorable occasion in the Garden of Eden, when Sight was first brought into antagonism with Faith, till the present time, the history of the world is but a succession of events attesting the superior excellence of Faith. Sight, when followed beyond its legitimate sphere, has ever led mankind astray. Its dazzling beauty, its splendid attire, and its fascinating charms are well calculated to captivate those who trust in appearances. But it is only necessary to examine the records of the past, and our own experience, to understand how deceitful is all this display, and how unworthy it is of our confidence.

Not so of Faith. It offers no enchanting prospects in this life. Its promises here are self-denial, toil, struggle, sorrow, and disappointments; but its history is full of immortal heroes and glorious triumphs. After a while its work will be accomplished, and then those who "have kept the faith" will, with the Apostle Paul, receive a "crown of righteousness" which shall never fade away.

But let us now consider wherein consists Faith's superiority.

1. *It has a more extended view than Sight.*

Whoever attempts to walk by Sight will not be long in finding out the shortness of his vision. He will find that life is full of labyrinths he can not thread, while everywhere he will meet untold mysteries he can not explain.

Discouraged by his failures, and bewildered by the difficulties of his situation, he will very possibly despair of
relief, and accept one of the inevitable alternatives of des-
peration, viz.: dissipation, solitude, or suicide, either of
which will unfit him for the land of the great hereafter.

But the horizon of Faith is not so limited. The apostle's description will help us to understand its extent:
"Faith is the foundation of things hoped for, the conviction of things not seen." (Heb. xi: 1.) That is, it stands
under all the future, and convinces of all the past. It
is, therefore, master of the invisible world, and is to the
spiritual world what Sight is to the material. With this
wonderful telescope we can survey every step of human
progress, and understand every path of human duty.

2. *Faith is more truthful than Sight.*

Things are not here what they seem to be. Deception
lurks in the most inviting prospects. We see only the
outside. We do not penetrate to the real *essence.* We are
intoxicated with *qualities,* and show our aptness by com-
pounding *relations,* but we only deceive ourselves, and demonstrate that—

> "This world is all a fleeting show,
>   For man's illusion given;
>   The smiles of joy, the tears of woe
>   Deceitful shine, deceitful flow,
>   There's nothing true but heaven."

Sight takes cognizance of things as they *appear;* Faith
sees them as they *are.* Sight sees that which is *visible;*
Faith sees only the *unseen.* One deceives, and often leads
astray; the other deals honestly with us, and tells us the
truth. When was any one ever disappointed who walked

by Faith? You will search the records of the past in vain for a single example. On the contrary, however, you will find that the "obedience of faith" has always been richly rewarded. I can refer to only a few instances.

As the children of Israel journeyed from Mount Hor, by the way of the Red Sea, to compass the land of Edom, they became much discouraged because of the way, and complained bitterly against God and Moses for having brought them out of the land of Egypt to die in the wilderness. And the Lord sent fiery serpents among them, to punish them for their unbelief and hardness of heart. From the bite of these serpents, many of the people died. After which, those remaining confessed their sins, and besought Moses that he would pray the Lord to have the curse removed. The Lord instructed Moses to make a brazen serpent, and set it upon a pole, and said it should come to pass that every one who was bitten, when he looked upon it, should live.

Could any thing have been more unphilosophical than this remedy? How unlike the *materia medica* of Sight! Suppose some modern physician were to suggest such a remedy for the bite of serpents now, what, think you, our learned doctors of medicine would say of him? Would they be likely to regard him as sane? Not unless they should exercise more charity than they are in the habit of doing toward adventurers in their profession. But these Israelites were not to seek for the reason of the command; they were to walk by Faith—simply to *look and live*. When they had obeyed, were they disappointed? No matter how unpromising the thing appeared, was not the Faith of every poor, suffering Israelite, who looked to the remedy instantly and amply rewarded?

The destruction of the walls of Jericho is another striking illustration of the fidelity of Faith to her promises. What if some modern Joshua should establish a school of military tactics in accordance with the programme of that siege? Does not the very thought excite a smile on the face of every war-worn veteran in all the land? Nevertheless, when the Israelites had compassed the city, as commanded, their Faith met no disappointment—the walls of the city fell

3. *Faith is more powerful than Sight.*

There is nothing, perhaps, in which we are so constantly cheated as in our estimate of power. We are accustomed to look for it in noise and great display; but nothing could be more unwise, for *real* power moves in silent courses. It is not in the thunder's deep, portentous roar, but in the lightning which sleeps in the storm-cloud. Sight is forever thundering in our ears its arrogant boasts, while it is only able to make display; but *Faith goes on in silence, and overcomes the world.*

It would be both a pleasant and profitable exercise to notice the many conditions in life where Faith manifests its superior power, but a few must suffice.

The most self-sacrificing service, which God requires of us, Faith can make easy. Abraham offering up his son Isaac is a fine illustration of this. What could have more severely taxed Abraham's fidelity to God than the act he was required to perform? It was paternal love and Faith in conflict; a struggle between a father's affection for his son—his only son—and respect for the commandment of God. Faith gained the victory; and, on this account, Abraham is called the "father of the faithful."

Faith also enables us to endure the severest trials without murmuring. The Bible is full of splendid examples

illustrating the truth of this statement, and the history of
the Church bears overwhelming testimony in its favor.
With what eloquence does the long list of martyred saints
speak on this subject! The names of such glorious heroes
as John Huss, John Rogers, and William Tyndale, tell
how true it is that faith in Christ is able to sustain us
through the darkest hour of trial.

Again: it is a glorious fact that, when we are exposed
to the greatest dangers, Faith gives us courage, and lights
up our pathway. During a storm at sea, a ship, which
had for a long time breasted the fury of the waves, was,
at last, apparently about to go down. All on board were
in the wildest state of excitement, except one man, who
remained perfectly composed, and seemingly indifferent to
the danger which threatened him. His wife, noticing his
calm demeanor, and not understanding the meaning of it,
asked him how he could appear so resigned in the presence of so great peril. He immediately drew a dagger,
and presented it at her heart. Said he: "Are you not
afraid of this dagger?" "No," she answered, as the tears
streamed down her pale cheeks. "And why are you not
afraid of it?" he continued. "Because," said she, "*it is
in the hands of my dear husband.*" "Neither am I afraid
of the storm," said he; "*because it is in the hands of my
heavenly Father. I know that he loves me, and doeth all
things well.*" This man walked by Faith, and Faith gave
him perfect resignation. "Though he slay me, yet will
I trust him," is not the language of weak, hesitating, stam-
mering Sight.

Finally: Faith's conflicts, though they may seem doubtful for a time, never fail to end in victory. How many
sad and weary hearts, worn down by the long, long night
of toil, are inspired with a new hope and new life by the

quickening rays of this blessed assurance! All along the
lines of the struggling soldiers of the Cross, I see unmistakable evidences of a forward movement, as they unitedly
pronounce the cheering words of the apostle: "Thanks
be to God, who giveth us the victory, through our Lord
Jesus Christ."

It is difficult to conceive how our heavenly Father could
have given us more evidence than he has that Faith is
stronger than Sight. We have seen that philosophy clearly
suggests it; that history speaks but one voice on the subject, and that the heroes of the Bible, to whom we have
referred, exemplify it in their lives. "And what shall I
more say? For the time would fail me to tell of Gedeon,
and of Barak, and of Samson, and of Jephthae; of David
also, and Samuel, and of the prophets: who, through
Faith, subdued kingdoms, wrought righteousness, obtained
promises, stopped the mouths of lions, quenched the violence of fire, escaped the edge of the sword, out of weakness were made strong, waxed valiant in fight, turned to
flight the armies of the aliens." (Heb. xi: 32–35.)

I feel that enough has been said to convince the most
skeptical mind that only Faith is able to lead us to certain
and glorious victory.

And now, in conclusion, let me urge upon you the importance of following the lead of Faith. The things of
Sight can never bring happiness, though the world, with
all its stores, were placed at your feet. The history of
Solomon is re-enacted in the history of every man who
seeks for happiness in the unsubstantial pleasures of this
world: "All is vanity and vexation of spirit, and there
is no profit under the sun."

But, even allowing that there is a degree of real pleasure
in pursuing the things of Sight, they can not remain with

you long, for decay is written upon them all—all is changing, passing, fleeting—

> "The sweetest and dearest, alas! will not stay."

Where are the companions of your youth? "The fathers, where are they? and the prophets, do they live forever?" Look back upon the past. How many of life's fondest treasures lie buried there! How many cherished hopes and dazzling prospects sleep within that tomb of ages! When, O when, will the world understand the folly of trusting the things of Sight!

Dear brethren, let us heed the voice of heavenly wisdom, and "look not at the things which are seen, but at the things which are not seen: for the things which are seen are temporal; but the things which are not seen are eternal." "Let us not be weary in well-doing," but toil on and suffer, if needs be, *yet a little while;* "for in due season we shall reap if we faint not."

> "Soon shall close our earthly mission,
> Soon shall pass our pilgrim days;
> Hope shall change to glad fruition,
> Faith to Sight, and prayer to praise."

Fraternally.
A. R. Benton

ALLEN RICHARDSON BENTON.

A LLEN RICHARDSON BENTON was born in the town of Ira, Cayuga County, New York, October 1, 1822. Very early in life he had an ardent desire for learning, which was fully gratified by his parents until, from too much mental labor, his health failed, which made it necessary for him to give up his studies, and seek the restoration of physical strength in laboring on a farm. This was a severe stroke to his youthful ambition; but he submitted to it as gracefully as he could, with the hope that he would yet be able to complete his education.

At the age of fifteen, under the preaching of Dr. S. E. SHEPARD and JOHN M. BARTLETT, he became a member of the Christian Church.

At the age of twenty-one, having entirely recovered his health, the old desire for learning revived, and, after due preparation at the Fulton Academy, New York, in the fall of 1845, he was matriculated in Bethany College. While at college, he was distinguished for close application to his studies, integrity of character, and a faithful discharge of all his obligations as a student and Christian. He was graduated Bachelor of Arts in July, 1847, dividing the first honors of his class with ROBERT GRAHAM, now Presiding Officer of the College of Arts in Kentucky University, he delivering the Greek, and GRAHAM the Latin salutary.

In the fall of 1848 he became permanently established as Principal of Fairview Academy, Rush County, Indiana, in which place he continued six years, during which time he succeeded in building up a highly prosperous school. He was married, June 26, 1851, to SILENCE HOWARD, daughter of Dr. HOWARD, of Volney, New York.

Having been elected to the Professorship of Ancient Languages in Northwestern Christian University, he spent part of the year 1854 attending the Rochester University, New York, in the study of the Hebrew, under the instruction of Dr. CONANT.

In the spring of 1855, he opened a preparatory school in the Northwestern Christian University buildings, and, in the fall of the same year, the college was opened. He continued in the discharge of the duties of

(559)

the Chair of Ancient Languages until the summer of 1861, when he was elected President of the University, which position he still occupies.

During all the time he has been engaged in teaching, as opportunity offered, he has done good service as a preacher of the Gospel, and has been, for several years, an efficient elder in the Church at Indianapolis.

President BENTON has a somewhat feeble physical organization, but possesses a strong, vigorous, active intellect. He is quick in his movements, and his mind is characterized by very sharp angles. He throws his whole soul into whatever he undertakes; and his career demonstrates that he is not deficient in executive talent and mental power.

RETRIBUTION.

BY A. R. BENTON.

"For what a man soweth, that shall he also reap."—GAL. VI: 7.

IN the formation of character, and in the practical concerns of life, it is of the highest importance to keep in
mind the natural connection between cause and effect—between an action and its consequences. That there is a natural tie, which inevitably binds an act to its consequence,
is a truth obvious in every department of nature. This,
also, is the plain inculcation of our text—that *whatever* a
man sows, *that* he also shall reap.

According to the reasoning of the apostle, it is no more
natural to gather a crop after the kind of seed sown, than to
look for definite and invariable results in our moral husbandry. Whatever of certainty in results is incorporated
into the physical economy of God, the same certainty is an
invariable constituent of his moral system; and it is as
difficult to elude and baffle the latter as the former.

It is a pleasing truth for our contemplation, that the
Great Designer of all things has given, in his physical universe, some intimations of what he is in his moral administration—that the excellencies of a spiritual life may be
reflected from the relationship of earth; and that material

things may become to us sacred hieroglyphics, by which to read the things that are spiritual.

Upon this conception of the relation of the material to the spiritual, are the parables of the Savior founded. Like the tabernacle, which was made after the form of a heavenly pattern, so the earth, with all its forces and processes, is a copy and intimation of a higher state. Thus a harmonious and lasting unity runs through all the works of God, binding heaven and earth in one glorious universe —demonstrating the oneness of creative power, and the oneness of administration, by Him "who filleth all in all."

Nothing, perhaps, would deter more effectually from the commission of crime—nothing would restrain more vigorously the obliquities of human conduct, than a decided conviction that God's moral and spiritual laws are as immutable as his physical laws. No man, in contempt of the law of gravitation, plunges down a precipice; yet millions eagerly leap down all the steeps of sin into the very abyss of Tartarus and perdition.

Is it because men prize less highly, or conserve less carefully, their spiritual concerns? By no means. It is because the consequences of vice, folly, or shameless wickedness are not believed as being certain, and, by the constitution of nature, inevitable. Heaven and earth *may* pass away, but the word of God shall *never* pass away. His moral system will continue with its primal and perennial freshness, when the present physical order of things shall have undergone an entire change.

It is not to be denied, that an impression is widely prevalent, with respect to the dissimilarity of God's moral and physical government. In the physical economy, his laws are admitted to be fixed and immutable; and no sane man expects to evade the penalty of outraged law. "The thou-

sand ills that flesh is heir to" are conceded to be the natural sequences of personal or ancestral transgression. Tell
a man that health and longevity depend invariably on the
observance of laws in which there is no chance—no arbitrary interference of some capricious power—and it will
receive his unqualified assent. Tell him that every gratification of inordinate appetite—that intemperance and dis-
soluteness will bring with them a train of ills fearful and
indescribable, in the eclipsing of the flaming brilliancy of
the mind, and in paralyzing and prostrating the powers of
the body, and he can give it no denial.

But, on the other hand, when you come to speak of the
retributions which inexorably pursue the man who violates
the laws of his *moral* being, you are met with distrust and
chilling skepticism. In this department of God's universe,
multitudes see nothing but chaos, disorder, and capricious
chance. The hectic hue of health is upon the face of their
pursuits and enjoyments, while the virus of death lurks
in the vitals. In their vocabulary, there is no such phrase
as the "evil of sin." They have perturbations and dis-
quietudes of mind, it is true, but these are charged to
physical, rather than to moral causes.

Because of this lurking and pervading distrust, a false
and fatal indifference to the moral quality of actions is
painfully evident in the pleasures and pursuits of life.

In our daily experience we have a proof of God's intolerance of sin, and an incontestible evidence that he will
not allow it to go unpunished.

If his displeasure at sin was as transient as our concern;
if his estimate of its guilt as small as our sense of danger,
why does he visit us all with death, to us the most certain
and inexorable of all events? This experience, unknown
to sinless angels, and one from which the whole sentient

creation shrinks, is inflicted with pitiless constancy on every child of Adam.

If God regards the moral evil of the world with that complacency with which the world regards it, why such a hard dispensation to the children of men? For death, with remorseless certainty, as a keen scytheman, cuts down the fair and blooming in all the successive generations of men.

In the moanings of pain, in the tortures of remorseful despair, in the wild agonies of death, we have emphatic testimony that God hates *moral* evil, and will certainly punish it, if not abandoned with penitence. The *sting* of death is *sin*. It is, therefore, delusive to cherish the imagination, that retribution for infraction of God's moral law is not certain. It is the most certain of all, for most of all is he incensed at the violation of his moral laws. The great central truth of God's moral government is, that he governs actively toward *moral*, and not *physical* ends; and hence, every thing which conduces to this result will especially please him, and not go unrewarded.

As a Creator, God may be said to have physical plans and ends to reach; but as a Father, which is the highest relation revealed to us, or concernable by us, he has moral purposes to serve. And is it not reasonable to suppose that he will certainly smile with benignity upon such as act in harmony with his *moral* purposes, and frown with indignant displeasure upon such as seek to subvert his moral order and designs?

That the evil of sin, and the certainty of its punishment, may stand out more vividly before the mind, we pass from these general considerations to more minuteness of specification.

I. And first, with respect to the evil of sin. It is, without doubt, true that the tone of general literature is in palliation of the turpitude of sin. Its sharp, harsh outlines of offense are softened down by the euphemisms of a skeptical imagination. Again, it is often looked upon as a theological subtlety of professional interest, and a subject for cloister meditation; while, by others, its existence may not be denied, it is regarded as something born with a man, a kind of moral taint, that no moral disinfectant can wholly remove—a transmitted virus that corrupts and poisons all with which it comes in contact.

In the Bible, the nature of sin, and the magnitude of its evil, receives no such complacent handling. It is represented as the sting of death—that it can kill the soul, and inflict unrespited torment forever. All voluntary wrong-doing is sin. It is to resist our sense of right, to neglect acknowledged duty, or to disregard the laws of justice, integrity, and benevolence toward men, or, in the highest sense, to fail in our duties to God.

The Scriptures are full and explicit in affirming that all pains, afflictions, and losses are light matters compared with the guilt of voluntary wrong-doing; that to lose a right eye or right hand would be preferable far to a stain upon the soul, which may tarnish its beauty forever. This uniform testimony of Scripture is in perfect accord with human reason and experience. Take a man who has never occupied himself with the study of questions of morality and religion, and set before him the case of a man who has become rich by extortion and fraud; and the example of another, who has carefully abstained from these, and, in the discharge of acknowledged duty, has borne great suffering. Will he not decide that the latter has made a wise choice? The admiration of our souls for what is disinterested and heroic in human conduct, is proof of the excellence of virtue and the unnaturalness of sin. In our personal experience, those things which sting with the keenest pang are the occurrences in which, so to speak, we gained the world, but lost our soul; in which temptation triumphed over our moral principles, or in which selfishness or passion degraded us below our proper level.

There is no sting so sharp as remorse; no loss like the loss of innocence; no crimson so deep as that of shame, in view of remembered follies and vices. This is the voice, not of a single man, nor of a single age, but it is the universal sentiment of humanity. The Furies, brandishing in one hand the torch of vengeance, and in the other a scourge of writhing, wriggling vipers, and bearing aloft a Gorgon's head, that could turn every beholder into stone, are terrific representations of the heinous nature of moral evil, as revealed in the universal consciousness of men. But the culmination of this evil will not be realized in the present life; but, like the envenomed robe of Nessus, will cling with burning and consuming potency to the blackened and charred soul forever.

There is a kind of parchment, on which the characters, faded by time, are so perfectly restored by chemical reagents as to reveal, after the lapse of centuries, the secrets and forgotten lore committed to it. Such a parchment is the human soul, on which will be restored, in lines of ineffaceable light, the desires and the deeds of the unremembered past. The continuity of our being will not be interrupted by death. "Dust to dust" was not spoken of the soul. As our lives to-day are the resultant of past affections, aspirations, and pursuits, so our character beyond the stream of death will be the product of the influences that control us from day to day. Though we may be blind now to the turpitude of moral evil, through the fascinations of pleasure, or the anxious cares of active life, in *that* day, if given up to a sinful life, we shall feel with Milton's Satan, that "whichever way I turn is hell—myself am hell."

II. In the next place, we consider the *certainty* of God's retributive justice. The nature of moral evil lays the foundation for such justice. God's nature is the foundation of its certainty. This certainty is affirmed with the positiveness of dogmatism in our text. "Whatsoever a man sows, that *shall* he also reap." It is not hypothetical or uncertain. He *shall* reap: not as a mere prediction, but as of positive appointment. To many, no doubt, this inflexible certainty of sequence seems a hard and stern decree. Like the man who had received but one talent, they complain of God as an austere Master, who reaps where he has not sown. It is obvious that our complaining does not and can not alter God's plans; but it will be our highest wisdom to learn his plans, and to conform to them.

Even if one should be unable to explain them, or construe them satisfactorily to his mind, this will absolve him in no measure from the penalty incurred by violating known law. Approve or disapprove as we may, of the sanctions which God has annexed to his laws, this will, in no respect, bias or change the Divine course. Go and work, and whatever is *right* I will give you, is the universal law underlying all his economies. From this his immutability can not allow him to swerve.

In illustrating and enforcing the truth of the certain connection between our acts and their pre-ordained consequences, we shall appeal to matters that intimately concern the young, as youth is, in the order of nature, the period in which the seed is sown which will ripen with pestiferous fruit, or into a glorious harvest.

1. In the first place, we invite attention to one of the lowest and least reprehensible forms of transgression—the mistakes of the young.

If there were any cases in which we might reasonably expect that the rigor of law would be relaxed, surely we might expect some mitigation of penalty in the case of simple mistakes. But do we find such to be the case? Does even involuntary error lead to no pernicious result? Does ignorance snap the ligament that binds effect to cause? The answer is found in our own experience.

How often do we find men in situations that they have a special unfitness for. In such conditions they labor on for years, without suspecting for a moment their inaptitude for their calling. They blame their mischances, the infelicity of their conditions, while they are simply the victims of their mistakes. They, perchance, mistake their turbulent pride, and enormous self-consciousness, for the measure of their practical force; and hence are arrogant in all their demands on society. Inordinately desiring a life of ease and elegance, and believing themselves, by birth or culture, fitted to shine in the highest positions, with singular pertinacity they claim for themselves the special consideration of the world. This great mistake with regard to what the world owes or will accord, paves the way to their ultimate ruin. The common callings of life, in which downright, earnest work is demanded, are shunned, and without aptitude or ability for those positions which they seek, they fall peevishly into a driveling mediocrity.

There is a law of adaptation in the affairs of life which we may not violate with impunity. While something in our failures may be charged to circumstances, and to the infelicities of our lot, still this great organic law, Adaptation, is the main operative principle that controls our fortune; and no plea of mistake will undo the mischief which inevitably follows the infraction of this law.

2. In the next place, indolence and disregard of the opportunities of life are visited with certain punishment. For a time these things may sit easily, and life may glide along jauntily; but in the end their results will sting like adders, realizing to the transgressor that whatsoever he sows, *that*, and nothing else, shall he reap. There are a great many in this world, of whom more might have been made; but all their vain regrets over what might have been will be unavailing to bring back the neglected past, or squandered opportunities. If a young person makes a mistake here, no degree of industry in after life will fully retrieve the losses of the past; and painful losses they will remain forever.

Am I asked what are the special inflictions visited upon this easy and seductive vice? They are poverty, beggary, loss of self-respect and public esteem. Should I place before you two classes of circumstances, one of ease, affluence, and indolence, the other of hardship and the reward of persistent evil, most, I presume, would choose the former.

One comes into life the expectant heir of countless advantages. He has no want unsupplied or unanticipated. He walks the easy path of indolence—the petted, the indulged, and, generally, the spoiled child of mistaken parental love. This bleached, etiolated scion of doting parents, harboring all the selfishnesses and meannesses of an unoccupied life, is fitted, by the lessons of indolence, for all covert or public transgression of law.

The other is born, perhaps, under the dispensation of rags. From early life he falls into the eddies of society, and is thrown from one side to another—sunk at one time, then coming to the surface; and, with fearlessness and fortitude, at last begins to get hold on li e, and, in the words of Emerson, he "teams it, farms it, peddles, keeps school, edits a newspaper, goes to Congress, buys a township," and so forth. This discipline develops something better than wealth or position. It develops manhood, and, by its attritions, polishes the jewels of character until they shine with splendid luster.

Given these circumstances and careers from which to choose, would not many young persons choose the life of indolence and magnificent worthlessness? We need not now stop to trace indolence through all its labyrinths of dishonesty—to which it most surely leads—its swindlings, its forgeries, thievings, and the sensual indulgences which fill up the interstices between these crimes.

3. In the third place, there is certain retribution consequent upon the dissipation of life. One of the most alarming exhibitions of unbridled desires, is that pursuit of pleasure called, with great significance, *dissipation*. This is a species of self-gratification that assumes Protean forms —the idol of modern society, and the constant pursuit of restless and unoccupied minds. Such persons, in constant pursuit of some new titillations of pleasure, seek to drown their time, thoughts, and restiveness in the whirl of endless dissipation. They stand along the high road of life as sad examples of self-anarchy and internal misrule.

These "wild oats" of dissipation may be sown—thousands do sow them—but the reaping will be according to the sowing. Not more certainly will the husbandman reap tares when tares are sown, than will he reap shame and disappointment who makes pleasure his pursuit in life. All the steps taken on this road must be retraced with pain-

fulness and cross-bearing, if ever safety or happiness in
this life be found.

Were I to specify with particularity those forms of dissipation most hurtful to the moral welfare of the young,
I should mention the saloon, the theater, the gambling
hell, and the haunts of sensuality to which modesty denies
a name. Of some of these, it may be said, that their gross-
ness is so great, that none but the most hardened in depravity are reckoned among their votaries; while the theater may be a source of rational and innocent satisfaction.
It is often asked, with an air of conscious triumph, what
specific law of morals is violated by attending the theater?
It may be true that it has been refined from the excesses
of intemperance, from the execrations of profanity, and
the jeers of infidelity, and yet be practically pernicious
to moral culture. Then comes the groveling question:
What mysterious harm in frequenting such a place as this?
It is a fallacy to suppose that no substantial objections
may exist against a practice which infracts no specific command.

A man might be unwell, and the physician be unable to
give a specific name to his complaint. So with the scenic
representations of the stage. The ailing is general; and
even if unable to impeach them for specific guilt, they are
to be condemned for their complicities and general results.
In the words of an apostle, "An idol may be *nothing*, and
the meats offered to it may be *nothing*," and still it may
be unlawful in morals to visit its temple, or to sit at its
table.

It is, no doubt, well that the Christian religion gives
no dogmatic utterances on points like this; but that it
aims to supersede the luxury, the license, and the giggling
folly of such entertainments by new tastes, new affections,

and a nobler manhood. The *new* wine of tastes and principles must be put into new bottles, if both are to be preserved.

"Rejoice, then, young man, in the days of thy youth!
But *know*, that for *all these* things God will bring you into
judgment."

4. There is also certain retribution for the dishonesties of
life. There is, in our time, not only a tolerance, but there
are even encomiums upon some of the dishonesties of men.
The moral significance of deeds is charged, and what was
formerly, and in truth, esteemed a vice, is now canonized
as a virtue. This is the involuntary homage that men are
compelled to pay to virtue. If rascality is called tact or
business sagacity, it is because men wish to give a creditable account of themselves; if mendacity, in all its forms,
is called a prudent defense against the impertinence or
overreaching of others, it is because they wish to gloss
over the repulsiveness of lying. The danger of dishonesty comes not in some hideous, colossal form, but often
attenuated and gay, rallying the fears or piquing the pride,
until, admitted to the hospitality of human hearts, it suddenly swells into gigantic proportions, and with its Gorgon
head of horror, affrights every impotent struggle to exor-
cise the demon. Then honor, integrity, and purity perish;
and, with these, all is gone but the stinging disappointment, the useless remorse. Instead of the anticipated
harvest of respect, and honor, and life eternal, there is
the fruit of tyrannous and insatiable desires, which will
constitute forever a man his own tormentor.

Among our own countrymen, I know no more melancholy example of warning to aspiring young men, that they
beware of the dishonesties of life, than that of Aaron Burr.
Sprung from a noble ancestry, and bearing an honored

name; endowed with a mental tact and brilliancy that eclipsed
all competitors; of speech as fluent and fascinating as that
which angels use; of ambition towering as Lucifer's; of an
iron will that bent all, even bodily infirmity, to its own im-
periousness, he was fitted, by nature and liberal education,
to become a blessing to his race. But, losing his hold of
moral and religious principles, which had shed their hallowed and sweetening influences on his early life, he fell
from bad to worse, until, in his infinite progression toward
evil, he conspired to dismember his country, was exposed
in his wicked career, and is now gibbeted by the execrations of his countrymen.

Thus it ever will be, that it may be known how God
watches the flow of our daily life, its honesties and dishonesties, asserting his approbation of the one, and his
condemnation of the other.

5. In the last place, consider the application which the
apostle himself makes of this doctrine of retribution.
"He that sows to the flesh, shall of the flesh reap corruption; he that sows to the spirit, shall of the spirit
reap life everlasting."

No labor is expended to prove that it is wrong to sow
to the flesh, or that it is right to sow to the spirit. He
affirms a universal truth, with its certainty and momentous
import, and leaves it for us to apply. That it is always
criminal to sow to the flesh is clear; but in this connection the apostle endeavors to enforce the evanescent and
perishable nature of its objects.

The whole round of pursuits, tastes, and affections of
mankind are generalized by the two words, flesh and spirit.
The former are temporal and evanescent; the latter are
commensurate with the life of God—they are eternal.

What, then, is the boundary-line that separates the spirit

from the flesh? Is it that by which the dissipations or dishonesties of life are separated from its decencies and uprightness? Is it that by which the man labeled all over with uncanceled wickedness is separated from the genteel and affable?

There is no need for one to possess Satanic eminence in moral turpitude in order to define his spiritual status. The jurisprudence of heaven requires no such glaring contrasts to fix the character or destiny of men. It is possible to belong to the category of the flesh without any of the forms of gross delinquency. We might conceive of a man possessing a lively relish for the amenities of social life; of public spirit and activity; of keen relish for the sensuous beauties which have been spread with lavish prodigality on the face of nature, and yet, with all these, he may be on the side of the flesh. In his tendencies, habits, and practical concerns, he may be altogether carnal. God may not be in any of his thoughts. Like Mammon, "whose looks were always downward bent," the earth may claim all his affections, and be the theater of all his aspirations and all his hopes. Far better would it be to be destitute of worldly schemes and ambitions than to be destitute of religious affections and a sensibility for spiritual things. The flesh and corruption; the spirit and life eternal. The choice is ours. The ample apartments of the soul may become dismal and dreary from sheer emptiness of this spiritual furnishing, or they may become bright and refulgent by the garnishing of spiritual inclinations and holy affections. May no treacherous delusions or errant philosophy beguile us from the simplicity of this truth, that "Whatever a man sows, that shall he reap;" and may God graciously grant, that we may sow to the Spirit, and bring us at last to partake the felicities of everlasting life.

Yours truly,
Joseph King

JOSEPH KING.

J OSEPH KING was born in Kinsman, Trumbull County, Ohio, July 9, 1831. At seven years of age he was left an orphan, and was thrown on the world entirely upon his own resources. This fact subjected him to many privations and severe trials; but his energies were correspondingly quickened, and the self-reliance and patience which have since characterized the man were developed and strengthened thus early by the struggles of the boy. The money he expended in acquiring an education was earned by his own efforts: first, by manual labor on a farm, and, afterward, by teaching. No one helped him to a dollar.

He began the study of English grammar, and, indeed, all the common branches of an education, after he entered his eighteenth year, and graduated, with distinguished honor, at Bethany College, in 1855.

His early religious training was thoroughly Presbyterian, and he had no accurate knowledge of the Disciples, or of their views, till he was twenty years of age. When in his twenty-first year, after going through a long and terrible ordeal in seeking the way of salvation, he was brought to see and understand the truth, and was immersed, in Mahoning County, Ohio, in 1852.

After graduating at college, his first year in the ministry was spent at Warren, Ohio; the next three years were spent in the State of New York, in connection with the Williamsville Classical Institute. He was afterward pastor of the Church in New Lisbon, Ohio, four years; he then removed to Alleghany City, Pennsylvania, and took charge of the Church in that place, where he has been for nearly five years, and which is his present field of labor.

Brother KING is of medium stature, and very slight, but has shown himself capable of a large amount of hard work. He has brown hair, gray eyes, and weighs one hundred and twenty-five pounds. His physiognomy marks him as a man of equitable temper, large benevolence, but very decided and firm in reference to all his plans of life.

His preaching is chiefly practical, and his discourses are generally characterized by much that appeals directly to the conscience. He has very little imagination, and is not, in the popular sense, an orator, but his success in the ministry demonstrates that he wields an influence more potent than that which belongs to the most gifted speakers. Every-where he has labored, the Divine blessing has attended his preaching, and he is now doing a work in Alleghany City which is worthy to be recorded as among the most splendid successes that have crowned the pastoral labors of the ministry.

THE JUDGMENT TO COME.

BY JOSEPH KING.

"And he commanded us to preach to the people, and to testify that it is he who has been ordained of God to be Judge of the living and dead."— ACTS X: 42.

THESE words were spoken by the Apostle Peter, in the house of Cornelius, at the opening of the Gospel dispensation to the Gentiles. Peter was preaching, declaring the testimony of God, and, after affirming the resurrection of Christ, saying: "Him God raised up on the third day, and showed him openly, not to all the people, but to witnesses chosen before of God, even to us who ate and drank with him after he rose from the dead;" he also affirms, saying: "He commanded us to preach to the people, and to testify that it is he who has been ordained of God to be judge of the living and dead."

The apostles profoundly respected the authority of Christ. They obeyed his commands. They faithfully executed his will. They were his ambassadors, his plenipotentiaries, clothed with full power to treat with offending man, and make known the terms of reconciliation with an offended God. The text informs us that the apostles were commanded to do two things: First, to preach to the people. In preaching, they were subject to the will

37   (577)

of Christ. They preached, not to gratify their own ambition, or because the work of preaching was light and irresponsible, but because the *obligation* to preach was upon them. All authority in heaven and on earth had been given to Jesus. By that authority he commanded them, saying: "Go ye into all the world, and preach the Gospel to every creature." There is the obligation imposed— the duty solemnly enjoined. How deeply did Paul feel in reference to the work given him to do! And, no doubt, all the apostles felt as did he. "Though I preach the Gospel, I have nothing to boast of: for necessity is laid upon me; yea, woe is to me if I preach not the Gospel." (1 Cor. ix: 16.)

Secondly, they were commanded to "testify that Jesus had been ordained of God to be the Judge of the living and dead." The word "testify" scarcely does justice to the original. The word means, in the Greek tongue, to make solemn, public affirmation; to declare earnestly; to urge and enforce, under a deep sense of the truth and importance of what you say. Hence, the Judgeship of Christ was a capital item in the apostolic testimony. The apostles were commanded to proclaim to "all men every-where" that Christ is to return to judge the world in righteousness. Jesus is not only "Lord of all;" he is Judge of all, and to him every knee must bow, and every tongue confess. He is King, Lord, and Judge. His Lordship and Judgeship grow out of his offices as King. As "King of kings, and Lord of lords," he proclaims the law of pardon, governs the Church, rules over his people, and is also the Lord of providence. All things are in his hands. As King he is to judge the world.

I ask your attention, therefore, to this subject, growing immediately out of Christ's coronation and investiture with supreme authority, viz., *his advent to judgment*—his coming to reckon with every man, and "pronounce the sentence of eternal woe or bliss."

Your attention is invited to the following points:

I. THE CERTAINTY OF A FUTURE JUDGMENT.
II. THE JUDGE.
III. THE PERSONS JUDGED.
IV. THAT FOR WHICH WE ARE TO BE JUDGED.

I. Beloved hearers, listen while I speak to you. Let me ask: Do you believe in a future and eternal judgment? Do you believe that *you* are to stand before God, to give "account to him who is ready to judge the living and the dead?" Do you really accept it as a truth of Divine revelation, that Christ will come to reckon with you; to make solemn inquiry as to the improvement you have made of the talents given you; as to what you have thought, and said, and done during this life; and that the "hidden things of darkness will be brought to light, and the counsels of every heart made manifest?"

Do you believe this to be a part of God's great revelation? O, I say to you, men need to believe it: but multitudes do not; and, because they do not, they are going down to a fearful end. Let us inquire, then, will there be a future judgment? To this question there can be but one answer. *There certainly will be. An approaching judgment is certain.* And I proceed to establish the certainty of it.

1. In the first place, let us examine the "book of conscience." Man's mental and moral constitution furnishes evidence of the judgment of God. The sentence—God will judge every man—is written on every man's heart. Let us search the records within. Every one has evidence—evi-

dence quite satisfactory, too, if he but take the pains to examine it—in his own soul, in the constitution of his moral nature—that God will sit in judgment upon him. To illustrate: Suppose you do right; suppose you pursue a right course of conduct, such a course as is in harmony with the word of God and the principles of eternal rectitude, there is that within which approves your conduct—in other words, you have the testimony of a good conscience. On the other hand, suppose you do wrong; you sin; act contrary to that which you know to be right; do those things which you ought not to do, or leave undone those things which you ought to do, there is that within which disapproves your conduct; there is inward pain, mental uneasiness, and a consciousness of unhappiness arising from wrong-doing. You have done wrong, and you know it, and *feel* it. Now, what is that which approves one course of life, and disapproves the opposite course? It is conscience, or the moral sense. It is what the Apostle Paul calls the "law written in the heart;" *i. e.*, in the hearts of the Gentiles, those who had not a written revelation of God's will. And, as the guide-board points out to the traveler the way he must go to reach the desired place, so conscience, rightly interpreted, points, with unerring certainty, to the "righteous judgment of God." It is God's law in the soul, "written in the heart," testifying in favor of truth, and justice, and righteousness, and against sin, and wrong, and disobedience. (Rom. ii: 12–16.) And in the first and second chapters of the letter to the Church at Rome, the apostle clearly shows that conscience and the works of creation—"the things that are made"—furnish such a plain revelation of at least some of the attributes of the Supreme Being, that the others are left "without excuse." And of them he writes:

"Who," (without the Bible,) "knowing the *judgment of God*, that they who commit such things are worthy of death; not only do the same, but have pleasure in them that do them." (Rom. i: 32.)

2. The justice of God requires that there be a day of judgment. Justice is not here meted out to every one. Injustice abounds in this world, and God, for wise reasons, permits it. In every civilized country there are what are called "courts of justice." All men will not, of their own accord, act justly. Hence, courts are organized for the one purpose of seeing that justice shall be done between man and man. And yet, it can not be truthfully said that, in a single court, from that held by a country squire, or a village mayor, up to the Supreme Court of the United States, justice is always and absolutely done. A man may have injustice done him in, and by what is called a court of justice. Indeed, the fact is notorious that fraud and injustice are often perpetrated by those who are themselves set to administer justice. All over this world the innocent are oppressed, the just are treated unjustly.

The wicked are generally in great power; the righteous poor are trampled upon and kept down. And, during the ages that have passed away, how many of God's chosen and just ones have been persecuted, maltreated, injured in their person and property, oppressed, bound to the stake, and the life violently crushed out of them? and yet God, the infinitely just One, suffered their persecutors to live, and did not come forth openly to vindicate the cause of his suffering and oppressed people. How often is it the case that great criminals go unpunished in this world? Every-where the laws of God and the principles of justice are disregarded—iniquity, transgression, and crime run riot.

Is there a just God in heaven? Will the "Judge of all the earth do right?" If so, things being as they are in this world—injustice abounding, and justice mocked and trampled under foot in ten thousand instances; if God be just, (and who can doubt it?) if justice and judgment are the habitation of his throne, then there will come a day—there *must come* a day—when God will come forth as Sovereign, and openly, publicly, visibly, in the presence of all his accountable creatures, punish sin, reward righteousness; search out sins secret and concealed from the knowledge of men; make solemn investigation into the character of every one; examine his life; scan his purposes; scrutinize his heart; explore the deep recesses of his being; penetrate behind the vail of that which is outward; and, having weighed, examined, sifted, searched, scrutinized, exposed, will do what infinite justice determines and says ought to be done. Such a judgment, fearful, searching, far-reaching, awaits every man. None will escape. It will come. It is certain as that you live and hear me speak. God's justice requires it. It will not suffer the guilty to escape. Before Felix, Paul "reasoned concerning righteousness, temperance (self-control), and the judgment to come." (Acts xxiv, xxv.)

If Jefferson could say "I tremble for my country when I remember that God is just," every one may well tremble for himself when he remembers that God will sit in judgment upon him.

3. Turning now from conscience and Divine justice, we ask, What says the Word of God? What does God say in his Word concerning a future judgment? Not turning just now to the Old Testament for a single passage—for space will permit me to quote but a few—I cite the words of our Divine Lord in Matt. x: 15: "Verily,

I say to you, it will be more tolerable for the land of Sodom and Gomorrah, *in the day of judgment*, than for that city." Our Savior often speaks of the *day of judgment*. I need not multiply quotations. (See Matt. xi: 22–24; xii: 36–42.) Would Jesus unequivocally speak of that which is never to be? Nay; there is, therefore, to be a day of judgment; and sins committed thousands of years since, if not forgiven, will be had in remembrance in that day. It will be a day of wondrous revelations.

The Apostle Paul, in his discourse to the Athenian philosophers, as you will see recorded in Acts xvii: 30, 31: says, "God now commands all men every-where to repent: because he appointed a day in which he will judge the world in righteousness by the man (Christ Jesus) whom he ordained"—appointed to be Judge of all men. And the proof of Christ's having all judgment committed to him is his resurrection from the dead. God, therefore, has appointed a day; *i. e.*, he has fixed a time—a set time —a time that will be given up to the solemn work of judging men, and determining the destiny of each one. Nothing else will then absorb the mind of either the Judge or the judged. Now, Christ is governing the universe, administering the affairs of his vast empire, and interceding for his people; but there draws near a time when he will come, with "his mighty angels, in flaming fire," and, laying aside other things, will devote the necessary length of time to one thing—judging "the world in righteousness." When he comes, "every eye shall see him, even they who pierced him: and all the kindreds of the earth shall wail because of him." (Rev. i: 7.) Gloom and dismay will overspread the world; horror and anguish will seize men. "And the kings of the earth, and the great men, and the rich men, and the chief captains, and the mighty men, and every bondman, and every freeman, hid themselves in the dens and in the rocks of the mountains; and said to the mountains and rocks, Fall on us, and hide us from the face of him who sits on the throne, and from the wrath of the Lamb: for the great day of his wrath is come, and who shall be able to stand?" (Rev. vi: 15–17.)

This day is approaching, and no power of man or angel can prevent its approach. Men may laugh, treat the matter with ridicule, and "make light of it;" they may say: "Peace and safety;" "Where is the promise of his coming?" and "Away with your notions about a future judgment and the conflagration of the world;" but "sudden destruction will come upon them, and they shall not escape." The antediluvians mocked Noah, a preacher of righteousness, and treated his solemn warnings with indifference; yet the "flood came and swept them all away." So will it be with all the ungodly in the great day of final reckoning.

O, beloved, write it upon the tablet of your heart; receive the solemn truth; and, from this hour, practically believe that you are to appear before the Judge of all the earth, to receive according to the deeds done in the body.

In proof of a future judgment, many other passages might be quoted; but it is not necessary. (Rev. xx: 12, 13.) "In the mouth of two or three witnesses shall every word be established." John, Paul, and, above all, our Savior himself, assert the fact of a "day of judgment."

II. The Judge.

This is our Lord Jesus Christ. Jesus is the Judge of the living and the dead. "The Father judges no one; but has committed all judgment to the Son; that all should honor the Son, as they honor the Father. He that honors not the

Son, honors not the Father who sent him." (John v: 22, 23.) All judicial authority has been given to Christ; and the Father's purpose, in giving him such authority, is that his Son may be honored equally with himself. Christ is to receive equal adoration with God; and, wearing our nature as well as the Divine, he is thus an "impartial Judge."

III. WHO ARE TO BE JUDGED?

We pass to consider the subject of the Divine judgment.

1. *Fallen angels.* There has been sin in heaven among the angels as well as on earth; and as angels are accountable beings—subjects of moral government—and as "*all* judgment" has been given to the Son, the fallen angels will be judged by the Son of God. (2 Pet. ii: 4; also Jude 6.)

2. *All men will be judged.* Not one will escape the righteous judgment of God. "All who, at Christ's coming, shall be living, or shall ever have lived." The judgment will be universal, embracing not only one tongue or kindred, but all tongues and kindreds of men. The beggar and the millionaire; the king on his throne, and the humblest of his subjects; the prince and the peasant; the master and the servant; the old and the young; the judge on the bench, and the prisoner at the bar: *all men* standing now on the same level, robbed of every earthly distinction; their former position and supposed greatness lost sight of, and with nothing but the character they formed during life, are to stand before the omniscient, omnipotent Judge of all. "*We* must *all* appear before the judgment-seat of Christ; that every one may receive the things done in the body, according to what he has done, whether it be good or evil." (2 Cor. v: 10.) "Every one of us shall give account of himself to God." (Rom. xiv: 12.)

Professors of religion sometimes say: "Why, we are not to be judged, are we? Are we not Christians? Are we not members of Christ's body? Have we not been forgiven? Are not the promises ours? Will Christ judge us?" I answer: Yes. Yes, *you* will be judged. There lives not a man who will escape the final judgment. Not one—not *one*. Does not the apostle say: "The Lord will judge his people." And, in reference to this very judgment to be passed upon the Lord's people, Paul says: "It is a fearful thing to fall into the hands of the living God." Fearful, because the Judge is omnipotent; fearful, because he is the searcher of every heart; fearful, because many who are expecting to be acquitted will be condemned; fearful, because the Judge has power "to destroy both soul and body in hell." Well may we tremble, in view of that day; and thousands will tremble then who never trembled before. Like Belshazzar, they will turn pale; their knees will smite one against another, and horror and anguish will seize them. O, may we be prepared for that great day—day of God Almighty!

The question is sometimes asked, Whether the sins of God's people will be published in the day of judgment. This is one of those "secret things that belong to the Lord our God." It is certain their sins will not be alleged against them *to their condemnation;* nevertheless, "the Lord will judge his people."

IV. For what are we to be Judged?

1. For our works, our deeds, conduct, actions. All the deeds of your life will be subject-matter of inquiry and judicial investigation in the day of final retribution. Not some actions, not some deeds—but *every* action, *every* deed of *every* man. Nothing will be left out of the ac-

count. The Judge will take cognizance of every act. *He is Omniscient.* His knowledge of your whole life, and of every thing you do, during life's continuance, is perfect. No *act*, no *deed* will escape his notice.

I have observed that business men, in making out their bills, to distribute for collection, are careful to specify every item purchased. They forget nothing. Of *this*, so much, at so much per unit of measurement. Of *that*, so much, at so much per unit of measurement; and so on, to the end. And often you forget that you bought so much; and when the bill is presented to you for payment, you are surprised to find it so large, and are disposed to dispute its correctness; but the books show it. Here it is—the date and the full account in order.

Now, God keeps a strict account of all we do. He forgets nothing. All is written in the book of his remembrance. You sin, but you soon forget that you sinned. You drive a hard bargain. You cheat some ignorant one in dealing with him; you falsify for base gain; you give way to passion, and storm about; or you yield to the power of appetite, and drink that which intoxicates. These "little sins," as you call them, are soon forgotten, (you do not retain them in mind long enough to repent of them;) and you flatter yourself you are living a consistent life. Thus life passes on. The day of judgment comes. "The books are opened." And here, in God's great Book of remembrance, is the record of your whole life. Every action is therein recorded, and "every work God will bring into judgment."

2. But the Divine judgment will extend farther, and reach deeper, than *actions*. For their *words* men are to be judged. The Judge says: "Verily, I say to you, that every idle word that men shall speak, they shall give ac-

count thereof in the day of judgment." (Matt. xii: 36.)
Solemn, startling revelation! "A man's words are the
evidence on which he is to be tried before God." His
speech—the words that proceed out of his mouth—are an
indication of the true principles of his heart. By words
the heart is made known, as the tree by its fruit. (Matt.
xii: 34.)

Reader, do you believe this? Do you believe that your
words are recorded in God's great Book, and that they will
be brought up for judicial investigation in the final day?
Take heed to your speech. Restrain your tongue from
evil. Pray that God would set a watch upon your lips.

3. But the Divine judgment goes still farther and
deeper than "every work," and "every idle word." Your
secret thoughts and purposes; your hidden life—which is
every one's true life—must pass the scrutiny of the omniscient Judge. Hear the word of God: "Let us hear the
conclusion of the whole matter: Fear God, and keep his
commandments: for this is the whole duty of man." And
what is the reason assigned? The fear of God, and obedience to his commandments, are urged by the most powerful reason. "For every work God will bring into judgment, together with *every secret thing*, whether it be good
or evil." (Eccl. xii: 13, 14.) Every *secret* thing! *Every*
secret thing, both good and evil! "God will judge the
SECRETS of men (τα κρυπτά τῶν ἀνθρώπων) by Jesus Christ,
according to the Gospel." (Rom. ii: 16.) God will "bring
to light the hidden things of darkness, and will make manifest of every heart." The heart makes man what he is,
and determines his character.

O, my hearers, the judgment of God, the solemn scru-
tinies of the Great Day, the searchings of Jehovah, go
to the depths of your being; to your thoughts, desires,

purposes, aims, the moral tendencies of your life, and a full revelation of the whole will be made. Does it not become you to strive after holiness; to be terribly in earnest in seeking conformity to Christ, and in aiming to have your *thoughts*, as well as *words* and *actions*, pure?

The poet says: "Things are not what they seem." And we may say, some men are not what they seem. They are masked. They are one thing externally, and another thing internally. Their true life you do not see. They manage to conceal it. But in that day, to which we haste, vails will be rent away, and every man will appear before God and the world in his true character.

My brethren, do not be false. BE what you profess to be. Be true men; and, above all things, seek to be clear of the last vestige of hypocrisy. Let your light shine.

And now, in conclusion, let me ask: Are you prepared for this searching, righteous judgment of God? O man, dying man, accountable man, "Prepare to meet thy God." Delay not the work of preparation. The day of which I have spoken; the final day; "the dying day of the world;" "the day which none unholy ought to name," the *Day of Judgment*, will come. It is drawing near. Soon it will come upon the whole world. May God, the Judge of all, approve thee in that day. *Amen.*

THE END.